A History of Wollaston

'HOW'
History of Wollaston (Group)

A
H OW
Publication

Preface

As Member of Parliament for Stourbridge I am delighted to have been asked to do this preface, but it is as a resident of Wollaston that I can write with enthusiasm. Everyone who lives in this urban village knows it has a special atmosphere and a unique character. Its architecture is eclectic. Domestic buildings include desirable Victorian terraces, flats, modern houses, and estates of semi-detached homes and detached dwellings of varying sizes. There are much loved specialist shops serving local people, small enterprises and some quite large factories. With such diversity it is hard to pinpoint what makes Wollaston tick. But I can say with some certainty, as both Member of Parliament and resident, that it has something to do with its people. People who live and work in Wollaston care about their urban village. They are interested in their surroundings; they are protective of its special character. The place is undoubtedly its people. I am therefore particularly pleased to see the production of this history of Wollaston come to fruition. Researched and written by local people as a result of winning £5,000 worth of Lottery funding.

This history gives the reader an insight into the people and the place. I congratulate all those who worked to create it. They've made a unique contribution. A book by the people of Wollaston for the people of Wollaston.

Debra Shipley MP
Member of Parliament for Stourbridge
Wollaston Resident

Front: Anthony Graham produced this picture of Wollaston Hall in 1892. His oil painting gives probably the best impression of what the building must have looked like. The timber framing was dark brown in colour and the rendering that infilled it a brownish white. Painted for the Firmstone family, who then owned the Hall, the artist was clearly harking back to earlier times, because a conservatory, added by William Blow Collis in the early 1850s, is conspicuously absent on the left. *H Jack Haden*

Rear top: Don't believe everything you read on postcards! As every Wollastonian will tell you, this is not High Street but Bridgnorth Road. Most of these buildings remained in 2003, but the trams have sadly gone. Sometime in the first decade of the 20th century, Kinver Light Railway car No 46 curves away left en route to The Fish, whilst smartly dressed young ladies disembark from the rear platform of Dudley & Stourbridge car No 21, which was working the Enville Street line.

Rear bottom: The Church of St James, Wollaston, was the gift of William Orme Foster, and consecrated on 17 September 1860. This is one of the earliest photographs of the church. If the clock is to be believed the time was 14:05. The blurring of the top of the trees suggests that there was also a bit of a wind, but the churchyard is almost empty.

First published 2004

ISBN 0 9547053 0 0

© History of Wollaston Group 2004

Published by HOW (History of Wollaston Group), 151 Bridgnorth Road, Wollaston, Stourbridge, West Midlands DY8 3NU

Printed by Ian Allan Printing Ltd, Hersham, Surrey KT12 4RG.

Contents

Introduction: HOW and Why

This book, and the group that produced it, had a most unusual beginning. In the summer of 1998 someone came into Stepalong Shoes in Bridgnorth Road Wollaston, and asked the owner, Pat Burrage, if she could remember the name of one of Wollaston's lost pubs. This sparked an interest in Wollaston's history in Pat and her customers. They started bringing in old photographs, some of which showed school classes, which Pat put in her shop window with requests for people to put names to faces. As more and more items appeared, so, too, did some people with an interest in actively researching Wollaston's history. A meeting was called on 24th September 1998 and a research group formed, with Dr Paul Collins as Chairman. They decided to take their name from the subject they were researching – so the History of Wollaston (Group) became known as just 'HOW'.

Pat Burrage made the body of her shoe and craft shop available to the group for its meetings. As it turned out, a shoe shop made a remarkably good venue for meetings – lots of room, and chairs! For the first year or so HOW only met one evening a month, but as interest and information grew it was decided to meet more often, and a regular pattern of meeting at 7:30pm on the second and fourth Tuesday evening became established.

By the summer of 1999, HOW had decided on two things: one was to work towards the production of a book; the other was to apply for a Millennium Awards For All grant to help to pay for its publication. The latter application was successful, and on 25th September 1999 HOW learned that they had been awarded the maximum grant of £5,000 towards publication of their book. At around the same time the group also received a £500 Millennium grant from Dudley MBC towards the cost of staging an exhibition of their work in 2000.

The only publication on Wollaston to this time was a booklet by Geoffrey Beard in 1946. HOW wrote to Dr Beard, who now lives in Bath, and sought permission to quote from his work. He replied on 12th January 2000, saying: '*use anything from my little 1946 booklet. I was little more than a schoolboy at the time, and there are many occasions since that I know I could have done better!*' Dr Beard closed by wishing HOW all the best for their work.

News of HOW and their research began to spread. The group set up a website, which brought enquiries and information from around the world. They were also approached by The Black Country Society to host one of their Summer Walks. This was held on 28th June 2000, and over 80 people were conducted around Wollaston, visiting places associated with its history and development, much to the amusement and bemusement of some local residents, who could not understand why 80 people were standing outside their house while they were watching Coronation Street!

HOW's Exhibition was held in Wollaston Church Hall every weekend in September 2000. Members of HOW were on hand to answer any questions and to note any comments or suggestions visitors made. Over 600 people visited the Exhibition, which proved most successful. Many offered additional information, photographs or other items, and a lot of HOW's time was subsequently spent in following these leads up. The Exhibition also marked the public launch of HOW's intention to publish this book, and advance orders were taken, with the 'carrot' of the first 100 subscribers having their names printed in the book. Doubts were cast as to whether there would be any takers for this offer, but by the time the Exhibition closed, so had the subscription list!

The Exhibition also produced much additional information, and many loose ends. One of the greatest of these was, and remains, the fate of Wollaston Hall. Eastern Pennsylvania repeatedly cropped up as the destination of the Hall, and early in 2001 Dr Paul Collins decided to bombard preservation societies, local history groups and newspapers in this region with e-mails. This produced a torrent of replies, which at their peak came in at over 100 a day! It also brought HOW to the attention of the producers of an Open University series on the use of the Internet. And so it was that on 27th March 2001, TV Presenter Mariella Frostrup was in Wollaston, filming in Apley Road – the former site of Wollaston Hall – and around the Church and in various other locations in the village. The programme featuring HOW – *Well Connected* – was screened on BBC2 at 9:00am on 15th September 2001, and repeated at the same time on 23rd March 2002.

Thursday 5th April 2001 saw the 100th anniversary of the public opening of the Kinver Light Railway (KLR) that connected The Fish with Kinver via Wollaston. HOW felt this important anniversary should not go unmarked, so members of the group, plus a representative of the Kinver Historical Society, met at The Fish at 7.00pm and walked the route of the line – up to Wollaston, through the village to The Ridge, and down to The Stewponey, where a toast was drunk to the tramway. Five weeks later, on 16th May 2001, members of HOW led another Black Country Society Summer Walk along the same route. An estimated 86 people came along to share a little of the KLR's history.

Thereafter all of HOW's efforts have been directed towards production of the book you are holding. All concerned the endeavour hope that, whether a Wollastonian or not, you find something to interest and surprise you in the continuing History of Wollaston – that's HOW!

A note on currency

Most of Wollaston's history happened in the days of pre-decimal currency, before 15 February 1971 when the UK's money went decimal. No attempt has been made to convert the old money values included in this book, but a word or two of explanation may prove useful for those who only know our decimal currency. Before 1971 a pound was divided into 20 shillings, equivalent to 5p. Each shilling was divided into 12 pennies, and halfpenny coins were also in circulation. Before January 1961 there was also the farthing, a coin worth ¼ of a penny! There are a number of websites that provide information about pre-decimal currency, including Jo Edkins' Weight & Measures: www.gwydir.demon.co.uk/jo/units

Chapter One

WOLLASTON'S DEVELOPMENT TO 1850

Early History

It is thought that the name Wollaston was derived from that of 'Wulfgar', a personal name, and 'aston', an Anglo-Saxon word meaning 'east town' or settlement. Wulfgar was one of the kings of Mercia, one of the seven Anglo-Saxon kingdoms into which England was divided in the 7th century. However, there is no documentary or archaeological evidence of any settlement at this time, indeed the village is not even mentioned in the Domesday Survey of 1086, when it was recorded that the manor (or feudal estate) of Oldswinford was held by Acard, who in turn held it from his overlord William Fitzansculf, the Norman builder of Dudley Castle. From later records it is known that the manor of Oldswinford originally included the land that is now known as Wollaston.

The first recorded mention of the name of 'Wollaston' was in 1241, when it was known as 'Wullaston.' The document recording this name was a conveyance of land from William de la Platte to Peter de Prestwood. This is preserved in the Public Record Office. In the same century in the Assize Rolls (court records) for Worcestershire there is mention in 1275 of 'Wollaueston', whilst in the Lay Subsidy Rolls (taxation records) for 1327 the name of Christina de 'Wolarston' is listed. These different spellings reflect the fact that there was no standardised spelling, especially of place names, before the 19th century, until then spelling was dependent on the whim and education of the writer or scribe. Not surprisingly a number of spellings of Wollaston have been recorded.

- 1241 Wullaston
- 1275 Wollaueston
- 1305 Wollaston
- 1327 Wolarston
- 1368 Wolaston
- 1572 Wollastone
- 1708 Woolweston
- 1830 Woolestone

The earliest known lease relating to property in Wollaston is dated 25 October 1552 in the reign of Edward VI when:

'*Roger Pyrote* (or Perrott), *Lord of Wollaston, yeoman, granted to William Tayler of the same, one cottage and two acres of land lying in the ville* (or village) *and fields of Wollaston of which one acre lies in Withybrook field... .*'

The term 'Lord of Wollaston' clearly implies that Wollaston was then a manor, or the estate of a nobleman. Unfortunately there are no known records of such a manor's legal existence, even though there are numerous direct and indirect references to the manor of Wollaston between 1442 and 1672. In 1442 the Perrott family held the manor before it passed by marriage to the Persehouse family, who sold it

in 1592 to George Liddiatt, a London merchant. The manor disappeared without trace after 1672 when it was acquired on behalf of Thomas Foley, the founder of Oldswinford Hospital School, and became part of the vast Foley estate. After his death in 1677, his eldest son, also called Thomas, leased the manor to his brother Philip in 1678. For a detailed discussion of Wollaston's claim to be a manor see: R L Chambers (1978) '*Oldswinford, Bedcote and Stourbridge manors and boundaries.*' In all likelihood Wollaston was just a hamlet or small village, and if a manor at all, then one inferior to, and dependent on, the Manor of Bedcote.

A survey of Wollaston in 1637

One of the earliest surviving accounts of Wollaston is contained in a handwritten survey of the hamlet headed:

Below: One of the earliest surviving accounts of Wollaston is headed: '*Wollaston – A true survey of certain parcels of land meadows and pastures there taken the 25th day of February Anno domini 1637.*'

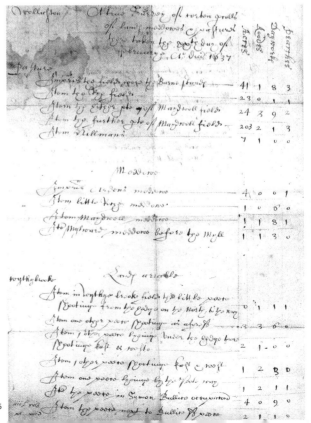

'*Wollaston – A true survey of certain parcels of land meadows and pastures there taken the 25th day of February Anno domini 1637.*' The area, then still mainly fields, is described in terms of its acreage, which is measured in acres (a), roods (r) and perches (p), plus the even more arcane means of 'daywork'(d) – i.e. how many day's work each field took to plough. (see above right.)

This document summarises 351a 2r 21p of Wollaston's 386 acres, the balance probably being accounted for by the land not in cultivation, such as that surrounding the Hall and the other buildings there.

Wollaston in the late 17th century

The first real glimpse of Wollaston as a community comes from fragmentary documents dating from the second half of the 17th century, and from the map drawn by Josiah Bach in 1699. An inventory of the possessions left by John Payton, miller of Wollaston, who died in 1661, shows that he was a wealthy businessman and therefore it is not unreasonable to infer from this that Wollaston was a prosperous community. This inference is reinforced by a number of documents detailing property repairs in the period 1678-1680. These reveal that lime, new millstones and timber were required for repairs to the windmill, whilst elsewhere a well was being sunk, a barn was being built and houses were being thatched.

Above: In 1442 the Perrott family held the manor of Wollaston before it passed by marriage to the Persehouse family, who sold it in 1592 to George Liddiatt, a London merchant. This document is part of an early legal document relating to the Liddiatt family's ownership of Wollaston Hall and Manor, dating to 1663. The words 'John Lyddyatt de Wollaston' can clearly be seen in the third line.

The accounts, compiled by Dan Rowley, land agent to Philip Foley of Prestwood, are very detailed, giving dates, descriptions of the work done, amounts and costs of materials used, names of workmen and their pay, as well as the names of some of the house holders. Thomas Oliver had a barn built and work was done to buildings rented by Thomas Moody, John ffranks, Thomas Hurtle, Humfry Whiles, John Ainger and William Eginton, including glazing, thatching and general building work. The workmen included: Thomas Hurtle, who was paid £3 5s for mason's work; John Davis and Humfrey Davis were the thatchers;

Pastures	a	r	p	d
Imprimis (first of all) the fields near the Barn stands	41	1	3	8
Item the rye fields	23	0	1	1
Item the hither part of Maydwell fields	24	3	2	9
Item the further part of Maydwell fields	203	2	3	1
Item nillmans'	7	1	0	0
Meadows				
Imprimis Arden's meadows	4	0	1	0
Item little Roche's meadows	1	0	0	6
Item Maydwell meadows	1	1	1	8
Item Maynards meadows before the mill	1	1	0	3
Withybrook				
Lands arable				
Item in Withybrook fields the little piece shooting from the hedge on the north to the way	0	1	1	1
Item one other piece shooting as aforesaid	3	3	0	6
Item 1 other piece lying under the hedge there Shooting east and west	2	1	0	0
Item1 other piece shooting east and west	1	2	0	3
Item one piece lying by the pool way	1	2	1	1
Item one piece in Symon Bullins occupation	4	0	0	9
Item one piece next to Bullins aforesaid piece	2	1	0	1
More in Wythybrook fields				
Item Alice Parrs piece	2	2	0	4
Item the piece lying on the west side of Alice Parrs piece	1	3	0	8
Item one piece shooting on the pool head	1	1	0	4
Item one piece shooting to the aforesaid pool	1	0	2	0
Item one piece shooting on Wythybrook meadow	5	3	3	2
Item Wythybrook meadows				
Item the parcel of meadow under the pool	0	2	0	2
Item a little gobbett at the pool head	0	0	0	4
Item the piece close within the pool	16	0	3	5

Above: This document itemises the rental value of the Manor of Wollaston in the year 1680. The 20 elements of land and buildings, including the Hall, come to a total value of £206 13s 8d. Last of all is the intriguing 'Glasshouse', which, at this date, is unlikely to refer to a greenhouse or conservatory, and almost certainly refers to a glassworks.

Left: The original script of the first of Dan Rowley's letters to Philip Foley.

Thomas Hurtle and his boy were also masons, and they were paid 4s 6d for three days' work; John Allis, was a carpenter who received £1 2s 2d for work at William Eginton's; Job Cadick supplied hair for building at Thomas Oliver's barn for £14; Richard Badger supplied bricks, and Richard Smallman supplied 5,000 roof tiles and 27 crests for £3 19s 6d. Timber and boards were brought from Prestwood, Compton Park or Arlys Wood, and were usually carried by Philip Foley's own team. The cost of sinking a well and supplying a chain and bucket was 18s, and 8,700 bricks and their carriage cost £6 9s. The total expense on just one of the accounts amounted to £112 11s 10d alone!

The following letters, written by Dan Rowley to Philip Foley, also show that building disputes and late payers are as old as time itself:

'*This is as just account as I can give except these houses had been finished which had been before this time but we have had bad weather which hath prevented them – John Angeworth would have the shed which is at the end of the barn in Beanall* (a field name shown on Josiah Bach's map of 1699) *removed to the mill which I told him could not be done except you would grant it, which I desire your resolve in your next – I would very willingly have differences composed betwixt Mr Oldbury and me for it is of a long standing – I very much wonder I hear not from him – I thank God we are all well and things go well with us. I hope it is the like with you. This is all at present*

from him who is
Sir your obliged faithful servant
Dan Rowley
Prestwood the 17 November 1680'

'*Hon. Master*
This is a true and full account of all the charges laid at Wollaston since you went to London and if I had understood your will in the first I could the better have satisfied your desire before this time but I hope this will serve your purpose – Sir, I have not as yet had anything from Mr Oldbury neither can I imagine what he intends to do, therefore I desire you would be pleased to order Mr Hall to make another tender to him of £6 13s 2d before witnesses and then I know not what he can do unto me. This is all at present.

From your obliged servant
D. Rowley
December 1 1680'

Another glimpse of life in Wollaston at that time comes from the papers concerning a legal dispute between Thomas Foley and John Sparry in 1696 over rights of ownership to the Washing Pool and the fields adjoining it. In describing this pool, which was situated by the side of what is now Mamble Road on the ancient border between Bedcote and Wollaston, Thomas Foley wrote:

'*Whereas your orator is and for severall years last past hath been lawfully seized in fee of and in the manor or lordship of Wollaston within the parish of Old Swinford ... and of and in a certaine field called Poole field ... and a ground called Poole piece in the North West part of a certaine great Poole or Pond called Washing Poole ... all lying and being within the said Manor of Wollaston, which said Poole ... hath been used by the Tenants and inhabitants of the said Mannor and the Townshipp of Wollaston as a common poole for watering their cattle ... there was an ancient withey tree grew at the Tail of the said Poole, and neare the said Tree there was an ancient Gutter or Trench which ran to and through the said Poole neare opposite to the Bolt at the head thereof and ... through the lands beneath the head of the said Poole, and the said Trench or gutter was and was allwayes reputed and taken to be the Bound and division between the said Mannor of Wollaston and the Towne of Stourbridge.*'

Josiah Bach's map

Josiah Bach mapped Oldswinford Parish in 1699, including Wollaston. His map clearly shows that the original settlement was at the Barley Mow end of the High Street. The only roads shown are what are now called Vicarage Road, High Street, Bridgnorth Road and High

Right: Josiah Bach mapped Wollaston in 1699. Compared to later maps, his is very accurate when overlaid by modern Ordnance Survey maps of the area. This first portion shows the north and west boundary of the manor, which was formed by the River Stour. Wollaston Hall is seen at the bottom, at the end of a road leading diagonally up from it (later Vicarage Road), which was where most of the houses forming the hamlet of Wollaston stood. At the southern extremity of the hamlet stood Wollaston windmill, which is shown as a small pictogram on the extreme left.

Windmill Lane. Interestingly one plot of land is called Mount Carmel, a Biblical name suggesting high ground. This land is at the top of the steep (Withy) bank rising from the River Stour and in 2003 is where the Village Hall (formerly the Senior Citizens' Centre) stands.

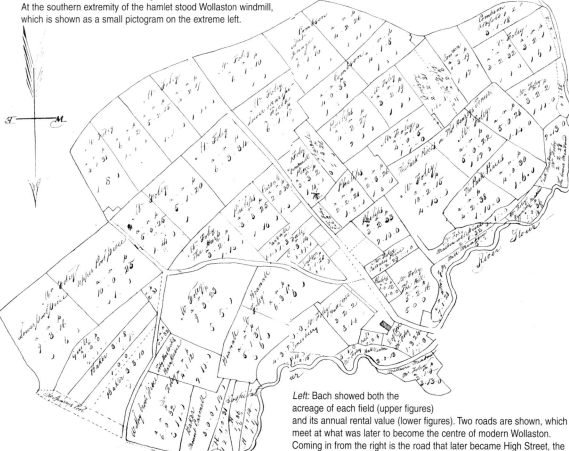

Left: Bach showed both the acreage of each field (upper figures) and its annual rental value (lower figures). Two roads are shown, which meet at what was later to become the centre of modern Wollaston. Coming in from the right is the road that later became High Street, the road it joins later became Bridgnorth Road. Many of the field boundaries would also become roads: the straight upper boundary to Lower and Upper Pool Pieces is now High Park Avenue.

Park Avenue. The primary objective of this map was to show land ownership. The boundary of each plot of land is drawn such that the map has the look of a patchwork quilt. Each of the plots shows the name of its owner, its size measured in acres, roods and perches, and its value in pounds, shillings and pence. The only habitation shown is Wollaston Hall, which was built in the early 17th century, judging from its style of architecture as depicted in 19th century illustrations. It is conceivable that there was an even earlier hall on this site, which is now covered by some of the houses in Apley Road. The only other building shown is the windmill, which stood approximately on the site of today's vicarage, and not surprisingly the road (today's Vicarage Road) was known to many generations as

Harry Court's map

A map drawn in 1782 by Harry Court, nearly a century after that of Josiah Bach, confirms the position of the Hall. It also shows a cluster of farm buildings and, almost certainly, cottages around the junction of what is now High Street and Vicarage Road. The most important building in this cluster was the Hall.

It is difficult to estimate the population of the hamlet, but taking together this cluster of houses around the Hall and a smaller one around Wollaston Mill on the River Stour, in all probability this would not have exceeded 100 in 1782.

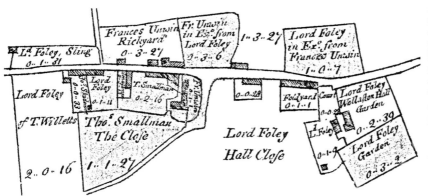

Left: Harry Court's map of 1782 provides more detail of the nature and position of Wollaston Hall. It also shows a cluster of farm buildings, and the cottages forming the hamlet of Wollaston, clustered around the junction of what is now High Street and Vicarage Road. Again, the figures shown are the acreages of each plot.

Below: L O Davies' map of 1827 provides a very detailed picture of Wollaston. It shows there had been a modest expansion of the village since Harry Court's survey in 1782. In the old village, in addition to the Hall, there were 24 houses, two shops, the windmill, and The Barley Mow Inn, standing near the junction of the two roads.

Apart from those employed as servants in the Hall and those working in the water powered slitting mill on the River Stour, the remainder of the inhabitants would have worked on the land, for Wollaston had not yet felt the impact of the Industrial Revolution. In all probability the interests and activities of the Hall dominated the life and work of the hamlet. It was a small, compact, somewhat isolated, rural community.

The 'Old Village'

A map drawn by L O Davies in 1827 provides a more detailed picture of Wollaston. It suggests that there had been a modest expansion of the village since Harry Court's survey in 1782. In addition to the main settlement of the 'old village', adjacent to the Hall, there was a cluster of six houses around the watermill, on land occupied by the Sunrise Medical factory in 2003, a smaller cluster of three

Left: Isaac Taylor's map of 1772 is the first consistently to distinguish between different types of mill. In this extract the windmill is clearly shown as a tower mill, one with a brick tower base. Also shown is a simple house, representing Wollaston Hall, and a watermill, a house with a wheel attached, representing Wollaston Mills.

Left: In his less detailed map of 1830, Christopher Greenwood also shows Wollaston's windmill, plus waterwheels representing Wollaston Mills and, at the bottom, Gig Mill. By this date, the small cluster of black dots along the newly turnpiked Bridgnorth Road, which runs left-right.

Above: This is the only photograph discovered to date of cottages in the old Wollaston village. The scene is the High Street end of Vicarage Road, at the rear of The Barley Mow. The houses on the extreme right were built in 1904, but those in the foreground are much older. Characteristic of Wollaston Old Village was the use of highly crenulated Dutch or Queen Anne gables on the buildings, seen very clearly here.
Stourbridge Library

Above: A sketch of houses in the Old Village at Wollaston, which was produced in 1951, at the time when these buildings were being demolished. Unwin Passage can be seen receding into the background between the houses. The view is from Vicarage Road.

Above: A third view of the Old Village provides a different perspective, and fixes the relationship between the cottages seen in the previous illustrations and The Barley Mow. The asymmetry of the gables mentioned above is also highlighted.

houses on the site occupied by Wollaston Garage in 2003, and another cluster comprising The Gate Hangs Well, a farm and six houses. In the old village, in addition to the Hall, there were 24 houses, two shops, a windmill and The Barley Mow Inn, which, standing on the junction of two roads, had in all probability been an alehouse for many generations, long before 1827. The population of the old village in 1827 was probably in the region of 150 to 250, out of a total of between 300 and 400 for the much larger area regarded as Wollaston in 2003. By the time of the 1851 census the population of the old village had risen to 373, out of Wollaston's total population of 1,172.

The Stourbridge Canal

Wollaston's rural isolation was not to last long. Plans for the proposed route of the Stourbridge Canal, drawn by James Brindley in 1766, and by Robert Whitworth in 1774 and 1775, show that Wollaston would soon have a direct link to the Staffordshire & Worcestershire Canal and thence to the wider world, whilst locally it would be linked with the growing industrial areas of Wordsley, Pensnett and Brierley Hill. These three plans, like Harry Court's map of 1782, all show the old village as a cluster of houses near to the Hall. The Stourbridge Canal, which eventually opened in 1779, was an important factor in determining the location of John Bradley & Co's ironworks.

John Bradley's Ironworks

Established in 1800 by the side of the canal, near to the modern road, Bradley Road, that commemorates the name of the firm's founder, John Bradley. This ironworks was to transform Wollaston's shape and identity. As the company prospered and grew in size, it attracted workers from the heartland of the Black Country, as well as from further afield. The old village began to grow so much so that by the time of the 1851 census it had extended as far as the New Street that was built to connect Windmill Lane with the High Street. New Street was later renamed Firmstone Street. The old village was now effectively triangular in shape, bounded by High Street, New Street and Windmill Lane (later Vicarage Road), the original vicarage was not built until the 1860s. That this area was the original village is confirmed by the 1851 census in which the address of houses within this triangle is given simply as 'The Village.'

Stourbridge to Bridgnorth turnpike

Another important factor in the growth of Wollaston, and in determining its subsequent physical shape, was the turnpiking of the Stourbridge to Bridgnorth Road in 1816. Houses were eventually built along both sides of the road as far as the Ridge Top and The Forester's Arms. A consequence of this ribbon development was the creation of a new village centre away from the old village that had grown up near Wollaston Hall, at The Barley Mow end of the High Street.

The turnpike (or toll road) was established by an Act of Parliament, which empowered a group of trustees to levy tolls for the improvement and maintenance of the road. Along the road at irregular intervals barriers or gates were erected; to travel beyond the gate a toll or charge had to be

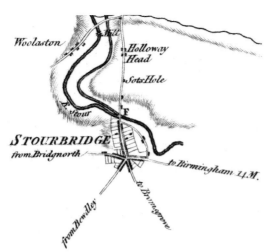

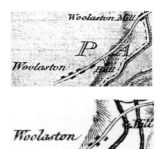

Left and right: Plans for the proposed Stourbridge Canal show that Wollaston as a cluster of houses near to the Hall. There is a good consistency between the way that the village is represented on all three maps The Stourbridge Canal eventually opened in 1779.

Left: The seal of The Company of the Proprietors of the Stourbridge Navigation (Canal). Passing very close by the old village of Wollaston, this canal opened on 3 December 1779. Its proximity to the River Stour was an important factor in determining the location of John Bradley & Co's ironworks.

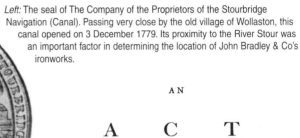

AN

A C T

For making and maintaining a Turnpike Road from the High Street in the Town of *Stourbridge*, in the County of *Worcester*, to the Boundary Stone between the Parish of *Worfield*, and the Liberties of the Borough of *Bridgnorth*, in the County of *Salop*.

[ROYAL ASSENT, 11 *April* 1816.]

𝖂𝖍𝖊𝖗𝖊𝖆𝖘 the Road leading from the High Street in the Town of *Stourbridge*, in the County of *Worcester*, to the Boundary Stone, situate upon the said Road, between the Parish of *Worfield*, and the Liberties of the Borough of *Bridgnorth*, in the County of *Salop*, through the several Townships, Parishes, Liberties or Hamlets of *Stourbridge* and *Old Swinford*, in the said County of *Worcester*; *Kinver*, *Enville* and *Bobbington*, in the said County of *Stafford*; and *Alveley*, *Claverley* and the said Parish of *Worfield*, in the said County of *Salop*, is not only much out of Repair, but in many parts narrow, circuitous, and otherwise incommodious to the Public; and the same Road cannot be properly amended, widened, turned, improved and kept in Repair, by the Laws now in force:

And whereas it would be of great Convenience to the Neighbourhood, and of great public Utility, if the said Road was amended, widened, altered, turned, improved, and kept in Repair: BUT the same cannot be effected without the Aid and Authority of Parliament;

15.   A   May

Above: 'The Iron Works of Mr W O Foster, Stourbridge' was first published in Measom's Guide to the Great Western Railway in 1860. The engraving is rich in detail and shows how much the John Bradley ironworks had developed in its first 60 years. Despite its association with Stourbridge, the greater proportion of the land the works occupied was in fact in Wollaston.

Above: If one factor had to be singled out for being responsible for the relocation of Wollaston and its subsequent growth, that would have to be the turnpiking of the Stourbridge to Bridgnorth Road in 1816. This is the first page of the Act that the turnpike's promoters obtained, showing that their bill gained the royal assent on 11 April 1816.

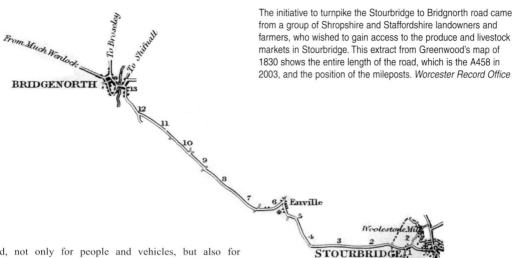

The initiative to turnpike the Stourbridge to Bridgnorth road came from a group of Shropshire and Staffordshire landowners and farmers, who wished to gain access to the produce and livestock markets in Stourbridge. This extract from Greenwood's map of 1830 shows the entire length of the road, which is the A458 in 2003, and the position of the mileposts. *Worcester Record Office*

paid, not only for people and vehicles, but also for livestock, cattle, sheep and pigs. Approaching Wollaston from Stourbridge there were chains at Beauty Bank, and near The Waterloo Inn, plus a gate near The Gate Hangs Well, whilst further along the road, on the way to the Stewponey, there was also a tollhouse near New Wood.

The initiative to turnpike the road came from a group of Shropshire and Staffordshire landowners and farmers who wished to gain access to the produce and livestock markets in Stourbridge. At the beginning of the 19th century, Stourbridge was not only the business and social centre for much of North Worcestershire and parts of the Black Country, it was also an important communications centre; it was the hub of a number of major turnpikes, and was linked to the canal system. The list of 26 investors, who collectively raised £3,400 to launch the turnpike trust, was headed by Lord Stamford of Enville Hall who subscribed £600.

The map of the original survey made for the turnpike trust shows that the road coming down from Beauty Bank to cross the Withy Brook (near to the pub known at different times as the Golden or Stourbridge Lion, and most recently as Katie Fitzgerald's) had to be straightened out. The original alignment of the road was probably in line with the frontage of the flats that face Enville Street. When the road was turnpiked the sharp bend was removed by the construction of a small embankment that in turn created the steep slope at the end of Mamble Road that motorists invariably curse still in 2003.

By 1834 there was a coach service running three times a week, but whether it carried sufficient passengers or packages to ever make it profitable is not known. The turnpike trust certainly struggled financially and was eventually wound up in 1877 when the road was dis-turnpiked, and the barriers and gates were removed.

William Scott's survey

William Scott published his *'Stourbridge and its Vicinity'* in 1832. This detailed survey of Stourbridge and its surrounding area includes a vivid picture of Wollaston. It is a snapshot in time of what was once a compact, self-

Below: As with other turnpikes in the country, towards the end of its existence the collection of tolls on the Stourbridge to Bridgnorth Road was let to 'toll farmers', who agreed to pay the trustees a guaranteed sum each quarter. This notice is valuable as it lists the gates along the road, most of which were not near Wollaston.

STOURBRIDGE & BRIDGNORTH
TURNPIKE ROAD.
"Stourbridge and Bridgnorth Road Act, 1854."

TOLLS
TO BE LET.

NOTICE IS HEREBY GIVEN that the Tolls arising at the several Toll Gates erected upon the Turnpike Road leading from the boundary stone of the Township of Stourbridge, at the commencement of the Hamlet of Wollaston, in the County of Worcester, to the boundary stone between the Parish of Worfield and the Liberties of the Borough of Bridgnorth, in the County of Salop, and called or known by the respective names of Prestwood, Stewponey Bridge, Broad Oak, and Old Lodge Gates, WILL BE LET BY AUCTION, at the STAMFORD ARMS HOTEL, ENVILLE, in the County of Stafford, upon *Tuesday the 19th day of November, next*

between the hours of Twelve o'clock at noon and Two in the Afternoon, in the manner directed by the Acts passed in the third and fourth years of the reign of his Majesty King George the Fourth, "for regulating Turnpike Roads."

THE Tolls were Let for the year ending upon the 31st day of December next, at the sum of £ *455* above the expenses of collecting them, and will be put up at that sum, ~~or at such other sum as the Trustees of the said Road shall think fit.~~

WHOEVER happens to be the best bidder, must, at the same time, pay one month in advance of the rent at which such Tolls may be let, and give security with two sufficient sureties to the satisfaction of the Trustees for payment of the rent agreed upon, either monthly, or at such other times and in such other proportions as they shall direct.

JOHN HARWARD,
CLERK TO THE TRUSTEES.

Stourbridge, *October 15th 1867*

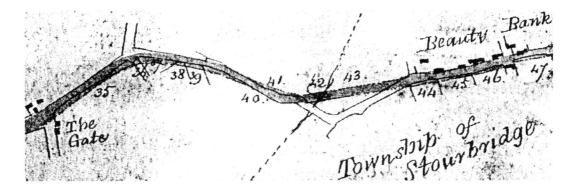

Above: A portion of the map of the original survey made for the Stourbridge to Bridgnorth Road showing the original alignment of the road and the course of the small embankment that was constructed to overcome a dip by the Withy Brook. This created the steep slope at the end of Mamble Road that motorists still invariably curse in 2003.

contained, rural community on the brink of transformation as industrialisation began to spread from the nearby John Bradley ironworks. Scott describes the village as follows:

'*The ancient rural village of Wollaston, is situated near to the turnpike road from Stourbridge to Bridgnorth* (in 1832 the road did not pass through what was then considered to be the village), *and contiguous* (adjoining) *to a branch of the first district of Stourbridge roads* (this was High Street), *leading from Kidderminster to Dudley. The site of the Barley Mow, in the centre of the village, is supposed by some, to have been that of an ancient family residence.*'

Scott describes what could be seen when walking across 'The Rough', the land between Wollaston Hall (its site was approximately the cul-de-sac end of Apley Road) and Mount Carmel. The route indicated by Scott can be traced in 2003 by following the path that leads from the end of Wyre Road, and then runs parallel to the River Stour before climbing the grassy slope at the rear of the Village Hall:

'*The Rough is traversed by a winding path, exhibiting through several avenues in different directions, a pleasing prospect of the subjacent vale* (the valley below), *with manifold meanderings of the river, bordered by opposite acclivities, extending into the mining and manufacturing parts of the country, to which the ornamented heights of Hagley* (referring to the obelisk) *and its vicinity are contiguous. The churches of Stourbridge and Oldswinford are conspicuous objects. This miniature picture, previously to the establishment of extensive iron works near the base of the brow, possessed a more beautiful exterior. The northern acclivity* (slope of the river bank) *forms a more rural appendage to the demesne* (the grounds of the Hall) *than the last described eminence. It is well planted with*

Above, top: This rural scene would have been familiar to William Scott, who published his '*Stourbridge and its Vicinity*' in 1832. In this he provided a detailed topographical description of Wollaston. Astonishingly, this photograph was taken in the late 1950s and shows John Bradley & Co, viewed from the old Wollaston road, which led on past the Hall to the old village. John Rastrick's New Foundry can be seen in the centre of the works, between the two chimneys. *Harry Cartwright/Stourbridge Library*

Above. lower: The old Wollaston road skirted the edge of Wollaston Hall, whose grounds were protected by this high brick wall. In the distance is Wollaston Mill (see Chapter Five), and, behind the trees, The Barley Mow. In 2003 the road is a footpath and cycleway.

Above: A page from the enumerator's book in the 1841 census showing Withy Bank. There is a good mix of trades, such as shoemaking, but the greater proportion of the men are down as 'foundry man' or 'forgeman', almost certainly at John Bradley & Co., where 33% of Wollaston men worked that year.

CHAIR MAKERS.

Higgins Samuel, Coventry-street
Jones Richard, Withy Bank
Mills Thomas, New Road
Parker William, Seven-dwellings

Above: An extract from Bentley's Directory of Stourbridge for 1841.

*Above:*The 1841 census shows the development of King Street, which began in the mid-1830s. Originally there were two parts to it, Upper King Street, which led from the new village, and Lower King Street, the part leading off Withy Bank. By 2003 there were just these few original houses left in Lower King Street, the rest having been cleared in the 1970s.

Below: Bridgnorth Road, formerly Withy Bank, in 2003. The houses on the left were built together with those in Lower King Street in the mid- to late-1830s.

timber and its varying undulations admit a tasteful display of landscape gardening.'

Scott describes the Hall in the following terms:

'The mansion called the Hall, of the Elizabethan age, is dated 1617. An avenue of Sychamors, in the style (from which the Gothic architecture is supposed to have derived its origin), fronted by two pillars surmounted by two figures of lions rampant, forms the side entrance; the front is half-timbered, with a lawn at the entrance. ... the adjacent garden, laid out in a gradation of terraces, covering the descent to the meadows beneath.'

These terraces can still be seen in the steep slope that runs from Apley Road down to Sherwood Road.

The 1841 Census

To William Scott's subjective picture of Wollaston in 1832, can be added the objective statistics of the 1841 census in order to obtain a much clearer idea of what sort of community Wollaston was, as it made the transition from a small, predominantly rural community into one whose prosperity and development would be inexorably linked with industrial activity. An analysis of the census information shows that of the 165 men in employment 55 (33%) worked at the ironworks, ten worked in the glasshouses of nearby Amblecote and Wordsley, and nine

Above: Again, these four houses are all that remain from many similar ones built along Withy Bank and Lower King Street in the 1830s. In the centre of the row is a date stone ...

Right: ... which reveals that the houses were built in 1837. 'R. W.' are probably the initials of the builder. It was quite common for builders to commemorate their efforts in this codified manner.

changing as Lower King Street and Withy Bank became residential areas. Exactly when the building of houses in these two locations began is not known, but in all probability it was in the 1830s, as these houses are not shown on the 1827 survey drawn by Davies, nor does Scott make any reference to them. Further support of this view can be seen on a stone tablet set into the eaves of No 5 Bridgnorth Road, which bears the legend '*R. W. 1837.*'

Sale of Lord Dudley's Wollaston Estate

Despite this growth, housing development was restricted by the fact that in the 1840s most of Wollaston belonged to the Dudley Estate. Exactly when it acquired land in Wollaston is not clear, but the Trustees who managed the Dudley Estate from 1833 to 1845 bought land from the Foley estate, which in the early 19th century owned much of Stourbridge and Wollaston. The reasons for the sale of the Dudley land in Wollaston can only be guessed at. Perhaps the new Lord Dudley was responding to the critical comments that had been expressed by James Loch, an acknowledged authority on estate management

Below: This sale, on 25 January 1848, of the Wollaston part of the Dudley Estate was a milestone in the village's development. Within two years houses were being built along Bridgnorth Road, advancing from King Street towards The Gate Hangs Well, whilst, at right angles to Bridgnorth Road, Cobden Street and Duncombe Street were also beginning to evolve.

Plan and Particulars
OF

A Freehold Estate,

Tithe-free, and Land-Tax redeemed,

The Property of the Trustees of the Will of the late Right Honourable JOHN WILLIAM, EARL of DUDLEY, deceased,

SITUATE IN THE

PARISH of OLDSWINFORD, in the COUNTIES of WORCESTER & STAFFORD,

COMPRISING A MANSION, CALLED

WOLLASTON HALL,

WITH

The Gardens, Pleasure-Grounds, and Plantations attached;

ALSO, THE

WOLLASTON ROLLING-MILL, with the Yard and Buildings belonging thereto;

Two Valuable Farms,

CALLED

HIGH PARK & EGGINGTON FARMS,

AND

DIVERS PIECES OF ARABLE, MEADOW, AND PASTURE LAND;

THE WHOLE PROPERTY

Containing 386 Acres,

OR THEREABOUTS,

Which will be Sold by Auction,

(Except as to such parts thereof as may be previously disposed of by Private Contract),

BY

Mr. JOHN DAVIES,

AT THE TALBOT HOTEL, STOURBRIDGE,

On *TUESDAY*, the 25th day of *JANUARY*, 1848, at Three o'Clock,

In 22, or such other number of Lots as may be agreed upon at the time of Sale.

Particulars and Plans may be had, on application, of Messrs. BOURNE & WAINWRIGHT, Solicitors, Dudley; of the Auctioneers; of Mr. JOHN HENRY BENBOW, Solicitor, 1, Stone Buildings, Lincoln's-Inn, London; and of JOHN MAUGHAM, Land Agent, Dudley.

worked in the small spade making works on the banks of the River Stour, whilst in contrast agriculture provided employment for only 26 (14.2%). It can be assumed that by 'the ironworks' the enumerators were referring to John Bradley & Co.

1841 Census summary
Total number of inhabitants 578
Total number of male inhabitants 299
Total number of female inhabitants 279
Total in employment (male and female) 183
Employment by occupation:
- Clerical/professional 2 (1.1%) *
- Building trades 7 (3.8%)
- Spade works 9 (4.9%)
- Glass industry 10 (5.5%)
- Domestic service 20 (10.9%)
- Service trades 24 (13.1%)
- Agriculture 26 (14.2%)
- Iron industry 55 (30.1%)
- Miscellaneous 30 (16.4%)
  * (*Note: These percentages are of the total in employment, both male and female*).

The census also shows that Wollaston was physically expanding not only in terms of population, but also in terms of new houses. It confirms that the shape of the village was

and auditor to the Trustees, who had pointed out that the rental income from their agricultural land was low; or, perhaps, it was the lure of a good price for land for house building and Lord Dudley judged that the time was opportune to sell his Wollaston Estate. The sale took place at the Talbot Hotel in Stourbridge on 25 January 1848.

The sale in 1848 of the Wollaston part of the Dudley Estate was a milestone in the village's development and undoubtedly led to the formation of two land societies to take advantage of the opening up of the land market. Within two years of this sale, houses were being built along Bridgnorth Road, advancing from King Street towards The Gate Hangs Well, whilst, at right angles to Bridgnorth Road, Cobden Street and Duncombe Street were also beginning to evolve.

Land Societies

A phenomenon of the Black Country around 1850 was the establishment of Land Societies, modelled on the Birmingham Freehold Land Society founded in 1847. Each of the following districts: Oldswinford, Wordsley, Pensnett, Kinver and Brierley Hill, witnessed the establishment of such a club, whilst in Wollaston there were two – the North Wollaston Land Society and The Gate Hangs Well Land Society. At face value these land societies were simply the forerunners of today's building societies, enabling people to buy land on which a house could be built.

Important though the acquisition of land was for the building of a house, it was equally important in obtaining a vote. Unlike today the right to vote in a parliamentary election in the early 19th century depended on the ownership of land or property, thus the land societies had a political objective as well as a social one of providing housing. By an Act of Parliament passed in 1430 the owners of freehold land with an annual value of 40 shillings (i.e. the land, if put out to rent, would produce an income of 40s or £2) were entitled to vote. This act was still in force in 1850. The land societies sought to take advantage of this situation. A block of land was bought by a society and then sold off to members in plots with an annual value of not less than 40 shillings. The member who purchased one of these plots was then entitled to vote. The political aspect of these land societies is clearly revealed in the following report on the North Wollaston Land Society which appeared in the *Worcester Chronicle* of 9 January 1850:

'*In the afternoon of Tuesday week a general meeting of this society was held at Mr Baker's, the Barley Mow Inn, Wollaston, when a piece of land which had been purchased by the society was balloted for and transferred to the respective owners. The land, which contained about eight acres, was divided into 39 lots of £30 each. After the transaction of the business about 24 of the members sat down to an excellent dinner* (the gift of the vendor of the land and of the surveyor) *which was served up by the respected host in good style, and a very pleasant evening was enjoyed under the presidency of Mr Lightbourne, the president of the society, who together with Messrs W Brierly, Sedgley, Dykes and Paris, delivered addresses on the importance of possessing a freehold and a vote for the county, and also pointed out the value and advantages of the land in question.*'

The fact that the North Wollaston Society met at The Barley Mow was not unusual; most land societies had their headquarters in a local pub, as this was often the only place where a non-religious meeting could be held. Indeed, the other Wollaston land society took its name from the pub where its meetings were held. The *Worcester Chronicle* of 24 April 1850 carried this report on the Gate Hangs Well Society:

'*This society, the members of which have had only three previous meetings, assembled on the 8th instant, when an eligible piece of land, either for garden or building purposes, comprising ten acres, situate in the immediate locality, which had been purchased by the society from Mr John Yardley, was balloted by the members. 48 shares were allotted, and the possession given to the allottees.*'

The monthly subscription paid by members eventually created a large aggregated capital sum that could then be used to purchase land and, in some cases, finance building operations. The allocation of land and houses was, as the above newspaper report illustrates, by a ballot of the members. When a society had achieved its objectives it was wound up by its members; most societies had a life span of about ten years. Exactly how long Wollaston's two societies existed is not known, but they certainly made an important contribution to the provision of homes for a growing community.

Right: Wollaston had two land societies, the North Wollaston and The Gate Hangs Well. Allocation of land and houses was by a ballot of the members. This photograph shows the rear of one of the four houses built in this way alongside The Gate Hangs Well.

Chapter Two

WHATEVER HAPPENED TO WOLLASTON HALL?

For at least 700 years (c.1230 to 1926) Wollaston Hall, its accompanying estate and various owners exercised great authority over life in Wollaston and the growth and development of the village.

Wollaston Hall stood opposite the end of Vicarage Road, facing the old village, in a position that corresponds to that occupied in 2003 by Nos 42-38 Apley Road, with adjoining buildings that stood in what are the back gardens of Nos 36-30 Apley Road. The hall that was dismantled in 1926 bore the date '1617', but there had clearly been an earlier building, presumably on the same site, for at least four centuries.

The early history of the Hall

Specific mention of a 'Wollaston Hall' is first made in a deed of sale of the reputed Manor of Wollaston to George Liddiatt, a merchant tailor of London, which is dated c.1230. What form this hall took is unknown. In February 1967, Eileen Blades and Don Hooson, both grandchildren of the last owner of Wollaston Hall, Caleb William Roberts, expressed the opinion that:

'*the date 1617 refers to the time when the house was built on to a medieval hall, and the ancient castellated tower and extensive arched cellaring were remains of the earlier building, probably already 300 years old.*'

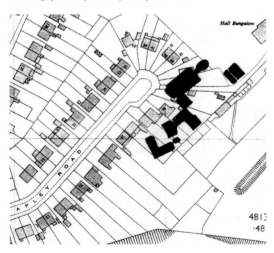

Above: The precise location of Wollaston Hall has sometimes been the subject of conjecture. This map shows the exact position of Wollaston Hall in relation to the later street pattern. It stood opposite the end of Vicarage Road, in a location that corresponds to that occupied in 2003 by Nos 42-38 Apley Road, with adjoining buildings that stood in what are the back gardens of Nos 36-30 Apley Road.

Eileen Blades, who was 13 when the Hall was sold in 1924, added that:

'*There were some rooms, particularly in the old tower (fortified, castellated, three-storey), with walls so wide and hollow that one could walk right along to come out at another secret exit.*' She also recalled that she was: '*forbidden to go into the tower as she was told she would fall through the floor if she did!*'

The ownership and occupancy of Wollaston Hall changed with that of the reputed manor and estate of Wollaston, as outlined in Chapter One. In 1592 George Liddiatt, a London merchant, bought the Manor of Wollaston, including the hall, plus 20 acres of land and 30 acres of meadow, for £341. A John Lyddyatt is recorded as living there in 1578, and in 1616, just before the Hall was rebuilt, one John Liddiat of Cannock, conveyed it to Thomas Banneste, but this was probably only a temporary move as part of a settlement, because it was conveyed back to him the same year.

The rebuilt hall of 1617

The following year, 1617, Wollaston Hall was rebuilt, possibly from the '*medieval hall*' referred to by Eileen Blades in 1967, to the form in which it stood in the village until 1926.

Above the window over the front door Wollaston Hall bore the legend: '*Restored 1643*', which some people have taken to relate to damage it may have incurred during the Civil War. This is however unlikely, as there is no known Civil War action in the area before 1644, although it does

WOLLASTON HALL, STOURBRIDGE.

Above: Eileen Blades recalled that the old tower, which survived from the first Wollaston Hall, had walls so wide and hollow that she could walk right along to come out at another secret exit. She also recalled that she was forbidden to go into the tower as she was told she would fall through the floor if she did. This engraving from 1851 is the only one that shows the tower to good advantage.

seem odd for someone to have had to restore a house that was built only 26 years before! Whatever the case, Wollaston Hall remained in the Liddiatt family until 1672, when Thomas Foley acquired it.

The Foleys and Wollaston Hall

This sale appears to have been a most protracted business, conducted through an intermediary, Samuel Hunt, who was Thomas Foley's Attorney. Indeed it appears that Hunt lived at Wollaston Hall between 1669 and c.1678, possibly leasing it from 16 April 1669 onwards.

Foley family papers, held in Hereford Record Office, show that Samuel Hunt bought the Hall and Estate on 30 September 1672 for £5,000. Of this:

'£1,000 was to be paid at or before the Feast of St James the Apostle next ensuing; £1,000 at or before the feast of All Saints next ensuing, and £3,000 at such time as the now son of John Liddyatt shall be 21. Additional yearly rental of one rose flower payable at the Feast of the Nativity of St John the Baptist.'

Completion of these 'staged payments' seems to have taken four years, and on 3 August 1676, John Liddiatt, presumably now aged 21, sold to Samuel Hunt:

'all that manor or reputed manor of Wollaston, with the Manor House called Wollaston Hall, and meadows in Wollaston and Amblecote and now in the possession of the said Samuel Hunt or his tenant.'

Above: Wollaston Hall was rebuilt in 1617 into the form in which it would remain in the village until 1926. This event was recorded in a date painted onto one of the gables, seen here in an enlargement from a postcard view. Allegedly, above the window over the front door, the Hall also bore the legend: '*Restored 1643*', but this does not show up in photographs.

This was not all that Samuel Hunt possessed, for on 21 February 1676 he, his wife, and two servants were also granted: '*liberty to sit in the seats in the loft of Oldswinford Church belonging to Wollaston Hall.*'

In 1678 Wollaston Manor, the Hall and Estate, were finally transferred to Thomas Foley, who, on 1 December that year, leased to his brother Philip: '*All that reputed Manor of Wollaston, the capital messuage called Wollaston Hall, and all stables, etc.,*' for £332 per annum. It is very doubtful that either Foley brother ever lived at Wollaston Hall, Thomas residing at Witley Court and Philip at Prestwood. Indeed it is known that between 1678 and 1680 a Mr Chelsham rented Wollaston Hall and some of the lands attached to it for £108 per annum. During his tenancy, in October 1680, it is recorded that bricks to the value of 15 shillings were delivered to him, and lead for repairs to a gutter cost 18 shillings. These works were part of the major programme of repairs undertaken with great energy and diligence for Philip Foley by Dan Rowley, as described in Chapter One.

The 18th century was unremarkable so far as Wollaston Hall is concerned. The freehold remained in the ownership of the Foleys, but the leasehold changed hands three times by sale and once by marriage:

- 1703 – Leasehold sold to John Wheeler, JP
- 27 November 1708 – John Wheeler dies, his eldest son John, inherits
- 1711 – Leasehold sold to Edward Kendall
- 1731 – Leasehold sold to Francis Homfray
- 1758 – John Homfray, son of Francis, marries Mary Addenbrooke
- 21 February 1792 – John Homfray, son of John, grandson of Francis, changes his name to Addenbrooke

Below: The Manor of Wollaston disappeared without trace after 1672, when it was acquired on behalf of Thomas Foley, the founder of Oldswinford Hospital School, and became part of the vast Foley estate. After his death in 1677, his eldest son, also called Thomas, leased the manor to his brother Philip in 1678. Dated 2 November that year, this document is an acknowledgement of monies owed him by Philip Foley, the settlement of which formed part of the change of ownership of the manor and hall.

• 29 April 1795 – Tenancy of Wollaston Hall granted to John Addenbrooke by Mary, daughter of Jeremiah Addenbrooke.

John Addenbrooke remained at the Hall during and after the sale of the leasehold by the Foleys in 1809. Wollaston Hall was sold by auction at 3.00pm on 12 June 1809 in The Talbot Inn, Stourbridge. The sale was divided into 14 Lots, of which:

LOT X. – Comprises the beautiful MANSION of WOLLASTON HALL, with the Stables, Barns, Out-offices, Gardens, Lawns, Plantations, Pleasure Grounds, Arable, Meadow, and Pasture Lands, lying on the East side of the turnpike-road leading from Coalbourn Brook through Wollaston towards Kidderminster, containing 68 Acres and 39 Perches, now in the possession of the aforesaid Mr Addenbrooke, together with Six Tenements and a Barn, in Wollaston village, let to different persons.

The leasehold of Wollaston Hall was probably purchased by Thomas Hill of Dennis Hall, whose will (dated 29 June 1822) gives his executors powers to dispose of his possessions, including:

'all my capital Messuage or Mansion House called Wollaston Hall with the gardens pleasure grounds land and appurtenances thereto belonging... purchased by me of the Rt Hon Thomas Lord Foley and now late in the several possession of John Addenbrooke and others and being in Wollaston...'

Thomas Hill died in 1824. It seems clear from various references in contemporary newspapers that during the preceding 15 years the Addenbrooke family had continued to reside at Wollaston Hall. One example comes from Berrow's Worcester Journal of 6 November 1823, which recorded: 'Married on the previous Thursday, J A Addenbrooke of Wollaston Hall to Mrs Lea of The Hill, nr Stourbridge.'

Wollaston Hall sold to the Dudleys

Lord Foley sold many of his Worcestershire holdings to Lord Dudley in 1826, the Wollaston Estate being included amongst the 634 acres purchased at that time. This made little or no difference in Wollaston or at the Hall, where the Addenbrookes continued to live, under an annual tenancy agreement. John Homfray Jr died at Wollaston Hall in 1837, aged 78, but a Mrs Addenbrooke remained there until the late 1840s. The Trustees of the will of the late John William, 1st Earl of Dudley, who had died in 1833, sold the freehold of the Wollaston Estate at an auction held at The Talbot Hotel, Stourbridge, at 3.00pm on 25 January 1848. The significance of this sale to the development of Wollaston, and especially of the new village, has already been described in Chapter One. It signalled the break-up of the Wollaston Estate and the sale of the freeholds to the lands and properties comprising the 22 lots into which the 386-acre estate was divided. Wollaston Hall was Lot 10 and, in addition to the hall, included 21 acres of land.

William Blow Collis and changes to Wollaston Hall

William Blow Collis, a local solicitor, bought Wollaston Hall for £3,500, and moved in shortly afterwards. Collis was born on 12 November 1808 at Cannock, and had married Anne Hooman on 17 September 1835 at Oldswinford. On 14 August 1849 he took out fire insurance cover for Wollaston Hall with the Law Fire Insurance Society of London. The sum insured was £480, for which £1 5s 9d was paid annually each 25 December, comprising:

'£400 on his private dwelling house and Brewhouse, fowlhouse and other offices all communicating... brick timber and plaster or wattle built and tiled or slated except the small Greenhouse which is of Glass; a small stove in the Butler's pantry allowed. £80 on Lodge brick built and tiled or slated at the end of the plantation leading to Stourbridge.'

Wollaston Hall was the home of William Blow Collis for about ten years, between 1848 and 1858, during which time he made a number of changes to the fabric of the building. On the front of the house this included repositioning the front door, which thereafter gave the house an asymmetrical appearance, plus the addition of bargeboards and finials to the gables. At the rear the wall was covered with roughcast concealing the original timbering, and a brick-built projecting wing was added to the east side of the house, containing a kitchen and offices. The interior was also restored and modernized, although in a rather ruthless manner, stripping out much of the original detail on the ground floor. It is likely that these alterations were made quite soon after Collis acquired the Hall, as they appear on a series of three engravings made of the Hall

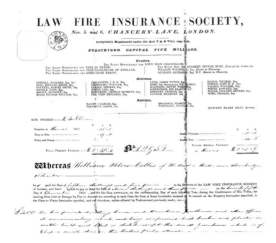

Left: On 14 August 1849, shortly after buying Wollaston Hall for £3,500, William Blow Collis took out fire insurance cover for Wollaston Hall with the Law Fire Insurance Society of London. The sum insured was £480, for which £1 5s 9d was paid annually each 25 December. This is a copy of the insurance certificate with which he was issued.

during the 1850s, the earliest of which is dated 1 October 1851.

The Firmstone family at Wollaston Hall

William Blow Collis died at Wollaston Hall on 27 August 1858, aged 49. His will and codicil were proved at the Principal Probate Registry on 7 October that year by oath of his widow Anne Collis, Charles Evers Swindell, an ironmaster of the Quarry near Stourbridge, and William Cochrane, an ironmaster, three of his executors. His effects were under £45,000. Anne Collis continued to live at Wollaston Hall for just over a year after her husband's death, before selling it to Henry Onions Firmstone on 29 September 1859. Firmstone was born in Bilston on 23 February 1815, the eldest of 14 children. His family were ironmasters. His father, William, and uncle, George,

Above: Wollaston Hall was the home of William Blow Collis for about ten years, between 1848 and 1858. During his time there he made a number of changes to the fabric of the building, including repositioning the front door. At the rear a projecting wing was built, containing a kitchen and offices. Collis also commissioned several engravings of his revamped home, which, like this one, portray a somewhat idealised view of the building and its grounds.

Below: The interior of Wollaston Hall was also restored and modernized, although in a rather ruthless manner, stripping out much of the original detail on the ground floor. It is likely that these alterations were made quite soon after Collis acquired the Hall. He commissioned this engraving, which shows the line of trees forming the main avenue approach to the hall to the right.

acquired the Leys Iron Works, Brockmoor, and when Henry was 16, and still at school in Bridgnorth, his father died; whereupon he left to work at the Leys, running the business after George Firmstone retired until 1894, when the works was closed owing to the bad state of the iron trade. His other business interests included: the Great Bridge Iron & Steel Co.; Glascote and Amington collieries, near Tamworth; Crookhay Furnaces at Hill Top, West Bromwich; the Hyde ironworks, near Kinver; Oak Farm Works, near Dudley, and iron ore mines at Froghall, in North Staffordshire. He was also one of the first commissioners under the South Staffordshire Mine Drainage Act. H O Firmstone was a churchman, a JP for Worcestershire and Staffordshire for nearly 30 years, and a feoffee of Oldswinford Hospital Charity and a governor of Stourbridge Grammar School. In his earlier years he was an enthusiastic amateur actor. He was also an able chess player. Stourbridge Chess Club was formed at his house in 1852, and he was its first President for life. He was also a supporter of the Volunteer movement, and was the first Captain of the Brierley Hill Company.

The Firmstones owned Wollaston Hall for exactly 40 years, and many of the stories of life there emanate from this period. One concerns a dining ritual. Every Wednesday the dining room, which was panelled floor to ceiling in fine-grained English Oak, was the scene of a party attended by about 30 family members. On one occasion only 13 arrived, and because of a belief that if 13 sit down to dine the first to rise will die within the year, it was suggested that some members of the party should sit at another table. Unfortunately, this suggestion was ignored, and 13 sat down to dine. First to rise was Henry Onions Firmstone's sister, Francis Ann (Mrs Alexander Baxter), who died within 12 months. Another concerns a brown pony, used to pull the family phæton (an open four-wheeled carriage), which one day ran into one of the gate pillars at the Hall and was so badly injured that it had to be destroyed. Its hindquarters were roasted at the nearby Barley Mow!

Tragic times

Sadly, Henry Onions Firmstone's time at Wollaston Hall was not without tragedy. His first wife, Ann Onions, who was also his cousin, died there in 1874, and his second wife, Phoebe Palmer Claridge, died at the Hall on 7 January 1893. But perhaps most tragic of all was the suicide of his son, Arthur George Firmstone, at the Hall on 24 April 1890. This was reported by the *County Express* of 26 April:

'*A tragic affair occurred this morning at Wollaston Hall, the residence of Mr H O Firmstone…. One of his sons, Arthur George Firmstone, breakfasted with the family as usual, and about twenty minutes past ten left the breakfast-room, and proceeded to his bedchamber. He was subsequently found there lifeless. A breechloader lay near him, and its discharge had inflicted a terrible wound in the head. No reason is known for the act. Mr Firmstone, sen, is a well-known ironmaster, and much sympathy is felt for him.*'

As a gruesome reminder of this event it was said that the marks on the ceiling left by this gunshot remained until the hall was dismantled. The effect of this tragedy also left its mark on H O Firmstone, and it is probably not a coincidence that he made his will just two months later, on 27 June 1890.

The Roberts family at Wollaston Hall

Henry Onions Firmstone died at Wollaston Hall on 5 April 1899, aged 84, and he was interred in the family vault at St Mary's Church in Kingswinford on 10 April. His son, Thomas Alfred Firmstone, continued to live at the Hall until it was sold by auction at The Talbot Hotel, Stourbridge, at 4.00pm on 30 June 1899. The purchaser was Caleb William Roberts, another local ironmaster. He was born on 14 April 1851, and with Ebenezer Elias Cooper founded the firm of Roberts & Cooper in 1870. In 1881 they bought the Brettell

Below: Henry Onions Firmstone bought Wollaston Hall on 29 September 1859, and his family owned it for exactly 40 years. This is the oldest known photograph of the Hall, which was taken during the Firmstone's time there. For once it shows the Hall without the distorted perspective often applied to it by artists.

Above: Henry Onions Firmstone died at Wollaston Hall on 5 April 1899. His son, Thomas Alfred Firmstone, continued to live there until it was sold by auction at The Talbot Hotel, Stourbridge, at 4.00pm on 30 June 1899. Caleb William Roberts, a local ironmaster, bought it. This is the title page to the sale particulars.

Right: The Plan of the Wollaston Hall Estate from the 30 June 1899 sale particulars. This shows both the Hall and its outbuildings, plus both of its lodges.

Plan of WOLLASTON HALL ESTATE STOURBRIDGE.
For Sale by Auction on
FRIDAY, JUNE 30TH 1899
BY
H. KING & SON.

Lane Ironworks from Thos Webb & Co, in March 1898 they acquired the Great Bridge Iron & Steel Co, and later the Leys Iron Works at Brockmoor, which had formerly belonged to H O Firmstone. The company also owned timber businesses at the Nine Locks and the Old Wharf, Stourbridge. Ebenezer Cooper retired in 1900, and Caleb Roberts continued the business on his own. Late in 1911 a private limited company was formed under the title of Messrs Roberts & Cooper Ltd.

Caleb Roberts paid £4,300 for Wollaston Hall, which was conveyed to him on 29 September 1899, 40 years to the day after H O Firmstone had bought it! During his period

Below: Caleb William Roberts, who paid £4,300 for Wollaston Hall on 1 July 1899. It was conveyed to him on 29 September 1899, 40 years to the day after Henry Onions Firmstone had bought it!

there, Wollaston Hall seems to have featured much more in village life than at any other time, particularly in the years immediately before the Great War. A large number of fetes and meetings seem to have been held there, reflecting the great degree of involvement both Caleb Roberts and his wife Mary had in Village affairs, as the following examples show:

- 17 August 1908 – Garden Fete held in the grounds of Wollaston Hall to raise funds for the purchase of a Parish Room,
- 19 July 1913 – First Carnival and Fete held by the Wollaston Benevolent Committee in the grounds of Wollaston Hall on behalf of the proposed Public Hall,
- 2 July 1914 – Carnival and Fete held in the grounds of Wollaston Hall: '*The splendidly kept gardens were quite an attraction, and many inspected the giant holly tree which grows out of the side of the hall*', (*County Express* 11 July 1914)

Given this greater public access to the Hall, it is probably not surprising that a number of descriptions of it and its grounds began to appear in print. The *County Advertiser* of 3 January 1914 had an article on:

'*The beautiful Elizabethan Mansion of Wollaston Hall with its noble avenue of sycamore trees and its fine grounds which have been recently opened on numerous occasions to Wollaston residents, never fails to win admiration from visitors to the district....*'

The gardens were laid out in a gradation of terraces, covering the descent to the meadows and river beneath. They must have been a memorable sight, as a Mr Jennings of Mamble Road, who saw the Hall as a boy, told *The Black Country Bugle* of May 1998 that he: '*never saw such well cared for lawns.*'

Above: Caleb Roberts can be seen again at the heart of his extended family on the occasion of his daughter Elsie Mary's marriage to Alfred Ernest Marsh on 22 April 1903. The real value of this picture lies in the fact that it was taken at the rear of Wollaston Hall, and represents the only known view of this side of the building.

Below: A copy of the marriage certificate of Alfred Ernest Marsh and Elsie Mary Roberts.

Below: Whilst some of the dates of the various photographs of Wollaston Hall can be estimated, such as from the postmarks on postcards, few can be dated more precisely that this one. It was taken to illustrate what is probably the best-known description of the house, which appears in a volume of the *Victoria County History of Worcestershire*, published in 1913. *National Monuments Record*

A contemporary description of Wollaston Hall

From this same period also comes the best description of the house. It was in a volume of the Victoria County History of Worcestershire, published in 1913, and was clearly written by someone who had visited the Hall:

'Wollaston Hall, a much modernized early 17th century house of half-timber, L-shaped on plan, and two stories (sic) *in height, facing north-west. The main limb of the L is two rooms in depth, and in the centre of the principal front is a recessed entrance porch, which probably opened in the first instance directly into the large room, which occupies the southern end of this side of the building, out of which the present entrance corridor appears to have been taken. On the north side of the entrance are two large rooms en suite, making up the rest of the frontage, while to the rear of them are two narrower rooms of equal length. The stairs, which are of original date, are on the south side of the entrance corridor, at the back of the original entrance hall. The projecting wing on the east side of the house, containing the kitchen and offices, is of brick, and appears to be a later addition or rebuilding. With the exception of the stairs and some linen-pattern panelling in one of the*

Below: The lodge and drive to Wollaston Hall. This was at the corner of what is the junction of Apley Road with High Street in 2003. The roof of the lodge can be glimpsed on the left, whilst an avenue of tall trees affords a small peak at the Hall in the distance.

rooms at the back, little original detail remains on the ground floor. In some of the first floor rooms the original roof-timbers are exposed, and the construction displays great ingenuity. The rooms to the south of the staircase are reached by a narrow and lofty central passage lighted by dormers. Generally the interior has been ruthlessly restored and modernized. The front elevation is crowned by a range of five gables, filled with ornamental half-timbering disposed in quatrefoil panels with flat baluster-shaped uprights above them. On one of the beams is carved the date 1617, and in the apex of the southern gable are the initials R M. The bargeboards and finials appear to be modern, but the carved brackets at the intersection of the gables are probably original. The back elevation is also gabled, but the wall has been covered with roughcast, so that the timbering is concealed. The windows have in nearly every case been renewed and enlarged. The original brick chimney shafts have for the most part survived. The roofs are tiled. The garden slopes down in a succession of terraces to the valley of the Stour.'

Above: A view looking back along The Avenue at Wollaston Hall, with the house immediately behind the photographer. The maturity of the trees, evinced by their gnarled trunks, attests to the centuries for which it had stood in the village. On the right a lady peers out from a porch window.

Below: The Avenue ended in a circular gravelled forecourt in front of Wollaston Hall, part of which can be seen in this photograph. By this time ivy had taken quite a hold on some parts of the building.

This description failed to mention the Hall's two lodges: the Lower Lodge, which stood on the Hall's southern boundary by the River Stour, next to the old Wollaston Road, and the Main Lodge, which stood by the gates leading off High Street.

Wollaston Hall in the early 20th century

Life at Wollaston Hall in the early part of the 20th century appears to have been pretty idyllic. Eileen Blades, Caleb Roberts' granddaughter, recalled in February 1967 that:

'the highlight of the year was Christmas Day at Wollaston (arriving there in true Dickensian style by horse and carriage). I did so enjoy that. I particularly remember Auntie's radiantly happy face and very merry laugh, which added greatly to the festivities. I remember, too, the lovely Christmas cakes she made and iced herself.'

The Tragic Death of Caleb Roberts

Caleb William Roberts Jr served with distinction on active service in France, and was awarded the French Cross of Honour in August 1916. Sadly his father did not live to see the Armistice. On 25 September 1918 Caleb Roberts was supervising the removal of a boiler at the Leys Ironworks, when an attached metal chimney came loose and struck him a fatal blow to the head.

Although he had made his will in June 1917, it took until 23 September 1919, almost a year after his death, for probate to be granted to Caleb William Roberts' executors and trustees. His effects amounted to £160,977. In retrospect, this tragic turn of events can be seen as a critical turning point in the fate of Wollaston Hall.

The Decline of Wollaston Hall

Without Caleb Sr as both head of the family and its business interests, the Roberts were less able to cope with the difficult economic times that lay ahead. Within seven years Caleb's two eldest sons would die stress-related deaths, and his widow would also pass away, leaving Wollaston Hall surplus to requirements and a valuable capital asset to be liquidated. In the short-term life carried on much as before at the Hall. Mary Roberts continued to support both her late husband's and her own interests, and made the Hall and its grounds available for village functions. One late example was in early September 1923 when a Garden Party was held in the grounds in aid of a fund for the proposed public hall in Wollaston.

Some of the Hall Estate land fronting to High Street Wollaston was also sold off for housing on 5 July 1920. This comprised 22 building plots, seven of which lay between the junction of Vicarage Road and what is in 2003 the junction of Wentworth Road with High Street, the remaining 15 plots being between The Bull's Head Inn and the drive to Wollaston Hall, approximating to Apley Road in 2003. Later that year, on 11 October 1920, the mortgage on Wollaston Hall was finally discharged, and the freehold was conveyed to the Executors and Trustees of the Will of the late Caleb William Roberts.

In the early 1920s Roberts & Cooper's ironworks suffered considerably from the prevailing trade depression,

Right: During the Roberts' time at Wollaston Hall it seems to have played a greater role in village life than at any other period. It was regularly used as the venue for fetes and garden parties, many of which were held in aid of village activities.

putting great strain on those family members running the business. One day in mid-October 1923 Caleb Roberts Jr fell down the stairs at his home in Brierley Hill, and died two weeks later on 28 October from a cerebral haemorrhage; he was only 47. Adding to the late Mr Roberts' concerns had been the poor health of his mother, living alone at Wollaston Hall. Just prior to his tragic fall there had been a small fire at the Hall, caused by Mrs Roberts knocking over an oil lamp beside her bed, the Hall not having been wired with electricity, which was only just becoming available in Wollaston. The damage caused was

Left: This second view of the lodge, gates and avenue at Wollaston Hall was clearly taken in the winter. The leafless trees reveal more of the lodge, which appears to have had precariously tall chimneys. Slightly more of the Hall can also be seen at the end of the avenue, whilst at right a paling fence has been erected.

Below: Although there are quite a few three-quarter views of Wollaston Hall taken in this direction, this commercial postcard one shows more of the single-storey bay and, on the extreme right, the side of the tower.

Left: Three-quarter views of Wollaston Hall taken in this direction are much more rare. In fact this postcard is the only known view taken at this angle, which obscures the tower behind later additions.

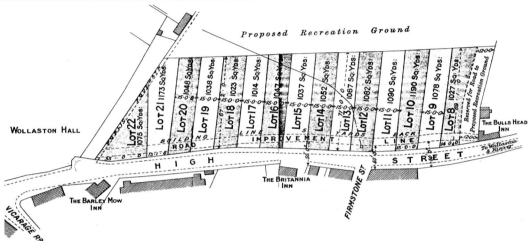

Above: Times became harder for the Roberts family following Caleb Roberts' death in 1918. On 5 July 1920 some of the Hall Estate fronting to High Street was sold off for housing. This plan shows 15 of the plots between The Bull's Head Inn and the drive to Wollaston Hall, the remaining seven lay between the junction of Vicarage Road and what, in 2003, is the junction of Wentworth Road with High Street.

Below: The sales particulars for the 5 July 1920 Wollaston Hall Estate land sale included this picture taken across High Street from near the corner of Vicarage Road. The poles and wires of the Kinver Light Railway can be seen, and, through a gap in the trees, the Hall itself can be glimpsed.

slight, but the concern this incident generated was great. Mary Roberts did not leave the Hall after her son's death, except on one occasion in early March 1924, when she presided at a tea held after the annual meeting of the circuit branch of the Women's Missionary Auxiliary at Hill Street Church in Brierley Hill. She died at Wollaston Hall on 31 March 1924, aged 71. The housekeeper and gardener were kept on at the Hall, but, as no other members of the family desired to live there, a decision was taken to sell it.

The struggle to sell Wollaston Hall

Once probate was granted on Mary Roberts' will on 23 April 1924, Wollaston Hall was put up for sale by auction at The Talbot Hotel, Stourbridge, at 4.00pm on 9 May 1924. The following is the complete description of the Hall taken from the sale catalogue. It is the most detailed description of the Hall known:

THE WOLLASTON HALL ESTATE is situated in the Borough of Stourbridge in the County of Worcester and divided from Staffordshire by the River Stour. Within a short distance of the South Staffordshire Industrial Area, 10 miles from Wolverhampton and 12 from Birmingham.

THE MANSION built in the early 17th Century, is a well preserved and beautiful type of Elizabethan Architecture of Historical interest (mentioned in Scott's *Stourbridge*). The Reception Rooms which are mostly panelled and of large dimensions and some of the Bedrooms with quaint oak beams and recesses will be found a

Above: Following Mary Roberts' death on 31 March 1924, the housekeeper and gardener were kept on at Wollaston Hall, but, as no other members of the family desired to live there, a decision was taken to sell it. This remarkably sharp commercial postcard view of the Hall dates from that period, and shows the building looking a little run down and unloved.

particularly attractive feature. Much of the original oak carving and beams, together with two studded doors in the Hall remain intact.

THE GROUNDS with fine Forest Trees, Plantations, Old World Gardens and Rich Pasture Land, are such that only time can produce.

SPORTING Hunting with two Packs, the 'Albrighton' and 'Woodland.' Stourbridge Golf Course 18 holes, one of the finest in the Midlands, is within easy distance. Good shooting in the district.

FIXTURES A List of Tenants Fixtures will be produced at the time of the sale, which the purchaser will be required to pay for in addition to the purchase money, at a sum to be named by the Auctioneers.

GENERAL The Auctioneers call special attention to the Estate, which, while possessing all the amenities of a Country Residence, offers exceptional facilities to a business gentleman.

POSSESSION On Completion.

PARTICULARS The Valuable and Attractive Freehold Residential Estate consisting of the Fine old Elizabethan Mansion in a wonderful state of preservation and equipped with Modern Conveniences, known as WOLLASTON HALL.

THE MANSION approached by a long Carriage Drive, guarded at the entrance by a Convenient Lodge through an avenue of matured sycamore trees, presents a most picturesque half-timbered front and contains:-

On the Ground Floor – Vestibule, Tiled Entrance Hall, opening on to a Massive Oak Well Staircase with domed roof.

Handsome Panelled Dining Room with open chimneybreast and modern grate, and sideboard recess, 27ft x 21ft.

Partly Panelled Lounge with two fireplaces, one with carved oak mantel, and the other carved white marble, divided by sliding and folding doors, in all 35ft x 21ft, opening into an Elegant Conservatory.

Morning Room (Panelled), and Study with two modern fireplaces and Adam Mantels, also divided by sliding doors, in all 41ft x 12ft.

Lavatory and W.C.

The Domestic Offices: Back Hall, two large Cooking Kitchens both with excellent ranges and saddle boilers connected with the hot water system for Bath Room and Domestic purposes, glazed sink cupboards, etc. Larder, Housemaid's Pantry with lead washing and fitted cupboards.

Outside Wash House and Coal Stores with Fruit Rooms over.

Dairy, Wood House, etc.

Basement – Extensive arched Cellaring with brick wine bins.

On the First Floor – Off a square landing with West Wing having a quaint old Timbered Glass Roof, are Nine Bedrooms, three Dressing Rooms and Box Room, mostly fitted with cupboards; Bath Room with Lavatory Basin and enamelled Bath, W.C., etc.

Second Floor – Three light Attic Rooms.

The Outbuildings include Large Motor House with sliding door, Two Coach Houses with hot water pipes, 3-stall stable and Loose Box with lofts over. Four Tie Cow House, Potting Sheds, Tool Houses, etc., Pigsties. In an Arch Cellar under the Yard is an independent Heating Apparatus for Coach House and Vinery 26ft x 16ft.

GLASS HOUSES in addition to the CONSERVATORY adjoining the House. LEAN TO GREENHOUSE in three sections, 70ft x 12ft 6in, with three Vines and two Peach Trees, and FORCING PIT 31ft x 13ft, all heated by a powerful independent Ideal boiler, which also supplies a radiator in the Lounge.

IN THE GROUNDS are most delightful Old World Gardens and Lawns with terraced and woodland walks, ornamented with ancient sculptured figures; Rose Pergolas, Evergreen Shrubs and old Yew Trees. Two productive Kitchen Gardens, Orcharding, &c.

THE REMAINDER is rich, well watered Meadow Land, and a Valuable Sand Mine on the East side.

There are TWO CONVENIENT LODGES, one at the Entrance Gate and the other on the Southern Boundary.

Bedrooms as follows:-
1. Birch Room – Dressing Room (adjoining)
2. Bachelor's Room
3. Mrs Roberts' Room - Dressing Room (adjoining)
4. Green Room – Dressing Room (adjoining)
5. Pink Room
6. Linen Room
7. Little Pink Room (with Bathroom)
8. Bedroom
9. Bedroom
10. Sewing Room
+ three Servants' Bedrooms (in Attic)

To everyone's surprise at the auction, the Hall failed to reach its asking price, and the sale did not go ahead. Undaunted, the Roberts' arranged to auction the Hall's contents in a sale to be held at Wollaston Hall over three days, 26-28 May 1924. The sale began at 11.00am each morning:

- Monday 26 May – 289 lots comprising the contents of the Hall, Morning Room, Study, Dining Room, Lounge and Inner Lounge, with separate sales at 3.30pm of books, and at 4.00pm of Motorcars and Carriages;
- Tuesday 27 May – 346 lots comprising the contents of the Birch Room No.1, Dressing Room (adjoining), Bachelor's Room No.2, Mrs Roberts Room No.3, Dressing Room (adjoining), Green Room No.4, Dressing Room (adjoining), Pink Room No.5, Linen Room No.6, Little Pink Room No.7, Bathroom, Bedroom No.8, Bedroom No.9, Sewing Room No.10, Landing and Staircase, Glass and China, Silver and Plated Articles;
- Wednesday 28 May – 272 lots comprising the contents of Attics Nos. 1-3, Upper Landing, Back Hall, China Pantry, Office, Servants' Hall, Larder, Cooking Kitchen, Curtains, etc., Fruit Room, Laundry, Dairy, Saddle Room, Yard and Outside, Garden, Bedding Plants, Long Greenhouse, Conservatory and the Vinery.

Although all of the lots were sold, many failed to realise their true value. Reporting the sale, the *County Express* of 31 May 1924 commented that: '*No fancy prices were realised, but plenty of bargains were obtained.*' These included the motorcars, a 1914 Sunbeam going for £100, a 1913 Daimler sold for £31, and a 10hp Standard two-seater, which went for just £15. The names of Roberts, Darby, Hooson and Marsh also occur frequently against the purchases, the last three being the married names of Caleb Roberts Sr's daughters, suggesting that the family purchased a number of the items themselves.

Thus by June 1924 Wollaston Hall was unoccupied and empty, but its disposal was just one of many concerns for the Roberts family. The general depression in the iron trade had led to the closure of the Leys Ironworks, and in late 1924 it was dismantled. A few months later, in mid-1925, Roberts & Cooper Ltd went into voluntary liquidation.

Concern was also expressed about the fate of Wollaston Hall from outside. At its meeting on 30 June 1924 Stourbridge Council discussed the Wollaston Hall Estate. After its meeting on 11 June, the Finance Committee had approached Messrs King & Son (the auctioneers) and one of the executors of the estate, with regard to the purchase of the back land adjoining Wollaston Playing Field, forming part of the Wollaston Hall Estate. Cllr Guest reported that they:

'*would much prefer to sell the land as a whole and not in portions, but that if such a course was not possible they would approach the Council in regard to the portions required by them.*'

The Committee decided to leave the matter in abeyance. Alderman Cook thought that this was a '*very great mistake*', and he was certain that '*the town would regret the property was not purchased.*' Alderman Taylor said that '*the non-purchase of the Hall was reported at the last meeting of the Town Council.*' Unfortunately, Stourbridge Council does not appear to have discussed the fate of Wollaston Hall at all after this, apart from reporting at its meeting on 27 April 1925 that Wollaston had returned a low rate income because the Hall was vacant.

Wollaston Hall was advertised for sale '*by private treaty*' in a series of adverts run in the *County Express* during July 1924, but no interest was shown. The Roberts family were either extraordinarily patient about this matter, or some in the family, possibly Ebenezer Elias John Roberts, Caleb Roberts Sr's eldest son, had a sentimental attachment for the Hall. Its ownership was conveyed to Amelia Blanche Cooper Darby, one of Caleb Roberts Sr's daughters and wife of Walter Samuel Darby, for £3,000 on 26 March 1925. Four months later, on 4 July 1925 the *County Express* carried another advert for the Hall, describing it as:

'*this old Elizabethan residence with a quantity of old oak fitments and delightful pleasure grounds*' which was: '*to let with immediate possession.*'

Again there can not have been any interest shown, as the *County Express* of 1 August 1925 carried a further advert for the Hall, which this time was: '*to be let as a whole or subdivided.*'

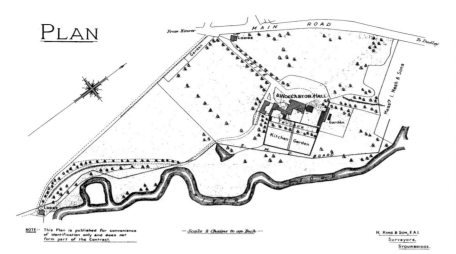

PLAN

NOTE:- This Plan is published for convenience of identification only and does not form part of the Contract.

— Scale 2 Chains to an Inch —

H. KING & SON, F.A.I.
Surveyors,
STOURBRIDGE.

Left: Once probate was granted on Mary Roberts' will on 23 April 1924, Wollaston Hall was put up for sale by auction at The Talbot Hotel, Stourbridge, at 4.00pm on 9 May 1924. To everyone's surprise at the auction, the Hall failed to reach its asking price, and the sale did not go ahead. This is the plan of the Hall and its grounds from the catalogue for that sale.

This tack having also failed, agreement must have been reached to consider the demolition of the Hall and to sell its fabric as building materials. The *County Express* of 12 September 1925 carried an advert addressed to:

TO ARCHITECTS, BUILDERS, DEMOLITION
CONTRACTORS AND OTHERS.
WOLLASTON HALL,
Near STOURBRIDGE.
IMPORTANT SALE OF BUILDING
MATERIALS,

comprising LEAD, Flats and Gutters, many thousand beautifully-weathered hand-made Tiles, Oak Window Frames, Oak and Pitch Pine Doors, Constructional Timber, Valuable OLD OAK BEAMS and HALF-TIMBER WORK Oak and Elm Floor Boards, IMPOSING OLD-OAK STAIRCASE, Pair of Valuable Antique and Massive STUDDED OAK ENTRANCE DOORS, Antique Carved Mantelpiece, Glass Conservatories and the General Material of which this Early XVII. Century Mansion is constructed.
TO BE OFFERED FIRST AS A WHOLE.

A note at the foot of the advert further qualified the circumstances under which the demolition sale would proceed:

'*The Auctioneers specially invite Offers for this Residential Estate, comprising THE HALL AND 21 ACRES AS A WHOLE, and are prepared to deal with same up to time of sale, failing which the Fabric will be Sold Piecemeal as above, and the Land, a considerable portion of which is ripe for immediate building development, will be offered under the hammer, together with the Timber thereon, at a later date.*'

The sale date was given as '*EARLY IN OCTOBER*', but once again this sale does not seem to have taken place as Wollaston Hall was still standing in the autumn of 1925.

Matters in the Roberts' family business do not seem

to have been any better. Despite the demise of Roberts & Cooper Ltd, E E J Roberts fought back by buying the Nine Locks Sawmills in Mill Street Brierley Hill on 20 November 1925, with the intention of carrying it on as '*Messrs Roberts & Cooper, Nine Locks Sawmills, Brierley Hill.*' Unfortunately he did not have much of a chance. For some years he had been battling a deteriorating heart condition, and he died of this on 24 December 1925, aged 51. Under the terms of his will his estate, amounting to £14,990, passed to his widow Kate Roberts, probate being granted to her on 25 February 1926.

Ebenezer Roberts' death may have paved the way for something finally to be done about Wollaston Hall, but its owner, Amelia Darby, does not appear to have been in any great hurry to act. No sales notices relating to the Hall can be found in the *County Express* through 1926, until a brief note appeared in the *Notes & News* section of the edition of the paper of 16 October 1926 reporting that:

'*Wollaston Hall has been sold and is being demolished. It dates from 1617 and has been vacant since the death of Mrs Roberts, the wife of the late Mr C W Roberts.*'

The 'demolition' was a slow process, because its product, a series of building materials, was not offered for sale until December. On 14 December 1926 Amelia Darby sold Wollaston Hall to her husband Walter Darby and one William Kayley for £3,000. A week later, on 21 December 1926, a sale of Building Materials was held on the Hall site at 11.00am. The notice for this sale contained a clue as to why it had taken so long to 'demolish' the building, saying that: '*the above Hall having been dismantled*', presumably to recover the materials for resale.

The Wollaston Hall Estate

At this point the story of Wollaston Hall splits in two: that of its site, and that of its materials. Of these, the story of what happened to the site of Wollaston Hall is the clearer. From its edition of 5 March 1927 the *County Express* carried a series of adverts for the: 'WOLLASTON HALL

BUILDING ESTATE, STOURBRIDGE', which was described as:

'*valuable freehold building land in choice lots to suit purchaser ranging from 583 to 1065 square yards, situate in a good central position between Stourbridge, Brierley Hill, and Wollaston, within a few hundred yards of the 'Bus routes to Wolverhampton, Kinver, Stourbridge, and Wednesbury. The sewer, water, electric light, and gas are down the main road.*'

A road is shown, but named 'The Grove.'

Once again the 'delay' that seemed to surround anything to do with Wollaston Hall appears to have intervened, because the first homes on the 'Wollaston Hall Estate' were not put up for sale until they were advertised in the *County Express* of 22 March 1930, priced at between £500 and £900. More houses were advertised in this way on 3 January 1931, priced at: '*£700 detached; £650 semis*', and they were clearly selling as on 14 March 1931 there were: '*only 4 houses remaining.*' The reason for there being a ten month gap between the first and second lot of houses being offered for sale is probably explained by the builders not being able to redevelop the actual site of the Hall. This is confirmed by a sale of land on Wollaston Hall Estate, owned by William Kayley, to Walter Samuel Darby for £782 10s on 3 February 1930. According to the terms of this sale, the land concerned:

'*formed the residue of the premises formerly known as "Wollaston Hall"*' and was: '*firstly conveyed to the parties thereto by a conveyance of 14th December 1926.*'

The land equates to that occupied in 2003 by Nos 29-35 Apley Road, but the plan accompanying the sale shows no houses to have been built past No 12 on the even-numbers side of the road. Wollaston Hall and its outbuildings formerly occupied land beyond this point, and it seems reasonable to assume that building could not proceed there until they had been cleared. The Hall stood where 42-38 Apley Road stand in 2003, and the east wing, added during W B Collis' time at the Hall, stood to the rear of Nos 36-32 Apley Road. All of these are houses that are noticeably different in style to the rest in the road, suggesting that they were built at a different date to the rest.

Below: After two years of trying to sell, let or sub-divide Wollaston Hall, the Roberts family took the decision to dismantle the building and sell the site for housing. The use of the phrase '*the above Hall having been dismantled*' is deliberate, and gives a strong clue to the ultimate fate of the building.

"WOLLASTON HALL,"
Near Stourbridge, Worcestershire.

JOHN STANLEY BELL,
AUCTIONEER,

will Sell by Public Auction in Lots

On Tuesday, December 21st, 1926,
At 11 a.m. precisely,

BUILDING MATERIALS,

the above Hall having been dismantled, including

Roof Timbers, Floor Boarding, Floor Joists, 40 Pine Doors, Oak Doors, 50 Window Fitments, Chimney-pieces, Oak and Pine Staircase, 2 Ranges, Stoves, Anthracite Stove, Radiators, Sanitary Equipment,

HANDSOME PINE PANELLING & DOORS
from room 16ft. × 16ft. × 7ft.,

Stain Glass Panels, 6 Galvanised Tanks, 50 Corrugated Sheets 6ft. × 3ft., Large quantity of Timber, including Oak Spars, Beams, Joists, Beading, Boarding, &c.,;

100,000 BRICKS
cleaned and stacked,

Stone Paving, Garden Ornaments, Vases, 6 Old Figures 5ft high, Garden Frames, 20 Iron Archways, 2 " Ideal " Boilers, Piping,

CONSERVATORY AND GLASS HOUSES, VALUABLE OLD ROOFING TILES,
and a large quantity of miscellaneous effects

NOW ON VIEW.

Auctioneer's Offices :
3, GORE STREET, PICCADILLY, MANCHESTER.
'Phone: City 1599.

N.B.—Owing to shortness of time Catalogues will not be issued.

Henry Blacklock & Co.,Ltd., Printers, Albert Square, Manchester.

'Wollaston Hall' was disappearing from the village. One way of preserving at least a link with it would have been through the name of the new road built on its site, but at the Stourbridge Council meeting held on 28 June 1932, the Highways & Improvements Committee instructed the Town Clerk to make an order assigning the name of 'Apley Road' to the new road on the Wollaston Hall Estate. Cllr Jones suggested that 'Wollaston Hall Road' would be a more appropriate name as:

'*they ought not to forget that Wollaston Hall, a fine old Elizabethan building, occupied that place, and the next generation would know nothing of this unless something was done to preserve its name.*'

Sadly, Cllr Jones' proposal did not have a seconder, and his prediction has come true. The last tangible links with the Hall were its two lodges. Wollaston Hall Lower Lodge was demolished in 1938; Stourbridge Council's Highways & Improvements Committee accepting a tender

Left: Walter Darby, who was instrumental in the final disposal of Wollaston Hall and items from it, taken on the occasion of his marriage to Caleb Roberts' daughter Amelia. It was she who sold Wollaston Hall to her husband, and one William Kayley, for £3,000 on 14 December 1926.

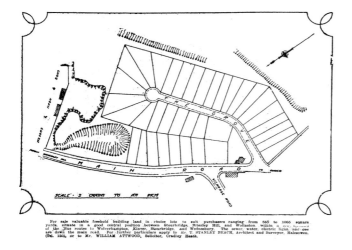

For sale valuable freehold building land in choice lots to suit purchasers ranging from 585 to 1066 square yards, situate in a good central position between Stourbridge, Brierley Hill, and Wollaston, within a few hundred of the Bus routes to Wolverhampton, Kinver, Stourbridge, and Wednesbury. The sewer, water, electric light, &c. are down the main road. For further particulars apply to Mr T. STANLEY BEACH, Architect and Surveyor, Halesowen. (Tel. 1201), or to Mr. WILLIAM ATTWOOD, Solicitor, Cradley Heath.

Left: Following its dismantling, the story of Wollaston Hall splits in two: that of its site, and that of its materials. From its edition of 5 March 1927 the *County Express* carried this advert for the: '*WOLLASTON HALL BUILDING ESTATE, STOURBRIDGE*' for several weeks. Named initially 'The Grove', the road shown conforms very closely to the way that Apley Road was built eventually.

Below: Left standing after Wollaston Hall was dismantled, and Apley Road developed, were its two lodges. The lower one, close to John Bradley & Co's works, was demolished in May 1939, but the upper one, on High Street, Wollaston, stood for another 23 years, before being demolished in November 1961. These two toddlers were snapped inside the gates of this lodge on a sunny day in 1956.

from F T Smith of Grange Road for its demolition on 25 April 1938. The Apley Road Lodge stood for another 23 years, before being demolished in November 1961.

The fate of Wollaston Hall

Many stories persist locally concerning the fate of Wollaston Hall. In essence these come down to one of three options, either that it:
- burned down,
- was demolished, or,
- went to America.

Of these the first can be dismissed. True, there was a fire there in October 1923, but this did minimal damage, and the fact that the Hall was advertised for sale on many occasions afterwards serves to prove that fire did not destroy the Hall. The second option is in part true, the Hall was 'demolished', but this took the form of a dismantling in order to recover its materials for resale. Writing to *The Black Country Bugle* in May 1998, Elsie Gail, who was 33 in 1926, recalled seeing: '*numbered boxes on the site*', other local residents could recall seeing: '*men painting white numbers on the timbers*', and some of the first residents of Apley Road 'inherited' numbered timbers and piles of bricks in their back gardens when they moved in. All of these memories lend support to the view that the Hall was dismantled rather than being demolished.

The third option, of the Hall going to America, is a remarkably persistent story, but where? The late Frank Firmstone, an ironmonger in Warwick, and a member of the family who once owned the Hall, wrote on 25 September 1995 that:

'*after the fire it was removed brick by brick and re-erected in Salt Lake City USA ... and I believe the Mormon Church purchased it and it is in private hands.*'

HOW contacted the Mormon Church concerning Frank Firmstone's suggestion, but in a reply dated 24 June 1999 they stated that they had no evidence of the whereabouts of Wollaston Hall.

Other suggested places the Hall went to include California, Eastern Pennsylvania, Las Vegas, Quincy Massachusetts, and Virginia.

The search for Wollaston Hall

As part of HOW's on-going research into the History of Wollaston, its members set about trying to find out what happened to Wollaston Hall. Many local stories were followed up and in this way a number of pieces of the Hall were identified locally. The Hall's conservatory was taken down and re-erected at Wollaston Court, then the home of Trevor Guest, who was married briefly to Valerie, the daughter of Ernest Marsh and Elsie Mary Roberts. Elsewhere in the village, small pieces of panelling, encaustic floor tiles and items bought in the May 1924 sale have also been located, together with sales catalogues and other artefacts, but nothing came to light which indicated the possible whereabouts of the Hall itself.

Books and other sources relating to American houses and architecture were combed for clues, but to no avail. By late 2000 it seemed that the trail had gone dead, but HOW Chairman, Dr Paul Collins, was determined to have one last go at finding Wollaston Hall. The most persistent location suggested for it was Pennsylvania, and in particular Eastern Pennsylvania. This was a region favoured for home building by industrialists and bankers, and it had been established that they also preferred English styles of architecture for these. How better then than to import the

Where is Wollaston Hall?

To the editor:

I am chairman of a local history group in Wollaston, Stourbridge, West Midlands, UK. We are trying to trace the whereabouts of our former manor house – Wollaston Hall – which was dismantled and sent, we believe, to eastern Pennsylvania, around 1927 or 1928.

Wollaston Hall stood overlooking the works of John Bradley and Company where the "Stourbridge Lion" locomotive was made in 1828. So far we have been able to substantiate that the hall – a timber Tudor building – was bought by an American, dismantled, and exported to eastern Pennsylvania. The hall bears the date 1617, carved into one of the main timbers over its front door.

I have already received and a great deal of information from people in the USA,

especially in Pennsylvania, since I began this search only two weeks or so ago. A recurrent theme is that some respondents recall Wollaston Hall being featured on A&E's TV series "America's Castles." It may well have been a building that was imported to the USA but never re-erected, and could be lying around in cases somewhere. I have contacted A&E.

I would be grateful for any help/advice you could give. If there is any truth to this story, someone, somewhere, may know something about this building. One story concerning it is that it was the first such export of a building from the UK to the USA.

Paul Collins
Wollaston, U.K.
e-mail: paul.collins@

Left: HOW's attempts to discover the fate of Wollaston Hall were greatly aided by use of the Internet. In early 2001 newspapers in the eastern part of Pennsylvania, where the Hall was then believed to have been removed to, were 'bombarded' with letters and stories. This one appeared in the *Carlisle Sentinel* on 21 February 2001.

real thing? The wider availability of the Internet and of e-mail around the turn of the 21st century made it possible both to identify and to contact newspapers and historic preservation organisations in various parts of the USA. Attention was directed at all of the places mentioned above, and in particular Salt Lake City in Nevada, and Eastern Pennsylvania. There, 49 state and regional newspapers were identified, most of which published either a letter or an article based upon information and images e-mailed to them.

The response was unexpected and overwhelming. HOW's e-mail was forwarded around the USA, and at its peak, in late January 2001, in excess of 100 replies were received each day. (The more persistent correspondents are listed separately in the *Acknowledgements* section). Much new and useful information was collected in this way. Many houses were suggested as being 'Wollaston Hall', but none checked out on further enquiry. Nonetheless more was learned about the architectural 'plundering' of English houses for panelling, staircases, etc. to be installed in American homes, which was, if not commonplace, then at least not unusual in the 1920s. Had this happened to Wollaston Hall? In a letter to HOW Geoffrey Beard had mentioned hearing that panelling from the Hall was in the Edsel & Eleanor Ford House near Detroit, Edsel Ford being Henry Ford's eldest son.

The Edsel & Eleanor Ford House, Grosse Pointe Shores, Michigan

Contact was made with the Edsel & Eleanor Ford House, which is now a museum open to the public. The basic history of the house fitted the timescale for the dismantling of Wollaston Hall. Eleanor and Edsel Ford had decided to build a new home for their family on Lake St Clair in Grosse Pointe Shores in 1926. They planned a traditional home that would blend excellent design and craftsmanship with modern conveniences, set in an inspirational, beautiful and peaceful place where they could

raise their young family. The couple engaged Albert Kahn, one of the world's great architects, to design and build their home, and travelled with him to England to survey various styles of residential architecture and ultimately chose the Cotswold style. It is known that both Edsel Ford and his father were no strangers to England. Henry Ford had stayed in Dudley in July 1924 when he was on one of his visits buying up artefacts for his Henry Ford Museum in Dearborn. Esdel was also a frequent visitor to England, as he had charge of the project to build the company's new factory at Dagenham in Essex.

Edsel & Eleanor Ford's 60-room house took shape as a cluster of structures, resembling a village. It took three years to design, build, and custom-fit. Imported antique architectural pieces, carved fireplace mantels, wood panelling, and even the main stairway, were built into the house. English craftsmen laid the stone roof shingles, and a traditional English style was authentically reproduced in much of the interior space, with stone or wood-panelled walls, hand-plastered ceilings with decorative motifs, and leaded-glass windows with stained-glass medallions. The Fords moved into their new home at the end of 1929.

Josephine Shea, Curator of the Edsel & Eleanor Ford House, was able to confirm in 2003 that panelling and a fireplace in the house's gallery did indeed come from Wollaston Hall. She took and e-mailed digital photographs of these, and also found the following entries in account books kept in the house, which gives a timescale for their removal, transportation and reinstatement that fits in with the pattern of events described above:

- 28 September 1926 – 3 panelled rooms from England
- 30 June 1927 – 1st (one third) payment for panelled room
- 23 March 1928 – 2nd (one third) payment for panelled room
- 13 June 1928 – 3rd (one third) payment for panelled room
- 22 October 1928 – balance of payment of panelling
- 6 November 1928 – additional freight Gothic Stone fireplace.

The agents were C Roberson & Co Ltd, fine art dealers of London, who also had offices in New York in the 1920s. They appear to have been the sole agents involved in any similar move of architectural features, or even complete buildings, between England and the USA at that time. Josephine Shea also confirmed that Roberson & Co fitted the panelling in the house. This opened up a new line of enquiry, into Roberson's archival material. Fortunately the company had an extensive but un-catalogued archive, which it had recently donated to The Fitzwilliam Museum,

Above: HOW's strongest lead to the fate of at least part of Wollaston Hall came from Geoffrey Beard. In 2003, Josephine Shea, Curator of the Edsel & Eleanor Ford House Museum in Grosse Point Shores, Michigan, was able to confirm that panelling and a fireplace in the house's Gallery did indeed come from the Hall. This view shows a general view of the Gallery looking towards the fireplace and panelling. *Edsel & Eleanor Ford House Museum*

University of Cambridge. Unfortunately, as of 2003, this archive was inaccessible.

HOW's interest in the panelling from Wollaston Hall led the Edsel & Eleanor Ford House to revise their catalogue and website (www.fordhouse.org) to include this new information:

Gallery

At 25 x 60 feet, the Gallery is the largest and one of the most impressive rooms in the house. It was planned this way to allow for large gatherings such as dances, parties and family celebrations. The room resembles an English baronial hall with its architectural details, such as a richly carved plaster ceiling and antique 'linenfold' English panelling. **The panelling and the huge Gothic chimneypiece came from Wollaston Hall in Worcestershire, England**.

The Hearst Connection

What then of the rest of Wollaston Hall? As tantalising a prospect as it may be, it seems unlikely that the Hall is standing at the end of a drive somewhere in the USA, looking much as it did when it was in Wollaston. A

house of its age and provenance would be appreciated and celebrated, thereby showing up in searches. Parts of it could have been used in various buildings, which could take a long time to trace. There is however one further possibility. Many of HOW's American correspondents mentioned *America's Castles*, a 26-part TV series produced by A&E Television Networks in the USA between 1994 and 1996. This looked at the grand homes built by the generation of America's 'royal' families that included the Vanderbilts, Rockefellers and Hearsts. Some recalled mention being made in the edition focussing on 'Hearst Castle – San Simeon*'*, of an English Mansion still being in store in crates in San Simeon, California. William Randolph Hearst (1863-1951) was a newspaper tycoon, and the person upon whom Orson Welles based his character Charles Foster Kane in his debut film Citizen Kane (1941). Hearst built his castle at San Simeon from 1919 onwards, and the project remained uncompleted when he died. The house grew to 165 rooms and had 127 acres of gardens. An avid collector, Hearst acquired antique ceilings, English furniture, oriental rugs, pottery, silver, statues, and tapestries, many of which remain un-catalogued – is Wollaston Hall amongst them?

Postscript

Whilst Wollaston Hall was a great loss to the village, it is worth speculating on what might have happened to it under different circumstances. Might it still have been standing in Wollaston? A number of other Black Country houses (Bradley Hall, Kingswinford, for example), have also been lost. Large houses of this kind are expensive to maintain, and it is difficult to find alternative uses for them. Large grounds also tend to surround them, land which has greater commercial value when developed for housing. Therefore, if Wollaston Hall had remained in the village, it is likely that houses would have been built in the grounds around it, and, it may well have found another use, as a residential care home for example, a fate that has befallen a number of the other large houses in Wollaston.

Above: Josephine Shea also took some detailed photographs of the panelling from Wollaston Hall, of which this is an example. A selection of these photographs appears in the colour section of this book.

Below: Much evidence remains of Wollaston Hall in and around Apley Road, including the terracing from the gardens. Another example is the walling referred to in Chapter One. In places this even retains its wrought-iron spikes.

Chapter Three

WOLLASTON'S DEVELOPMENT 1851 TO 1939

1851 – A snapshot in time

A study of the 1851 census and of contemporary trade directories shows that Wollaston was transformed, from an isolated rural hamlet into a rapidly growing urban community, in the 50 years following the opening of Bradley's Ironworks in 1800. Its population increased substantially from an estimate (based on the number of houses shown on L O Davies's survey) of between 300 and 400 in 1827, to 578 by the time of the 1841 census. It then doubled in the next ten years, so that by 1851 Wollaston had a population of 1,172. Whilst most of this increase can be explained by immigration from neighbouring communities in North Worcestershire and South Staffordshire, and to a lesser extent from Shropshire and Warwickshire, there were also newcomers from much further away, such as Yorkshire, Durham, Ireland and Scotland.

In the 1841 census 26 people were recorded as working in agriculture, or 14.2% of the working population. In 1851 the corresponding figures were 16, or 3.7%, although there were additionally 28 general labourers some of whom would undoubtedly have been employed on the land, even if only on a casual or seasonal basis. This decline in agricultural employment was offset by an increasing number of jobs in industry. In 1841 there were only ten glassworkers living in Wollaston (5.5% of the working population), but ten years later the figures had risen to 60 and 14.0% respectively. The ironworks in 1841 had 55 employees (30.1% of the working population); by 1851 these figures had risen to 160 and 37.3%. Taken together the number of employees in the glass and iron industries in 1851 account for over half of the working population.

The ironworkers were employed by John Bradley & Co in the works where the famous locomotives *The Agenoria* and the *Stourbridge Lion* were built in 1829. The glassworkers would almost certainly have been employed in the nearby glasshouses of Amblecote and Wordsley. Given that workers in 1851 had no alternative but to walk to work, it was, therefore, highly desirable to live near the workplace. By far the biggest concentration of ironworkers was in King Street, within easy walking distance of John Bradley & Co: 68 ironworkers lived in this street compared with only nine glassworkers. Conversely, the biggest concentration of glassworkers was in the old village area where 34 lived within easy walking distance of Amblecote and Wordsley.

The most significant feature in terms of housing was the growth of King Street and the complementary development along Bridgnorth Road, from the bottom of Withy Bank as far as The Gate Hangs Well. (Withy Bank was the name given to the rise along Bridgnorth Road, stretching from the former Golden or Stourbridge Lion, where the road crossed the Withy Brook, now culverted, as far as the Cottage Spring pub.) A contributory factor in this ribbon development was, undoubtedly, the enhanced status of Bridgnorth Road as a consequence of it being turnpiked in 1816. Then, as now, an improved road surface invariably leads to an increase in traffic, which in turn encourages building development and commercial activity. Thus, not surprisingly, the majority of shops were to be found in this area. Checking the trade directory entries against the census returns reveals that most of the shopkeepers and beer sellers had another occupation, either working in the iron or glassworks, or plying a trade such as basket maker or scythesmith.

A comparison of trade directories shows a slowly expanding range of shops and services. *Bentley's Directory of Stourbridge* published in 1841 has only eight entries for Wollaston, whilst *Kelly's Directory* published in 1850 has 12, including three public houses, The Barley Mow, Britannia Inn and The Gate Hangs Well. A further insight into this evolving community is provided by *Melville's Directory of Dudley and the Mining Districts*, published in 1852, which has 21 entries for Wollaston; clearly this was a time of continuous expansion. Most of the business premises listed in *Melville's Directory* are located on Withy Bank, with a few along High Street, but significantly there is also an entry for a provision dealer in what is the row of shops on Bridgnorth Road, between Wollaston Garage and Cobden Street, in 2003. This entry is a clear indication that Wollaston's centre of gravity was moving inexorably from the old village to its present position. It was the lure of employment, principally at Bradley's Ironworks, that attracted people to the village and,

Left: Here and there glimpses of Wollaston as it must have looked in 1851 survive. This is one example, a stretch of old walling outside the vicarage in Vicarage Road that may even date from the period when Wollaston's windmill stood on the site.

Right: Kelly's Directory published in 1850 has 12 entries for Wollaston, including three public houses: The Barley Mow, seen here, the Britannia Inn and The Gate Hangs Well. The building probably dates from around 1820. Unwin Passage, linking High Street with Vicarage Road, runs to the left, whilst the chimneys to the right belong to houses from the original old village.

significantly, houses were being built at a rate commensurate with the increase in population, such that there appears to have been no housing shortage and, most importantly, no overcrowding. This latter factor undoubtedly played an important role in ensuring the good health of Wollaston's inhabitants and giving it the lowest death rate of all the surrounding districts as the table below shows:

District	Total deaths in last 7 yrs	Average No. of deaths per year	Population in 1851	One death to every	Annual deaths per 1000 living
Stourbridge	1292	184.6	8333	45.14	22.15
Lye	855	122.1	4448	36.42	27.45
Wollaston	140	20	1229	61.45	16.27
Wollescote	294	42	1456	34.66	28.81
Upper Swinford	424	60.6	2728	45.01	22.21
Amblecote	316	45.1	2053	45.42	21.96
Whole District	3321	474.4	20247	42.67	23.43

A summary of census information

	1841	1851	1861	1871	1881	1891
Population	578	1172	2041	2166	2414	2333
Total No of houses	141	259	445	502	546	559
No of houses inhabited	115	250	418	464	509	536
Persons per occupied house	5.03	4.91	4.88	4.66	4.74	4.35

Wollaston in 1851 was only a fledgling community. Although its population and range of shops and services were increasing, it lacked those two key elements, which shape and give focus to a community, a church and a school. Fortunately by the time of the next census, thanks to the generosity of William Orme Foster of the ironworks, Wollaston had become the proud possessor of a church and a school on a site overlooking the very ironworks, which had contributed so much to the growth and prosperity of the village.

The evolution of the 'new' village

Although there was a considerable increase in both population and houses in the decade following 1851 the remaining decades of the century saw only a modest increase as the village, after its initial growth spurt, began to consolidate and stabilize in terms of size and shape. By the end of the century a 'new' village had evolved with the following streets being shown on the 1890 *Stephens and Mackintosh's Business Street Map of Stourbridge*. Their names, if different in 2003, are shown in brackets:

Left: Wollaston's housing in 1851 included some rows of terraces. One was Field Terrace in Mamble Road, seen overleaf, and another was Yardley's Row, in Firmstone Street, which was caught in the background of this family snap of a small child playing with a teddy bear.

Right: A second snap of Yardley's Row shows one of its tenants standing in her doorway. The stone block to the right was probably used to chop firewood against. Yardley's Row was demolished to make way for Firmstone Court in the early 1960s.

Left: This view, of the back of a house in High Park Avenue, would have been echoed in many places in 19th century Wollaston. Outhouses, including an outside privy, and a brewhouse, where washing was done, would have been found in large numbers. The large white area in the foreground is most probably a rudimentary cucumber frame.

Right: The aforementioned Field Terrace in Mamble Road, photographed in the early 1960s, with The Swan Inn in the background. The road was probably unadopted because it went nowhere! All of these buildings were cleared for the erection of low-rise maisonettes. *Harry Cartwright/Stourbridge Library*

- Bowling Green Lane (Park Road)
- Bridle Road (Gladstone Road)
- Cobden Street
- Cross Street (Bright Street)
- Duncombe Street
- Enville Road (Bridgnorth Road)
- High Park Road (Avenue)
- High Street
- King Street
- Mamble Road
- Swan Street
- Upper Bridle Road (Bridle Road)
- Upper King Street (King Street)
- Wood Street
  [see map overleaf]

Becoming a desirable place to live

This process of development and consolidation was also to be seen in the social composition of the population and in the increasing range of trades and services available. *White's Directory of Staffordshire*, published in 1873 has no fewer than 118 entries for Wollaston. Impressive though the number of entries is, in comparison with the directories of the 1850s and 1860s, this large number is more significant in its composition. It shows that the village was beginning to attract managerial and professional people who obviously thought that Wollaston was a desirable place to live. Such a view was confirmed by the statistics published in 1884 showing the number of births and deaths in Stourbridge and in the surrounding districts of Amblecote, Lye, Upper Swinford, Wollescote, Wordsley and Wollaston. Wollaston was without doubt the healthiest district, with the lowest death rate. A comparison with the neighbouring parish of Amblecote on the other side of the River Stour is revealing, as both parishes had roughly the same population at the time of the 1881 census (Amblecote: 2,808; Wollaston: 2,414) and the workforce of each community was largely employed in foundries or glassworks, yet life

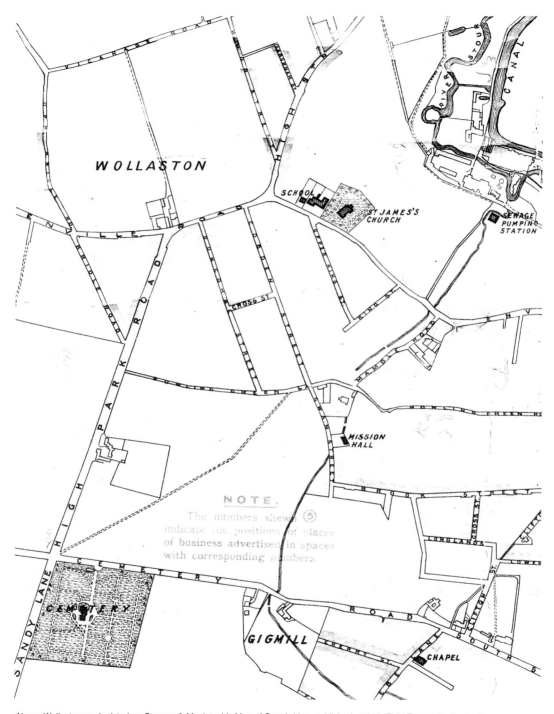

Above: Wollaston as depicted on Stevens & Macintosh's Map of Stourbridge, published c.1893. Field Terrace is clearly shown projecting down from Mamble Road, and Bright Street is still shown under its original name of Cross Street. Both High Park and Eggington farms are also marked. *H Jack Haden*

Parish	Year	Births	Deaths	Deaths under one year	Deaths above one and under 60 years	Deaths over 60
Amblecote	1880	99	42	6	26	10
	1881	91	54	9	32	13
	1882	89	64	14	39	11
	1883	86	64	14	33	17
Totals		365	224	43	130	51
Wollaston	1880	75	32	8	17	7
	1881	66	26	7	9	10
	1882	76	46	7	21	18
	1883	63	50	5	29	16
Totals		280	154	27	76	51

expectancy in Wollaston was better, as the above table shows. This strong recommendation of life in Wollaston was reinforced by the statistics published by the Stourbridge Poor Law Union for the period 1873–1883. These figures show that the number of paupers (destitute people) in Wollaston applying for poor relief was substantially lower than in Stourbridge itself and the outlying districts. Not surprisingly the trend of people moving into Wollaston, because it was thought to be a good place to live, was well established by the end of the 19th century.

The role of the Vestry

In the formative years of the new village the provision of public services was organised and managed by the Vestry on behalf of all who lived within the boundary of the parish. The word 'Vestry' is derived from the Latin word 'vestiarium' meaning 'robing room'. The Vestry was originally a room in the church where the vestments or robes of the clergy and choir were kept. From the habit of parishioners meeting in the Vestry and discussing parish business when they met, the word 'Vestry' is now used to describe both the body of the parishioners as well as the meeting itself. From the 17th to the 19th centuries various acts of Parliament had encouraged vestries to take on an ever-increasing range of local government responsibilities, which varied from parish to parish. The annual meeting of the Vestry was open to all and in Wollaston it was usually held in the village school. The customary practice was for the meeting to elect a Vestry Committee that would meet, as circumstances dictated, to discuss issues concerning the parish. Although the date of the first meeting of the Wollaston Vestry is not known, it is not unreasonable to assume that it became operational shortly after the church was opened in 1860. The very first entry in the Wollaston Vestry Committee minute book was the record of its decision on 8 February 1867 to select and return a list of: '*9 men qualified and able to serve as constables in this hamlet.*' On 14 February 1867 the following were selected:

- Joseph Hill, King Street, Forgeman
- Henry Pardoe, Wollaston Lane, Moulder
- Samuel Merchant, Ridge Top, Glass Cutter
- Goodwin Sergeant, Cobden Street, Forgeman
- William Short, Wood Street, Bricklayer
- John Green, High Street, Shoemaker
- William Pearce, Bridgnorth Road, Glass Cutter
- Henry Kitchen, King Street, Dresser
- Henry Breeze, Duncombe Street, Gas Fitter

It is interesting to note that all these nine constables were skilled workers, the elite of the working class. In all probability they already commanded the respect of their fellow citizens and thus their election as parish constable would be a further mark of social distinction, even though the title was, by then, largely honorary. They had few law enforcement powers, as Worcestershire's own constabulary had policed the county since 1839.

Left: By the 1880s Wollaston had become a very desirable place to live, with some very fine houses. This example is typical of a number built in High Street around that time, preserved for posterity courtesy of whoever photographed this smartly dressed young lady. All is however not what it appears. The house is in fact two houses, with 'front' doors opening off midway down the passageway seen to the right.

However, not all the Vestry appointments were simply honorary in nature. The Surveyor of the Roads and the Collector of the Highway Rate were paid for their work, because the parish had a responsibility for road maintenance and consequently the collection of the highway rate to fund this work was essential. Equally important in the life of the community were the Overseers of the Poor who were responsible for the welfare of the poor. They supervised the distribution of charitable funds and gifts in kind, as well as collecting the poor rate. This was used to contribute towards the running costs of the workhouse at Wordsley, which provided accommodation for the homeless poor who lived within the boundary of the Stourbridge Poor Law Union.

An on-going concern of the Vestry Committee was the provision of street lighting. As early as August 1866 they discussed the siting of lamps additional to those already in existence. In all probability these lamps would have been oil burning, as it was not until 1882 that gas lighting was considered. On 24 January the Vestry Committee endorsed Job Short's proposal that: '*it is desirable that the public roads in this parish should be lighted with gas.*'

By 1886 it was clear that the number of lamps, which had been installed, was considered inadequate, as the '*Extra lamps sub-committee*' recommended on 8 March an additional 17 lamps. Two amendments to this proposal increased the number to 19. Another safety concern of the Vestry was that the village should be equipped to deal with the outbreak of fire and thus on 27 April 1888 the Committee agreed that:

'*six fireplugs be fixed on the mains of the Water Works company, in such positions as may be recorded after inspection of the township by Captain Turney of Stourbridge Fire Brigade.*'

These fireplugs gave the fire brigade access to the water mains. By 1890 the number had been increased to ten and, to ensure that their location was easily identifiable, the committee agreed that nameplates should be fixed on the walls immediately opposite the fireplugs.

On 24 March 1890 the Committee took responsibility for giving what it regarded as an official name for a street, where there was no doubt or confusion. In some cases the committee merely confirmed an existing name, such as High Street, King Street, Cobden Street and Duncombe Street. Wollaston's Victorian streets, unlike those on modern estates, had not been planned or developed systematically, but had grown, at times haphazardly, over a

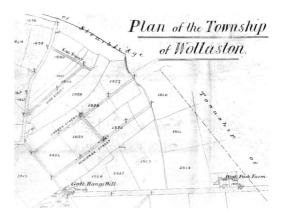

Above: For many years Wollaston's Vestry Committee were concerned with the provision of street lighting. They discussed the siting of lamps, additional to those already in existence as early as August 1866. Most likely these would have been oil burning, as gas lighting was not considered until 1882. Dated 1890, this map shows the location of all the gas lamps installed the new village area by that time. Wollaston had 50 gas lamps overall.

number of years. In some case more than one name was used for the same street, or the street took its name from a family who lived there. Among the nine recommendations that the committee made were that:

- '*the road now called Bridle Lane be styled Bridle Road*',
- '*the lane leading from the Ridge Cover towards Coalbournbrook be styled Vicarage Road*',
- '*the road from the brook near the Golden Lion Inn to the Ridge Top be styled Bridgnorth Road.*'

HIGH PARK AVENUE

Above: On 24 March 1890 the Vestry Committee took responsibility for giving official names to Wollaston's streets. In some cases more than one name was used for the same street, or the street took its name from a family who lived there. After making its decisions, the Vestry Committee decided to purchase enamelled iron street nameplates to be fixed to the walls of houses. One of the last survivors is this one which is affixed to The Gate Hangs Well.

Above: The Vestry Committee decided to purchase number plates so that all 532 houses then in Wollaston could be numbered consecutively. These means of identifying properties would help not only in the sorting and delivery of letters, but would also be of benefit to the community as a whole. This is one such example of an original 1890 house number.

As part of this rationalisation and tidying up process in 1890, the Vestry Committee decided to purchase enamelled iron street nameplates to be fixed to the walls of houses and also to purchase number plates so that houses could be numbered consecutively. These measures of identifying properties would help not only in the sorting and delivery of letters, but would also be of benefit to the community as a whole.

The following illustrations give a fuller insight into the role of the Vestry Committee:

NOTICE

The inhabitants of this Hamlet are requested to meet in the Public Vestry, at the National School, on Thursday the 31st day of March 1881 at seven o'clock in the evening, to make out a list of persons fit and proper to serve the Office of Overseers of the Poor for the year ensuing, to be returned to the Justices of the Peace for the Hundred of Lower Halfshire. And at the same time and place the said Meeting will likewise appoint a Surveyor of the Highways.

Thomas Faulkner
Joseph Taylor

Overseers of the Hamlet of Wollaston
March 25th 1881

Posted a true copy of this Notice upon each place of public religious worship within the Township of Wollaston on Sunday March 27th 1881 by me.
Thomas Faulkner

Mr Thomas Bishop in the Chair at a Vestry Meeting of the inhabitants of the Township of Wollaston holden at the National School in the aforesaid Hamlet on Thursday the thirty first day of March 1881 pursuant to the foregoing notice.
The following persons being substantial Householders within this Township were nominated as fit and proper

Above: The back of the same house number shows that it was made by Archibald Kenrick & Sons of West Bromwich, and was type No.7 in their catalogue.

persons to serve the Office of Overseers of the Poor for this Township for the year ensuing viz:-
Joseph Taylor
George Rew
Joseph Burton
Edwin Steward
Henry Addenbrooke Cook
Proposed by Mr Benjamin Ryder and seconded by Mr Joseph Astley that a paid Surveyor be appointed. Carried unanimously.
Proposed by Mr Benjamin Ryder and seconded by Mr Thomas Noxon Bishop that Mr John Edwards be appointed the paid Surveyor. Carried unanimously.
Proposed by Mr Henry Richards and seconded by Mr T N Bishop that the Surveyor's salary be twenty five pounds for the ensuing year. Carried unanimously

It was proposed by Mr T Lea and seconded by Mr J Lewis that Mr John Edwards be reappointed paid surveyor for the ensuing year at the same salary as before viz. twenty three pounds to include the making and collecting of the Highway Rate. Carried.

Proposed by Mr D Skidmore and seconded by Mr J R Elcock that the highway leading from Vicarage Road to Bell's Mill be repaired by the Surveyor from Vicarage Road to the cottage opposite New Wood Farm House. Carried.

Proposed by Mr W W Pagett and seconded by Mr Pugh that a letter be sent to W O Foster Esq asking him to have the foot road put in repair between the Barley Mow Inn and the Iron Works. Carried.

Resolved that application be made to the Rural Sanitary Authority for two additional lamps to be placed in the road called Fir Grove. Carried.

6th April 1893

The legacy of the Vestry Committee
Although superficially democratic, the Vestry Committee was in reality a self-perpetuating body, with little change in its membership from year to year. Despite these limitations it had nevertheless stimulated an interest in local government and had prompted some villagers to become involved in managing the affairs of their community, thus preparing the way for Wollaston's voice to be heard on a wider stage if Wollaston were to join Stourbridge.

Wollaston joins Stourbridge
Wollaston became part of Stourbridge after much soul searching and careful financial calculations. Until 1894 the Vestry Committee was the final authority in all parish matters, whether civil or ecclesiastical, but the Local Government Act, passed in March of that year, severely curtailed its powers. The Act authorised the creation of parish councils and required that the civil functions of the Vestry be transferred to them. Furthermore the same Act also established urban district councils for towns such as Stourbridge.

Ten years before this momentous Local Government Act was passed, Stourbridge had been seeking to improve its status by becoming a borough with an elected council and a mayor. Those who supported this idea thought that Stourbridge's case for borough status would be helped if its population and boundaries were increased by absorbing the outlying, but separate districts of Amblecote, Lye, Wollescote, Wordsley, Upper Swinford, Pedmore and Wollaston. They believed that the Privy Council, which had the responsibility for recommending or rejecting

The County Council of Worcestershire.
Local Government Act 1888.
Stourbridge Extension.

WHEREAS a proposal has been made to the County Council of Worcestershire for the transfer of the Parish or Township of *Wollaston* in the District of the *Stourbridge* Union Rural Sanitary Authority the said District being a County District within the meaning of Section 57 of the Local Government Act 1888, from such District to the District of the *Stourbridge* Urban Sanitary Authority and for the increase of the number of Members of the said Urban Sanitary Authority from *Eighteen* to *Twenty-one ;* and the said County Council have directed Inquiry to be made in the locality into the subject matter of such proposals :

NOTICE IS HEREBY GIVEN that JOHN WILLIAM WILLIS BUND Esquire, Chairman of the said County Council, the Person appointed to hold the said Inquiry, will attend for that purpose at the *National School, Wollaston,* on *Tuesday* the *Thirty-first* day of *July* 1894, at *Half-past Seven* o'clock *p.m.*, and will then and there be prepared to receive the evidence of any Person interested in the matter of the said Inquiry.

Wm. Nichols Marcy
Clerk of the said County Council.

County Hall, Worcester,
14 *July* 1894.

E. B. & S. 150 18.7.94.

Above: On 3 May 1894 the Vestry Committee appointed a sub-committee to investigate the implications of a merger with Stourbridge. This reported back the opinion that joining Stourbridge would mean better government, better road maintenance, cheaper gas lighting and a reduction in the poor rate. Overall, the rates would also be one penny cheaper. Before the union could take place there had to be a public enquiry held in the village, for which this is a public notice. *Worcester Record Office*

Stourbridge's bid to become a borough, would be more likely to be impressed by an enlarged Stourbridge rather than by the existing town. There was, however, strenuous opposition to this proposal from the outlying districts where it was strongly suspected that Stourbridge would be the only real beneficiary, whilst they would not only lose their independence, but would have to pay for amenities and improvements that they did not want. In view of the hostility that this proposal aroused in all districts, the Stourbridge Town Commissioners were forced to abandon it in October 1884.

The Local Government Act of 1894 forced Wollaston Vestry Committee into making a momentous decision: should the village remain independent and establish a parish council, or should it merge with Stourbridge? As Wollaston considered its future, Stourbridge was reviving its plan for enlargement, but this time a great deal of statistical information was collected and published in order to persuade the people of Wollaston that their future lay with Stourbridge. The most important of the six statistical tables compiled by Harry Mills, Clerk to the Stourbridge Improvement Commissioners, was that which showed the many services and facilities that Stourbridge and Wollaston shared, namely: water, gas supply, post, main drainage, courts, banking, medical, market, secondary education, poor law relief, county council and parliamentary representation.

On 3 May 1894 the Vestry Committee appointed a sub-committee to investigate the implications of a merger with Stourbridge. It reported back the following week on 11 May. At this full meeting of the Vestry Committee, held in the village schools, Isaac Nash Jr, on behalf of the sub-committee, reported that not only had there been comprehensive discussions with Stourbridge on the financial implications of joining, but also that it had persuaded Stourbridge to make concessions such that if Wollaston joined Stourbridge its rates would be one penny cheaper than if it chose to remain independent. In addition the sub-committee was of the opinion that joining Stourbridge would mean better government, better road maintenance, cheaper gas lighting and a reduction in the poor rate. In the light of this very favourable report Mr T Grazebrook proposed, seconded by Mr T Guest: '*that this meeting empowers the committee to take steps for the joining of Wollaston with Stourbridge.*'

The following document is a copy of the agreement between The Stourbridge Improvement Commissioners (a forerunner of Stourbridge Urban District Council) and Wollaston's Vestry Committee:

This Indenture made the 29th day of May 1894 between the Stourbridge Improvement Commissioners hereinafter called the Commissioners of the one part Isaac Nash (scythe manufacturer) Chairman and The Revd George Gilbanks (Vicar of Wollaston, Clerk in Holy Orders) John Richard Salter Elcock (Solicitor) Edward Parsons (Farmer) Job Till Short (Engineer) Joseph Jordan (Solictr.) Walter William Pagett (Accounts Clerk) Tom Grazebrook (Architect) and James Albert Lycett (Assistant Clerk to

Guardians) all of Wollaston near Stourbridge in the County of Worcester and all of whom are included in the term of and are hereinafter called "the Committee" of the other part. Whereas the Committee were recently appointed by the Vestry for the parish of Wollaston in the County of Worcester hereinafter called 'the rural parish' to consider whether it was expedient for that parish to become included in and form part of the Urban District of Stourbridge. And whereas the committee having duly investigated and considered the subject reported to an adjourned meeting of their said Vestry held on the 11th day of May 1894 recommending the adoption of terms as or to the effect hereinafter stated and such report was adapted at such meeting 'that this meeting empowers the Committee to take steps for the joining of Wollaston with Stourbridge.'

The proposal to join Stourbridge was carried by a large majority, but before the union could take place there had to be a public enquiry. This was held in the village school on 31 July 1894 before J W Willis Bund, Chairman of Worcestershire County Council, on behalf of the County Council as the parish came under its jurisdiction.

In his report Willis Bund made it clear that the real and perceived links between Wollaston and Stourbridge had led him to recommend: 'that the District of the Stourbridge Urban Sanitary Authority be extended so as to include the Township of Wollaston', and thus Wollaston officially became part of Stourbridge on 11 September 1894. In December 1894 the first elections for the newly created Stourbridge Urban District Council were held; of the 21 new councillors, three were elected to represent Wollaston –Isaac Nash, junior, Joseph Wooldridge and Joseph Bridgwater. Wollaston was now truly part of Stourbridge, but with a voice of its own.

Wollaston councillors

In the early years of the 20th century Wollaston was fortunate in having a number of outstanding and long serving representatives. The quality of Wollaston's representatives was highlighted in 1908 during the council debate on whether the village was under-represented and deserved an extra councillor. The *County Express* of 4 January reported that Councillor Fiddian (West Ward) said that he had always been under the impression that Wollaston had been wonderfully well represented. He then commented:

'Since Wollaston came into Stourbridge he was perfectly certain he was well within the mark when he said they had had two pence for every penny into Stourbridge. That fact was complimentary to the Wollaston representatives – they had never failed, when anything was wanted for Wollaston, to let them know about it. He had not seen this from other wards, whose members considered they represented the town generally; but the Wollaston representatives had gone out of their way to get as much as possible for Wollaston. Perhaps it was all the better that Wollaston had only three representatives, because these three could put their heads together and get pretty well all they wanted.'

The. Local Government Act, 1888.

Stourbridge Extension.

STOURBRIDGE & WOLLASTON.

PUBLIC ENQUIRY

TO BE HELD AT WOLLASTON, ON THE 31ST JULY, 1894, BEFORE J. WILLIS BUND, ESQ., J.P., BARRISTER - AT - LAW, CHAIRMAN OF THE COUNTY COUNCIL OF WORCESTERSHIRE, ON BEHALF OF SUCH COUNCIL.

Statements and Tables

(PREPARED BY MR. MILLS, CLERK TO THE STOUR-BRIDGE IMPROVEMENT COMMISSIONERS,) FOR USE AT THE ENQUIRY.

Above: This is the cover of the evidence presented before Willis Bund's enquiry on 31 July 1894. In his report, he made it clear that the real and perceived links between Wollaston and Stourbridge led him to recommend: 'that the District of the Stourbridge Urban Sanitary Authority be extended so as to include the Township of Wollaston', and thus Wollaston officially became part of Stourbridge on 11 September 1894.

Outstanding councillors

- Isaac Nash, Jr, head of the spade and edged tool works, located at Wollaston Mills, represented Wollaston on Stourbridge UDC from 1895 until his death in 1908.
- Frank Taylor, head teacher, served from 1889 until 1935 continuously, except for one three-year break.
- Frank Mason, head teacher, served from 1910 until his death in 1927.
- Joseph Pearson, head teacher of the village school, served from 1922 until his death in 1946.

In addition to the aforementioned councillors on the newly created Stourbridge UDC, which became Stourbridge Borough Council in 1914, Wollaston was also represented on Worcestershire County Council, which was established in 1889. Wollaston's first County Councillor was Alfred William Worthington who held the seat virtually unopposed for 18 years until his retirement from public life in 1907. Although born in Manchester in 1828, he had settled in Stourbridge in 1882. A former schoolteacher and Presbyterian minister, he was a lifelong member of the Liberal party.

Election campaigning

At the beginning of the 20th century Wollaston was a stronghold of the Liberal Party. On 4 January during the height of the 1906 General Election campaign Wollaston members of the Liberal Party organised a meeting in Edkin's Repository. Mr Edkins was a removals and storage contractor whose premises are occupied in 2003 by Wollaston Garage. The meeting was addressed by Cecil Harmsworth the Liberal Candidate in the forthcoming contest for the Mid-Worcestershire constituency, which then included Stourbridge and District.

A suffragette in Wollaston

Reporting on Harmsworth's vistory, the *County Express* of 27 January 1906 included the following observation:

'The lady voter, Edmot Bradley, of Wheeler Street, Stourbridge, who was admitted by the Revising Barrister to the Wollaston voting register, under the impression that 'Edmot' must be a man, succeeded in registering her vote at the Wollaston booth* on Tuesday. She went to the poll early in the morning and applied to the presiding officer, Mr W B Hulme, of Worcester, for a voting paper, and he, after the usual searching of the rolls, found that everything was correct. Before, however, taking upon himself the responsibility of giving her the stamped paper, he decided to telegraph for instructions to the Under-Sheriff at Worcester, Mr Brown. The telegram was despatched and an answer received that the vote might be admitted, and 'Edmot Bradley' on returning to the booth later in the morning, received her voting paper and registered a vote for Mr Harmsworth. We may say that the Presiding Officer could have refused the lady's vote, but if he did so it would have been on his own responsibility. In his speech at the Stourbridge Liberal Club on the evening after his election, Mr Harmsworth alluded to the fact and the pleasure he felt at being one of the very first MPs to receive a lady's vote.'
(*The voting booth was in Wollaston Schools.)

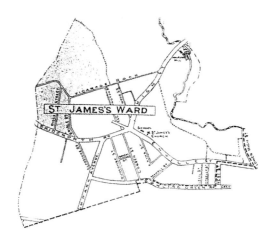

Above: From 11 September 1894 Wollaston became an electoral ward of Stourbridge. The boundaries of this were revised in 1914 when a new St James's Ward was created. The broken line on this map shows its boundaries.

Viewed from 2003 'Edmot's' action in casting a vote does not seem remarkable, but in 1906 it was not only unthinkable, it was earth shattering, because women were not allowed to vote in parliamentary elections. How 'Edmot' had managed to get her name on the voting register is a mystery, but in doing so she posed a problem for the Presiding Officer, because he could not legally refuse to give a ballot paper to someone who was listed on the electoral roll and had not already voted. The deliberate nature of 'Edmot's' action is a clear indication that she was a suffragette and that her action was designed to draw attention to the campaign, launched by the Women's Social and Political Union in 1903, to obtain a vote for women. It was not until 1918 that women received a vote. What happened to 'Edmot Bradley' and whether that was her real name remains an unsolved mystery.

An extra councillor for Wollaston

On 30 December 1907 at the monthly meeting of Stourbridge UDC, Cllr Frank Taylor raised the matter of the representation of Wollaston on the town council. He argued that as Wollaston was growing rapidly it needed greater representation on the town council. This issue, far from being settled that day, was to divide the council for the next six months and was resolved only after there had been two public enquiries chaired by J W Willis Bund, the Chairman of Worcestershire County Council.

At the enquiry Mr W W Goddard (Town Clerk) put forward the key facts on which the case for additional councillors for Wollaston was based. He pointed out that the Wollaston Ward had only three councillors whereas each of the other four wards had six councillors. He added that Wollaston's population and voters were similar to those of Upper Swinford and actually exceeded those of West Ward.

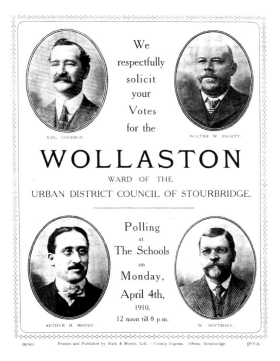

We
respectfully
solicit
your
Votes
for the

WOLLASTON

WARD OF THE

URBAN DISTRICT COUNCIL OF STOURBRIDGE.

Polling
at
The Schools
on
Monday,
April 4th,
1910.
12 noon till 8 p.m.

EMIL COOKSON. WALTER W. PAGETT. ARTHUR H. MOODY. W. SOUTHALL.

(95291) Printed and Published by Mark & Moody, Ltd., " County Express" Offices, Stourbridge [P.T.O.

Above: At the 30 December 1907 meeting of Stourbridge UDC, Cllr Frank Taylor argued that as Wollaston was growing rapidly it needed greater representation on the town council. As a result of this, by May 1908 Wollaston gained an extra councillor, whilst each of the other wards had their number of councillors reduced. The additional seat was first contested in the 1910 elections, which was a significant event in Wollaston's history. When the list of candidates was originally drawn up there were 11 nominations, four of whom produced this leaflet. On the day none of them was elected!

This lack of consistency in terms of the relationship between voters and councillors was commented on by the Chairman, who said that it was an anomaly that there should be a member for every 99 electors in the East Ward, and one for every 244 in Wollaston Ward. Frank Taylor argued that population alone or rateable value, the current yardstick employed by the council, was not a good basis for determining the number of councillors. He believed that the number of households in the ward was a more reliable basis and in support of his argument produced statistics to show that Wollaston had experienced the greatest increase in house building in the last three years: in East Ward 21 new houses had been built, in Upper Swinford Ward 42, in South Ward 64, in West Ward 79 and in Wollaston 93!

No decision was made by the first public enquiry and so a second one was held in May. Eventually the County Council ruled that Stourbridge Council had too many councillors and called for a reduction from 27 to 21. The consequences of this reduction was a re-distribution of the number of councillors for each ward, hence Wollaston

gained an extra councillor whilst each of the other wards had their number of councillors reduced. These changes would be put into effect at the next triennial elections in 1910.

Wollaston's success in winning the argument over representation was not greeted with enthusiasm in the other four wards, so it was not surprising that contest for the Wollaston Ward in 1910 aroused much interest and feeling.

The Council Election of 1910

The 1910 Stourbridge UDC election was a significant event in Wollaston's history. It was recognition of both Wollaston's growth and its contribution to Stourbridge's development. The campaign to secure greater representation for Wollaston, led by Cllr Frank Taylor, had polarised the opinions of the councillors into those who thought Wollaston deserved an extra member and those who vehemently opposed it. The *County Express* believed that in most wards the outcome was predictable, except for Wollaston where a keen contest was anticipated. The latter view was confirmed by the large number of candidates and the turnout of the 777-strong electorate, 594 (or 76.45%) of whom voted. It was in fact the highest percentage turnout of all the wards.

When the list of candidates was originally drawn up there were 11 nominations, but three withdrew, to leave the following eight candidates to fight for the four Wollaston seats:

- Alfred Brookes, Duncombe Street, edge tool foreman
- Emmanuel Cookson, 23, Wood Street, iron-works manager
- Benjamin Francis Mason, 73, High Street, schoolmaster
- Arthur Hatfield Moody, 'Stranraer', Greenfield Avenue, journalist
- Walter William Pagett, 11, High Street, ironfounder
- William Southall, The Grange, New Road, retired brewer
- Francis (Frank) Taylor, 13, High Park Avenue, schoolmaster
- Harry Unitt, 60, Bridgnorth Road, turner.

Although party labels did not feature in the election, Taylor and Brookes were well known Liberals, whilst Unitt was a Conservative. The four candidates, Cookson, Pagett, Moody and Southall, who issued a joint manifesto, campaigned on a 'ratepayers and businessmen' platform. Despite their well produced leaflet they all finished bottom of the poll, which was headed by Frank Mason who stood as an independent. The votes were cast as follows:

Elected Votes for	
B F Mason	415
F Taylor	336
A Brookes	252
H Unitt	247

Not Elected	*Votes for*
W W Pagett	175
E Cookson	162
A H Moody	162
W Southall	154

Significantly the two candidates who topped the poll were both schoolmasters who undoubtedly benefited from public support for the proposal to increase the number of elementary schools in Stourbridge, whereas the four defeated candidates were all opposed to increasing the number of schools because of the costs likely to be incurred.

The provision of Public Services

During the second half of the 19th century as the new village was taking shape there was a growing demand for those essential services that are taken for granted in 2003, principally the provision of water, gas, and later electricity. As a consequence of these services becoming available, the physical links between Wollaston and Stourbridge increased to such an extent that by 1894 there was, as shown above, an overwhelming case for Wollaston to join the newly created Stourbridge UDC.

Water was supplied by the privately owned Stourbridge Water Works Co, which, although formed in 1854, did not become operational until 1857. A pumping station on the Amblecote side of the River Stour was used to pump water from natural springs to a reservoir on Amblecote Bank. By 1863 the company's pipes had reached as far as the Crown Inn in Enville Street, reaching Ridge Top by 1867. To meet the increasing demand for water a new pumping station was opened in 1880 at Coalbournbrook on the Wollaston side of the Stourbridge Canal (near to the entrance of Richardson Drive in 2003).

Initially, as with water, gas was supplied by a private

company, the Stourbridge Gas Co, established in Amblecote in 1835. In 1893 their Gas Works were bought by the Stourbridge Town Commissioners on behalf of the town, although long before that time, as *Bentley's Directory of Stourbridge* for 1841, makes clear, gas lighting in public places was well established in Stourbridge by the 1840s: '*This useful and brilliant vapour is now introduced into places of worship, inns, shops, etc., and the streets are lighted thereby.*'

Exactly when piped gas reached Wollaston is not known, but given that in 1882 Job Short urged the Vestry Committee to press for gas street lighting and by 1886 the Vestry Committee was wanting additional street lights, it is not unreasonable to assume that piped gas reached Wollaston in the mid 1880s. However, as with the water supply, the fact that certain streets had piped gas and water did not guarantee that individual households had gas and water supplies.

In contrast to neighbouring Black Country towns there was a delay in the supply of electricity, because some members of Stourbridge Council thought that the introduction of electricity would threaten the commercial viability of the municipally owned gas works. In 1909 The Midland Electric Corporation for Power Distribution Ltd (the forerunner of the Midlands Electricity Board) began distributing electricity in the Stourbridge area. As a consequence of this delay Wollaston was not electrified until the 1920s; Nash's works at Wollaston Mills were the first premises to be supplied in October 1920, whilst St

Right: In 1884 the Stourbridge Mains Drainage Board erected a pumping station alongside the Withy Brook, near to where it joined the River Stour, in what would become Lowndes Road in the 20th century. This date plaque was recovered from the building when it was demolished and was incorporated into the new installation that performs the same function there in 2003.

Below: The date plaque can be seen in this photograph of the pumping station, to which a refuse destructor was added in the early 1900s. The massive chimney of John Bradley & Co dominated the skyline behind.

Right: Mains water came later to Wollaston's streets. This is a portion of a plan from the Stourbridge & District Water Board's Bill to Parliament dated 30 November 1908, showing the route of the main down Cobden Street. *Worcester Record Office*

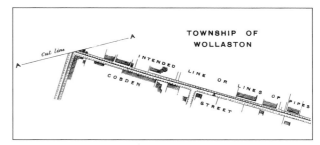

Below right: Exactly when piped gas reached Wollaston is not known, but Job Short urged the Vestry Committee to press for gas street lighting in 1882, and by 1886 the Vestry Committee was wanting additional street lights, it is not unreasonable to assume that piped gas reached Wollaston in the mid 1880s. One of the original gas lamps is seen in this view of the end of High Park Avenue c.1920.

Below: It was not until 1909 that The Midland Electric Corporation for Power Distribution Ltd (MEC) began distributing electricity in the Stourbridge area, but Wollaston was not electrified until the 1920s. Their distinctive 'device', incorporating their initials and slighly alarming lightening bolts, is seen on the switch house in Bridgnorth Road, seen below.

James's Church was connected in October 1924. Thereafter there was a yearly progression of cables being laid in individual streets throughout the 1920s and 1930s.

The Kinver Light Railway

Between 1901 and 1930 Wollaston was linked to the Black Country and Birmingham by an electric tramway built to reach Kinver, an inland resort and the destination for many Birmingham and Black Country folk on Sundays and Bank Holidays. Wollaston was the junction of tramways from The Fish Inn, Coalbournbrook, and Stourbridge, and annually hundreds of thousands of people passed through the village to and from a day out in the place the tramway company branded '*The Switzerland of the Midlands*.' The effect of this 'exposure' upon the growth of the village can only be guessed at, but doubtless many thought what a nice place Wollaston would be to live as they passed through, and some hastily scribbled down the details of houses for sale, or 'Land Suitable for Building', as they rattled by.

Since 26 May 1884 a steam tramway had operated between the foot of Castle Hill in Dudley and the Amblecote side of the bridge over the Stour in Lower High Street that gives Stourbridge its name. Like many others in the country, in the late 1890s the British Electric Traction Co Ltd (BET), formed to electrify and develop steam- and horse-powered tramways, bought this line. Thus, in November 1897, Stourbridge Council received a letter from BET, stating that they intended to apply for powers to construct a line from The Fish Inn, Coalbournbrook, to Kinver. Issues surrounding the proposed Kinver tramway were aired at a Public Enquiry held in Stourbridge on 15 February 1898. Ahead of this debate the *County Express* of 12 February urged support for the scheme:

Below: There was a yearly progression of electricity cables being laid in Wollaston's streets throughout the 1920s and 1930s. Every existing property had access to an electricity supply by 1937, and all new properties built after this date were supplied with it from new. One consequence of this was the appearance of transformers and switch houses, such as this one on Bridgnorth Road.

'The (Tramway) Company means business, and we hope will be supported by the general voice of the community in their scheme.' It also noted that: *'at Wollaston there would be a station affording facilities for collection and distribution of goods sent by the cars.'*

The scheme was approved and BET obtained powers to construct the 'Kinver Light Railway' (KLR) on 7 March 1899. Like the other tramways in the Black Country the track was 3ft 6in gauge, because of the narrow streets, but Wollaston's streets must have been extremely narrow, because BET obtained powers to widen two lengths of road, each a furlong long, between five furlongs and a mile from The Fish Inn. Additional land had to be purchased for this, and the road was widened to 35ft between fences, half of the cost being borne by BET, the rest being divided between the County and Stourbridge councils. In addition, between the bridge over the Stour and The Ridge, the road was to be widened by BET to 23ft, by setting back the kerbs and channels.

Construction of the KLR began in June 1899. By that August the track between Wollaston and The Hyde, Kinver had been temporarily laid, and estimates for work on the overhead wires had been prepared and materials requisitioned. Thereafter progress slowed, and the whole of 1900 was taken up in completing the line, which was single, with passing loops every 200 yards or so. BET had a trial run over the line on 20 February 1901, but the tramway between The Fish Inn and Wollaston was put to a sadder use ten days earlier. In the early hours of 5 February 1901, tram driver Martin Cadman finally abandoned his tram after trying for three hours to climb Bath Hill (Blowers Green Road) in Dudley during sleet and snow. He died a few hours later at home, and was buried on 10 February, as the *County Express* reported:

'When the procession started from Martin's late home at Queen's Cross there was quite a crowd of 2,000 present. It had been decided to bury the deceased at Wollaston, and the sight of so unique a spectacle was witnessed by many thousands of people, in fact the road from Dudley to Wollaston was practically lined all the way. At Coalbournbrook the procession had to be reversed, and proceeded to the junction of the roads near to Wollaston Church, from whence the body was carried by bearers to the Church.'

This sombre procession was probably the first use of the Kinver Light Railway.

The tramway was officially opened on 4 April 1901 and the public service began the following day, Good Friday, the first tram being driven by George Smith of High Street Wollaston. The

Above: Construction of the Kinver Light Railway (KLR) began in June 1899. Passing through Wollaston along High Street and Bridgnorth Road, past The Ridge it moved to the side of the road as it made its way down to The Stewponey. In this commercial postcard, a tram can just be seen beyond the approaching trap. *Brian Standish*

basic service was half-hourly in each direction. Cars started from The Fish Inn on the hour and half-hour, and the line was divided into four one penny stages, the through fare being three pence. Over 10,000 people travelled on the tramway's first day, despite torrential rain, requiring many extra cars to bring them back from Kinver.

Below: The KLR was officially opened on 4 April 1901 and the public service began the following day, Good Friday. The basic service was half-hourly in each direction. Cars started from The Fish Inn on the hour and half-hour, and the line was divided into four one-penny stages, the through fare being three pence. Car No 46, seen here, was one of three double-deckers rapidly cut down after their use was prohibited following the line's final inspection on 1 April 1901. *Brian Standish*

Tram Terminus, Wollaston

Enville Street line was operated as a shuttle service, usually by one single deck car; with through passengers changing to Kinver cars at Wollaston.

Far from easing matters, the new line brought both additional passengers and more complaints, especially regarding a desire for Enville Street cars to run right through to The Ridge. By 1904, only five of the 15 cars leaving Enville Street between 8.00am and 12.30pm ran through to The Ridge, fare one penny, the others terminated at Wollaston Junction, with passengers often facing a long wait before a car from The Fish Inn arrived to take them to The Ridge. For the remainder of the day each alternate car ran through to The Ridge. BET said that traffic was so heavy that the single line was inadequate and the difficulties could not be remedied until the line was doubled.

Above: Over 10,000 people travelled on the KLR's first day, despite torrential rain, requiring many extra cars to bring them back from Kinver. Car No 48, the third of the original cut-down double-deckers, is seen at the terminus there around 1912. Second left in the group is Inspector Horton, whose diligence made its mark on the running of the tramway.

The Enville Street tramway

Despite the KLR's evident popularity, the tramway company were bombarded with complaints about the service, particularly from Stourbridge people over having to travel to The Fish Inn, or walk to Wollaston, to use it. In response, in November 1901, BET announced that work would soon commence on a Stourbridge-Wollaston (Enville Street) branch line. 'Soon' turned out to be mid-March 1902, the work being complicated by the need to widen parts of Bridgnorth Road. By 31 May 1902 the *County Express* reported that:

'*the permanent way on the Stourbridge-Wollaston tramway would be completed in a few days*', and on 5 July 1902 it told its readers that: '*the permanent way on the tramway would be completed in a few days.*'

The line opened on 13 December 1902. It began at a single-track junction with the main Dudley-Stourbridge line near Stourbridge Clock and ran down Enville Street and Bridgnorth Road, a single line with passing loops, to a double track junction with the KLR in the centre of Wollaston, at a point called Wollaston Junction, a destination still seen on buses in 2003! Just seven-tenths of a mile in length, the

The 1905 track doubling

Early in 1905 BET acted to relieve the congestion on the KLR. They revealed plans to double the track from just beyond the River Stour bridge at Coalbournbrook, right through Wollaston to The Ridge, a distance of about a mile. This required much road widening, from which the growing Wollaston benefited. The work began in March, and on the 27th the Stourbridge Surveyor reported that:

'*that the Tramway Company had commenced doubling the track within the area at Wollaston ... and had broken up the road in several places along the route*', and by late April he noted that: '*the doubling of the Tramway track within the council's area was completed as far as Bridle Road by Easter.*'

Below: In response to public complaints, a connecting tramway line was built, between Stourbridge town centre and Wollaston, along Enville Street. The line opened on 13 December 1902. It was a single, but had a double track junction with the KLR in the centre of the village, at a point called Wollaston Junction, a destination still seen on buses in 2003! Just seven-tenths of a mile in length, the Enville Street line was operated as a shuttle service, usually by one single deck car; with through passengers changing to KLR cars at Wollaston.

Below: Far from easing matters, the new line brought both additional passengers and more complaints, especially regarding a desire for Enville Street cars to run right through to The Ridge. By 1904, only five of the 15 cars leaving Enville Street between 8:00am and 12:30pm ran through to there, the others terminated at Wollaston Junction, with passengers often facing a long wait before a car from The Fish Inn arrived to take them to The Ridge. This timetable is from 1905.

Kinver Light Railway.

CARS LEAVE KINVER for the Fish Inn, Coalbournbrook, at 5.30, 6.30, 7.25, 8.30, 9.30, 10.15, 11.15 a.m., 12 noon, and every 30 mins. until 10.30 p.m.
CARS LEAVE KINVER for Stourbridge Clock at 8 a.m.
CARS LEAVE FISH INN, COALBOURNBROOK for Kinver at 6.0, 7.0, 8.0, 8.55, 9.45, 10.45, 11.45 a.m., 12.30 p.m., and every 30 mins. till 11.0 p.m.

SUNDAYS.
CARS LEAVE KINVER at 9.0 a.m., and every 30 mins. till 10.0 p.m.
CARS LEAVE COALBOURNBROOK (Fish Inn) at 9.30 a.m., and every 30 mins. till 10.30 p.m.

Stourbridge and Wollaston.

CARS LEAVE STOURBRIDGE CLOCK for High Street, Wollaston (for Kinver) at 8.30 a.m., and every 15 mins. till 11.0 p.m.
CARS LEAVE WOLLASTON (High Street) for Stourbridge at 8.22 a.m., and every 15 mins. till 10.52 p.m.

SUNDAYS.
CARS LEAVE STOURBRIDGE CLOCK at 10.30 a.m., and every 15 mins. until 10 30 p.m.
CARS LEAVE WOLLASTON (High Street) at 10.22 a.m., and every 15 mins. until 10.22 p.m.

Below: The track doubling on the KLR was completed by the end of May 1905, in time for the Whitsun Holiday traffic. This was a good thing too, as passenger numbers hit an all-time high. The line carried 16,699 passengers on the Monday and 14,421 the following day, during an operating period of only 15 hours! A section of the doubled line can be seen outside Waldron's tobacconists in High Street. In 2003 this shop is Websters, better known as 'Marion's.'

Everything was completed by the end of May, in time for the Whitsun Holiday traffic. A good thing too, as passenger numbers on the KLR hit an all-time high. It carried 16,699 passengers on the Monday and 14,421 the following day, during an operating period of only 15 hours. A seven minutes' service was operated up to 11:30am, and a service of 'double cars', two cars leaving at the same time, operated for the rest of the day. Nonetheless, at one period on the Bank Holiday Monday there were about 300 passengers waiting at The Fish Inn for Kinver cars. Even greater pressure was put on the tram service for the return from Kinver in the evening, but by 10:20pm the terminus was almost clear of passengers.

Complaints

Improvements apart, it seems that the tramway company could not get the service right for some. An insight into the problem comes from this speech by The Chairman of Stourbridge Council at its meeting on 20 May 1912:

Right: Early in 1905 BET acted to relieve the congestion on the KLR. They revealed plans to double the track from just beyond bridge over the River Stour at Coalbournbrook, right through Wollaston to The Ridge, a distance of about a mile. This required much road widening, from which the growing Wollaston benefited. The doubled line is seen in Bridgnorth Road, just past Duncombe Street. The tramway company were responsible for making up most of the road surface!

'There is no part of the tramway system that is treated so badly as Stourbridge. At holiday times people for the most part shun coming via Stourbridge to Kinver simply because they are landed at High Street, Wollaston, and sometimes have to stop there 2 or 3 hours before they can get to Kinver. I see no reason why the company should not run a few trams from Enville Street to Kinver (hear, hear). It is a nuisance to people coming from Birmingham to find themselves landed at Wollaston until a car comes along on which there is some spare room. Sometimes they get on at Wollaston and ride down to The Fish Inn in order to retain their seat to come back, but the company try to avoid this by running straight through Wollaston on the home journey.'

On the other hand, Wollaston's shopkeepers and publicans probably welcomed *'people from Birmingham'* with *'2 or 3 hours'* to spare in the village!

Accidents

Over the years travel on the KLR, especially on its open-side trams, was not without incident. On 7 September 1902, when a tram became stuck on the Wollaston side of

Below: One of the KLR's traction poles, with the BET's magnet & wheel symbol, is seen in this photograph of Langstone's brake outside the Britannia Inn in High Street. This point was fare-stage 2 on the journey, as painted on the pole.

The Ridge, a second tram nudged it down the gradient to Stourton, but its brakes then failed, and it ploughed into the back of the first (formerly stuck) car, causing passengers to be thrown clear and damage to the two trams. More serious was the death of a tram conductor, Joseph Compson, as a result of an accident on 4 June 1917. Annie Harper, from the dairy in Fir Grove, witnessed the incident. Two tramcars passed her as she was driving her milk float near The Bull's Head at about 1.30pm. She saw Compson fall from the tram on to the track as the other car passed the one he was on, and shouted to the driver of the first car: *"Your conductor has fallen off."* Both cars stopped at once, but Compson was found on the road unconscious, and died of a head injury in Corbett Hospital two days later.

Closure

The KLR continued to serve Wollaston throughout the 1920s, but from the end of 1925 onwards other lines were closed, reducing the number of people who could reach The Fish by tram, and as a result the KLR's passenger numbers fell. On 17 August 1925 Stourbridge Council considered complaints about trams not running in the mornings from Stourbridge to Wollaston, to which BET replied that this was a cost-saving measure. In response the Council reduced its rating assessment on the tramway from £100pa to just £10pa, but this did not prevent BET from proposing to abandon the Stourbridge-Wollaston line in 1926. When figures provided by BET were considered at an inquiry into the tramway service held in Stourbridge on 23 July 1926, it was disclosed that the line needed £4,900 for renewals and £2,400 to replace two tramcars, but that it only raised £400pa in fare income each year. Stourbridge Council did not oppose BET's proposal to close the Enville Street line, which it did on 16 November 1926, the KLR Winter service being reduced to just two cars per day from 17 November.

Thereafter, the service offered on the KLR declined, even during the summer months, provoking more complaints. The *County Express* of 17 August 1929 carried a letter from T G Hughes, Secretary of Kinver & District Horticultural Society, remarking on the poor tram service to Kinver on 7 August, the day of the Kinver Flower Show! But by this time BET was in advanced negotiations with the

Left: Despite the improvements of 1905, at one period on the May Bank Holiday Monday there were about 300 passengers waiting at The Fish Inn for Kinver cars. Even greater pressure was put on the tram service for the return from Kinver in the evening, but by 10:20pm the terminus was almost clear of passengers On Bank Holidays the Enville Street line was used to 'park' additional Kinver trams.

Below: The Rev E G Hexall founded Bethany Boys Home in Kinver, and when he died in January 1915, his body was carried by tramway all the way to Spon Lane Cemetery in Oldbury. The event, on 28 January 1915, was photographed as it made its way between The Stewponey and Wollaston ...

Below: ... and as it passed through the village. The tramway cortege has just passed the end of Cobden Street as PC Round holds back the crowds.

various Black Country local authorities over replacing the tramway services with buses operated by the 'Midland Red.' An agreement to this effect was signed on 10 September 1929. Under this BET did not lose out, they were a significant stakeholder in the 'Midland Red'! The KLR closed on 8 February 1930, the worn state of the track at The Fish Inn being cited as one reason for this. Three weeks later the last tram ran between Dudley and Stourbridge, driving one of them was George Smith of Wollaston, who had driven the first KLR tram 29 years earlier.

Telephones

Until the second-half of the 20th century few households had a 'phone. Telephone usage was largely confined to business matters. Although the National Telephone Co established an exchange in Stourbridge in 1894 few phones were installed in the early years of the 20th century, because some landowners and householders objected to telephone wires passing over their property, as the following passage illustrates.

In 1902 The National Telephone Co entered into an agreement with William Henry Foster, owner of John Bradley's Ironworks, concerning telephone wires extending over his land. The company agreed that during the time of the agreement the sum of £1pa, together with one-shilling per annum for each wire running across the property, should be paid to Mr Foster annually on 29 September. The company also agreed to repair at their expense any damage

done or caused to Mr Foster's property during the maintenance or removal of any wires. As Isaac Nash's factory at Wollaston Mills had the first phone installed in Wollaston (telephone number: Stourbridge 43), the likelihood is that the agreement relates to the National Telephone Co wishing to install a line from the centre of Stourbridge to Wollaston Mills, in doing so it would be necessary for a wire to pass over Foster's property, namely the ironworks.

That the telephone was a rarity at this time is borne out by the following notice that appeared in the *County Express* of 25 May 1912:

'IN CASE OF FIRE. Mr Edkins of the Repository, Wollaston, desires it to be known that in the case of fire in the village he will, on receiving word, gladly communicate by telephone with the Stourbridge Fire Brigade.'

Mr Edkins' telephone number was Stourbridge 81.

For those who had no access to a 'phone the quickest means of communicating with someone who lived or worked some distance away was by telegram. Reporting the monthly council meeting, the *County Express* of 31 October 1908 makes it clear that Wollaston's councillors had been pressing for the village to be connected to the national telegraphic system. The Clerk to the Council reported that:

'The Postmaster-General wrote that at present, a late collection of letters could not be made at Wollaston, but instructions had been given for an extension of the telegraphic system to the Post Office at Wollaston, and that work would be carried out as soon as it was practicable.'

Left: During the 1920s the KLR faced competition from a small fleet of Green Line buses, based at Wollaston Garage, but seen here parked by The Crescent at the end of Meriden Avenue. The KLR's tracks can just be seen in the foreground. The Enville Street line was closed on 16 November 1926, and the KLR closed on 8 February 1930.

At this time the post office was in High Street, although for the last 40 years of the 19th century there had been a 'letter receiving office' on Bridgnorth Road, kept by a Mrs Sneyd. On the 1903 Ordnance Survey (OS) map the Post Office is shown in a property on the corner of the junction of Wood Street with High Street, but a few years later according to *Kelly's Directory* for 1916, it had moved across the road, and Mr R A Rowley is listed as Sub-postmaster and grocer. From his premises '*telegrams could be dispatched, but not delivered.*'

Whilst the provision of water and gas had merely established physical links with Stourbridge, Wollaston councillors were determined that after joining Stourbridge in 1894 Wollaston should be treated as an integral part of Stourbridge. In the June Council meeting of 1898 Isaac Nash wanted to know why the Great Western Railway (GWR) Co delivered parcels in Stourbridge and Upper Swinford, but not in Wollaston! The Clerk to the Council was instructed to write to the GWR. Six months later the following item appeared in the *County Express* of 19 November:

'*THE DELIVERY OF PARCELS IN WOLLASTON. Mr Frank Taylor* (Wollaston Councillor) *writes: 'will you kindly make known to the inhabitants of Wollaston the decision of the Railway Company in this matter. There will be no charge for delivery on ordinary parcels when addressed to any house, etc within a mile radius (as the crow flies) of the Town Station.*'

Housing

'*Pleasantly situated, with electric trams connecting it on one side of the town, and on the other with the delightful district of Kinver, the place has become a popular residential neighbourhood.*'

This complimentary assessment was written by Cllr George Herbert Goodyear, author of *Stourbridge, Old and New,* published by Mark & Moody in 1908. The phrase '*a popular residential area*' accurately reflects the ongoing development of Wollaston in the early years of the 20th century before the outbreak of war in 1939. Just as the starting point for expansion in the second half of the 19th century had been the sale by Lord Dudley in 1848 of his Wollaston Estate, likewise the sale of the Eggington Farm Estate in 1903 meant that land for house building was now available close to the centre of the village. Thomas Rawson Vickers of Hollyberry Hall, Coventry, sold the land. He was the nephew of the previous owner, John Todd of Meriden House, Gladstone Road, who had died in 1895 leaving the estate to Vickers.

An immediate consequence of this sale was the building of houses along Bridgnorth Road, Bridle Road and Vicarage Road – the roads that enclosed the Eggington Farm estate – and also along the newly created Eggington Road and eventually Meriden Avenue. The public were invited to buy individual plots of land, as the following advert from the *County Express* of 22 August 1903 shows:

'*FOR SALE by Private Treaty Eligible Building Sites, fronting the Bridgnorth and Bridle Roads, from 2s to 3s 6d per yard, according to position.*'

Evidence gathered from the *County Express*, of building plots being offered for sale, and of the 'planning committee' frequently giving approval for houses to be built, clearly indicates that there was a property boom in Wollaston in the first decade of the 20th century, nevertheless there were still many people who could not afford either to buy a plot of land or a house.

In the early years of the 20th century, before the dream of municipal housing became a reality, the building of low rental houses was the result of private enterprise. Sometimes a factory owner would build houses for his employees near to their place of employment, but more usually small-scale builders, with the sole aim of making

Right: In the 20th century, Wollaston expanded most through the break up and sale of its farms. The first to go was Eggington Farm, which was sold in 1903. This plan is from the particulars of that sale, and shows eight lots along Bridgnorth Road. Ten years later Lot 1 would become The Crescent. Development did not take place right away as Buffalo Bill performed on this same field on 28 April 1904.

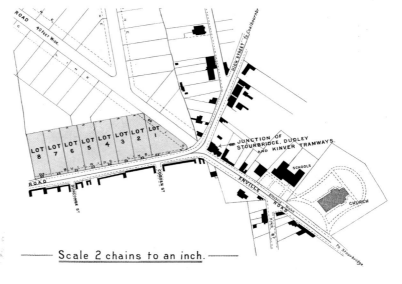

Scale 2 chains to an inch.

money, built houses for low rental. Given their limited capital it was rare for such builders to build more than a small terrace of perhaps four or six houses. Even though the building of low rental houses had been discussed by Stourbridge Council as early as 1898, the first council estate was not built until 1920. For Wollaston there had been a proposal in 1915 to build 13 council houses in Vicarage Road, but the scheme was abandoned because of the national war effort and so work on Wollaston's first council estate, High Park, did not begin until 1928.

As early as 1903 Cllr Frank Taylor had written to *Brierley Hill Advertiser*, highlighting the need to provide houses for small wage families, see page 55.

Similar views were expressed by Alfred Worthington, Wollaston's County Councillor, who had a deep interest in the problem of housing for the working class and not surprisingly he gave his full support to the Stourbridge Workmen's Dwellings Syndicate.

Stourbridge Workmen's Dwellings Syndicate

The Stourbridge Workmen's Dwellings Syndicate was the name adopted by a group of businessmen who:

'believing there is a need for dwellings suitable for the working classes in and near Stourbridge have agreed to combine under the style of 'The Stourbridge Workmen's Dwellings Syndicate' to supply such need by purchasing land in the vicinity of Stourbridge and erecting thereon dwelling houses suitable for the occupation of working men.'

The agreement they signed was dated 20 July 1905. Heading the syndicate was William Henry Foster of Apley Park, Bridgnorth (head of John Bradley & Co and son of W O Foster, who was responsible for building St James's Church, the vicarage and the village school). Other members were Philip Pargeter, (retired glass manufacturer and property developer with interests in Wordsley and Amblecote); Isaac Nash, Jr, (edge tool maker whose Wollaston Mills works employed over 200 men and boys); William Young, (builder); Walter Baylis, (another builder); Alfred Worthington, (Wollaston County Councillor); William Fiddian, (Surveyor for Stourbridge UDC); Albert

Above: Council houses were first proposed for Wollaston in 1915. There had been a plan to build 13 council houses in Vicarage Road, seen in this sketch plan, but the scheme was abandoned because of the national war effort, and Wollaston did not get its first council housing estate, High Park, until 1928.

Moyle, (grocer), and Richard Lowndes, (manager of John Bradley & Co). The syndicate was limited to 20 members. The syndicate's architect was Tom Grazebrook of Stourbridge, and its secretary was John Donaldson Harward, a Stourbridge solicitor.

Any thoughts that the Syndicate was motivated by philanthropic concerns for the welfare of working men and

Below: This is the site, as it appears in 2003, where it was proposed to build 13 council houses in 1915, by the corner of Somerset Drive.

THE HOUSING QUESTION AT STOURBRIDGE.

TO THE EDITOR OF THE " ADVERTISER."

Sir,—I have obtained permission to publish the enclosed letter, which I received on Tuesday, the day after the Council meeting. Mr. Turner's remarks only afford yet another proof that the need of houses for persons earning small wages is as keen as ever it was. The opponents of municipal housing tell us with painful reiteration that " private enterprise " can be relied upon to build the houses necessary ; meanwhile trade is being crippled, and money earned in the town is being spent outside, because those earning it cannot get residences.— Yours obediently.   F. TAYLOR.

Wollaston, October 28th, 1903.

Above: Cllr Frank Taylor addressed the thorny problem of providing affordable housing for people with low incomes as early as 1903 in this letter to the *Brierley Hill Advertiser*.

Below: The design for the first houses built by the Stourbridge Workmen's Dwellings Syndicate in Vicarage Road, up from its junction with the newly laid-out Eggington Road. Their architect was Tom Grazebrook of Stourbridge. They were built in two-phases, between 1905 and 1907. *Dudley Archives*

agreement, 20 July 1905, they purchased 9,300 square yards of land fronting Vicarage Road. The land was part of the Eggington Farm Estate, then owned by Thomas Rawson Vickers. The sale of the land surrounding Eggington Farm, which fronted Bridgnorth Road on the opposite side to The Gate Hangs Well, had begun in 1903 when 28 building plots fronting Bridgnorth Road and Bridle Road had been offered for sale. The land purchased by the Syndicate lay in the right angle formed by Vicarage Road and what became Eggington Road, and is now, in 2003, occupied by a row of 18 terraced houses. The houses were built in two phases: the first agreement with a contractor, George Garbett, to build 12 houses was signed on 17 March 1905, whilst the second agreement with a different contractor, Herbert Bullock to build six houses was signed on 18 February 1907. Eggington Road did not exist in 1905 although the plan produced for the 1903 sale clearly shows a 'proposed new road', intended to be 12 yards wide. The building of houses at the Vicarage Road end of this proposed new road, stimulated development at 'The Crescent' end of this new road; the Highways and Improvements Committee of the council approved on 28 May 1906 the plan for a new house in Eggington Road and on 3 August 1907 the council adopted not only Eggington Road but also Meriden Avenue,

their families, could be discounted. This was purely a business venture, as their articles of agreement make clear:

'*We are of the opinion that if (as we have reason to believe) suitable sites at reasonable prices can be obtained, cottages may be erected at a cost that would provide fair interest for money invested and would at the same time meet a public need by providing housing accommodation at 3/6d per week upwards.*'

Rule 12 of their agreement stated:

'*Each member of the syndicate shall be entitled to one vote in respect of each £100 subscribed.*'

In other words money bought power: Foster subscribed £1,000, Pargeter and Nash £500 each and the rest of the members put in sums of between £100 and £500.

It is not known how many houses the syndicate built in total, but on the same day that they signed their

assuming full responsibility for their maintenance.

Council housing

In November 1927 Stourbridge Council approved in principle the construction of the High Park estate on the site of the former High Park Farm, but the go-ahead for development was not given until June 1928 when an advertisement for tenders appeared on the front page of the *County Express.*

On 30 July 1928 the Council accepted the tender of A M Griffiths & Sons of Wolverhampton and building work had started by September. In January 1929 the Housing Committee recommended a rent of 6s 6d per week for a three bed roomed house on the new estate. When the estate was completed in 1931 Wollaston had an additional 474 houses. In 1937 Wollaston's council houses increased by 80, when two further estates were built, comprising 12 houses in High Street and 68 on Bridgnorth Road, including Lowndes Road and Foster Place.

Other housing developments

The 1930s saw a considerable expansion in the number of houses in Wollaston; the growth in housing and population was on a scale far greater than any previous decade in the history of the village. In addition to the houses built by the council, new houses were also being added piecemeal to the existing ones in Vicarage Road and Meriden Avenue. A new residential road, Park Road West, with 64 houses was virtually completed by 1936, and by 1938 work was in progress on the development of Gilbanks Road and Gerald Road; in the case of the latter, where 100 new houses were planned, they were advertised for sale on a weekly basis in the *County Express*.

The Croft

This large house, set back from Bridgnorth Road, stands roughly opposite The Foresters. The Croft was built in 1916 by Albert Harry Guest, a building contractor of Coalbournbrook, Amblecote, and a member of a family long associated with the building trade. In 1913 when the Foley's Prestwood estate was being sold he bought $17\frac{1}{2}$ acres of land at The Ridge. This land, roughly triangular in shape, was bounded by Bridgnorth Road and Vicarage Road and on its third side by the houses already built in Ridge Street. Leonard A Harper, of Ewen Harper Bros & Co, Architects of Birmingham, designed the house. After the sale and demolition of Wollaston Hall in the 1920s The Croft took on the role of the 'big house' in the village and hosted garden parties, fetes and other charitable functions in much the

same way as Wollaston Hall had done in the past. Sadly, as this book was going to print, The Croft was being demolished to make way for smaller houses.

The 'Rec'

At the beginning of the 20th century the only designated play area for children was a council owned plot of land, an old gravel pit, situated approximately where modern day Wolverley Avenue has been developed. In June 1908 the Highways and Improvements Committee of the council recommended that this land at The Ridge be levelled and fenced to provide a children's play area. Two years later the council considered equipping the area with climbing frames suitable for children, but unfortunately this proposal was dropped on grounds of costs. Almost certainly this play area was underused because of its remoteness, in 1910 it was a long way from all the residential parts of the village.

This situation was remedied in 1921 when Harry Guest of The Croft gave to Stourbridge Council on behalf of the people of Wollaston $8\frac{1}{2}$ acres of land in the centre of the village in exchange for the council's old gravel pit at The Ridge. Befitting this 'Red-Letter-Day' for Wollaston, the park was opened with due pomp and ceremony. The proceedings started with a band concert on The Crescent and then the crowd, led by the band marched down High Street to the park's entrance by The Bull's Head. The opening ceremony was performed by the Mayor C S Hall and was attended by a crowd estimated at around 2,000.

Left: In November 1927 Stourbridge Council approved in principle the construction of the High Park estate on the site of the former High Park Farm, but the go-ahead for development was not given until June 1928 when an advertisement for tenders appeared on the front page of the *County Express.* This is High Park Avenue and its farm before the development began, looking towards the village.

Left: On 30 July 1928 Stourbridge Borough Council accepted the tender of A M Griffiths & Sons of Wolverhampton to build the houses on High Park Estate. Building work started in September 1928, and here houses on the Leonard Road side of the road are already standing, whilst a start has yet to be made on the farmhouse side.
Stourbridge Library

Above: In January 1929 Stourbridge Borough Council's Housing Committee recommended a rent of 6s 6d per week for a three bedroom house on the new High Park Estate. When this was completed in 1931, Wollaston had an additional 474 houses, some of which are seen here.

Below: In 1937 Wollaston's council house stock was increased by 80, when two further estates were built, comprising 12 houses in High Street and 68 on Bridgnorth Road, including Lowndes Road and Foster Place, the top of which is seen here in the early 1960s. *Harry Cartwright/Stourbridge Library*

Below: By 1938 work was in progress on the development of both Gilbanks and Gerald roads. In the case of the latter, where 100 new houses were planned, they were advertised for sale on a weekly basis in the *County Express*. This is the view from one of the back windows of the new Gerald Road houses – it really used to be all fields back then!

Some interesting street names

The centre of Wollaston, which was developed in the second half of the 19th century, contains a number of streets named after contemporary politicians. Interestingly they were all well-known national political figures sharing a similar Radical outlook and, moreover, were supporters of the Liberal Party or their predecessors, the Whigs. The likeliest explanation of this political bias in the choice of street names is that it reflects not only the standing and popularity of these individuals in mid to late Victorian Britain, but also reflects the strong pro-Liberal sympathies in Wollaston at that time.

Cobden Street. Named after Richard Cobden (1804-1865) who was born in Sussex. After establishing a successful textile business in Lancashire he entered Parliament in 1841 as MP for Stockport. He was the joint leader of The Anti-Corn Law League, a pressure group for economic reform.

Bright Street. John Bright (1811-1889) was born in Lancashire. He was the other joint leader of The Anti-Corn Law League. He became an MP in 1843 and for 25 years represented Birmingham. The partnership of Cobden and Bright played an important role in mid- 19th century politics.

Duncombe Street. Thomas Slingsby Duncombe (1796-1861) came from a wealthy Yorkshire landowning family. He was an MP for 35 years. He supported many radical causes, including parliamentary reform, trade union legislation and public health issues.

Gladstone Road. Originally known as Lower Bridle Road, it was renamed in July 1898 to commemorate William Ewart Gladstone (1809-1898) who had died earlier that year. He was leader of the Liberal Party for 30 years and was Prime Minister four times.

Below: In 1921 Harry Guest of The Croft gave 8½ acres of land, in the centre of the village, to Stourbridge Council on behalf of the people of Wollaston, in exchange for the council's old gravel pit at The Ridge. Befitting this 'Red-Letter-Day' for Wollaston, the park was opened with due pomp and ceremony. The proceedings started with a band concert on The Crescent and then the crowd, led by the band, marched down High Street to the park's entrance by The Bull's Head, seen here. Wollastonians have enjoyed the Rec' ever since.

Below: Wollaston Rec' was fenced off from the building plots fronting to High Street, which had been sold in July 1920, by this hoop-topped fencing, sections of which survive in 2003.

Hume Place. This name appears on the census returns from 1851 through to 1881. It was that part of Bridgnorth Road which runs from Wollaston Garage to the corner of Cobden Street. It was probably named after two campaigners for trade union reform, Joseph Hume (1777-1855) and Francis Place (1771-1854), whose names are always linked together because of their close political cooperation. This little 'in-joke' probably caused those responsible for this naming to give a little wry smile every time they passed by the building.

The importance of the iron industry in Wollaston's growth and development is remembered in four street names:

Firmstone Street. Named after Henry Onions Firmstone (1815-1899). He was an important Black Country coal and iron master. He lived in Wollaston Hall from approximately 1850 until his death in 1899.

Bradley Road. John Bradley (1769-1816) founded in 1800 the iron works between the River Stour and the Stourbridge Canal. For many generations the works were known as John Bradley and Company.

Foster Place. Named after the Foster Family, namely James Foster, William Orme Foster and William Henry Foster who owned and managed John Bradley & Co for most of the 19th century.

Lowndes Road. Richard Lowndes was the manager of John Bradley & Co in the first quarter of the 20th century. He lived at Beauty Bank House in Enville Street.

In contrast to the national figures who were honoured in the street names of the 19th century, local people who made an important contribution to the political and business life of Stourbridge in the first half of the 20th century have been commemorated by the following names: Francis, Gregory, Harmon, Palfrey and Leonard roads, whilst the intriguingly named Lady Grey's Walk commemorates the first

mayoress of Stourbridge, Lady Catherine Grey wife of Sir Henry Foley Grey of Enville Hall, who became Stourbridge's first mayor in 1914.

Interestingly some streets have had their names changed. The section of Bridgnorth Road from Mamble Road to where Wollaston Garage stands in 2003 was at various times in the late 19th century recorded on the census returns not only as Bridgnorth Road, but also as Withy Bank and, confusingly, as High Street on the 1861 and 1881 census returns. Similarly until the Vestry Committee in 1890 fixed the name of Vicarage Road, it had at different times

Above: Firmstone Street was named after Henry Onions Firmstone (1815-1899). He was an important Black Country coal and iron master who lived in Wollaston Hall from 1859 until his death in 1899. On this nameplate, the 'Firm' and the 'Stone' are in different sized letters!

been known as Windmill Lane, Mill Lane and Wollaston Lane. Bright Street which links Cobden Street with Duncombe Street was originally Cross Street, whilst Ridge Street had been known as Marsden's Lane, literally the lane leading to Marsden's house. Similarly Wood Street was originally Moore Street, presumably because the Moore family occupied the first or largest house in the street.

However, the place name with the richest history is that of 'The Crescent', an investigation of its origins gives an interesting insight into the social history of the village in the first 20 years of the 20th century.

BRIDGENORTH ROAD. WOLLASTON.

Above: Hume Place was the name given to the houses, later shops that run from Wollaston Garage to the corner of Cobden Street. It was named after two campaigners for trade union reform, Joseph Hume and Francis Place, whose names are linked because of their close political cooperation. This little 'in-joke' probably caused those responsible for it to give a little wry smile every time they passed by. The building is seen here in the 1920s.

The Crescent

'The Crescent' is the name popularly given to the car park area at the junction of Meriden Avenue and Bridgnorth Road, but intriguingly the name does not appear on road maps or on the official borough street plan. It would appear that the name has never had any formal recognition. The Crescent is an undistinguished area of tarmac in 2003. Its boundary on the Meriden Avenue and Bridgnorth Road sides is defined by nine mature London plane trees. The line of these trees is roughly crescent shaped and this, perhaps, is why the area has for generations been referred to as The Crescent.

On 30 September 1912 the Highways and Improvements Committee of Stourbridge UDC submitted its recommendations to the full council for what was then known as 'The Wollaston Improvement Scheme.' Some years earlier in 1908, after prompting by Cllr Frank Taylor the full council had discussed the desirability of purchasing a piece of land at the junction of High Street and Bridgnorth Road and of keeping that land as an open space. The recommendations of the committee, which were subsequently adopted, were:

'*that the footpath all around the land be properly paved; that the front* (Bridgnorth Road side) *be properly kerbed; that the surface of the land be concreted, with a round bed in the middle for shrubs; that on the back of the land there should be erected a rockery for shrubs; and that at the rear should be provided a public sanitary convenience for men.*'

The cost, including the purchase of land, was estimated at about £450. However, at the insistence of Frank Taylor, the council agreed, at an additional cost of £50, to provide a convenience for women!

Despite approval for the scheme being given in 1912, the implementation of it did not get under way until the summer of 1913, when the tender of Mr A Simmonds for the layout of the land and the street improvements, and that of Messrs Hill & Smith for the supply and erection of iron railings and gates were accepted. Before work commenced Joseph Wooldridge of Duncombe Street, suggested in a letter to the *County Express* that a drinking fountain be erected on the site as a memorial to the late George Gilbanks, Wollaston's first vicar, who had died earlier in that year. It is not clear what action, if any, the council took on this suggestion, but perhaps they chose to regard it as purely a church matter. Gilbanks, however, was commemorated the following July when a memorial window was dedicated to him in St James's Church, whilst at a later date it appears that a fountain was installed on The Crescent, as one is shown on the 1919 OS map. In reality no fountain was erected, although plans drawn up before work commenced made provision for a fountain. If erected, it would probably have been an ornamental one such as that in Greenfield Gardens. The fountain idea got no further than the construction of a circular pool in the centre of The Crescent as is revealed in a postcard of that period and confirmed by a contemporary eyewitness. By 1919 this pool was considered to be a danger to both children and adults and so the council took the decision to fill it in.

The 'Improvement Scheme' was officially completed in December 1913, giving the village a potentially attractive meeting point, especially when some benches were subsequently added. That this open space was envisaged as a recreational area is clear from the annual report of the Borough Surveyor in March 1915 in which 'The Open Space at Wollaston' is dealt with under the same heading as 'The Promenade Gardens' (also known as Greenfield Gardens). Referring to The Crescent he reported:

'*the trees and shrubs have made good progress and after a few more years' growth will be quite attractive.*'

Furthermore, in June 1919, when the Council was considering the future of the pool, the area around it was referred to as a '*playing space.*'

In those years before the motorcar was king and when the village was still very small, The Crescent would have been a pleasant place to watch the world go by. Horse drawn vehicles would stop to enable the horse to drink from the trough situated approximately where the buses stop in 2003. Apart from the clip-clop of horses' hooves and the roar from the occasional passing motorcar the only traffic noise to disturb this quiet meeting place would be the rumble of trams, metal grating on metal, as they approached Wollaston Junction. In 2003 the place where the tramlines from Stourbridge via Enville Street met those of the Kinver Light Railway is covered by a nearby traffic island.

In its first summer as a public recreation space and meeting place, The Crescent was host, in July 1914, to a public meeting and, perhaps, if it had not been for the outbreak of war in the following month there might have been many more. The *County Express* of 25 July reported that there had been an open-air debate, in which representatives of the Liberal, Conservative and Labour parties had debated the perceived strengths and weaknesses of each party's ideology. The debate was attended by a large orderly crowd, which listened attentively until the meeting ended just after ten o'clock.

Below: The 'Wollaston Improvement Scheme' was officially completed in December 1913. It gave the village an attractive meeting point, especially when some benches were added later. This open space was envisaged as a recreational area. In the Borough Surveyor's annual report in March 1915 he dealt with it under the same heading as 'The Promenade Gardens', also known as Greenfield Gardens. Here 'The Crescent' is seen shortly after completion.

The Crescent, Wollaston

A different use was made of The Crescent on 22 September 1917 when, according to the *County Express* it was the venue for a military band concert. Whether there were other band concerts during the war years is not known, but the precedent for using The Crescent as a venue for band concerts had been established as a report in the *County Express* of 30 April 1921 clearly shows. The Baths and Parks Committee informed the Council that it had consented to Wollaston Band playing at The Crescent during the summer. The concerts were to be held on Sundays after the evening service at St James's Church.

Unfortunately for Wollaston the vast increase in the use of cars led to the loss of The Crescent as a recreational space in the centre of the village.

Wollaston's Public Hall

Few people in 2003 know of the existence of Wollaston's Public Hall, but from 1920 to 1930 it was the centre for social life in the village. The hall was situated in

Above: In July 1914 The Crescent was host to a public meeting at which representatives of the Liberal, Conservative and Labour parties debated the perceived strengths and weaknesses of each party's ideology. The debate was attended by a large orderly crowd, which listened attentively until the meeting ended just after ten o'clock.

Below: Its Baths and Parks Committee informed Stourbridge Borough Council in April 1921 that it had consented to Wollaston Band playing at The Crescent during the summer. The concerts were to be held on Sundays after the evening service at St James's Church. Seen here in the early 1930s, The Crescent's plane trees were maturing nicely. Immediately behind the group of men was the site of Wollaston's Public Hall.

Meriden Avenue, opposite The Crescent. 'Galen' the house built for Cecil Hawkeswood, whose family owned a number of chemist shops in the neighbourhood, occupies its site in 2003.

The decision to build a public hall was taken at a public meeting on 8 February 1913. The meeting was convened by the Wollaston Benevolent Committee and held in the village school. There had been earlier attempts in 1908 and 1909 to provide: '*a parish room in connection with the church*', but after a few money-raising activities, notably a fete in the grounds of Wollaston Hall, the scheme was abandoned. The Benevolent Committee, which convened the meeting in 1913, had evolved out of the Coronation Committee that had been established in 1911 to organise celebrations for the Coronation of George V. By 1913 the Benevolent Committee, which existed to raise and distribute money to the needy families of the village, was acknowledged as the only truly public body in the community. The previous year Mr C S Hall of Eggington Farm (occupied in 2003 by Hamilton Avenue) had written to the Benevolent Committee arguing that Wollaston needed a public hall and institute (Stourbridge, Oldswinford and Amblecote already had institutes — adult educational and recreational centres) and offered to make a substantial contribution towards building one. Mr Hall's argument struck a chord with the Committee who had found difficulty in obtaining a room for their meetings and, perhaps, stirred the memory of the older inhabitants of the village into recalling that there had been an institute 40 years earlier, probably housed in the village school, when Edward Hackwood was the headmaster. *Littlebury's Directory for Worcestershire* (1873) records that:

'*the Wollaston Institute is open every evening. It has a good library, and is well supplied with periodicals and daily papers. Its secretary is Mr Edward Hackwood.*'

The meeting on 8 February 1913 elected a Public Hall Committee charged with the responsibility for building a public hall and institute for Wollaston. Within a few months

Below: For many years there was a tobacconists and confectioners at the Bridgnorth Road end of The Crescent, whose railings can be seen on the right. In the 1930s this was run by the Martin family. The shop did a roaring trade from children going to and from school.

the committee had second thoughts and decided that it would be better to leave out the 'institute' part of the programme and concentrate all their efforts on the building of a public hall. The committee, chaired by Cllr Frank Taylor, Chairman of Stourbridge UDC, moved swiftly to organise money-raising activities, of which the highlight for 1913 was the procession and fete held on 19 July. Led by the Stourbridge Military Band, a procession of decorated vehicles, costumed pedestrians, Scout troops from Oldswinford, Brockmoor, Wordsley and Wollaston and a contingent of the Wordsley Boys' Brigade left Eggington Farm on Bridgnorth Road and then proceeded via Cobden Street, Brook Street, Greenfield Avenue, New Road, Stourbridge High Street, Enville Street and thence by Wollaston High Street to Wollaston Hall. The fete was to be held in the grounds of the Hall, at the invitation of its owner, Caleb Roberts. This event was so well supported that it was repeated with equal success in July 1914.

By August 1914 the Public Hall Committee had high hopes that building work would soon commence, as in addition to the money raised by the fetes and other activities, there had been a number of substantial donations headed by that of £100 from W H Foster of Apley Park, Bridgnorth. Moreover the site in Meriden Avenue had already been purchased, whilst at a meeting in May, held in Bright Street Chapel, the committee had unanimously chosen one plan from the four put before them – the future

Above: The idea for a Public Hall in Wollaston came from Charles Hall of Eggington Farm, who wrote to the Benevolent Committee in 1912 arguing that the village needed a public hall and institute (Stourbridge, Oldswinford and Amblecote already had these), and he offered to make a substantial contribution towards building one. Charles Hall went on to become Mayor of Stourbridge in 1920-21. *Stourbridge Library*

Public Hall would be built of brick, with either a stone or terracotta facing and would accommodate 300 people. Unfortunately the Great War began in August 1914 and so building plans were *'put on hold'* for the duration of the war.

Although the war ended in November 1918 the building scheme was not revived until 1920, when the *County Express* reported on 6 March:

'owing to the high price of building materials and labour, it has been decided to modify the original scheme, and as a temporary measure to purchase one of the sectional army buildings which are now for disposal.'

The hut that was purchased measured 82ft by 29ft and came from Sutton Coldfield. This purchase aroused much excitement in the village and there was renewed enthusiasm for the scheme now that it could be clearly seen that the dream of many years was about to become reality. Everyone rallied round to raise money. The local traders, at a meeting chaired by Charlie Smalley, the newsagent, agreed to raise money for the furnishing of the Hall. Some ladies joined the weekly sewing party to make goods for a sale of work. Whist drives and dances were held in the village school and in late July 1920 Mr and Mrs Harry Guest held a garden party in the grounds of The Croft in aid of the Hall fund. At the garden party the Vicar of St. James's, the Rev Hugh Wanstall, publicly reiterated that the Hall was for everyone; he said that he:

'was pleased that they were to have a public hall for Wollaston, that it was not to be a Church Hall, a Chapel Hall, or even a Labour Hall, but a Wollaston Public Hall for the people of Wollaston.'

Randle L Mathews officially opened the Hall on 2 September in the presence of a large and representative attendance of local residents, traders and councillors. Reporting the event the *County Express* described the Hall as having:

'wood flooring on a cement foundation. It will seat about 500 persons, is brilliantly lit by four incandescent gas lights of 600 candle power each, and there are six gas radiators for heating purposes. There are two retiring rooms and altogether the Hall is cosy and comfortable.'

Although the opening of the Hall was a milestone for all those villagers who had worked so hard to bring it about, their task was not yet finished. There was still a debt of £400 to be cleared, as the cost of purchase, transportation and erection had come to £1,000 and so far only £600 had been raised. Accordingly a two-day bazaar was held in December to raise the outstanding money, the net proceeds after deducting expenses were £420! For ten years the Public Hall met the social needs of the village, hosting dances, concerts, whist drives, wedding receptions, furniture sales, evening classes and public meetings. However, by 1930 the trustees were faced with liabilities of £235 and a possible repair bill of £150. The Hall had outlived its usefulness. Lettings and consequently income had fallen substantially since 1925. The Hall could not compete with the attractions of Stourbridge, especially the increasingly popular cinemas, which were only a penny bus ride away. Moreover, the building, which was essentially a wooden hut, was in need of urgent and expensive repairs. Reluctantly, at a public meeting in the Hall in February, the trustees were empowered to sell the building, its contents and the site. This was an ignominious end for what had been a much used, multi-purpose building, but as the *County Express* pointed out on the 22 February 1930: '*the very small attendance which responded to the summons to the meeting was itself indicative of no real desire for the Hall's continuance.*'

All that remained was to wind up the affairs of the Public Hall, accordingly a public meeting was held in

Above: There is no known photograph of the outside of the Public Hall in Wollaston. For ten years the venue met the social needs of the village, hosting dances, concerts, whist drives, wedding receptions, furniture sales, evening classes and public meetings. One such occasion was this children's play in the 1920s, which has preserved the only known view of the Hall's interior. *Nellie Perry*

Above: Randle L Mathews, seen here, officially opened Wollaston's Public Hall on 2 September 1920. The event was attended with due ceremony and was held in the presence of a large and representative attendance of local residents, traders and councillors. *Stourbridge Library*

Wollaston Schools on 16 October 1930 to discuss how to dispose of the assets. The Treasurer's report showed that after selling the Hall, its furniture, fittings, the site, and paying all outstanding bills, there was a balance of £59. After much discussion, during which it emerged that both the Guides and Scouts met in unsuitable and unsatisfactory premises, the meeting voted unanimously to give the money to the two associations to enable them to purchase a suitable meeting hut.

Exactly what happened to the Hall is not known, although there is evidence that at least a section of it was re-erected alongside the Robin Hood Inn at Drayton, near Belbroughton, in Worcestershire to serve that community in a similar way to that in which it had served Wollaston.

The movers and shakers of the interwar years

In the period in between the two world wars a group of local businessmen played a pivotal role in Wollaston village life. Their business premises were literally a stone's throw from each other and they all lived on the premises. This proximity and their common interest forged a strong bond and, moreover, the fact that they all lived and worked in the heart of the village meant that they were in tune with the concerns of the community.

They were influential in Wollaston's social life, especially in raising money for good causes and they also acted as an unofficial forum for raising matters concerning the village. With this background it is not surprising that three of this group were elected, at different times, to serve as councillors for Wollaston on Stourbridge Borough Council. Together they constituted 'the village elders.'

Joseph Pearson the headmaster of Wollaston Boys' School (1919-1946) who lived in the School House (opposite Wollaston Garage), was elected to the Council in 1924.

Sydney Parker owned a grocer's shop on Bridgnorth Road in the 1930s, opposite the Church. These premises are occupied by a veterinary practice in 2003. Around 1938 Sid Parker moved into a shop opposite Wollaston Garage. When he died in 1951 Harrison & Sons a Black Country grocery firm acquired the premises and continued to trade there until 1984. In 2003 this shop is Fletcher's Drinks Cabinet.

Eric Heynes founded Wollaston Garage in 1924. In 1938 he was elected to the Council and later he became Chairman of the Governors of Wollaston Schools.

Norman Rabey established in 1928 a ladies' and gentlemen's hairdressing business in premises on Bridgnorth Road next to The Waterloo Inn. He was still cutting hair in the same shop 50 years later!

Left: Following its closure and removal in 1930, exactly what happened to Wollaston's Public Hall is not known, although there is evidence that at least a section of it was re-erected alongside the Robin Hood Inn at Drayton, near Belbroughton, in Worcestershire for use as a tea rooms, seen here in a contemporary advert.

Left: This aerial view of the Robin Hood Inn at Drayton, near Belbroughton, shows the former Wollaston Public Hall to the left of the main pub. This was removed around 1995.

C. SMALLEY, *Newsagent and Tobacconist,*

THE CRESCENT, WOLLASTON.

Pure Sweets, Tobacco & Stationery,

SATISFACTION GUARANTEED.

Above: Charles Smalley was the village tobacconist and newsagent for over 30 years. On his retirement in 1939 his shop next to the chip shop on Bridgnorth Road was acquired by Arthur Cooper and later run by his son Peter. As a sideline Charlie Smalley also published postcards showing views of Wollaston landmarks a number of which appear in this book.

Charles Smalley was the village tobacconist and newsagent for over 30 years. On his retirement in 1939 his shop next to the chip shop on Bridgnorth Road was acquired by Arthur Cooper and later run by his son Peter. An interesting sideline to Charlie Smalley's main business activities was the publication of two sets of postcards. Each postcard had a photographic view of a Wollaston landmark, such as the tram terminus, St James's Church and The Gate Hangs Well.

Cecil Hawkeswood owned the chemist shop on the Bridgnorth Road which used to face the zebra crossing and the bus shelter Eventually from his Wollaston base he controlled a chain of chemist shops which, at its peak, included branches in Brettell Lane, Amblecote; Hagley Road, Oldswinford; The Broadway, Norton; and Market Street, Stourbridge.

William Harris owned the butcher's shop on Bridgnorth Road that still bears the family name in 2003. He was also the landlord of the adjoining public house, The Alexandra, known as The Princess in 2003. He was elected to the Council in 1925.

Self-help and community service

In the first half of the 20th century, before the creation of the Welfare State and social mobility became the norm, Wollaston was essentially a small close-knit community, which still retained the feel and characteristics of a village, even though it had been, since 1894, technically part of Stourbridge. The village ethos was seen at its best in the way in which the community looked after its own members, the rest of the community cared those for in need, whether young or old. There was a strong tradition of community service in not only raising money for good causes, but also in supplying the volunteers and expertise to make things happen.

At first sight the Coronation, Benevolent and the annual Old Folks Reunion Dinner committees appear to be very different organisations with totally different aims, but in reality they represent a continuum of community service over a number of generations.

By the time of George V's Coronation in 1911 the tradition of celebrating a royal occasion was well established in Wollaston. When Victoria celebrated her Diamond Jubilee in 1897 80 villagers aged 60 or over were provided with a celebration dinner. Similarly in 1902, on the occasion of Edward VII's Coronation, 113 of the over 60s were entertained to dinner in the village school, whilst a tea and games were provided for 630 children. The committee established to celebrate George V's Coronation was chaired by Charlie Smalley. He was to play a pivotal role in not only the work of the Benevolent Committee, but also in the organisation of the annual Old Folks Reunion Dinner.

When the Coronation Committee was being disbanded in July 1911 the *County Express* records that:

Below: William Harris owned the butcher's shop on Bridgnorth Road that still bears the family name in 2003. He was also the landlord of the adjoining public house, The Alexandra, known as The Princess in 2003. He was elected to the Council in 1925. He is seen here outside his shop with his delivery van.

'*the hope was expressed that the committee might continue under another name if necessary, for the purpose of carrying out any scheme for the relief of necessitous cases or for the benefit of the whole parish, and a resolution was passed to that effect. The secretary, Mr W Davis, was asked to convene a meeting shortly.*'

The first Annual General Meeting of The Wollaston Benevolent Committee was held on 16 September 1912 in The Foresters' Arms. The annual report showed that money had been given to needy families and, in particular, food had been provided for hungry children during the coal strike. The view was also expressed that: '*widows and orphans, aged men and women, looked upon the committee as a godsend.*'

At the close of the formal proceedings Councillor Mason was re-elected President and Charlie Smalley was re-elected Chairman of the Committee. The second AGM was held on 11 September 1913 in The Plough Hotel. The Secretary W Davis reported that all the money that had been given out had gone to Wollaston residents only. He said that their work:

'*was to help homes made sad by sickness and death, and by this means 20 destitute families had been relieved and 40 children's wants had been attended to. He thought he interpreted the feelings of Wollaston right, judging from the help they had received - that no destitute family should be allowed to want, or widow or orphan to starve.*'

In addition to their money-raising activities such as concerts, fetes and whist drives the Benevolent Committee also helped in the promotion of the projected Public Hall. The Benevolent Committee rescued the scheme to build a parish room, which had been first proposed in 1908, but had since failed to make any progress. In 1912 Mr C S Hall of Eggington Farm (later to be a Wollaston Councillor) wrote to the Benevolent Committee asking it to give support to the idea of a public hall. This request is a clear indication that the Benevolent Committee was regarded as the only body in Wollaston that effectively represented all sections of the community. In response to this request the Benevolent Committee convened a meeting on 8 February 1913 to discuss the feasibility of building a public hall and elect a Public Hall Committee.

Exactly when the Benevolent Committee ceased to exist is not known, although the reports on its activities in the *County Express* show that it was still active in the spring of 1915. A fundraising New Year's Eve Party and concert was held on 31 December 1914 at which Belgian refugees were guests of honour. A fortnight later the County Express of 16 January reported on a meeting of the committee held at The Gate Hangs Well in which the Chairman Charlie Smalley explained to members that:

'*... owing to the increase in the price of foodstuffs, coal, etc. a large number of cases were brought forward and grants were made to what were considered the most needy.*'

At the same meeting the Secretary, W Davis, reported

Above: The Wollaston Benevolent Committee grew out of a group established to celebrate George V's Coronation in 1911. Charlie Smalley, seen holding his bowler hat on the right in the second row, chaired it, and the president was Frank Mason, seen seated in the centre of the same row. Their fund raising activities were directed towards helping homes made sad by sickness and death. Although their activities ceased in 1915, many of the people involved formed an Old Folks' Reunion Dinner Committee, which ran until 1939.

that Christmas parcels had been distributed on Christmas Eve to the most needy cases in the village. Subsequently the *County Express* reported on two meetings in March and a whist drive in April; thereafter no further reports or references to the Benevolent Committee have been found. Possible clues to the fate of the organisation can be found in two of the meetings. On the occasion of the New Year's Eve party Councillor Mason, the President, said: '*considerably more work had fallen to the Benevolent Committee since the outbreak of war*', and a committee meeting had been convened in March to refute allegations of financial impropriety. Perhaps it was pressure of their day time work and possibly new commitments to fund-raising for war-related activities (the impact of the war on individual families and the community as a whole was considerable) that reduced the number of volunteers willing to work on behalf of the Benevolent Committee, or did the rumour of financial impropriety lead to a loss of credibility?

Fortunately for Wollaston, although 1915 appears to be the year in which the short-lived Benevolent Committee died, there arose 'phoenix-like' from the ashes of that organisation what came to be known as The Old Folks' Reunion Dinner Committee. This further instance of community care and self-help was to manifest itself on an almost unbroken annual basis until the outbreak of war in 1939. Not only did the Old Folks' Reunion Dinner continue the idea of community spirit, but also many of the people who had figured prominently in the work of the Benevolent Committee and its predecessor, the Coronation Committee, were to occupy similar roles in the organisation of what became an important annual event in the Wollaston year.

The credit for initiating the Dinner belongs to Caleb Roberts of Wollaston Hall. On 5 January 1915 he entertained the wives and mothers of Wollaston men on active service, as well as the over 60s of the village, to dinner in Wollaston Schools, at his own expense. Over 170 attended. The following year there were nearly 200 guests when Mr and Mrs Roberts hosted a similar dinner and concert on 4 January 1916. Councillor Mason, who acted as Secretary and general organiser for the event, said that Mr Roberts, when asked whether he would give the dinner this year replied: '*It is the annual dinner, and there you are.*'

In 1918 owing to the difficulty in obtaining food, the meal was dispensed with, but each of the 220 guests who attended a concert in the school hall received the sum 2s 6d in lieu of the meal. For the 4th year in succession Councillor Mason acted as Secretary and organiser.

After this very successful beginning the annual Old Folks' Reunion Dinner came to an abrupt halt when Caleb Roberts was killed in September 1918. No record or reference has been found of a dinner in either 1919 or 1920, no doubt because Caleb's death deprived the event of its sponsor. Fortunately for Wollaston Mrs Roberts, remembering the pride and interest that her husband had taken in what was essentially his creation, stepped in to continue his work and in 1921 entertained 105 guests in the new Public Hall. Similarly in 1922 and 1923 Mrs Roberts and her family provided a dinner and a concert for the over 60s in the Public Hall. Sadly she died in March 1924 and, not surprisingly, no reference has been found to a dinner in that year.

The death of Mrs Roberts might have ended the event, but for the determination of a group of public spirited villagers to keep alive the idea of an annual dinner. Under the chairmanship of the Vicar, the Rev Hugh Wanstall, the group met at the vicarage to discuss the feasibility of reviving the dinner and, more importantly, the means of raising the money to finance the event. Cllr Joseph Wright, who lived in Wood Street, attempted to solve the financial problem by suggesting that if each member of the group promised to collect £5 they would be able to meet the costs of a dinner. All agreed to do so. This decision to accept responsibility for organising and financing the annual dinner was a turning point in the history of the event.

The dinner that was held on 7 January 1925, attended by 120 Old Folks, was the first of an unbroken run of annual dinners, which lasted until the outbreak of war in September 1939. During this period the organisation of the dinner and the coordination of the collection of money from the growing number of those who regularly gave donations was formalised, with the tireless Charlie Smalley acting as Secretary, backed up by a large committee, which, at times, numbered over 40! After the closure of the Public Hall in 1930 the dinner reverted to the school hall, and from this point Councillor Pearson, the school's headmaster also played a strong supporting role in ensuring the continuing success of this event.

In the 1930s the event was so highly regarded that it was invariably honoured by a visit from the current mayor and mayoress and, as its popularity and standing increased,

so did the support from the business community with donations of meat, vegetables and cakes. By the late 1930s the well-known Stourbridge coach firm of Sammy Johnson's Supreme Coaches was providing transport to collect some of the Old Folks from the outlying parts of the village and then taking them home after the dinner and concert.

At the last dinner, held on 4 January 1939, tributes were paid to Charlie Smalley. It was widely agreed that it was almost entirely due to him that the dinner had taken place and that: '*it was practically a one man show.*' Responding to the tributes Charlie Smalley said that he had been doing the job for about 12 to 13 years and as he was nearing 65 thought that it was time for him to stand down and for someone else to take his place.

Whether someone did respond is not known, but by September 1939 the question of Charlie Smalley's successor was immaterial as the outbreak of war changed people's priorities. Moreover the introduction of food rationing, on a more comprehensive scale than during the Great War, meant that the organisation of a public dinner was no longer possible.

Above: The Old Folks' Reunion Dinner was instigated by Caleb Roberts of Wollaston Hall in 1915 and was supported by his widow until her death in 1924. At this point the event almost foundered, but for the efforts of Cllr Joseph Wright, who suggested that if each member of the group collected £5, they would be able to meet the costs of a dinner. This decision was a turning point in the history of the event. Joseph Wright went on to be Mayor of Stourbridge in 1933-34 and 1934-35. *Stourbridge Library*

Chapter Four

EDUCATING WOLLASTON

Before 1859, the education available for children in Wollaston was either at a number of schools some distance from the village or at Dame Schools. The latter were small classes set up in their own homes by women who could read and write but had not had any formal teacher training. In the 1851 census there were two dame schools recorded, both in King Street. Maria Price and Mary Foxhall both had '*Dame School Governess*' recorded as their occupations.

William Orme Foster, the owner of John Bradley & Co, saw the need for a better educated work force and endowed the schools and church. He also paid for the building of the vicarage and the headmaster's house. In 1858 work started on the building. On 28 February 1859 the schools opened and the buildings housed a mixed Infants' School and separate schools for boys and girls who were seven and older.

The infants started school from four years of age and the older children could leave at any time up to 14. When the

Boys' School opened 88 boys were admitted, their ages ranging from seven to 13. The school was clearly fulfilling a need, for by the end of July 1859, 141 boys had been enrolled.

Edward Hackwood, the first headmaster, had previously taught at St Mary's School, Bilston. Miss Elizabeth Evers was in charge of both the Infants' School and the older girls until the Girls' School opened later. The first headmistress of the Girls' School was Mary Cortis.

Although many of the pupils came from Wollaston, the reputation of the schools soon spread and by the 1870s the addresses recorded in the Admissions Registers included: Brierley Hill, Coalbournbrook, New Wood, Norton, Oldswinford, Prestwood, Stamber Mill, the Stewponey and Stourbridge town.

The early days at the schools were hard work as the only qualified teacher was the head. The assistants were unqualified and often pupil teachers were in charge of classes, helped by monitors. The pupil teachers were apprenticed for five years and were often only 13 when they started. An insight into their lives comes from the deed of apprenticeship for James Hands, who became a pupil teacher on 1 July 1864. His day began before school, and his pay was £8pa, with annual rises of £2. James Hands was expected to work for no more than six hours a day or more than 30 hours a week. Outside of school hours, or in the evenings, he was also expected to receive five hours' of training from one of the

WOLLASTON
NEW SCHOOLS,
WITHY BANK.

THE

BOYS' & INFANT'S SCHOOLS
Will be OPENED
ON MONDAY, FEBRUARY 28th, 1859,

When it is hoped the Inhabitants of the District will avail themselves of the opportunity thus afforded them of giving their children the advantages of a sound Education.

MR. HACKWOOD, of St. Mary's School, Bilston, is engaged as Master of the Boys' School, and

MISS ELIZABETH EVERS, late of the Red Lake Schools, near Wellington, Shropshire, as Mistress of the Infant School, and until the Girls' School be opened, she will also undertake the teaching of the elder Girls.

COURSE OF INSTRUCTION.

SECTION 1.—At Two-Pence per Week—Reading, Writing, and Arithmetic.
SECTION 2.—At Three-Pence per Week—Reading, Writing, Arithmetic, Grammar, and Geography.
SECTION 3.—At Four-Pence per Week—Mensuration, Mechanics, Book-keeping, Drawing, History, Mental Arithmetic, and Letter-Writing, together with the ordinary subjects included in Sections 1 and 2.

Hours of Attendance.—From 9 o'clock in the Morning till 12 o'clock, and from 2 o'clock in the Afternoon till 5 o'clock.

Children to be admitted should be brought by their Parents or Friends, who may obtain more particular information on applying to the Master, at the Schools, on or after February 28th, 1859.

R. BROOMHALL, PRINTER & BOOKSELLER, STOURBRIDGE.

Above: Wollaston New Schools opened on 28 February 1859. The buildings housed a mixed infants' school, and separate schools for boys and girls who were seven and older. The infants started from four years of age and the older children could leave at any time up to 14. By the end of July 1859, 141 boys had been enrolled. Mensuration is a branch of applied geometry that gives rules for finding the length of lines, the areas of surfaces, or the volumes of solids. *St James's School*

Above: This is the oldest known photograph of pupils at Wollaston Schools. It is dated to c1861. As it only shows girls it may have been taken on the occasion of the opening of the Girls' School. It is known that Elizabeth Evers was in charge of both the Infants' School and the older girls until the Girls' School opened, and that the first headmistress of the latter was Mary Cortis. Possibly it is both of these ladies who are seen here. *Stourbridge Library*

Memorandum of Agreement between William Orme Foster Esq. M.P. of Stourton Castle Rev. George Gilbanks M.A. of Wollaston, and Jacob Stokes Esq. of Kent, herein-after called the Managers in behalf of the Wollaston National School and George Hands herein after called the surety, the Father of James Hands herein after called the pupil teacher.

Above: Some of the teaching at Wollaston School was provided by pupil teachers, who were bound to their duties by a deed of apprenticeship. This is part of such a deed for James Hands, who became a pupil teacher there on 1 July 1864. He was expected to work for no more than six hours a day or more than 30 hours a week. Outside of school hours he was also expected to receive five hours' of training from one of the certificated teachers in subjects on which he was next to be examined. His pay was £8pa, with annual rises of £2. *St James's School*

certificated teachers in subjects on which he was next to be examined. Dismissal for '*idleness, disobedience, or immoral conduct of a gross kind*' would be without notice, but if either party wished to end the apprenticeship they had either to give six months' written notice, or to pay a sum between £3 and £6 depending upon the length of study completed. Some pupil teachers left for other occupations at the end of their apprenticeships but others went on to teacher training colleges.

Nonetheless, Edward Hackwood set and maintained a high standard, as exemplified by one of the school's first inspections, conducted by Rev H M Capel, and reported in the *Brierley Hill Advertiser* of 30 March 1861: '*The efficiency of this school is most creditable to Mr Hackwood. I was particularly pleased with the religious knowledge, arithmetic and geography.*'

The schools had very close links with the Church, and Edward Hackwood and George Gilbanks ran a savings club for the people of the village. Many of the boys in the church choir regularly took part in choir outings. The schools frequently closed for one or two days when the buildings were

Report of H. M. Inspector . (Mr Hernaman)

"The general efficiency of the School is remarkably good. The writing & Arithmetic are excellent. The fact of not a child's failing in any subject bears the highest testimony to Mr Hackwood's power & success."

Above: To date no photograph has come to light showing Edward Hackwood, but his handwriting is preserved in the schools' logbooks. This is his record of an inspection in 1864, which showed '*not a child's failing in any subject*', great testimony to Hackwood's abilities. *St James's School*

needed for a church bazaar or tea, and for special occasions connected with the church or with the Foster family. For example, the *Brierley Hill Advertiser* of 14 January 1865 reported that on Monday 9 January a '*grand concert*' had been held in the schoolroom:

'*for the purpose of raising funds to purchase a clock for the parish.*' The report continued: '*the schoolroom was profusely decorated for the occasion. The attendance was large and many of the principal families in the neighbourhood were present. Misses Foster, Annesley, Addenbrooke, Dixon and Mrs Freer were the vocalists. ...They were accompanied on a grand piano lent for the occasion by Mrs Foster of Stourton Castle.*'

The grand piano would have been conveyed to the school from Stourton Castle by wagon and horses, via Ridge Top. Edward Hackwood also recorded in the school logbook that there was no school on Monday 9 January to enable preparations to be made for the concert to be held later in the day in aid of funds for the church clock. The logbook also reveals that a further day's holiday was given on 26 July 1865 to celebrate the inauguration of the church clock and bells.

Another example was on 13 March 1874, when there was a holiday to celebrate the marriage of Mr W H Foster. The Foster family always retained their interest in the progress of the schools and pupils. Mrs Foster and her children paid regular visits and presented annual prizes for good work and attendance. Collections were made for presentations to members of the Foster family on the occasion of 21st birthdays and weddings.

The school logbooks

The old school logbooks give a unique picture of life in Wollaston during the second half of the 19th Century. The summer holiday was timed so that the boys could help with the harvest or go hop picking, and when the schools reopened in September there were often children still absent. Celebrations of May Day included the girls choosing a May Queen and the boys parading around the village with glass trumpets. Sports were also a feature of school life from its earliest days. Advantage could be taken of the many surrounding fields, such as in August 1892, when Henry Nickless, whose family ran a coal delivery and cart hire

23 Coal & Iron Masters' Prize scheme list arrived and as usual we are at the top of the tree in this district Our Boys take 7 Prizes out of 19 Corngreaves the next to ours takes 3

Above: Edward Hackwood's meticulous records in the school logbooks also reveal how successful Wollaston Schools were in relation to others in the district. This is his account of the annual Coal Masters' Prizes in 1868. Corngreaves was a not dissimilar area to Wollaston, partly rural with a large ironworks nearby. *St James's School*

Apr. 13

M.ᵣ Foster's Annual Prizes 1891

| Scripture | Arithmetic | Writing & Dict.ⁿ |
| | | |

Standard
I A. Timmins
   Geo. Parker   Jas Smith   C. V. Morton
II Wilf. Walker   Hor. Guest   Herb. Hankle
III Arth. Hitchin   Geo. Rabone   Arch. Chappele
            W. Eddkin
IV John. Willis   Har. Parker   Fred. Bowen
V Percy Marson   Frk. Dalloway   Har. Harrison
VI Howard Brooks   W.ᵐ Edwards   Harry Brooks

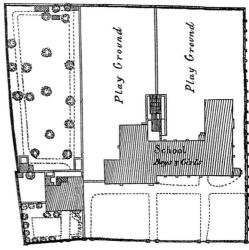

Above: Prizes donated by local businessmen rewarded School achievement. In Wollaston none were more important that those given by W O Foster. Here is Edward Hackwood's record from the school logbooks of these prizes as awarded on 13 April 1891. *St James's School*

Above: Wollaston's growth in the late 19th century put pressure on school accommodation, as did a new requirement in 1897 to admit children aged three years and over rather than five and over. Schools with overcrowded infants' departments had to provide additional accommodation for 60 to 70 pupils. At Wollaston the cost of this amounted to £300. This plan of the schools dates from the late 19th century.

Dec. 1 I flogged my own son (P.T.) for making

Above: Charles Hackwood, Edward's son, was one of the pupil teachers at Wollaston Schools. Edward's fairness in his treatment of everyone even extended as far as flogging his own son on 1 December 1868 for making one of his boys cry! *St James's School*

business directly opposite the school, gave them the use of his field in High Park Avenue for a sports day.

While Edward Hackwood was to remain at the Boys' School for 40 years, the Girls' School saw seven head-mistresses in the same period. Mary Cortis left in August 1864, being temporarily replaced by Elizabeth Evers. Elisabeth M Lucas, who was to hold the post for 36 years, retired in 1891. She came to Wollaston after a distinguished career at Whitelands College, Chelsea. There were three short-term appointments until Ada Aughtie was appointed in 1895. She remained headmistress for 33 years.

The need for larger schools

The growth of Wollaston in the late 19th century put pressure on the accommodation, as did new requirements from the Education Department. This meant that schools with overcrowded infants' departments must provide additional accommodation for 60 to 70 pupils. This applied at Wollaston, and a public meeting was called to discuss the matter on 11 January 1897. George Gilbanks chaired the meeting, which was only thinly attended, with just nine others present. He explained that at Wollaston the cost would amount to £300. The problem had been exacerbated by a recent change that required them to admit children aged three years and over rather than five and over. He said:

'This was a nice convenient thing for the mothers; it was a kind of nursery when they wanted to get the children out of their way. As the school was a voluntary one, it could not benefit from a compulsory rate.'

Even in the 19th Century education was subject to the pressure of party politics. The Liberals, who had many non-conformist supporters, disliked church schools. Non-conformists objected to paying rates to finance schools in which there was denominational teaching:

'The Wollaston Liberal Association,' said Rev Gilbanks, *'had passed a resolution hoping that no Liberal would be called upon to subscribe, or would subscribe even if called upon.'*

He went on to say that it was contemptible meanness that people should act against the best interests of the Parish. Not all the non-conformists agreed and there were many more who had benefited from their education and who might have subscribed a little for the benefit of others.

There were two courses of action; either for the school to join the local School Board, which would cost local people four to five times as much, or to levy a voluntary rate of one shilling, which would raise £340. After a discussion in which it was pointed out that the opening of the Jones & Attwood foundry in February could lead to an expansion of the village, George Gilbanks stated that Wollaston was not a place of stagnation and further building would take place. The poor attendance, however, meant that the meeting was adjourned. It resumed on 26 January, with 17 attending. Informally canvassed opinion was that a voluntary rate was not popular, and only a few would pay. A committee of 24 was formed (pretty good at a meeting with only 17 present!), which was to meet on 22 February to report progress. Another public meeting was held on 1 March, with 15 present, and after much discussion, means for visiting all the ratepayers were considered, and canvassers were appointed for the work. Thus the money was raised and the schools enlarged.

The retirement of Edward Hackwood

On 28 February 1899, the 40th Anniversary of the school, Edward Hackwood announced his intention to retire in June. Such was the esteem in which he was held in Wollaston that it was decided to make some recognition of his long and faithful service. A circular was issued among old boys, and a testimonial fund set up, to which there was a great response. On 20 October he was presented with a

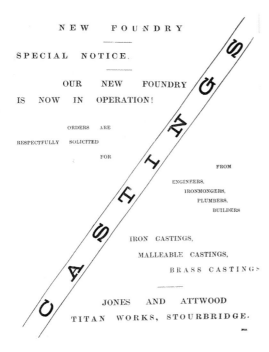

NEW FOUNDRY

SPECIAL NOTICE.

OUR NEW FOUNDRY
IS NOW IN OPERATION!

ORDERS ARE
RESPECTFULLY SOLICITED
FOR

FROM
ENGINEERS,
IRONMONGERS,
PLUMBERS,
BUILDERS

IRON CASTINGS,
MALLEABLE CASTINGS,
BRASS CASTINGS

JONES AND ATTWOOD
TITAN WORKS, STOURBRIDGE.

Above: Also of concern to the managers of Wollaston Schools in 1897 was the imminent opening of the Jones & Attwood foundry in Amblecote that February. This was seen as possibly leading to an expansion of the village. George Gilbanks acknowledged this at a public meeting held on 11 January, also saying that Wollaston was not a place of stagnation and that further building would take place. *Stourbridge Library*

cheque for £60. In his speech at the presentation George Gilbanks praised Edward Hackwood's achievements, particularly the successes of the boys in winning many of the prizes awarded by the iron and coal masters. Many appreciative messages were received from past pupils and the new head teacher, Arthur T Spiers, a former pupil and pupil teacher, bore testimony to the early training received at Wollaston.

In his response Edward Hackwood remarked on the preference often given by businessmen to Wollaston boys. Coming from Bilston, what had astonished Mrs Hackwood most was the personal cleanliness of the children. He recalled how disappointed George Gilbanks was when Wollaston boys gained only 11 out of 24 prizes, that their schools did not take more, and so claim half. There was also reference to the Government Inspectors and their visits to the schools, and, speaking of a pupil teacher who had come out top of the Queen's Scholarship list, he asked if they had ever heard of another case in the district. He concluded by thanking those who had contributed to his handsome present and said that the great lessons he had tried to teach were '*Humility, Truth and Honesty.*'

On 15 February 1900, at the height of the Boer War in South Africa, the beleaguered British Force in Kimberley was relieved and the following day the new playing field behind Wollaston schools was opened by George Gilbanks and named 'The Kimberley Recreation Ground.'

New buildings at Wollaston schools

As the school numbers grew the Board of Education demanded an increase in the Girls' Department. Plans for erecting a room at the cost of £160 were submitted to them, and approved. Yet another public meeting was held on 18 February 1901 to consider how the money could be raised. The cold weather may have resulted in only nine people attending, leading George Gilbanks to say that the people of Wollaston did not seem to appreciate education much and a response to the Managers' appeal should be made by the people of Wollaston who had made full use of the education without any cost to the public. Arthur Spiers stated that space was available for 263 infants, 197 boys and 156 girls and, as the Census Returns showed that girls outnumbered boys, the need for more accommodation was in the Girls' Department. The meeting was adjourned and resumed on 27 February, when, perhaps because of better weather, 70 attended. In the discussion, when asked if a guarantee could be given that the need for expansion would not occur again, George Gilbanks replied that this was impossible unless a guarantee could be given that Wollaston population would not increase. Another query was made about the number of children who attended the schools from outside the district but Arthur Spiers explained that no child could be refused admission on other than reasonable grounds, but if the schools were crowded, preference would be given to the children of Wollaston. Ultimately it was resolved unanimously that the additional accommodation be added to the present schools, and that the inhabitants and property owners should be asked to subscribe towards the amount necessary, some £200. Arthur Spiers was asked to act as secretary and treasurer. Subscriptions of between £30 and £40 were promised

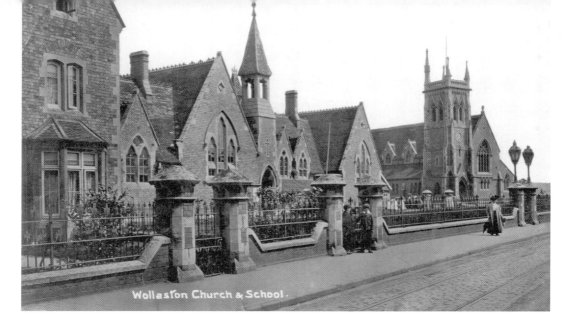

Wollaston Church & School.

Above: Edward Hackwood retired in June 1899, having served Wollaston Schools for their first 40 years. Arthur T Spiers, a former pupil and pupil teacher at the school, succeeded him. At an event to celebrate Hackwood's retirement, Spiers bore testimony to the early training he had received at Wollaston. This commercial postcard shows the schools in the early 20th century, at the time that Spiers took over as head of the Boys' School.

Above: A view inside the Boys' School at Wollaston Schools in the early 1900s, during Arthur T Spiers' brief career there as Head. The boy on the extreme right is holding up a slate with the class number on. Behind the back row of boys is a folding wooden partition, which allowed a larger room to be created if the need arose.

Above: Private education was also available in Wollaston. One provider were the Misses Southall, who ran a preparatory school for boys and girls from their home in Wood Street. Here, six attentive pupils, and a distracted boy, pose at the rear of the Southall's house-cum-school.

including several from 'the working classes.' George Gilbanks, responding to a vote of thanks, said:

'*Although the working men present might think I am flattering them, I can say that wherever I go, I never saw a finer set of children, or a better behaved set, than those in Wollaston.*'

The Education Act, 1903

On 1 April, the schools came under Worcestershire County Council as non-provided schools, under the Education Act, 1903. At the end of the school year in April the head wrote in the logbook that the Age & Attendance Clause of the byelaws had affected attendance. This clause allowed boys, on reaching their 13th birthday, to claim a certificate of exemption, which meant that they could leave school. Nearly every boy had immediately done this.

At the same time some parents had the choice of having their children educated privately in Wollaston. The *County Express* of 12 September 1903 carried the following advertisement:

'PREPARATORY SCHOOL FOR BOYS AND GIRLS, WOOD STREET, WOLLASTON. MISSES SOUTHALL wish to remind their pupils that School Duties will be RESUMED SEPTEMBER 15th'

How many people took up this option is unknown, but the village school remained popular as the same edition of the newspaper also carried a note regarding the '*Enlargement of Wollaston School*' which reported that an increase in numbers in the Boys' Department had led to work in progress to enlarge one of the wings of the premises.

An outbreak of scarlet fever closed the schools for some weeks in 1902 and in 1903 the same followed an outbreak of chicken pox. Throughout the early years of the 20th century there were many outbreaks of measles, flu and mumps and the schools were closed either to disinfect the buildings or until the epidemics had ended. In 1904 the schools were again closed for six weeks due to yet another outbreak, this time of measles.

For many years there were glowing reports of the standards in the schools from the regular inspections and there were no hints of any problems, either with the pupils or the staff. The schools marked the death of Mrs Gilbanks on 14 December 1903 when staff and pupils attended the funeral. On 8 February 1905 the schools were closed for the day in honour of the 21st birthday of W A Foster, grandson of the founder. Two months later, on 18 April 1905, the Foster family visited the schools on what the *County Express* of 22 April styled a 'red-letter day':

'*Tuesday was a red-letter day to those attending the Wollaston National Schools. In the afternoon Mrs W H Foster attended to distribute prizes for the year, accompanied by Mr W H Foster and their son Mr W A Foster. Mr Spiers presented an illuminated address to Mr W A Foster who had just come of age. It was signed by Arthur T Spiers; Edward Hackwood; Ada Aughtie and E J Lucas.*'

Mr Foster subsequently wrote to George Gilbanks enclosing £1 to be given to a boy he had noticed wearing four medals for unbroken attendance. On checking it was found that there were three other boys who each had a record of five years' unbroken attendance. George Gilbanks wrote to tell Mr Foster this. In reply he sent a sovereign for each boy, which George Gilbanks presented when he visited the school on 17 May.

There was continued success on the academic front too, and the *County Express* of 5 January 1907 carried an account of the Annual Prize Giving, which included prizes for attendance and achievement. At this Arthur Spiers quoted from the report of H M Inspector, which said: '*The school is conducted with energy and considerable success.*' He also quoted the words of the Diocesan Inspector, who, at the close of a lengthy and eulogistic report, said: '*It was not easy to put any question that puzzled the children. Teaching evidently thorough and skilful.*' Many individual pupils who were high achievers, were named, and past pupils who had won prizes elsewhere were mentioned.

The disappearance of A T Spiers

Yet, despite these glowing reports, in August 1907 the Vicar, as Chairman of the School Managers, wrote in the logbook:

'*A T Spiers formally dismissed by the managers (with the approval of the County Council) at their meeting held on 27th August. Signed G Gilbanks, Chairman.*'

Above: Arthur T Spiers both maintained and built upon the achievements of Edward Hackwood. He can be seen back row left in this photograph of boys class No 1 taken in 1906. Standing at the back on the right is Charles Rowberry, whose career at Wollaston would be in marked contrast to that of his Head.

Above: Pupils at Wollaston Schools were rewarded with prizes for both achievement and attendance. One of the latter was awarded to Joseph Westwood for the academic year 1906-7. The certificate must have been presented during the following academic year as it is signed by George Whitmore, Arthur Spiers' rapidly appointed successor.

There is no further reference to Arthur Spiers, but his daughter continued to attend the Girls' School until April 1908 when she left the district. The family emigrated to Canada and made a successful life there, although Arthur Spiers did not work as a teacher but instead was employed by the Canadian National Railway. The family kept in touch with their English relations, and on a visit during World War II, his grandson was encouraged to visit Wollaston to see the house where the family had lived.

Above: Despite glowing academic reports, in August 1907 George Gilbanks, Chairman of the School Managers, summarily dismissed Arthur T Spiers, seen here. No reason was stated at the time, but it subsequently emerged that he had 'borrowed' £75 from the Schools' Penny Bank on an 'informally agreed flexible term' basis!

The Managers had an important vacancy to fill, quickly, and the Situations Vacant of the *County Express* of 10 August contained a notice requesting applications for this unexpected vacancy, which had to be filled by 2nd September. Reproduced opposite, the notice stated that applicants had to respond by 24th August, enclosing copies of three testimonials, to George Gilbanks, chairman of the School Managers. Ironically, the adjoining adverts were for foundry workers and farm managers in Canada, where Arthur Spiers went! On 27 August, at the same meeting that recorded Mr Spiers' dismissal, the School Managers met to scrutinise the applications, 111 had been received; nine men were short-listed for interview. The successful applicant was George E Whitmore, who had trained at Saltley College and spent nine years as headmaster of Offenham School near Evesham.

A month later some light was shed upon the sudden dismissal of George Whitmore's predecessor. A meeting was held in Wollaston Schools on 21 October concerning the Wollaston School Penny Bank. The room was filled, chiefly with mothers of the children, and, as the *County Express* reported on 26 October:

HEAD MASTER (experienced) **Wanted** for September 2nd for Boys' National School, Wollaston, Stourbridge; average 196; salary as fixed by the Worcestershire Education Committee.—Applications, with copies of three testimonials, to be sent before August 24th to Rev. Geo. Gilbanks, Wollaston Vicarage. 7913

CANADA! CANADA!! CANADA!!!—Wanted, 25 to 30 good Labouring Men by the Canadian Iron and Foundry Co., Ltd., for their works at St. Thomas's, Ontario, Hamilton, Ontario, and Montreal. A splendid opportunity for intelligent Men to learn the Moulding. Wages from 6s. 3d. per day.—Apply Canadian Iron and Foundry Co., Ltd., Three Rivers, Quebec.[7901

Above: Following Spiers' dismissal the School Managers had an unexpected vacancy to fill – by 2 September 1907! This advert was hurriedly placed in the *County Express.* The irony of its juxtaposition with the one below, calling for emigrants to Canada, would not have been lost on some in the village – that was where Spiers had fled!

'*It was explained that subsequent to the disappearance of the late headmaster, Mr A T Spiers, who carried out the secretarial duties of the bank, a considerable sum of money subscribed by the children had been discovered to be missing. The Vicar and Mr Lowndes both expressed their regret, but intimated that they were unable to do anything in the matter. The meeting lasted a considerable time and was of an animated character.*'

By 2 November the School Managers claimed that they were unaware of the bank's existence, but they would try to raise the money, £75, to pay the depositors, and the following week it was reported that all the depositors would be repaid.

More improvements to the schools

In 1909 there was an architect's report regarding the building, the school organisation and the changes that were recommended. The classrooms were nearly all overcrowded and the condition of the cloakrooms, playground surface and offices (toilets) were all criticised. Improvements to the windows, the lighting and the size and surface of the playgrounds were proposed and it was suggested that one of the smaller classrooms in the Girls' School should be converted to a staff room. This however would mean that younger infants under the age of five would have to be excluded.

The Misses Lucas

The end of 1909 saw the end of a long association with the schools by the Misses Lucas. Elisabeth M Lucas, who had retired as headmistress of the Girls' School in 1891, died in mid-October at her home in Duncombe Street. The *County Express* of 23 October recorded the high respect and esteem in which her large circle of friends had held her. She had always taken part in church affairs and for a time had been the superintendent of the Girls' Sunday School. Her funeral was held on 23 October. One month later on 30

November 1909, her sister, Ellen J Lucas, the headmistress of the Infants' School, retired. Her friends and former pupils presented her with a purse containing £30 and an illuminated address, expressing the appreciation of the managers, teachers, scholars, parents and friends for her 42 years' service to the people of Wollaston. It was hoped that her retirement would be blessed with health and happiness.

Coronation celebrations

Celebrations were held to mark the Coronation of George V on 25 June 1911. The pupils were entertained to tea on the lawns at the front of the schools.

More money needed

The following year continuing pressure on the school accommodation needed to be addressed further. An appeal letter was sent out to raise the £250 balance outstanding for the £747 needed to alter the schools in line with the requirements of the Board of Education. The buildings and playgrounds needed many improvements. In addition a complete new heating apparatus for the three schools was needed. To this sum, W H Foster had pledged £300 in August 1912 and in other ways £200 had been raised, including £25 from Caleb W Roberts of Wollaston Hall. To raise the balance, letters were sent to employers, old boys, parents and rate pay-

Above: A total of 111 applications were received to replace Arthur T Spiers, of whom nine were short-listed for interview. The successful applicant was George E Whitmore, who had trained at Saltley College and spent nine years as headmaster of Offenham School near Evesham. He may well be included in this photograph of the celebrations held to mark the Coronation of George V on 25 June 1911. There appears to be a throne on the extreme left.

ers, signed by the School Managers: G Gilbanks; W Clark; F Fellows; R Lowndes; C W Roberts; W R Selleck. The schools were closed towards the end of 1912 so that alterations could be made.

Wollaston Schools suffered a terrible double blow in 1913 with the deaths, two weeks apart, of George Gilbanks, aged 87, on 4 January and Edward Hackwood, aged 81, on 18 January. Between them they had devoted 93 years to the service of the schools!

The Great War

During the Great War there were many problems in the staffing of the schools, particularly in the Boys' Department. Two of the staff, William Vaughan and Charles Rowberry, enlisted and there were difficulties in replacing them. A student teacher, Leslie Stanier, who had only commenced teaching in September 1916, was called up and left in March 1917. Women teachers were appointed to take their places and Mrs Whitmore taught in the Boys' School for many of the war years. Many of the replacements were unqualified but the schools could not have carried on without their help. There were other problems too, such as when the schools were closed in May 1915 due to scarlet fever. During the war there were frequent visits from past pupils who were in the services and an honours list was kept up to date. In 1921 a War Memorial Board was received from the County Council and on 13 April the memorial was unveiled and dedicated by the Vicar. Unfortunately it is not known what happened to the board.

Joseph Pearson appointed Headmaster

At the end of September 1919 George Whitmore moved to take up a post at Redditch. His successor was Joseph Francis Pearson, a former footballer with Aston Villa FC, and a member of their FA Cup winning team in 1905. He would go on to play a leading role in the development of Wollaston as a councillor and later as an alderman. Unsurprisingly, following his appointment, Joe Pearson encouraged the boys to play football and take up gardening.

After 43 years at the school, another long-serving teacher, the assistant master William T Vaughan, resigned on 31 October 1926.

Provision for more pupils

The perennial accommodation problems returned in the 1920s, and in mid May 1926 the County Education Authority

Above: At the end of September 1919 George Whitmore moved to take up a post at Redditch. His successor was Joseph Francis Pearson, a former footballer with Aston Villa FC, seen here in a team photograph from the early 1900s. *Aston Villa FC*

Above: The *County Express* of 26 June 1926 recorded that Wollaston Schools provided accommodation for 534 pupils and had a regular attendance of 437. By October 1927 this had risen to 471, and there was concern that if rumours of the imminent closure of St John's School in Stourbridge proved true, the number of pupils would reach the maximum of 534. This was the frontage of the Schools in the mid-1920s. The elaborate traction pole was for the Enville Street tramway, and it looks as though a horse has been by recently!

Below: Wollaston Schools' perennial accommodation problems returned in the 1920s. In mid-May 1926 the County Education Authority informed them that they were prepared to improve the lighting, ventilation and room for each class, the work to be carried out at the end of the year. Here is a look at 34 pupils, plus a teacher, in the Infants' School at around this time.

Above: Joe Pearson was a member of Aston Villa's FA Cup winning side in 1905, seen here with his teammates. He would go on to play a leading role in the development of Wollaston as a councillor and later as an alderman. Unsurprisingly, following his appointment, Joe Pearson encouraged the boys to play football, and also to take up gardening. *Aston Villa FC*

informed the schools that they were prepared to improve the lighting, ventilation and room for each class, the work being carried out at the end of the year. The *County Express* of 26 June recorded that the schools provided accommodation for 534 pupils and had a regular attendance of 437. By October this number had risen to 471 and there was concern that if St John's School in Stourbridge closed, as was rumoured, the number of pupils would reach the maximum of 534. By May 1927 the managers agreed that the only alternative was to mix the Boys' and Girls' Departments. This arrangement would give seven classrooms for seven classes. There was concern however, about Ada Aughtie's position, but assurance was given that she would remain as head of the Girls' School, and this was confirmed by an inspection in November 1927.

The decision to mix the classes caused some disquiet in the village, to which the vicar, Rev Hugh Wanstall, responded in the April 1928 *Parish Magazine*:

'The Managers have had a hard time lately. The only way we could save our Schools was by 'mixing' the departments. We have also been blamed because we were unable to support the idea of transferring our senior children to a condemned building in Stourbridge. ... Any attempt by the Stourbridge Parishes to provide Church Schools for their children will be supported by Wollaston, but we must think of our own Schools first. ... We have only to pull together to retain Wollaston Schools for the children of Wollaston.'

On 13-14 April 1929 a two-day bazaar was held to raise funds towards the £500 that was needed for alterations required by the Board of Education and for repairs to the

Above: In May 1927 the Managers of Wollaston Schools agreed that the only practicable solution to its accommodation shortfall was to mix the Boys' and Girls' Departments. This would give seven classrooms for seven classes. As a result, photographs such as this, showing Boys' class No 2 with Joe Pearson, would soon become a thing of the past. The variety of dress is remarkable.

Above: Celebrations held on 6 May 1935 at Wollaston School in honour of the Silver Jubilee of George V, and the event was recorded in a series of photographs. Here the pupils, staff and managers listen to speeches.

Below: The pupils at Wollaston School also enjoyed tea on the lawns as part of their celebrations of the Silver Jubilee of George V. *St James's School*

church. Mrs A A Marsh opened the bazaar and the *County Express* of 10 August reported a profit of £294 4s 2d, of which £100 was transferred to the managers' account.

During the early 1930s there were many discussions between the School Managers and the County Education Authority (CEA) about the future of the Infants' School. The County wanted to build a new school, and although the managers agreed in principle, they could not agree about a site. The managers proposed a site next to the church but the CEA proposed to use land that had been bought in Vicarage Road. The matter was deferred and finally shelved until after the war.

Silver Jubilee Celebrations

On 6 May 1935 there were celebrations held in honour of the Silver Jubilee of George V and the pupils were photographed on the lawns in the front of the school.

Other royal events were often recognised and a half or whole day's holiday was given for royal weddings. Photographs were taken of all the classes to celebrate the Coronation of George VI in 1937, and many of these have been traced.

Despite the overcrowded conditions, Wollaston children remained healthy, and a report by the Schools' Medical Service in May 1936 noted that:

'*Rheumatism appears rare in children attending Wollaston Schools. The majority of children live in houses that are situated at a moderately high altitude and with a sandy subsoil.*'

At least their houses were not damp!

Proposals for a new school

In June 1936 discussions on the enlargement of Wollaston School reached Worcestershire Education Committee. The school needed enlarging, but it was not possible to alter the existing building. One suggestion was to demolish it and rebuild on the playing field, but it was point-

Above: In this view of the celebrations of the Silver Jubilee of George V, the schoolteachers and managers flank the wall and railings. Behind the photographer has captured the end of (Upper) King Street. *St James's School*

Above: More details of the end of King Street can be seen in this view of Wollaston Schools' celebrations of George V's Silver Jubilee. *St James's School*

Below: This final view of Wollaston School's George V Silver Jubilee celebrations is looking towards Wollaston Junction. The house immediately above the school gateposts is Wollaston House, and in 2003 the area around this, where the trees are, is the forecourt to Wollaston Garage. *St James's School*

Above: In September 1938 Wollaston gained another private school with the opening of Miss, or 'Granny', Gaskins' School in Ridge Street. Grace Gaskins was an art teacher and she had retired from her post at King Edward VI Grammar School in 1938 after 22 years' service.

ed out that Mr Foster owned the land. A good site was said to be near the Vicarage, but as land in Wollaston was fast disappearing moves should be made to purchase land on Wollaston Farm before contractors started laying out roads. Stourbridge Council discussed the matter in October 1936 and it was suggested that a site be purchased while land was available there and negotiations were proceeding for ten-acres. It was priced at £6,000 and the price asked was £650 per acre, but the vendors imposed certain restrictions, which the sub-committee could not accept.

The debate continued into 1937 and the vicar, Rev Reg Bamber, commented in the August issue of the *Parish Magazine*: '*All children over the age of 11 are to be provided with separate secondary schools where possible.*'

The managers proposed that either the children over 11 should go to Brook Street School, or the present school should be remodelled, or a new infants' school should be built.

Wollaston gained another private school in September 1938 with the opening in Ridge Street of Miss, or 'Granny', Gaskins' School. Grace Gaskins had had a long career as a teacher of art at a number of schools and had retired from her post at King Edward VI Grammar School in 1938 after 22 years' service.

A partial solution to the schools' accommodation was found later in 1939. On 4 September children over 11 years old began to attend Brook Street School, and Wollaston became a junior and infants' school only.

Wollaston Junior School & World War II

One month later the country was at war again. This inevitably brought disruption as the schools were unable to open in September 1939 until air raid shelters had been built. Opening times were altered so that the children could get home in daylight during the winter months. Fuel was in short supply and air raids at night often meant that the children arrived late. Daytime raids also interrupted lessons, the first in August 1940. A number of evacuees arrived, mainly from Birmingham, Coventry and the London area. Altogether 41 boys came to Wollaston but only 15 girls. Some of the evacuees stayed only a short time, living with local families, but others remained in the village for much longer. Eleven children stayed for more than one year and two for longer than two years, the first having arrived in September 1940 and the last in August 1944.

School staffs were also drawn into the war. Mr A G Bayliss left the Boys' School to join the RAF in 1940 and Mrs Rowberry spent many of the war years as a temporary teacher in the Junior School. David Mallen, who was due to retire in 1942, stayed on until the end of the war. There are records of considerable sums of money being raised to help the war effort. Not all amounts were recorded but in 1944 the Junior School raised £1,025 for the 'Salute the Soldier' savings campaign.

Joseph Pearson, Mayor of Stourbridge

On a happier note, on 10 November 1941, Joe Pearson was made Mayor of the Borough of Stourbridge, a position that he held for two years. With the retirement of Gertrude Porter as headmistress of the Girls' School on 3 September 1943, the two junior departments were merged and Joe Pearson became head teacher of the Junior School. At that time, however, the two departments were still taught separately, and it was not until Joe Pearson retired that the boys and girls were taught in classes together.

Alderman Pearson resigned as head of the school in April 1946 through ill health. A presentation was made to him on 20 April, at which he made a lengthy and brilliant speech on his 27 years in Wollaston. The *County Express* reported the occasion at great length, over half a page, the rest of which was taken up by Alderman Pearson's obituary, as, sadly, he died on 26 April. The school's assistant master, David Mallen retired on 23 July 1946 after 43 years' service.

Joe Pearson's successor was Terence J J Kilby. He had recently been demobilised from the Royal Artillery with the rank of Major, having enlisted in October 1940.

Above: Joe Pearson resigned as head of the school in April 1946 through ill health. A presentation was made to him on 20 April, at which he made a lengthy and brilliant speech on his 27 years in Wollaston. Sadly, he died six days later. His successor was Terence J J Kilby, seen on the right in this 1947 photograph, who had recently been demobilised from the Royal Artillery with the rank of Major, having enlisted in October 1940.

The school's first open day & the formation of the PTA

An innovation in the immediate post-war years was a School Open Day, the first of which was held on 24 July 1947. It was a momentous occasion because at the same time a Parent-Teacher Association (PTA) was formed. Although one of its aims was to forge closer links, it was also hoped that money could be raised to purchase equipment for the school and some social functions would be held. In April 1952 Terence Kilby left and Percy B Troughton took over as head teacher.

The PTA has made an important contribution to the schools ever since, and has raised a great deal of money which has been spent on enhancing the facilities, as well as contributing to the social life of the village. For many years the copies of the New Testament presented to each school leaver were paid for from PTA funds. The biggest fund raising event every year was the Christmas raffle and bazaar. In 1970 the amount raised was a record £300 and by the end of the 1970s it had risen to nearly £700. During the years many social events were held at the school, which helped to bring together parents, staff, friends of the school and other visitors from the village.

Charles Rowberry's retirement

Over the years many teachers spent their entire working lives at Wollaston Schools. Another shining example was the deputy headmaster, Charles Rowberry who retired on 24 July 1952 after 44 years. At his farewell presentation

he thanked all his good, kind friends for their kind words and also for the cheque he had received. His years at the schools seemed but a few days he said. Through all the years he had received kindness, consideration and sympathy from all, and if he could re-live his life, he would choose to be '*a teacher at Wollaston*' once again.

1959 school extensions

During the post-war years, as the birth rate continued to rise, it was realised that the building in the village was no longer big enough to house all the children of primary age. On 6 April 1957 a church meeting heard that the church school would eventually become a two-form entry junior school. An architect was preparing a scheme of improvements to the buildings. The first stage was to begin that year with the erection of a hall on the playground.

The extensions to the village school, consisting of the hall, two classrooms, offices for the head and secretary and a toilet block were completed in 1959 and on 1 July celebrations were held in church. The official opening of the new buildings followed these, and an exhibition was held in the hall.

Above: Wollaston School held its first Open Day on 24 July 1947, and on the same occasion its Parent-Teacher Association was formed. Here, on 10 July 1974, founder member Maud Wheale, and Chairman Peter Guinness, make a presentation to retiring head teacher Percy B Troughton, who had succeeded Terence Kilby in April 1952.

On 31 August 1959 G Ruth Smith, who had been headmistress of the Infants' Department for 31 years, retired, and the new Infants' School on The Kingsway was opened. The youngest children became pupils at Meadow Park Infants' School, leaving only the juniors at Wollaston School.

When Stourbridge was still in Worcestershire, the school took part in the annual music festivals held in Worcester and music was a major activity in the schools after the war, with choirs, orchestras, bands and soloists playing and performing for their friends and parents.

In 1974, as a result of local government reorganisation, Dudley MBC took over responsibility for all the schools in Stourbridge from Worcestershire County Council.

When Percy Troughton retired in 1974, after 22 years as head, John E Porter took his place. Known as 'Jack', he had first joined the school in 1959 and had been deputy head since 1968. He retired in 1980, just four years before the vil-

Above: On 24 July 1952, deputy headmaster, Charles Rowberry, also retired, after spending 44 years at Wollaston School. He is seen here two years earlier in a group photograph. Back Row: Mr E Maurer; Mrs E Sutton; Miss W A Fisher; Charles Rowberry, deputy head; Miss E Reynolds or Miss M P Hand; Miss A H Davies; Mr A R Hayward. Front Row: T J J Kilby, headmaster; the Mayoress of Stourbridge, Mrs F G Gregory; the Vicar of Wollaston, Rev F Ingram Cox.

Above: Meadow Park Infants' School on Wollaston Farm Estate was built at a cost of £44,000 and opened on 1 September 1959, with Kathleen Corcoran as headmistress. It was officially opened on 2 July 1960. The old farmhouse, seen here, stood behind the school for some time, and it was here that the first caretaker lived, before a new house was provided next to the entrance drive.

lage school closed. His successor was Dorothy Gibson, who stayed at Wollaston for only three years. The last year of education in a building that had been in use for 125 years, was under the temporary headship of Lesley Prosser, who had been appointed deputy head at the same time as Dorothy Gibson.

Meadow Park Infants' School

On 23 December 1957 Stourbridge Council's Planning Committee examined plans for a proposed new Infants' School on Wollaston Farm Estate. These plans took two years to realise and the new school, which had been built at a cost of £44,000, opened on 1 September 1959 with Kathleen Corcoran as headmistress. The official opening took place on 2 July 1960. The old farmhouse still stood for some time behind the school. It was there that the first caretaker lived, before moving into a house next to the entrance drive, whereupon the farmhouse was demolished.

When the schools split in 1959, the numbers in the two departments were high and the new Meadow Park building of six classrooms soon needed another two. A wooden building, which is still in use in 2003, provided this and in Wollaston there were 12 classes in the Junior School, some of them containing well over 30 pupils. Links between the two schools were maintained and the infants for many years have taken part in the Infant Music Festival held for the Stourbridge schools.

In 1980, just prior to Kathleen Corcoran's retirement as head teacher of Meadow Park, the school celebrated its 21st Birthday with a party. Then in September 1980 Jeanette Stafford, who had been deputy head, took over as head, staying at the school until 1984.

Falling school rolls

However the numbers began to fall, until by the 1980s only four of the infant rooms were needed and the junior

numbers had halved. A Pre-School Play Group occupied a redundant classroom at Meadow Park. In 1982 the decision was made by Dudley MBC to merge the two schools and establish a new primary school on the Meadow Park site. This meant the closure of the building in the village and, under the terms of the original endowment by William Orme Foster, the building was sold and part of the proceeds went back to his descendants and part to Wollaston Church. The land, which for many years had been used by the school as playing fields, had been left to Wollaston Church and when that land was sold for house building, the money raised was invested for the church and some of it was eventually used to pay for the building of the church hall.

St James's Primary School

The move to the Meadow Park School site began in September 1984 when Anne Penn took over as head teacher of the new St James's Primary School.

After closure the old school buildings stood empty for five years, but in March 1990 work started on converting them into offices. The classrooms nearest the Church were demolished to create an access road, the end gable being reinstated with great skill.

The Kingsway site was not big enough to hold the remaining infants' classes and the juniors, so two new classrooms were built and the old barn of Wollaston Farm was converted into a library. Toilets and cloakrooms were built for the juniors, and one extra temporary classroom was erected on the playing field. A new playground was constructed and in February 1985 the last children left the site, which had served the village for 125 years. The playgroup moved into a new mobile classroom and the school settled down, with its official opening being held on 25 June 1985.

Over the next ten years the numbers of children applying for admission rose again until there was a two-form

Above: Three of the head teachers of Meadow Park and St James's schools were reunited in May 1990 on the occasion of the retirement, after 32 years service as a teaching assistant and school secretary, of Doris Totney. Seen here, left to right, are Anne Penn, Jeanette Hill (formerly Stafford), Doris Totney and Kathleen Corcoran. *St James's School*

entry, resulting in a school of 14 classes. The building was no longer adequate and for two years two more temporary classrooms had to be used. In 1992 the building of a new block of four classrooms was completed. The three temporary rooms were dismantled and removed and a new playground had to be constructed. Since then the numbers have remained stable. A cloakroom area has been converted into a computer base and all classes now have regular lessons there. It was soon found possible to add a nursery to the school, which would take children from four years old, and an existing classroom was converted for this use, while yet another new one had to be built for Year 1 children. In April 1997 the new nursery opened and the playgroup lost its older children but still takes three-year-olds.

The PTA continued to support the new St James's Primary School and the annual bazaar continued to be a money raiser. In Christmas 2000 this event raised over £2,000. In 2003 the money was still being spent for the benefit of the children: more books for the library, equipment for the reception class children, and funding for visits and visiting speakers, are all subsidised from PTA funds. The support of parents cannot be measured only in monetary

Below: In 1982 Dudley MBC decided to merge Wollaston's infant and junior schools and establish a new primary school on the Meadow Park site. This spelled the closure of the building in the village. The move to the Meadow Park School site began in September 1984 when Anne Penn took over as head teacher of a new St James's Primary School, seen here.

terms. The time spent by many generations of parents is greatly valued and their involvement in their children's education in so many ways helps the school to cater for activities that might otherwise be impossible.

Ridge Primary School

Ridge Primary School opened in 1968. It served the area around High Park Avenue to the south of the village. Children, who would previously have had to attend Meadow Park Infants', Gig Mill Primary or Wollaston Junior schools, now had one much closer to their homes. The site of the school is at the top of Gregory Road, next to Ridgewood School. It is a modern, two-storey building, and when it opened the head teacher was Harold Hoyle, a former bomber command pilot. He had previously taught in the Stourbridge area, and had been head of Stambermill School since 1962.

Harold Hoyle retired in 1975 and the new head teacher Mike Cruise remained there for 23 years until 1998. During this time the school built up a reputation in athletics, football, netball and cross-country. The children were encouraged to take up musical instruments, play in the wind band and school orchestra and join the school choirs. For many years they have taken part in the Dudley Music Festival. Over the years there have been frequent collections for charities, including the purchase of a guide dog for the blind.

In 2003 the school still caters for boys and girls from the age of five to 11. It has recently opened a state-of-the-art computer suite, which was visited on 8 June 1999 by the then Secretary of State for Education, David Blunkett, MP. There is an excellent library and close links with Ridgewood High School, where many of the children continue their education after the age of 11. There is a parent and toddler group, which meets regularly during term time and a kindergarten that operates in a separate building.

In July 1994 Ridge Primary School celebrated its Silver Jubilee with a programme of events that included a reunion party, an open day, a dance, the presentation of mugs to all the children, a service, a party and picnic for the children, and a balloon race. In 1997 a time capsule was buried in the school grounds. Since 1998 the head teacher has been Grahame Robertson.

Below: Grahame Robertson became head teacher at Ridge Primary School in 1998.

Left: Ridge Primary School opened in 1968 to served the area around High Park Avenue to the south of the village. The second head was Mike Cruise, who remained at the school for 23 years, until 1998. In 1997 he was photographed with a small group of pupils burying a time capsule in the school grounds, which was not to be opened before 2045.

High Park School

By the late 1950s a new secondary school was needed to serve the area of West Stourbridge, whose population had increased in the post-war period. A site was chosen at the end of Park Road West in Wollaston. It was the first new secondary school to be built in Stourbridge since the war, and was to be a secondary modern school, only the third of its kind in Stourbridge. Its intake was to be drawn mainly from Wollaston, but as it grew it included children who had been pupils at Amblecote, Beauty Bank and Gig Mill Junior Schools.

News of the new school reached Stourbridge Historical Society, who, at their meeting on 20 March 1958, suggested the name 'The Palfrey School' in honour of H E Palfrey, Stourbridge's distinguished historian and a past pupil of Wollaston School.

This suggestion was reached, and it was as High Park School that the new premises opened on 1 September 1958 with Fred Stanier as head teacher. As with many schools, its official opening came after it had been open for over a year, on 3 October 1959. The opening programme described it thus:

'The site of the School is a fine one with extensive views. It has been placed at the top of Park Road West, leaving the main area of the land to the south of the School as playing fields, and the high land behind for development as School gardens. The plan is a simple one, with the main teaching accommodation on the first floor in a single rectangular block. This block is linked by the entrance hall to a second building, which comprises a main hall, a small hall, art room, handicrafts room, and also kitchens and changing rooms. The site with its steep slope offers great opportunities for development and a great deal has already been done by way of preparation of the immediate surrounds of the School building.'

Steady progress was made, and at the first Speech Day on 15 October 1960 Fred Stanier gave a brief résumé of the first two years in the school's life. Throughout the 1960s the school maintained its numbers at between 300 and 400 pupils. The end of the 1960s saw the addition of a mobile classroom for the teaching of music.

A new access road to High Park School

Another growing problem was access to the site, which was still up the long and narrow Park Road West. In March 1972, the governors proposed to Stourbridge Council that a second access road be built to help alleviate congestion. Unfortunately the road could not be built without the Education Authority's permission, as it would limit the amount of space for playing fields. A petition was sent to Worcestershire County Council asking for a second access road to be built from Dunsley Road. On 3 November 1972 Stourbridge Council discussed suggestions for a car park with access from Dunsley Road allowing for 50 parking spaces with turning room at a cost of £10,000. In December the decision was made to go ahead with this proposal.

Above: High Park School opened on 1 September 1958, with Fred Stanier as head teacher. The buildings are seen here nearing completion. Its official opening came on 3 October 1959, after it had been open for over a year. Throughout the 1960s the school maintained its numbers at between 300 and 400 pupils. The end of the 1960s saw the addition of a mobile classroom for the teaching of music. *Harry Cartwright/Stourbridge Library*

Extensions to High Park School

The 1970s were to see huge changes in High Park School, both in accommodation and government education initiatives. At the prize giving held on 10 March 1972 Fred Stanier said that pupil numbers were 550, and were due to rise to 725 in the next two to three years. New buildings, for which they had waited six to seven years, were due to be opened in September 1972 consisting of a three-storey block to be built on the school playground. This contained classrooms on the lower floor and science labs on the upper floors. A new sports hall and craft rooms were also ready by 1972. The final phase of building was a new technology block and dining hall. By then the school had acquired extra land, with the purchase of a field adjoining the old school boundaries, which now became the new sports fields. A second playground was also built.

The raising of the school leaving age

Pupil numbers gradually grew during the 1970s, partly due to the increase in the school population, but also as a result of government legislation, which saw the raising of the school leaving age to 16. Since the 1960s High Park had always provided 5th Form education for pupils wishing to stay on beyond the leaving age of 15 in order to gain further qualifications. Now that all pupils had to stay until the age of 16, it was necessary to increase the building programme.

Comprehensive education in Stourbridge

The other main educational change occurred in 1976 when comprehensive education was introduced in Stourbridge and High Park became a comprehensive school from 1 September.

Fred Stanier retired in the summer of 1978 and on 1 September Ian Maddock took over as head teacher. By this time the numbers at the school had risen to between 800 and 900 pupils. During the 1980s the newly built dining hall was converted into classrooms and became the mathematics block.

Ridgewood High School

By the mid 1980s the pupil population of Stourbridge was in decline due to falling rolls and the numbers of children at all schools fell. The Local Education Authority

Below: Fred Stanier retired from High Park School in the summer of 1978. He is seen here at his retirement presentation. On 1 September Ian Maddock took over as head teacher. By this time the numbers at the school had risen to between 800 and 900 pupils.

(LEA) at Dudley decided to close one secondary school in Stourbridge. This happened in 1990, and from 1 September Longlands School (formerly Brook Street) was merged with High Park to form Ridgewood High School. At first lessons were held on both sites but by 1991 all pupils and staff were on the old High Park site and the Longlands building became part of Stourbridge College. Thus Ian Maddock became the first head teacher of Ridgewood High School.

The school developed a reputation in sport, and enjoyed many successes in team games, swimming, cross-country and athletics. Two former pupils of the school achieved notable sporting careers. Steven Cooper played professional football for Torquay United and Gavin Haynes played county cricket for Worcestershire. In the 1990s the English Schools Council granted the Sportsmark Award to the school.

In the 21st century the school has many specialist teaching areas which include four Information Communication Technology suites, each containing 20 to 24 computers, a drama studio, art rooms, a music suite and practice rooms, eight science laboratories, a sports hall, gym and playing fields, modern language facilities and a residential centre in Llanwog near Newtown in Wales.

There is a strong musical tradition in the school, which began when High Park first opened. The orchestra, choir and small groups all participated in the music festivals held in Worcester before 1974. About 20 public concerts are held every year and there are combined events in which the musicians from Ridgewood perform with the children from the feeder primary schools. Many members of the orchestra and band are also members of the Dudley Schools' Symphony Orchestra and other bands in the Dudley authority. In 1997 Ridgewood Rhapsody was invited to sing at the Queen Elizabeth Hall and the Royal Festival Hall. On three occasions in the 1990s the music department has visited the USA to perform to American audiences and has also travelled to France. There is a major annual school musical, bringing together all art forms. Recent performances have included 'Singin' in the Rain', 'Me and My Girl' and 'Grease.' The performances involve over 100 pupils as chorus members, soloists, orchestra members and technical crew.

Membership of the Duke of Edinburgh Award Scheme is encouraged, starting in Year 10 and continuing through Year 11. The residential centre in Wales is used for expeditions connected with the award.

Throughout the 1990s Ridgewood's numbers grew until by 2001 the school population was almost 1000. The buildings are being updated and refurbished and there are 196 places available annually in Year 7.

In August 2000, after 22 years as Headteacher, Ian Maddock retired and Sue Bates was appointed as the new Headteacher.

Since the early days of High Park School there has been a thriving and supportive parents' association, renamed Ridgewood High School Association. The members are all volunteers who are either parents of students or past students of the school. They give help at school events, providing stewards and refreshments at concerts. Money is raised to help finance the present pupils on exchange visits, sports events and the purchase of mini-buses. Furnishings have also been provided at the residential centre.

Chapter Five

WOLLASTON AT WORK

Wollaston's situation, on the edge of the Black Country, has meant that for many generations its inhabitants have found employment in both agriculture and industry.

Before the end of the 18th century the majority would have been involved in agricultural occupations, although a small number may have been employed in the glass industry across the River Stour in Amblecote, or in other trades in nearby Stourbridge.

The farms

Records from the early 19th century onwards show that there were four farms around Wollaston: Berkley's Farm, Eggington Farm, High Park Farm and Wollaston Farm.

Berkley's Farm was situated on High Park Avenue, almost opposite the end of Gladstone Road. The first reference to the farm was found in the 1871 census, when William Nickless and his family were farming seven and three-quarter acres. It continued in the hands of the Nickless family until 8 May 1896 when it was sold at auction at the Talbot Inn Stourbridge under the terms of the will of William Nickless. At the time of the 1901 census a glasscutter, Charles Nash and his family, occupied the house.

Eggington Farm was on Bridgnorth Road, opposite the end of High Park Avenue, and was first recorded in 1809 when it was advertised for sale by auction in *Berrow's*

Above: Wollaston had four principal farms, which originally formed part of the Hall Estate. There were also a number of other farming and produce operations in the village, including this orchard in Fir Grove, which still conveys a very rural scene as late as 1939 when this photograph was taken.

Below: Wollaston's smallest farm was Berkley's, situated on High Park Avenue, almost opposite the end of Gladstone Road, as seen in this sale plan from 8 May 1896. Up to that time it had been the home of the Nickless family, who tended its seven and three-quarter acres. The 'Homestead' survives in 2003 as a private house.

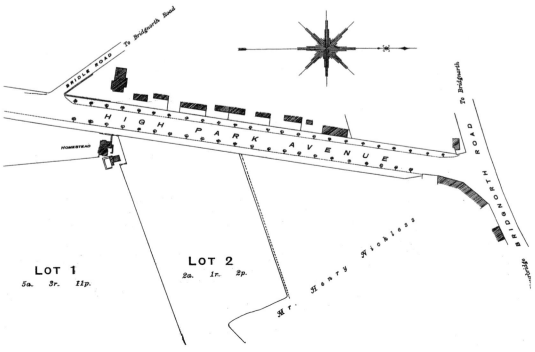

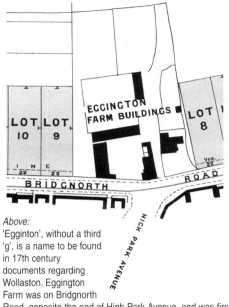

Above:
'Egginton', without a third 'g', is a name to be found in 17th century documents regarding Wollaston. Eggington Farm was on Bridgnorth Road, opposite the end of High Park Avenue, and was first recorded in 1809. After its purchase from the Wollaston Hall Estate in 1848 it was owned by a series of absentee landlords and occupied by tenant farmers. This plan is taken from particulars of a sale on 20 March 1903.

Below: After the sale of most of its land in 1903, Eggington Farm's buildings continued to be used, and the farmhouse lived in. Its most celebrated occupant was Don Despres whose motor spares business was based there for over 30 years. Wollaston Home Guard also used the barn seen to the left during World War II.

Worcester Journal. An 1827 map and schedule records Charles Grazebrook as the tenant of Eggitons (sic) farm and this was still the case when the executors of the Earl of Dudley sold Wollaston Hall and Estate.

The 1851 census records John Davis as the occupier, but he was described as a farm labourer. However, *Melville's Directory* of 1852 records Joseph Webb as the farmer. He was an absentee landlord as he lived at Springfield House, Wordsley. By the time of the 1871 census, Edward Elcock was in residence. Joseph Webb died in February 1873, and *Littlebury's Directory* of that year records H W Allin as the farmer. In 1881 it was in the ownership of the Nickless family and remained so until after 1891, according to the *Stourbridge Almanack & Directory.* However, the 1891 census shows Fanny Elcock and William Hubbill (a farm bailiff) in residence. Fanny Elcock was again present in the 1901 census, but the 1921 and 1925 electoral rolls record members of the Crampton family living there.

The 1936 edition of *Kelly's Directory* contains an entry for Don Despres who was trading as a '*scrapped car buyer*', and his company, Wollaston Motor Spares, continued to do so until the buildings were demolished to make way for the building of the houses in Hamilton Avenue (see below and Chapter Nine).

High Park Farm in High Park Avenue is first recorded on the 1841 census when William Ryland (a banker's clerk) and his family occupied it. In subsequent censuses, up to and including 1881, the occupants were a series of farm labourers and housekeepers, but contemporary trade directories record the farmer as Joseph Whitmore. By 1891 a Joseph Whitmore and his family were resident, but he was probably the son of the earlier farmer. The farm continued in the ownership of the Whitmore family until Stourbridge Council purchased it for housing in March 1927. The Whitmore's association with the land was perpetuated by the naming of one of the new roads built there as Whitmore Road.

Below: High Park Farm in High Park Avenue is first recorded on the 1841 census. William Ryland and his family lived there. Subsequent censuses, up to and including 1881, show that the occupants were a succession of farm labourers and housekeepers, but contemporary trade directories record the farmer as Joseph Whitmore. This is a detail from a commercial postcard showing the farm buildings, looking towards the village.

Above: Joseph Whitmore was still resident at High Park Farm in 1891, but he was probably the son of the earlier farmer. The farm continued in Whitmore family ownership until Stourbridge Borough Council purchased it for housing in March 1927. The Whitmore's association with the land was perpetuated by the naming of one of the new roads built on the land. Here, the farmhouse still stands but demolition of its outbuildings has begun. *Stourbridge Library*

Above: Wollaston Farm was plotted on a map of 1827, but no farmhouse was marked. The house, seen here in the early 1930s, was behind where the buildings of St James's School stand in 2003. The 1851 census shows that one of its residents was Frederick Stuart, of Stuart Crystal in Wordsley, who was the son-in-law of the farmer.

Wollaston Farm, which later gave its name to the housing estate circled by The Kingsway, was noted on the 1827 map mentioned above, but no farmhouse was marked. It was named as Mr Bill's Farm on the 1851 census, although the farmer was June Bill who was a widow. Also resident were Frederick Stuart (of Stuart Crystal, Wordsley), who was the son-in-law of June, plus his wife and young son. The farm remained in the Bill family until some time in the late 1870s when John Saunders took over. By 1886 he had been replaced by Edward Parsons who remained until the Great War. It then passed through the

Below: The side of Wollaston Farm, again in the early 1930s. After changing hands a number of times it was purchased for housing in 1935. Attempts to start a private development on the land did not come to fruition before World War II, and Stourbridge Borough Council finally developed it in the 1950s. If the photographer's vantage point could be located in 2003, all around would be houses.

Cooper and Cooke families and *Kelly's Directory* for 1932 placed Percy Edward Haines at Wollaston Farm, where he remained until the land was purchased for housing in 1935.

The mills

In the early 19th century the village had three different types of mill, in three different locations, but all within a mile of each other and all close to the old village, the original settlement that grew up around Wollaston Hall at the Barley Mow end of High Street. These mills reflected not only the close association of the industrial Black Country, with its green borderland, but also some of the technological developments of the 18th and 19th centuries.

Wollaston's windmill was situated in what is called Vicarage Road in 2003, but which in the early 19th century was known as Windmill Lane. It stood on the high bank on the north side of Windmill Lane, near to the site occupied by the modern vicarage. Josiah Bach was responsible for the first depiction found of the windmill, on a map of the village fields he drew in 1699. The windmill is shown situated in a field appropriately named 'Windmill Piece.' Exactly when the windmill was built, and by whom, is not known, but there was certainly a miller, John Payton, living in Wollaston in 1661, according to a document preserved in Birmingham Reference Library:

'A true and perfect indentured inventory of the goods and chattells of John Payton of Wollaston in the county of Worcestershire, miller deceased, taken and apprysed the fowerteenth day of September An Dom 1661 by Thomas Hilton, Robert Dudley, John Cartwright and George Darby.'

This inventory shows that John Payton was a wealthy businessman, judging from his many possessions and the list of substantial debts owed to him.

It is likely that the earliest structure was a timber post-mill, a construction typical of the 16th and 17th centuries. Probably sometime in the 18th century it was rebuilt as a tower mill, most likely of brick. The evidence for believing it to be a tower mill comes from Isaac Taylor's map of Worcestershire, published in 1772, which clearly shows a pictogram representing a tower mill. Such structures were commonplace in the West Midlands in the 18th and 19th centuries, and given the widespread availability of locally made bricks, a brick-built tower was the most likely structure at that time. Surprisingly the windmill does not appear on Harry Court's map of Stourbridge, drawn in 1782, but it was clearly in use in 1779 when among the Wollaston properties listed in an auction notice in *Berrow's Worcester Journal* of 18 February was:

'*Lot 2 – The Lease of a Wind Mill and convenient buildings, with about 4 acres of arable land and 5 acres of exceeding rich meadow land, for the remainder of the term of 21 years… situate in Wollaston aforesaid.*'

In the early 19th century the windmill was shown on a map of Worcestershire produced by Christopher Greenwood, published in 1830. It also appears on the first OS map of the area published in 1834. Moreover, it is mentioned twice in *Berrow's Worcester Journal* of 1 June 1809 in a list of Wollaston properties to be sold by auction on 12 June at the Talbot Hotel in Stourbridge:

'*Lot IX – One piece of arable and pasture land, in the possession, of Mr William Dewee, situate near Wollaston Windmill*'
'*Lot XIV – consists of a tenement and a windmill, two pieces of arable land, containing 4 acres, 2 roods and 5 perches, in the possession of Mr Hill and his undertenant.*'

It is not unreasonable to assume that the mill was sold as a going concern. Significantly it is not shown on the map that was produced for the sale in 1848 of the Wollaston Hall Estate by the Earl of Dudley, but Lot 6 in the list of sale particulars includes '*site of windmill.*' It is not known exactly what happened to the windmill; it was still standing around 1831-2 when the first OS map was drawn, but it is not known when it ceased operating. The reference to the site of the windmill suggests that the mill was either derelict or had already been demolished by 1848. Moreover, it is likely that the site was cleared to make way for the original vicarage which was built around 1861, as the plot of land containing the windmill site, shown on the 1848 map, is in almost the same location as that of the vicarage shown on the 25-inch OS map published in 1885, but surveyed in 1882.

Wollaston Mills is the name given to the area adjacent to the High Street and on the south (Worcestershire) side of the River Stour. This may well have been the site of Wollaston's first mill. There is documentary evidence from the 16th century linking it with the manor house, the predecessor of Wollaston Hall. In the Middle Ages the tenants of the lord of the manor would have been compelled to bring their corn to his mill for grinding. At a later date probably in the 17th century the river was harnessed to drive a slitting (iron) mill, possibly the one advertised for sale in *Berrow's Worcester Journal* of 1 June 1809:

Above: Wollaston's windmill stood where the vicarage stands in 2003, on a slight mound along Vicarage Road, which was known as Windmill Lane in the early 19th century. The only known miller was John Payton, who died in 1661. It is unlikely that his mill was a timber post one, but a brick tower mill, of the kind shown here, had replaced this by the late 18th century. The mill probably went out of use in the 1830s.

Below: A sketch of the bend in Stourbridge Canal close to John Bradley & Co, by the Wollaston-born artist, Sir Frank Short, showing, on the extreme right, some of the outbuildings of Wollaston Mills.

'Lot XIII – Comprises Wollaston Slitting Mill, water course, dam and (work) shops, and three tenements.'

Taylor's map of Worcestershire (1772) clearly shows a watermill on the Worcestershire bank of the River Stour close by the road leading to Amblecote (the end of High Street in 2003). It is also shown on Greenwood's map of 1830. During the 19th century it is likely that an additional water wheel was installed on this stretch of the river, hence the plural form Wollaston 'Mills' which appears on OS maps of the early 20th century.

According to trade directories, Samuel Hodgson & Co were making spades and shovels from before 1820 until at least 1865, at their 'Wollaston Works.' The *Brierley Hill Advertiser* of 4 January 1862 reported that on New Year's Day Messrs Hodgson & Co had given a treat to the hands in their employ, in one of the large warehouses, which had been cleared out and suitably decorated with evergreens for the purpose.

By the mid-19th century as the census returns show, the area had become associated with the making of spades and agricultural forks. The 1871 census shows that Alexander Norris was a spade manufacturer on this site and according to trade directories his company was manufacturing spades and shovels at Wollaston Mills in 1873 and continued to do so until at least 1912. Isaac Nash Sr began making scythes near Belbroughton in 1842. The business expanded rapidly and began making horse nails, a business which Isaac Nash Jr took over while his younger brother William Rusgrove Nash concentrated on the scythe business. In 1887 Isaac Nash Jr acquired Wollaston Mills, the home of the old established Norris business. For the next 70 years Isaac Nash & Sons manufactured a wide range of tools for agriculture and the building trade at Wollaston Mills.

Below: Some form of watermill may have been located on the River Stour, straddling Wollaston and Amblecote, since the 16th century. By the 17th century it was a slitting mill, and by 1820 it was the Wollaston works of Samuel Hodgson & Co, spade & shovel makers. Alexander Norris was working the mill by 1871, and Isaac Nash Jr acquired his business in 1887. This plan is from a valuation of the site Nash had prepared in 1900. It shows the mill, its outbuildings, and associated cottages. *Worcester Record Office*

Above: Inside one of the outbuildings at Isaac Nash & Sons was a workshop, where all of this belt-driven machinery was used to maintain the works' equipment. The smartly suited man centre left is probably one of the managers.

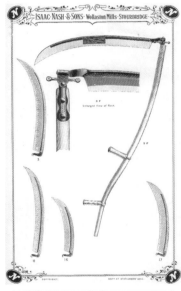

Left: The first of two pages from an 1897 Isaac Nash & Sons catalogue shows that the works was also used to make scythes…

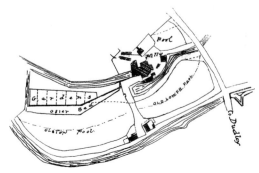

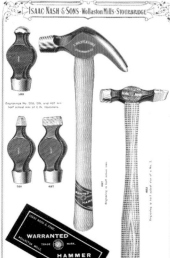

Left: … and hammers, of various shapes and weights. The label shown is also reproduced in the colour section of this book.

The *County Express* of 17 November 1900 recorded a serious fire at the Wollaston Mills works of Isaac Nash & Sons. The fire started in a new three-storey building, about 30-40yds long, which had been erected in the Yard in the centre of the works. The building was used to store among other things large piles of 'trees' for spades, shovels and other implements, quantities of varnish and other inflammable materials. This building was completely destroyed and other buildings and equipment were damaged. The cost of the damage was estimated to be between £10,000 and £12,000. It was hoped that some production would resume in about a week's time. It was said that the works employed about 300 men and boys.

On 5 October 1957 the *County Express* carried the following statement from Isaac Nash & Sons:

'WOLLASTON MILLS TO CLOSE – Isaac Nash & Sons' statement. A link with the Stourbridge of the last century is to be severed by a decision to transfer production of the Wollaston Mills works of Messrs I Nash & Sons to Oldbury. A statement was issued this week by Messrs Peter Boulton, Charles Boulton JP and Cyril Boulton (grandsons of the late Mr Isaac Nash who founded the business at Wollaston Mills.) It reads as follows: 'Some five years ago the Nash companies of Stourbridge and Belbroughton, together with the Tyzack company of Sheffield, joined forces with a third tool firm, the Brades of Oldbury. This new BNT group found itself with six fairly widely scattered manufacturing units. The first phase of a plan to co-ordinate all these interests was to establish at Oldbury a commercial centre to handle under one roof the world sales of the group; subsequently this was followed by the completion of a new central dispatch warehouse also at Oldbury. Now, finally in the interests of greater efficiency it has become necessary to concentrate some of the production units, and so the Wollaston Mills production is to be transferred to the largest factory in the group, which is also at Oldbury and adjacent to the central warehouse. There is no question of the Nash Company closing down – indeed in certain spheres, particularly overseas, a plan of expansion is underway. Key personnel are to be transferred to the Oldbury plant, and the company has done its utmost to take care of the interests of any cases of redundancy of workpeople and arranged pension rights for any of the older employees who have been retired."*

The third mill, still standing and often referred to simply as **Wollaston Mill**, was built at the end of the 19th century. At the monthly meeting of the Stourbridge UDC on 28 March 1898 the Highways and Improvements Committee reported that it had approved the plans submitted by Mr C H Parsons to build a mill. In 2003 it still stands at the junction of High Street and Vicarage Road, roughly midway between the windmill site and Wollaston Mills. Its small size suggests that it was a corn mill, producing animal feed, rather than a flourmill. Flour mills built at that time were usually larger, because space was needed for a number of 'dressing' machines which were necessary to provide the very fine white flour which had become fashionable. In the early years of the 20th century the mill was owned and operated by Charles H Parsons who in various local trade directories is described as a '*Corn Merchant*.' Originally the mill may have been steam powered given the availability of cheap local coal, although an oil-burning or gas engine cannot be ruled out, however, in its later years of operation electricity was installed. In this type of mill the cereal, usually oats and barley, was crushed between rollers rather than ground between two stones as in a windmill. During the first half of the 20th century the mill not only changed hands, but also its function. It was

Nash & Tyzac circa 1956

Above: Unfortunately, Wollaston Mills became a casualty of BNT's amalgamation process, closing at the end of 1957. Here is a plan drawn by an ex-employee at Wollaston, showing the layout of the site at the time of its closure.

Above: Wollaston Mill stands at the junction of High Street and Vicarage Road, roughly midway between the windmill site and Wollaston Mills. Its small size suggests that it was a corn mill, producing animal feed, rather than a flourmill. Charles H Parsons built it in 1898. The extension to the left probably housed an oil or gas engine, used to power the machinery.

CONTRACTORS TO H.M. GOVERNMENT

Seeds ~~~~~ *Fertilisers*

A. H. SUMMERTON LTD

CORN MERCHANTS, MILLERS
FORAGE CONTRACTORS

Telegrams & Telephone : STOURBRIDGE 5084

Wollaston Corn Mills · **S T O U R B R I D G E**

REG. OFFICE : SOHO MILLS, BIRMINGHAM, 18   (Tel. NOR 1539)

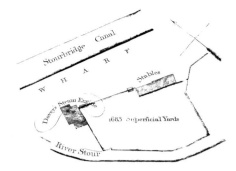

Above: On 29 September 1800, John Bradley purchased this plot of land between the Stourbridge Canal and the River Stour on which to construct his new ironworks. *Worcester Record Office*

Above: In the first half of the 20th century the mill changed hands and function. It was acquired by A H Summerton Ltd, corn merchants, who owned a number of mills in Birmingham and the Black Country, but long before its closure in the late-1950s it had ceased to operate as a mill, and was used simply as a grain store and as a distribution centre.

Left: When John Bradley died in January 1816 the running of his, by then, very successful ironworks passed to his stepbrother James Foster, seen here in later life.

acquired by A H Summerton Ltd who owned a number of mills in Birmingham and the Black Country, but long before its closure in the late-1950s it had ceased to operate as a mill and was used simply as a grain store and as a distribution centre.

From 1962 onwards, after its closure as a grain store, the mill housed the firm of Brazier & Jackson Ltd, who processed and distributed insulation materials, especially polystyrene, for 30 years. Towards the end of the 20th century it housed an antiques business, and at the beginning of the new millennium it took on a new role after conversion into a suite of offices for a number of small businesses.

John Bradley & Co

In 1793, on the death of his stepfather Henry Foster, John Bradley took over the family business of Stourbridge Forge, a hardware manufactory and producer of wrought-iron bar, on the east side of Lower High Street, Stourbridge.

John Bradley & Co was formed in 1800, when John Bradley went into partnership with Thomas Jukes Collier, a wine merchant from Wellington, Shropshire, and the trustees of Henry Foster's will. The company began construction of a new iron works between the River Stour and the Stourbridge canal on the west side of Lower High Street, Stourbridge. Within a few years the company was running a forge, steam engine, slitting and rolling mill and was producing nailers' rods as well as wrought-iron bars. The business continued to expand and, by January 1816 when John Bradley died, its products included: billets, boilerplates, merchant bar iron, hoop iron, iron strip and wire iron. James Foster, son of Henry, took over the running of the business and continued its expansion. In 1819, he formed a separate company in partnership with John Urpeth Rastrick. Styled Foster, Rastrick & Co, this was to be an

engineering division to manufacture steam engines amongst other products. One of Rastrick's first tasks was to design and build a new foundry, as the existing building was too small. This was erected on the other side of the river, just over the boundary into Wollaston, where it still stands in 2003. By 1825 the company had developed a standard list of cast components, which ran to many hundreds of items such as engine beams, cylinders, flywheels, domestic bedsteads and cooking plates, etc.

In 1826 James Foster proposed to build a railway to transport coal and other minerals from the mines he leased at Shut End to Stourbridge Ironworks. At the beginning of 1827, agreement was reached between Lord Dudley's Agent, Mr Foley (the landowner at Shut End) and James Foster about the line, and construction began under Rastrick's supervision. The operation of the line was to be by a combination of a stationary engine on an incline at

Above: In 1819, James Foster entered into a partnership with the engineer John Urpeth Rastrick. Run within John Bradley & Co, this partnership would last for just 12 years, but would yield some historic and heroic products, of which at least one would go down in history. For over 150 years this nameplate remained on one of the works buildings, before it was stolen, hopefully not for scrap. *Stourbridge Library*

Shutt End, a locomotive on the near level central section, and a gravity incline to the canal at Ashwood Basin. The locomotive, *The Agenoria*, was designed by Rastrick and built by Foster, Rastrick & Co. The Shutt End Railway opened on 2 June 1829. This was the same year that three other Foster, Rastrick locomotives, the *Stourbridge Lion*, the *Delaware* and the *Hudson*, were delivered to the Delaware & Hudson Canal Co's railroad in America. On 8 August 1829 the *Stourbridge Lion* entered history by becoming the first steam locomotive to run on a commercial railway in the USA.

All of these developments required a much larger workforce and also housing for them and their dependents.

Above: One of Rastrick's first tasks was to design and build a new foundry, as the existing building was too small. This was erected on the other side of the river, just over the boundary into Wollaston, where it still stands in 2003. Here is the building in its full glory, when it had six of these magnificent ladle cranes inside. *The late WKV Gale*

Above: Literally the crowning glory of the New Foundry is this cast- and wrought-iron roof. Rastrick pushed understanding of iron construction to its limits when he designed this in 1820. The inverted 'fish-bellied' beams are held in place by wrought-iron ties, and the original roof covering was iron plates, hinged at the top, so that they could vent any explosions that might happen inside safely! *The late WKV Gale*

This need was partially met by housing developments in the Withy Bank and King Street areas of Wollaston. By the time of the 1841 census, 30% of Wollaston's male workforce was employed in the iron industry, and in King Street the figure was 80% of the male inhabitants. By 1851 the percentage working in the iron industry had risen to 37%.

When James Foster died on 12 April 1853; the business was taken over by his nephew William Orme Foster. He was more openly generous than his uncle and in May 1856 he established a library and reading room at the Stourbridge Iron Works. He did not have the technical understanding of his predecessors and as a result the company failed to keep up with new developments, such as steel production, and began to decline; the effect of which was cushioned by the wealth of the Foster family. Various parts of their industrial empire were sold off and the profits invested in property, so that when William Henry Foster took over on the death of his father, Shut (sic) End Collieries and Stourbridge Iron Works formed the hub of the remaining business.

On 30 March 1901 the *County Express* reported '*Terrible Fatality at Stourbridge Ironworks.*' Two men were killed. They had been part of a team of four working on a pair of rolls in the rolling mill and had been using a large spanner to turn the rolls manually when the rolling mill accidentally slipped into gear and the spanner they were using hit them, killing one instantly while the second died later that day.

Above: More and more is being learned about the products of Foster, Rastrick & Co, but their most celebrated ones were four steam locomotives. *The Agenoria*, seen here at Round Oak in 1882, was the first to work on a railway in the Midlands or the south of England when she inaugurated the Shutt End Railway on 2 June 1829. Her sister engine, but with a chimney half the height, was the *Stourbridge Lion*, which became the first locomotive to turn a wheel on a commercial railroad in the USA on 8 August 1829. *Stourbridge Library*

The *County Express* of 19 October 1901 reported the opening of the winter session at Messrs Bradley & Co's Stourbridge Ironworks reading room, with a social evening and concert. Richard Lowndes, the works manager, said it was hoped that employees would find some activity to interest them. It was noted that they already had a bowls

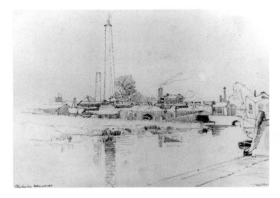

Above: When James Foster died, on 12 April 1853, the business was taken over by his nephew William Orme Foster. He was more openly generous than his uncle, and in May 1856 he established a library and reading room at the Stourbridge Ironworks. Soon afterwards he also endowed Wollaston with a church and school in memory of his uncle. This is Stourbridge Ironworks, as drawn by the Wollaston-born artist, Sir Frank Short, in the late 19th century.

Above: By the late 19th and early 20th centuries, the success of John Bradley & Co was as much down to its managers as its owners. One of its more successful managers was Richard Lowndes, who also became greatly involved in Wollaston life through being one of the Schools' managers. The naming of Lowndes Road, seen here in the late 1950s, marks his contribution. *Harry Cartwright/Stourbridge Library*

club and a cricket club was proposed for the coming summer, and suggestions for further activities were requested.

On 16 July 1919, William Henry Foster sold the last remaining part of John Bradley & Co, the Stourbridge Ironworks, to a limited company owned by Edward J Taylor, but linked with E Baylie & Co Ltd and Noah Hingley & Sons Ltd. Even after 45 years of contraction, the reputation of the firm was such that the new business retained the title John Bradley & Co (Stourbridge) Ltd. A Hingley's board member, J S Trinham, made a preliminary assessment of the works:

'I had another good look round on 29th (1919). The mills are no good with the present broken down state of the engine. Even with the engine in a good state of repair it would be hopelessly out of date on account of its speed. The engine ought to be realised as scrap & at present prices it would leave a sum of £1,500 to £2,000 to go towards a suitable electrically driven mill for rolling ¼in to ¹⁵/₃₂in diam. A 7in mill erected on existing 9in mill bedplates would do this work very well. The 14in mill ought to be scrapped... . The Forge could continue working making puddled bars of special quality for the special iron to be rolled at J B & Co and at Netherton. When the mills are taken off the steam the forge will work with a very much-reduced fuel cost.... The foundry is in good working order and has four air furnaces. The cupolas are no good. The cost of production would be greater than is our cost for ordinary castings, but high class work ought to be done quite cheaply.'

The first phase of the modernisation, a new forge-rolling department, was completed in 1923. Although this improved productivity, there was still room for improvement. However production was severely curtailed

in 1926 by the coal strike as shown by a notice in the *County Express* of 4 December which stated that John Bradley & Co were to resume work on 6 December, the works having been idle since the end of April. Further modernisation continued in the late 1920s with electrification of the mills.

The New Foundry appears to have fallen into disuse either just before or during World War II, and was subsequently leased to Sidney Smith in 1959 and brought back into use as a foundry. The *County Express* reported that a plaque to the Stourbridge Locomotives had been unveiled at John Bradley & Co on 27 May 1959. In 1964 part of the works was sold to Brockway Engineering, and the 'new foundry' was sold to Sidney Smith & Sons who operated the site until mid-June 2003. John Bradley & Co Ltd was voluntarily wound up in 1966.

On 13 March 1968, a chimney, which had stood at the new foundry for 150 years, was demolished. The event was thought sufficiently newsworthy to receive extensive coverage in both the *County Express* and *Express & Star*.

The spade works

Apart from Isaac Nash & Sons, there were numerous other smaller spade and shovel companies in the Stourbridge area. A group of three such companies was situated at the junction of Mamble Road and Bowling Green Road. These works were much smaller than Wollaston Mills, and tens of men rather than hundreds operated each. The longest-lived of these companies was **John Wooldridge & Sons**, which was formed in 1878 when John Wooldridge took over the works of Messrs Robinson & Pearsall who had previously used it for spade and shovel manufacture. The choice of this site was probably initially dictated by the presence of the Withy Brook as a convenient source of power. By the early 20th century a 30hp gas engine was the main source of power and this was itself replaced in the 1950s by a similarly rated electric motor.

John Wooldridge was formerly a foreman at The Brades works in Oldbury. He died in 1889 and his sons, Joseph, William, and John, continued the firm, which became a limited company in 1919. Joseph was the dominant partner. He served as a Stourbridge councillor and later became an alderman, and was a Methodist lay preacher for over 60 years. He died in 1943. After Joseph's death, the company was operated by his son Wilfred in partnership with Charles Sidney Hall until 1949, and then by the Hall family and Dennis Stringer, until its closure in 1988. In

Above: The New Foundry fell into disuse just before or during World War II. It was leased to Sidney Smith in 1959 and brought back into use. Sidney Smith & Sons subsequently bought the building and operated on the site until mid-June 2003. John Bradley & Co Ltd was voluntarily wound up in 1966, and on 13 March 1968, this chimney, which had stood at the works for 150 years, was demolished, an event thought sufficiently newsworthy to receive coverage in both the *County Express* and *Express & Star*.

Below: An extract from an 1885 map, showing the concentration of spade and shovel works around the junction of Bowling Green and Mamble roads. The location was deliberate, to make use of waterpower provided by the Withy Brook. At the bottom are the premises that were to become Durbar Works, at the top, John Wooldridge & Sons, and to the right the large works of John Hatton & Sons.

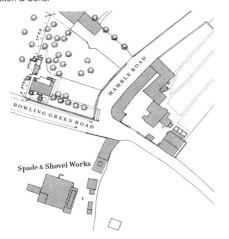

2003, the site of the works is occupied by a small housing development known as The Greenwoods.

A John Wooldridge & Sons catalogue from 1921 (overleaf) shows that a wide range of spades, shovels, forks and other garden tools, picks and mattocks, were offered for sale. At its peak the works employed about 15 people, but this was reduced to three at the time of its closure. The range of products had also been progressively reduced until only forks were made.

John Hatton & Sons operated from the mid 1880s until the 1960s on a site on the corner of Mamble Road and Bowling Green Road, where flats stand in 2003. Frank Hatton, one of the sons of John Hatton, died in July 1952 at the age of 75. He had two brothers, Arthur and Jack.

Above: John Hatton & Sons operated on this site, on the corner of Mamble and Bowling Green roads, from the mid 1880s until the 1960s. After the works was demolished these low-rise flats were erected on the site.

A third site in Mamble Road, adjacent to Wooldridge's, but nearer to Bridgnorth Road, was operated by the Fiddian family. **Benjamin Fiddian & Sons'** main works was situated in Brook Street, Stourbridge. In trade directories the Mamble Road works was attributed to Alexander Fiddian (son of Benjamin) around the time of the Great War and later to the parent company. It operated until about 1960 when it was taken over by Jenks & Cattell and production was transferred elsewhere. Under the heading '*Claim for Stourbridge spade and fork'*, the *County Express* of 18 November 1939 carried the following:

'*In August last while staying at Rhos-on-Sea, North Wales, Mr Alec F Fiddian of Wychbury, Pedmore, threw a watertight biscuit tin containing a note into the sea. The message stated that anyone finding the tin would receive from Mr Fiddian an Albion spade & fork manufactured by Messrs. B. Fiddian Ltd., Albion Works, Stourbridge. On November 10th Mr Fiddian received a letter from Miss Rita Thompson of Ballyfrench, Ballyhalbert, Co Down, Ireland, saying she picked up the tin & note on Ballyfrench beach. The tin must have travelled some 130 to 140 miles in about three months. The promised spade & fork have been sent to Miss Thompson.'*

From the Great War until July 1982 the firm of **Stourbridge Engineers & Ironfounders** occupied a site on the corner of Swan Street and Bowling Green Road, opposite Wooldridges. Although they did not make spades

Above: Called Durbar Works, Stourbridge Engineers & Ironfounders remained in production until July 1982. This photograph was taken on the final day. Following closure the site was cleared and housing built upon it.

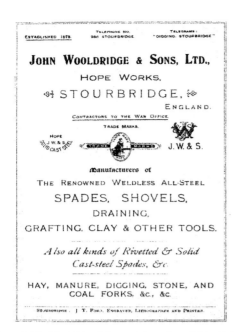

Above: A John Wooldridge & Sons catalogue from 1921, which shows that they offered for sale a wide range of spades, shovels, forks and other garden tools, picks and mattocks. At its peak they employed about 15 people, but this was reduced to three at the time of its closure in 1988. Houses forming The Greenwoods were subsequently built on the site.

and shovels, as part of their trade as general engineers and jobbing iron founders they made and repaired tools and machinery used in the manufacture of such items.

The Novelty Glassworks

The Novelty Glassworks once occupied a site in Gladstone Road, on the left-hand side when travelling from High Park Avenue towards Bridgnorth Road. Although there are no visible remains, there is documentary evidence of its existence. Property deeds, including a surviving site plan, show that it was purchased by Edward Edwards in 1888 and subsequently sold by auction in 1890 in The Gate Hangs Well pub nearby. The purchaser was James Marshall, who in 1892 set up a limited company with the principal objective of developing and extending the Novelty Glassworks. Unfortunately the company struggled to survive and was wound up at the Talbot Hotel in Stourbridge on 20 March 1893. The glassworks is listed in the annual editions of Mark & Moody's *Stourbridge Almanack & Directory* from 1886 to 1893, apart from 1890, the year in which it changed hands. However, there is no entry at all for the period 1894 to 1899 and then, intriguingly, there is an entry for Edwards & Co Glassworks, Gladstone Road in the 1900, 1901 and 1902 editions. Whether Edwards had managed to regain possession and in what circumstances is, as yet, unresolved.

How long the glassworks was operational is not known, although the late Cyril Manley, a well-known local glass collector and the author of *Decorative Victorian Glass*

(1981) suggested in his book that glass was produced between 1850 and 1900. The census returns of 1881 indicate that at that time Edward Edwards of Gladstone Road (then called Lower Bridle Road) was a glass manufacturer '*employing two men and a boy.*' The census 'address' matches exactly the location description given in the property documents. Edward Edwards, born 1840, was the son of Samuel Edwards (born in Amblecote) who in various local trade directories of the mid-19th century is described as a glass manufacturer and glass dealer of High Street, Stourbridge. Although Edwards was operating the glassworks in 1881, he did not purchase the premises until 1888. Nothing is known about Mr Grainger who sold the premises to Edwards, or of the identity of the person who began manufacturing on the site.

The Novelty Glassworks was clearly a small unit of production, with only a handful of employees, perhaps four to six at the most. Likewise the buildings, too, would have been on a small scale, such that the 'cone' which Manley claims was demolished in 1900 was in all probability no more than a narrow conical shaped chimney. Anecdotal evidence from Wollaston residents is that the glassworks was demolished 80 or 90 years ago. Perhaps the top of the

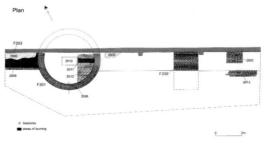

Above: The Novelty Glassworks site was redeveloped for housing in 2002, but ahead of this the Birmingham University Field Archaeology Unit recorded the standing buildings in November 2001, and also partially excavated the site in March and August 2002. Amongst their finds was a brick flue and the base of a small glass cone, seen here, which extended into the adjoining property.

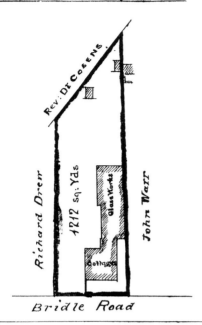

Plan before referred to.

Rev. Dr Cosens.

Richard Drew

4212 sq. Yds

Glass Works

John Warr

Cottage

Bridle Road

Above: Wollaston once had a glassworks: The Novelty Glassworks occupied a site in Gladstone Road, on the left-hand side when travelling from High Park Avenue towards Bridgnorth Road. Although there are no visible remains in 2003, there is documentary evidence. This site plan is from conveyance when Edward Edwards purchased the works in 1888. At that time Gladstone Road was still called Bridle Road.

Below: The buildings of the former Novelty Glassworks, photographed in March 2002. Clearly, only a handful of employees could have worked here. Joseph Forrest, who used the former glassworks as the base for his hay and straw distribution and haulage business, subsequently occupied the site. Briefly, it was also the headquarters of Wollaston Scouts.

conical chimney was lopped in 1900 because it was considered unsafe and then the rest of the structure was taken down at a later date. Joseph Forrest used the glassworks site as the base for his hay and straw distribution and haulage business following its closure. In the late 1920s it was also, briefly, the base for Wollaston Scouts. The site was redeveloped for housing in 2002, but ahead of this the Birmingham University Field Archaeology Unit (BUFAU) recorded the standing buildings in November 2001. They also partially excavated the site in March and August 2002. Amongst their finds was the brick flue and base of a small glass cone.

It is not known exactly what the Novelty Glassworks range of products included, although Manley's book has a photograph of three pink and orange coloured vases, standing between six and eight inches high. One of these vases (see colour section) is on display at Broadfield House Glass Museum in Kingswinford. A further clue to the range of products is in the descriptions of the patent designs that were registered by Edward Edwards and James Marshall. In 1885 Edwards registered a design, which was described as '*shape for relief on a vase*', whilst Marshall registered in 1890 a design for a vase, unfortunately no drawings of these designs have been found. One drawing that does exist is shown. It is design No 381369 registered by Edward Edwards on 23 May 1882, but unfortunately no description or dimensions were given. Perhaps the word 'novelty' aptly describes the output of The Novelty Glassworks, cheap

Ornamental Designs
Class 3 - Glass
Edward Edwards of Bridle
Road Wollaston near
Stourbridge

Above: Many of the products of the Novelty Glassworks remain to be discovered, but one that is known is this. It is design No 381369, registered by Edward Edwards on 23 May 1882. Unfortunately, no description or dimensions are given. Perhaps the word 'novelty' aptly describes the output of The Novelty Glassworks, cheap items of an unusual or gimmicky design.

items of an unusual or gimmicky design.

The glassworkers

Census returns show that quite large numbers of glassworkers were living in Wollaston. In 1851 the figure was 60. This had risen to 142 by 1871 and 160 by 1891. The majority of these were cutters, but there was also a wide representation of other skills in the glass industry, blowers, decorators, makers, stoppers, teasers, etc. Most were probably employed in the glasshouses of Amblecote and while most had been born locally, some had been attracted from other glassmaking areas in this country and some from even further afield, such as France and Bohemia (the latter forming part of the Czech Republic in 2003). Those who came from Continental Europe were all skilled in giving an artistic finish to a piece of glass. From France came glass

Below: In the 1880s and 1890s, Wollaston was the home to a number of highly skilled glass designers who had emigrated to this country from France and Bohemia. A number of the Bohemians lived in Duncombe Street. In 1881 the second house on the left was the home of Franz Hanke, whilst his compatriot, Theodore Kny, lived in a house opposite, since demolished.

painters such as Etienne de Villiers who lived in Duncombe Street in 1881, whilst the 1891 census records Louis Dausier living in Cobden Street, Paul Taillendier in High Street, Charles Hodam in Bridgnorth Road and Prosper Marcham in Laburnam Street. The Bohemians: Joseph Hackell in Wood Street, Franz Hanke, Theodore Kny, Joseph Palme and Fridolin Kretschmann, all in Duncombe Street, were highly skilled engravers.

The outstanding figure in this list of foreign-born craftsmen was Fridolin Kretschmann, regarded by glass historians as one of the most talented engravers of the late 19th century. He was born, around 1850, in Meistersdorf, Bohemia, then part of the Austrian Empire. After learning the basic techniques of engraving, Kretschmann came to London, where he lived from about 1869 until about 1878, working as an engraver for one of the London firms. During this period he married, and his first child was born. Then the family moved to the Stourbridge area when he obtained employment with Thomas Webb & Sons. Initially the family lived in Collis Street, Amblecote before moving to Duncombe Street where their second child was born in 1885. The 1891 census shows that both Fridolin's mother and a younger relative, Adolf, who was also an engraver, were living there with him and his young family.

According to the entries in the Webb pattern books Kretschmann worked primarily on cameo glass in the early 1880s and on copper-wheel engraved glass in the rock crystal style in the late 1880s and the early 1890s. One example of his work, a cameo portrait of Bismarck (see colour section), is in the collection of Broadfield House Glass Museum in Kingswinford. This piece is signed and dated 1886. Several other cameo objects, which are attributed to Kretschmann, are in American collections.

In 1892 Kretschmann moved to the USA where he worked for Corning Glass Co and later for Louis C Tiffany.

Another émigré to America was Frederick Jones. The *County Express* of 21 October 1967 contained the following article:

'A valuable addition to the Stourbridge Glass Collection is a crystal glass tankard, engraved with a view of Wollaston Parish Church and a monogram, which was taken to America over 70 years ago. This has been presented by Mr Frederick W Jones of Brooklyn, New York, a native of Brettell Lane who went to the United States with his parents in 1896. His father, Edward Pargeter Jones, was a glass engraver employed by his uncle William Pargeter, who had a glass decorating shop in Sutton Street (behind Brook Street School) in Wordsley. The tankard has been presented by Mr Jones in memory of his parents.'

The tankard is now in the Broadfield House Glass Museum, Kingswinford.

There was also an American connection for Charles Yates, of Vicarage Road, who was another highly skilled craftsman in the glass industry. He began his working life in 1936 at Stevens & Williams and later moved to Stuarts.

In 1971 his work was commissioned by Harrods and was shown in the White House. The exhibits consisted of glass plates, each depicting the likeness of American presidents. By now an assistant foreman at Stuarts, he specialised in an old technique called sgraffito, which involved scratching designs on the glass using a hard-tipped stylus. He produced 12 plates of each of the American presidents, a total of 444 plates, each taking about 15 hours to complete. The plates sold for £200 each.

Above: Charles Yates, of Vicarage Road, was another highly skilled craftsman in glass. In 1971 he was commissioned by Harrods to produce glass plates depicting American presidents. For these he used an old technique called sgraffito, in which he specialised, which involves scratching designs on to the glass using a hard-tipped stylus. He produced 12 plates of each of the American presidents, a total of 444, each taking about 15 hours to complete. The plates sold for £200 each, and were shown in The White House. This one shows John Adams, who was born in Quincey, Massachusetts, which has a district called Wollaston!

The dairies

The largest dairy-related concern associated with Wollaston was **Ashford Creameries Ltd**. Ronald Ashford began it in 1922, by investing in a pony, a milk float and utensils. He set up a milk round, and after about three months, a motor van was added in order to collect the milk from a farm near Bromsgrove. Ronald and his brother Edward then began milk wholesaling and other motor vehicles were bought. By 1924 premises were required, and Dunn's Farm in Bowling Green Road was acquired. In 1925 a milk cooling plant and storage facility were installed and cream production began. Butter production had been added by 1927 when another brother, Bernard, joined the company. Ice cream plant was purchased in 1928, and in 1929 a dairy shop was opened in High Street, Stourbridge the first of six. In 1935 the milk rounds were sold and the company concentrated on milk wholesaling and its retail outlets.

During World War II Ashford's were appointed as the milk-clearing depot for North Worcestershire and South Staffordshire. They also became a buffer depot for imported cheese, evaporated milk and other goods. The 14 years of food rationing meant that no expansion of the business was possible, although a modern ice cream plant and extra cold storage were installed in 1949. A boom in ice cream sales followed. With the end of rationing in 1954, cream production and butter making were resumed and sales again soared. A limited amount of frozen foods had been sold for some time, but in 1956 they began selling Findus frozen foods and sales increased, with a consequent need for increased cold storage and refrigerated transport. A new deep freeze store was built at Bowling Green Road in 1959-60, but this soon proved inadequate. Ashfords collaborated

Above: The might of Ashfords is seen to good effect in this nighttime shot of their newly completed long store, which opened in 1969. *Peter Ashford*

with John Thompson Transporter Division on the design of a new type of refrigerated van, which began production in 1964, and was to prove very successful. The problem of cold storage space was solved in the late 1960s when a former quarry site in Lowndes Road was purchased and new office accommodation and a cold store were built.

Cold storage capacity and distribution capacity both continued to be increased through the 1960s and early 1970s. Ashford's ice cream had been rebranded as Fiesta in 1962 and the whole company subsequently became Fiesta Foods, rising to become the third largest such concern in the UK. The company was taken over by Pillsbury UK in 1985 and the *Express & Star* of 20 November 1987 reported that Peter Ashford was leaving the company at the end of the year. Pillsbury subsequently sold their interest in Ashfords to Nestlé, who continued ice cream production in Lowndes Road. They in turn sold the site to Tudor Dairies, who ran the site until it was closed in the late 1990s.

There were a number of much smaller dairies that operated in Wollaston at various times:

The first mention of dairies or dairymen in local trade directories appears in *Littlebury's Directory* of 1873 which lists:

- **Joseph Burton**, dairy keeper, The Plough Inn
- **Joseph Cuttler**, dairyman & coal dealer, Upper King Street
- **John Horne**, dairyman, poulterer & coal merchant, Wollaston

Mrs Martin operated **Martin's Dairy** from Duncombe Street from the early years of the 20th century. In about 1907 she was joined by her husband, and later by their son, Arthur Henry, who was born in 1909. Older residents recall Arthur making deliveries with their horse called 'Billy.' *Kelly's Directory* last records the dairy of Mrs Arthur T Martin in Duncombe Street in its 1932 edition.

Kelly's Directory of 1916 records **George Fletcher** of Duncombe Street as a dairyman, and the 1921 edition of the same directory also lists **Harper's Dairy** in Fir Grove. Harry David Harper was married in 1911 at Kinver. In the same year he bought two cottages and a piece of land in Fir Grove to start his dairy business.

Harry had three milk rounds covering Wollaston, Stourbridge, Amblecote and Oldswinford. He worked one round himself with a Model-T Ford truck, while Frank Lane and his nephew Frank Harper worked the others with horse-

Above: One of the largest businesses that eventually moved to Wollaston was Ashfords Creameries Ltd. Founded in 1922, and based in Bowling Green Road, where Fox Covert stands in 2003, expansion into ice cream production and frozen food distribution after World War II created a demand for ever greater cold storage space. The problem this created was solved in the mid-1960s when a former quarry site was purchased in Lowndes Road for the erection of a new cold store. Here, Peter Ashford watches his son David cut the first sod on the site in September 1967. *Peter Ashford*

drawn floats.

At this time the milk was carried in churns and ladled into the customers' own containers. Frank Lane left in 1938 to set up his own business and Wilf Jones replaced him.

In 1941 the men were called up for war service, so the three rounds were consolidated to form two. In 1945 Frank Harper and Wilf Jones returned from the war, and a new dairy was built where milk was pasteurised and bottled. Subsequently the horses were retired and two vans purchased.

In 1958 the business was sold to W F Bache, for whom Bob continued to work until 1970 when they were taken over by Midland Counties Dairies. Whilst working for Bache's Dairy, Bob was voted the perfect milkman in a competition sponsored by a Birmingham newspaper. Bob was featured in an article in the *Evening Despatch & Mail*

Above: Mrs Martin operated Martin's Dairy from her house in Duncombe Street from the early years of the 20th century. In about 1907 she was joined by her husband, and later by their son, Arthur Henry, who was born in 1909. The sign reads; 'A J Martin – Wollaston Farm Dairy – Pure New Milk – Eggs, Butter, Cream & Poultry Fresh Daily.' Both children are standing on a very neat pavement formed from Staffordshire Blue Diamond pavers.

Left: Mrs Martin sitting outside at the back of her house-cum-dairy in Duncombe Street. Older Wollaston residents recalled her husband Arthur making deliveries with their horse, who was called 'Billy.' *Kelly's Directory* last records the dairy of Mrs Arthur T (sic) Martin in Duncombe Street in its 1932 edition.

Above: All members of the Martin family were pressed into service working the family dairy in Duncombe Street. Here are two of the younger members, suitably attired, with a milk churn, from which milk was ladled into the customers' own containers when the milk was delivered.

Below: In 1911 Harry David Harper bought two cottages and a piece of land in Fir Grove to start his dairy business. He had three milk rounds, covering Wollaston, Stourbridge, Amblecote and Oldswinford, one of which he worked himself in this van. After service in World War II a new dairy was built where milk was pasteurised and bottled, and the business was continued until 1958, when it was sold to W F Bache & Sons of Clark Street, Stourbridge.

of 25 July 1967.

Kelly's Directory of 1932 also records Harry Harper of Fir Grove and George Jones of Wood Street as dairymen.

There was also **Fisher's Dairy**, which had been started by Thomas Henry Fisher in the early 1920s. Thomas Fisher was born in Derbyshire in 1888 and worked for Darbys at Barrett's Coppice Farm from 1906. About 1914 the Darbys had a small dairy business, and in the early 1920s Thomas took this over and the family moved to Bridle Road and then, in 1934, to Ridge Street. Milk was delivered in churns by horse drawn float to houses in the Wollaston area. Before World War II, their son John had joined the business. After the war the horses were replaced by vans and by the 1950s all milk was delivered in bottles which required the dairy to be modernised to include bottling, washing and refrigeration facilities. An electric milk float was purchased in 1958 and in November 1960 the business was sold to W F Bache.

Before World War II milk rounds were also worked by **Noel Beddowes** in Bridle Road and by **George Wooldridge** in Wood Street.

Market gardens

In the last 30 years of the 20th century supermarkets have made available a year round supply of fruit and vegetables. Before the advent of supermarkets most communities were dependent on local market gardens for salad items, soft fruit and apples. These market gardens were located in an urban environment, invariably close to the centre of a town, not in the countryside. The produce of these market gardens was either sold by local greengrocers, or more often by the growers themselves, on their premises, direct to the public.

John Roberts, sometimes known as 'Scutchy' Roberts, was listed in *Kelly's Directory* for 1928, 1932 and 1936 as a 'Nurseryman.' He lived in Lawn Street and worked a market garden on the site occupied in 2003 by the houses of Gregory Road and the Ridge Primary School. Access to his premises was through two iron gates fronting High Park Avenue. Gregory Road follows the line of the central drive, which divided the market garden. Eyewitnesses recall walking up the drive and seeing a row of greenhouses along the left-hand side, and 70-year-old 'scrumpers' still vouch for the sweetness of the apples in the

orchard, especially those from the top of the drive!

Charles Layland and family had a nursery on Bright Street, between the Methodist Church and Duncombe Street. This was listed in Kelly's Directory for 1940. All the members of the Layland family: Charles, his wife Minnie, and their children, Chris, George and Annie, worked the nursery. Their contemporaries recall the growing of cucumbers, lettuces and 'cut' flowers, as well as tomatoes, which were grown in greenhouses.

Blacksmiths

Like most villages Wollaston once had a blacksmith, who, in addition to shoeing horses, would turn his hand to most odd-work that required a little bit of metal bashing. The best-known blacksmith was **Percy Wakeman**, whose forge stood next to The Gate Hangs Well, between it and 2003's betting shop. He is first encountered in the *Stourbridge Almanack & Directory* for 1913, where he is listed as a '*furniture remover*' in Bridgnorth Road. By 1915 this has changed to Bridle Road, where he lived at No 32, which was also known as 'Evesham Croft.'

Percy Wakeman is listed as '*blacksmith, Bridgnorth Road*' in Kelly's directories between 1924 and 1940. By 1932 he also had a 'phone (Stourbridge 5500), and had started to serve the needs of motorists. Some remember him best for the pump serving 'Zip' petrol that once stood outside his forge. Apparently local children used to egg each other on to say the brand name backwards! At some

Above: Thomas Fisher delivered his milk in churns by horse drawn floats like this one to houses in the Wollaston area.

Below: Fisher's Dairy purchased this electric milk float in 1958. This shot affords a good view of the Ridge Street Dairy in its final years of operation, because in November 1960 the business was sold to W F Bache & Sons of Clark Street, Stourbridge. 'T T Milk' referred to that which had been 'tuberculin tested.'

Above: Thomas Henry Fisher, who started Fisher's Dairy in the early 1920s. From 1906 he had worked at Barrett's Coppice Farm. About 1914 a small dairy business was started there, and Thomas took this over in the early 1920s, moving his family first to Bridle Road and then to Ridge Street in 1934.

Above: Charles Layland had a nursery in Bright Street, between the Methodist Church and Duncombe Street, in which all the members of the family worked. Their contemporaries recall the growing of cucumbers, lettuces and 'cut' flowers, as well as tomatoes, which were grown in the greenhouses seen in this view looking towards Cobden Street.

time **Billy Underwood**, who lived at 13 High Park Avenue, assisted Percy Wakeman. His son Jack later went on to found a successful motorcycle shop in Enville Street, Stourbridge. There is no evidence that Percy Wakeman carried on trading as a blacksmith after World War II, but he is recorded as a coal merchant trading from his home in Bridle Road as late as 1961.

The 1903 OS map also shows a 'Smithy' on the corner of Vicarage Road and the lane that was to become Gerald Road. Unfortunately, nothing is known about who ran this smithy, or when it ceased to work.

Transport

In the days before the tramway came to Wollaston it was difficult for most people to travel much beyond the distance they could conveniently walk. However, for special occasions, and when the need arose, there was the possibility of hiring some form of horse-drawn transport, such as a brake. **Frank Nickless** provided just such a service, from a cottage that stood near the junction of Bridgnorth Road and High Street. Nickless also sold coal from the cottage, which has continued to provide both fuel and/or transport to Wollaston ever since.

The cottage next became the base for **William E Edkins'** removal and storage business – Edkins' Repository, which relocated to the village from High Street, Stourbridge, in October 1902. For this he built a large storage warehouse to the rear of the cottage, which also came in useful when a large covered space was needed for public meetings, such as political rallies. Following Edkins, both the cottage and warehouse formed the basis of …

Wollaston Garage

Eric Arthur Heynes was born in Harborne in 1897, and served in the Great War as a despatch rider with the Highland Division. After the war he joined a motor trade

business in Sherborne, Dorset. Six years later he established Wollaston Garage as a vehicle repair shop and taxi service on a rented site in Bridgnorth Road. This had been a Green Line Bus Depot in front of which were two petrol hand pumps operated by Percy Smart of Kidderminster. The original Wollaston Garage Ltd went into liquidation on 26 June 1924, and Eric Heynes subsequently purchased the premises, including control of the petrol operation.

On 14 August 1926 the *County Express* reported a fire at Wollaston garage on the previous Tuesday in which cars, motorcycles and three motor omnibuses were damaged. These included a Morris Cowley car, belonging to Mr W Harris (butcher) of Bridgnorth Road, which had been

Above: Percy Wakeman was Wollaston's blacksmith. Sadly, no photographs of his forge have come to light, but this was its site, next to The Gate Hangs Well. By 1932 he also sold 'Zip' petrol, from a pump that stood outside the forge. Local children used to egg each other on to say the brand name backwards!

Below: The Langstone family ran a small haulage business from a yard behind the Britannia Inn in High Street. Here Langstone and son pose somewhat dubiously for the camera, whilst chickens and other birds run amok.

Above: Frank Nickless also provided a transport service, from a cottage that stood near the junction of Bridgnorth Road and High Street. He also sold coal from the cottage, which has continued to provide both fuel and/or transport to Wollaston ever since. His notice reads: '*F Nickless – Coal Sold Here – Brake Hire & Private Parties Accommodated*.' One of his brakes is parked resplendent in front of the camera, whilst a small boy peers out from beneath the horses' nether quarters! *Cary Nickless St Clair*

W. EDKINS,
REMOVER AND STORER,

WISHES to inform the public of Stourbridge and district that he has REMOVED to more commodious premises,

OPPOSITE THE CHURCH, WOLLASTON.

All orders left at 184, HIGH STREET, STOURBRIDGE, will receive prompt and immediate attention.

FURNITURE STORED IN HEATED ROOMS.
MODERATE CHARGES.

FURNITURE REMOVED ANY DISTANCE
By road or rail. Estimates Free.

Postcard will receive prompt attention.

Above: The cottage next became the base for William E Edkins' removal and storage business – Edkins' Repository, which, as this newspaper cutting shows, relocated to the village from High Street, Stourbridge, in October 1902.

Below: William Edkins built a large storage warehouse to the rear of the cottage, which also came in useful when a large covered space was needed for public meetings such as political rallies. Curiously, the sign on the roof refers to the business as a 'Depository.'

destroyed.

Eric Heynes married in 1926 and until 1936 the family lived at the garage. They then moved to Sherborne House in Wood Street. In the late 1920s franchises were obtained for the sale of Bedford and Dodge trucks, and by the early 1930s the firm was selling Morris and Wolseley cars and Morris Commercial vehicles. The business continued to prosper until 1939 when the supply of new cars dried up as a result of the war. The main activity during the war was the repair and maintenance of cars and commercial vehicles and the supply of reconditioned ex-War Department lorries.

Eric's sons, Paul and John, both joined the company in about 1950, and were later joined by their sister Mary. Having supplied Morris, Austin-Morris, BMC, and British Leyland (BL) cars, the firm was appointed a main BL car dealership in 1977. Although highly successful this dealership was terminated by the manufacturer in August

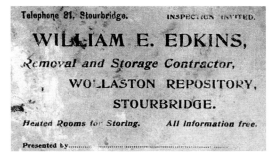

Telephone 81, Stourbridge. INSPECTION INVITED.

WILLIAM E. EDKINS,
Removal and Storage Contractor,
WOLLASTON REPOSITORY,
STOURBRIDGE.

Heated Rooms for Storing. All information free.

Presented by..

Above: One of William Edkins' calling cards. Following him both the cottage and warehouse formed the basis of …

Below: … Wollaston Garage. It had been a Green Line Bus Depot in front of which were two petrol hand pumps, operated by Percy Smart of Kidderminster. The original Wollaston Garage Ltd went into liquidation on 26 June 1924, and Eric Heynes subsequently purchased the premises, including control of the petrol operation. When this photograph was taken in the 1930s a showroom had been added to the front of the cottage, but Edkin's roof board is still in place, as is his repository to the right.

Above: Completing the series of pictures of the cottage, here it is, still standing in 2003 at the heart of Wollaston Garage. To the right, the finial atop Edkin's Repository is also still in situ and visible!

Above: A number of cars, motorcycles, and three motor omnibuses were damaged in the Wollaston Garage fire. These included a Morris Cowley, seen here, which had been destroyed. It belongied to Bill Harris, the butcher of Bridgnorth Road,

Below: A H Guest's Ridge sand and gravel mines provided gravel, building sand and stone chippings. Here they were photographed by the British Geological Survey in 1924. *British Geological Survey*

1982 and the search was on for an alternative franchise. In January 1984 the firm gained Vauxhall car and Bedford van franchises and these have subsequently proved to be successful. In 1988 Paul Heynes retired, but by this time members of the third generation of the Heynes family had joined the company.

Quarrying

As generations of Wollaston gardeners know, the village subsoil is mainly sand. Over the years this sand has been so abundant in places that it was extracted commercially. Sandpits or holes were once worked in the following places:

- between Cobden and King streets
- Lowndes Road
- the site of Wollaston Rec'
- Wollaston Farm, and
- The Ridge.

The latter was one of the most productive of Wollaston's sandmines, and an advertisement in the *County Express* on 1 March 1930 offered '*Rich red gravel suitable for garden paths, building sand and stone chippings.*' All were available from **A H Guest**, Ridge Sand and Gravel Mines, Wollaston.

Subsequently, **T & S Element** is known to have extracted sand and gravel from The Ridge, and for some time operated a 'cracker' or stone crusher. Local residents recall that during World War II, sandbags were filled at The Ridge by the same company and transported to the Birmingham area, especially Austin's Longbridge works. The sandmine on Wollaston Farm was also worked into the 1950s, and caused the first residents on the new estate some problems, which are detailed in Chapter Nine.

Midland Granolithic Co

On 23 February 1931, Stourbridge Council Highways & Improvement Committee approved a temporary erection in Bridgnorth Road for the Midland Granolithic Co. The company specialised in manufacturing a superior grade of

finish for application to concrete walls and floors to produce a smooth granite-like surface. The material used was cement based, but contained granite chippings. A stone crusher was erected on the Eggington Farm site to produce these chippings. The *County Express* of 25 June 1932 reported that: '*the Wollaston effort for the Stourbridge Carnival culminated in a sheep roast and funfair held on ground lent by Midland Granolithic Co.*'

Wollaston Motor Spares

One of Wollaston's most memorable businesses was Wollaston Motor Spares, owned and operated by Don

Left: This is how the Ridge sand and gravel mines were advertised in the *County Express* in the late 1920s. The sand was of a kind known as 'sharp', and was particularly prized for its special qualities by builders. It also came in useful during World War II when T & S Element & Co filled sandbags there, and transported these to the Birmingham area, especially to Austin's works at Longbridge.

Above: This advert for Don Despres yard appeared every week in the *County Express* for many years. It drew many people to Wollaston from far and wide in the paper's circulation area.

to rummage amongst the piles of dismembered cars to find the exact parts they were looking for. The yard was generally regarded as an Aladdin's Cave for obscure and elusive motor spares. Nothing was wasted either, any scrap metal left after the wrecked cars had been dismantled was sold to Round Oak Steelworks.

Responding to HOW's Bugle article, Sam Humphries from Lye recalled that Despres sold things other than motor spares. Mrs Despres was something of an antique dealer. He bought an old 'yard-of-ale' glass from her, and he and his brother also bought some old church bells there once! She also kept animals, including pigs and chickens, plus ducks, geese and guinea fowl. At Christmas orders were taken for the 50 or so turkeys that were fattened-up there each year.

The old Eggington Farm site was home to number of other businesses. Percy Smart, who was an agent for Petter Oil Engines, ran one of these, dealing in and servicing these engines. Midland Granolothic (see above) also occupied part of the old farm site, and in one of the buildings 'Darkie' the Oilman kept his horse. Known also as 'Ben' or 'Billy' the Oilman, he lived in Charles Road, but kept his horse at Eggington Farm and his cart at Wollaston Garage. In the 1940s this 'Oilman' traversed local streets, selling pots, pans, hardware and paraffin. During World War II, some of the Eggington Farm buildings served as the base for Wollaston Home Guard, where they practised their drill and firearm instruction. After the war the Home Guard's former base was occupied by the Midland Tile Co until the mid-1950s.

Don Despres sold his land and moved out in 1964, and went to live first in Fir House, High Street, Wollaston, and then in King William Street, Amblecote. The site was acquired and developed by L Spittle Ltd of 51 Constitution Hill, Dudley, and in March 1965 the name Hamilton Avenue was given to the road of houses built there, this name being formally adopted on 24 May 1967. The legacy of Wollaston Motor Spares still remains as the residents of Hamilton Avenue find from time-to-time when they dig up nuts, bolts and the odd car part in their gardens!

Despres. He was a French-Canadian by birth, and had come to the UK during the Great War after being wounded in France. His trade was engines and vehicles. He married a girl from Cheshire. In the late 1920s they were en route to Honiton in Devon to visit friends when they stopped off in Stourbridge, and got no further! Don Despres started his business in Wollaston around 1933. Initially he rented the Eggington Farm buildings from a Mr & Mrs Simpson who lived in High Park Avenue, although he later bought them. Called 'Wollaston Motor Spares', the firm dealt only with used vehicles, no new parts were bought, all the spares came from cannibalised 'wrecks', something characterised by a large sign at the entrance, on the left-hand side of the drive, which read:

YOU WRECK 'EM
WE FETCH 'EM
WOLLASTON SPARES

People visited Despres' yard from far-and-wide. An appeal by HOW for memories of the business that appeared in *The Bugle* for 13 September 2001 produced this recollection from Waldo Allchurch of Redditch, who was born in Wollaston. He remembered the entrance:

'opposite The Gate Hangs Well was a wide rough sandy drive, rising fairly steeply to the barns and outhouses. There were always old cars partly dismantled and I believe some form of machinery also, rusting away.'

Everyone seems to have 'mucked in' at Wollaston Motor Spares. Don Despres only had one full-time employee, Stan Squires, who lived in Ridge Street, and a part-timer, Albert Perks, who also helped with the animals the Despres kept on the farm. The Despres' daughters recall being paid 6d a bucketful for collecting up the many discarded nuts and washers that littered the yard. Customers too were allowed

Lion Garage

On 3 December 1934 Stourbridge Council Highways & Improvements Committee granted permission for a temporary building for use as a car showroom to Mr H Crumpton of Lion Garage, Bridgnorth Road, Wollaston. There were subsequent advertisements in the *County Express* of 25 January 1936 for Lion Garage and of 1 May 1937 for the Opel Cadet, which was then on show at Lion Garage. The site subsequently became Prestwood Garage.

Gladstone Road sawmill

Local residents recall a sawmill in Gladstone Road. Evidence of its existence was found in the *County Express* of 31 March 1934, which reported that Stourbridge Council Housing Committee had recommended that the Borough Surveyor accepted the tender of Messrs Johns & Westwood of Wollaston for supplying four garden frames for Mary Stevens Park.

Hewitt International Salvage Management

John Hewitt, who started Hewitt International in 1946, followed Don Despres' tradition. The business began in Queen Street, Stourbridge and has grown to become a major provider for the collection, storage, sale, dismantling and disposal of vehicles on behalf of insurance and fleet management companies. In 2003 their headquarters was based in Wombourne, but they had premises in Bridgnorth Road, Wollaston, next to Prestwood Garage, and just outside the village at Coalbournbrook.

of C & V Luxury Coaches Ltd was formed to acquire Cooper and Victor's business and, more importantly, their premises, which became Don Everall (Stourbridge) Ltd's operational base.

At its peak the C&V fleet comprised eight vehicles, all of which were second-hand, and all but two of which were built in the 1930s. Until February 1959 the livery was cream with dark brown lining and flares. In that month Don Everall also acquired the famous Stourbridge coach firm of Samuel Johnson (Supreme) Ltd, and thereafter that company's livery of olive, green and black was progressively adopted for all of Don Everall's Stourbridge coaches.

Away from outings and tours, the mainstays of Don Everall's Stourbridge operation were daily workmen's services from Stourbridge and Brierley Hill to Longbridge. These were worked by ex-London Transport RT class double-decked buses. The building of The Dell housing development in the mid 1960s reduced the size of Don

Above: Wollaston has had a few long-running motor repair garages. One was Lion Garage on Bridgnorth Road. This was begun in the early 1930s by Mr H Crumpton, who, by 1937 had taken an Opel franchise – perhaps a little unwise in the light of subsequent events. In more recent years the site became Prestwood Garage.

Above: George Alfred Cooper and Reginald Boyes Victor set up C & V Luxury Coaches in 1938. At first they operated from Amblecote, but by the end of World War II they moved to a garage at the end of Lower King Street, Wollaston. This is one of their striking adverts.

C & V Luxury Coaches

C & V Luxury Coaches was set up in 1938 as a partnership between George Alfred Cooper, who had previously driven for Samuel Johnson, and Reginald Boyes Victor. At first they operated from 44 Church Avenue, Amblecote, but by the end of World War II they had moved to a garage at the end of Lower King Street, Wollaston. Their advertisements for outings and tours appearing in the *County Express* in 1947 bore this as their address.

In February 1952 the Wolverhampton-based coach firm Don Everall secured a foothold in the Stourbridge area by forming Don Everall (Stourbridge) Ltd, to acquire the business of Albert Janes Ltd of 1 Brook Street, Lye. Thereupon Don Everall began to scout for other local coach firms to strengthen his presence in the area. It was in this way that C & V Luxury Coaches came to his attention. Approaches were made, and on 8 December 1952 the firm

Everall's King Street site, limiting the number of vehicles that could be garaged there. Accordingly, on 1 November 1968 they sold the site, together with the Longbridge services, to Watts of Stourbridge, who continued to use them for a few more years.

Reliance Garage

Harold Downing started this business, which became a limited company on 8 October 1953, in premises on the corner of Wentworth Road and High Street. William Owen Stevenson later joined him. For many years they were Citroen specialists. When Harold Downing left the firm Peter Thomas Foxall joined forces with W O Stevenson. In 1985 Peter Foxall's son Michael took over the running of the garage. William Stevenson left the firm in 1987 and Peter Foxall retired in 1988.

Stourbridge Stockholders Limited

Stourbridge Stockholders Limited was established in the mid-1950s in premises next to Isaac Nash's Wollaston Mills in High Street. The company specialised in the pickling and oiling of sheet steel, and also in shearing this, and transporting the finished product to any part of the UK. The company employed 25 people, and was part of David Fabb (Holdings) Ltd, which went into liquidation in June 2003.

Farley Steel Industries/John James

In 1957 Stour House was built for Farley Steel Industries on the banks of the Stour opposite Isaac Nash's Wollaston Mills works. In 1962 the John James Group, a nationwide firm of radio and TV retailers, bought it to house their hire purchase division. Reporting this the *County Express* of 19 May 1962 envisaged the creation of 100 jobs.

Above: At its peak the C&V fleet comprised eight vehicles, all of which were second-hand, and all but two of which were built in the 1930s. The livery was cream with dark brown lining and flares, and was quite attractive, as shown by this example, photographed on a tour.

Farley Steel Industries moved to a site opposite.

Dr Daniel McDonald acquired Stour House in 1972 when he set up a small factory in opposition to, and directly across the road from, his former company – BSR. Both firms subsequently became part of Astec, and in 2003 Palace Furniture occupied the Stour House premises.

Mamble Road Supply Company

The company was started by Arthur Williams on a site

Below: Reliance Garage was started by Harold Downing in premises on the corner of Wentworth Road and High Street. It became a limited company on 8 October 1953. For many years they were Citroen specialists.

in Mamble Road at the rear of the Golden Lion public house. The previous owner of the land had been a Mr Foley who sold roofing tiles and building parts. The site was levelled and the council later culverted the Withy Brook which ran through its centre. The company were originally landscape gardeners, but later became garden and building suppliers. Mr Williams' daughter ran the business from 1959-1963, and then her brother, Mel, joined her. Mr Williams Sr, who had run another business in Wollescote, rejoined them in 1971. By 1980 they had three lorries for deliveries, but business declined with the recession and the opening of the Merry Hill Centre. In 1993 they became a transport company, Mamble Transport, and relocated to Netherton. The original site, together with the bowling green from The Stourbridge Lion, plus other land at the rear of the pub that Mel Williams had owned for a short time, was sold and redeveloped for housing.

BSR/Sunrise Medical

Dr Daniel McDonald founded BSR as Birmingham Sound Reproducers in Blackheath in 1932. The increasing market for record turntables and changers meant the company outgrew its original site and moved to Powke Lane in Old Hill in 1954. The company name also changed to Better Sound Reproduction. Continued expansion meant the company needed an additional factory site and in 1959 the Wollaston Mills site formerly occupied by Isaac Nash & Sons was purchased. The building of the BSR works was the biggest factory development in the area for many years. It had a floor space of 200,000 sq ft and the cost was £650,000. The River Stour was diverted and culverted beneath the factory. As the river formed both the county boundary between Staffordshire and Worcestershire, and also the boundary between Amblecote Urban District Council and Stourbridge Municipal Borough Council, this created some legal and administrative problems.

In the heyday of the Wollaston factory, fleets of

Below: The Mamble Road Supply Company was started by Arthur Williams on a site in Mamble Road at the rear of the Golden Lion public house. They were originally landscape gardeners, but later became garden and building suppliers. This advert shows their range of products in 1970.

Above: Stour House was built opposite Isaac Nash's Wollaston Mills for Farley Steel Industries in 1957. The John James Group, a nationwide firm of radio and TV retailers, acquired it in 1962 to accommodate their hire purchase division. Stour House was then bought by Dr Daniel McDonald in 1972, where he set up a small factory in opposition to his former concern, BSR. In 2003 Palace Furniture occupy the premises.

Above: A BSR recruitment advert from June 1964. In its heyday the Wollaston factory drew fleets of coaches bringing in the mainly female workforce from surrounding districts as far afield as Kidderminster and Stourport.

coaches brought in the mainly female workforce from surrounding districts as far afield as Kidderminster and Stourport. But after production peaked in 1977, increasing competition from the Far East meant dwindling demand for BSR products and the labour force was reduced accordingly. In 1983 the Old Hill factories closed and the Wollaston factory became the sole producer of BSR record decks. Even this ceased in July 1984, although the company continued trading under the name Astec-BSR, manufacturing components for the electronics industry. This came to a close when Astec sold the site to Sunrise Medical in 1997.

In 1967 Ray Biddle produced the world's first folding electric wheelchair in the Black Country. The following year the 'Biddle Engineering Co' was formed. It prospered, and by 1972 had formed its own distribution company in the USA. Ray Biddle retired in 1983 and Biddle Engineering became part of Sunrise Medical Inc (USA). Sunrise went on to acquire other companies in related fields, manufacturing bathing and walking aids, oxygen equipment, personal hoists, and stair lifts. Sunrise extensively refurbished the BSR site and their whole manufacturing operation was brought under one roof in the new purpose-built building. HRH The Princess Royal formally opened the new building on 6 March 1998.

G R Price Motor Vehicle Repairs

Graham Price started his business as a motor vehicle repairer in Wentworth Road in 1969, just to the rear of Reliance Garage. He continued to trade in 2003.

Pugh Ceramics

Bruce Pugh moved from Birmingham to King Street in 1970. In August 1981 when the business was featured in the *County Express* they had come to specialise in dental crown and bridgework. They had some of the best equipment from the USA and Europe and were also the only firm of their type to be fully computerised. As a result they had attracted work from dentists from all over the UK.

Left: An aerial view of the BSR works which was developed around Isaac Nash's former Wollaston Mills from 1959 onwards. In the foreground, Stour House can also be seen.

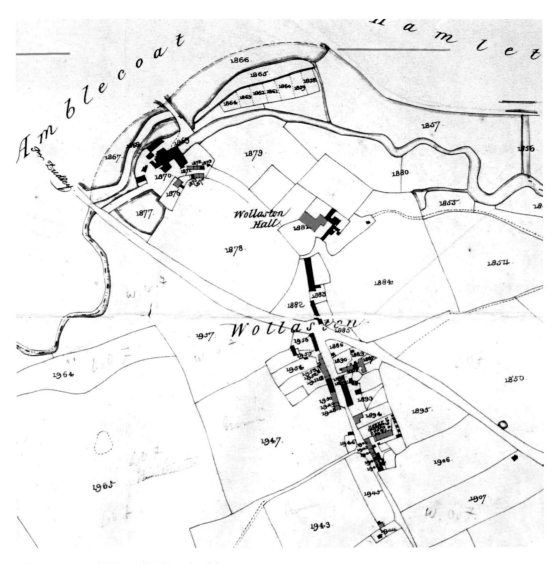

L O Davies' survey of Wollaston in 1827 produced the most detailed map of the hamlet to date. He identified inhabited properties by colouring them red, and gave each property or parcel of land a number. Starting at the top there is Wollaston Mills, at that date being worked by Samuel Hodgson & Co. Five of the cottages around the Mills were inhabited. Below is Wollaston Hall, where the Addenbrooke family were in residence, whilst in the hamlet itself there were 26 inhabited houses.

This series of three watercolours of Wollaston's farms gives a very good impression of what they must have looked like in their heyday in the 19th century. These are the buildings of High Park Farm, which was redeveloped for housing between September 1928 and 1931.

A close-up view of High Park Farm. Its last occupants were the Whitmore family, after whom one of the roads on the Studley Gate Estate was named.

Wollaston Farm was worked until 1935 when it was bought for housing, but work developing these did not commence until 1952. The farmhouse and some of the barns survived as annexes to Meadow Park School when it was first built in 1959.

Wollaston Schools' log-books provide a near daily record of life and events both there and in the village as a whole. This is the cover of the oldest surviving volume of the log-books, which starts in 1863. *St James's School*

Wollaston's Vestry Committee was instrumental in getting the village lit by gas. This plan was produced in 1890, and showed all 50 of the lamps installed to that time. The map's accuracy is proven by the scratched-out lamp at the bend in Laburnum Street, which was relocated into Wood Street.

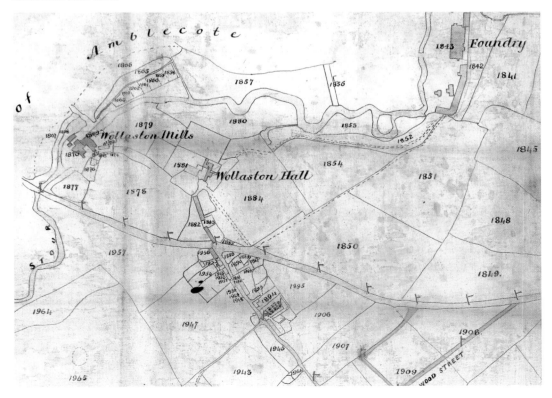

Much remains to be learned about the products of the Novelty Glassworks in Gladstone Road, but some of its output is known, and examples are held in local collections, including that at Broadfield House in Kingswinford. This vase was intact until the person donating it to the museum dropped it in the car park on her way into the building! Gilded red glass seemed to be a Novelty Glassworks specialty. *Broadfield House Glass Museum/Graham Beckley*

Although also red, this second piece of Novelty glass is a much more complicated piece. Its inside is white, and the shape was formed by blowing rather than through the use of a mould. The mottled pattern was formed within the glass itself. *Broadfield House Glass Museum/Graham Beckley*

Left: Glass historians regard Bohemian-born Fridolin Kretschmann as one of the most talented engravers of the late 19th century. From the mid-1880s to the early 1890s he lived in Duncombe Street, which also became home to a small clique of Bohemian glassmakers. Kretschmann worked primarily on cameo glass. One example of his work, a cameo portrait of Bismarck, is in the Broadfield House Glass Museum collection in Kingswinford. *Broadfield House Glass Museum/Graham Beckley*

Below left: Kretschmann's Bismarck piece is signed and dated 1886, when he was living at 10 Duncombe Street. *Broadfield House Glass Museum/Graham Beckley*

Right: Kretschmann moved to the USA in 1892, where he worked for Corning Glass Co. One of the pieces he engraved for them was this gourd vase, which also has gilding by Jules Barbe. Later, Kretschmann worked for the famous New York jeweller Louis Comfort Tiffany. *Jane Shadel-Spillman/Corning Museum of Glass, New York*

Before he left the area, aged 24 in 1881, the Wollaston-born artist Sir Frank Short painted this watercolour of a view of the Black Country from Kinver. *Graham Beckley*

Sir Frank Short won many awards and plaudits for his work. He was also a keen entrant of competitions, especially those held as part of the great expositions of the late 19th and early 20th centuries. He won this medal, which was designed by Louis Bottée, at the 1889 République Française Exposition Universelle.

Eleven years later, Frank Short won a second medal for his work, at the 1900 République Française Exposition Universelle. The exposition buildings can be seen beneath the figures in this design by J C Chaplain.

Frank Short was a member of the Fine Art Committee at the 1908 Franco-British Exhibition, but that did not prevent him from entering his works in competition, nor winning this handsome medal designed by F Bowcher.

Knighted in 1911, Frank Short specialised in etching and engraving, and so the award, in 1923, of this, the Art Institute of Chicago's Frank C Logan medal, given only for excellence in these fields, was a particularly special achievement.

The hand-tinting of postcards such as this tends to obscure detail in the original photograph, but at least whoever did this got the colours right! The same cannot be said of the overhead wires, which were clearly painted over and redrawn by pen. Sections are missing, notably that above the KLR tram on the left! On the right, not all the houses in Hume Place have been converted into shops.
Brian Standish

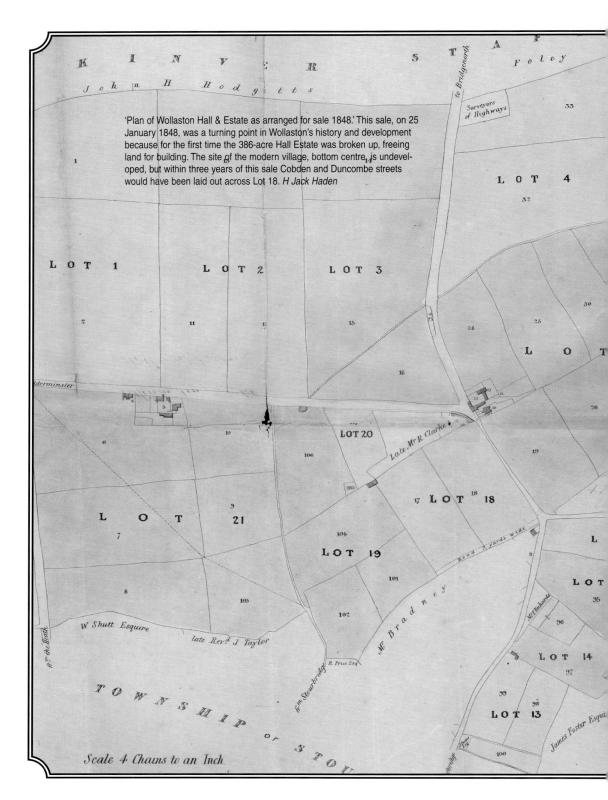

'Plan of Wollaston Hall & Estate as arranged for sale 1848.' This sale, on 25 January 1848, was a turning point in Wollaston's history and development because for the first time the 386-acre Hall Estate was broken up, freeing land for building. The site of the modern village, bottom centre, is undeveloped, but within three years of this sale Cobden and Duncombe streets would have been laid out across Lot 18. *H Jack Haden*

KINVER STAF Foley

John H Hodgetts

to Bridgnorth

Surveyors of Highways

33

1

LOT 4

32

LOT 1

LOT 2

LOT 3

LOT

2

11

15

24

25

30

...derminster

16

26

LOT 20

Late Mr R. Clarke

19

LOT

LOT 21

9

21

7

106

105

104

17 LOT 18

18

Road 9 yards wide

Mr Richards

L

LOT 19

101

8

103

102

Mr Bradney

LOT

95

96

W Shutt Esquire

late Revd J Taylor

R. Price Esq

LOT 14

37

TOWNSHIP OF STOU

39

38

LOT 13

James Foster Esqui

100

Scale 4 Chains to an Inch

112

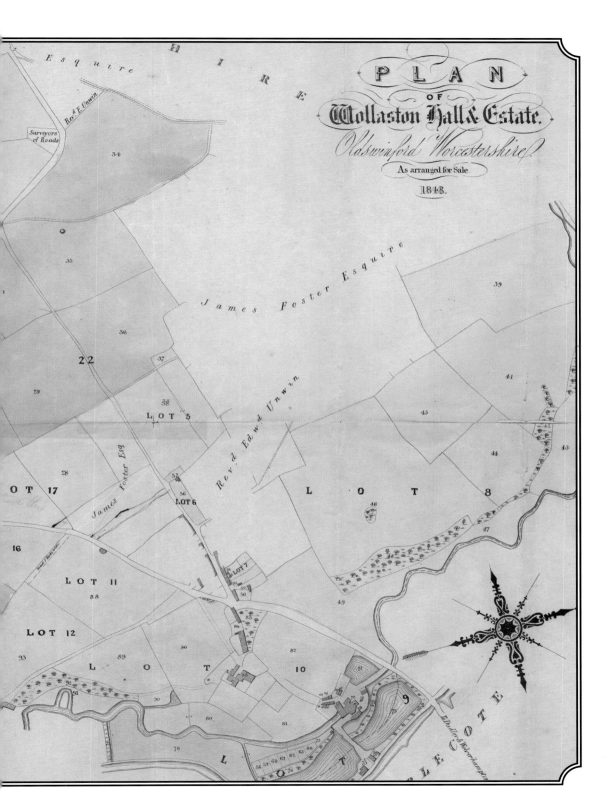

PLAN
OF
Wollaston Hall & Estate.
Oldswinford Worcestershire
As arranged for Sale.
1848.

Buffalo Bill's visit to Wollaston on 28 April 1904 would have been 'trailed' for many weeks beforehand by posters such as this.

The correct title for Buffalo Bill's tour was '*Buffalo Bill's Wild West and congress of Rough Riders of the World.*'

Half of a ticket used to see the 8:00pm performance of Buffalo Bill's Wild West and congress of Rough Riders of the World in Wollaston on 28 April 1904. As impressive as any of the acts was the electric light used to illuminate the performance. The figure '8' notes that this was the eighth show on that tour.

The main souvenirs for sale at Buffalo Bill's shows were pendants, and programmes such as this one.

Isaac Nash illustrated the products of his Wollaston Mills in richly decorated catalogues, of which this is a page from the 1897 edition.

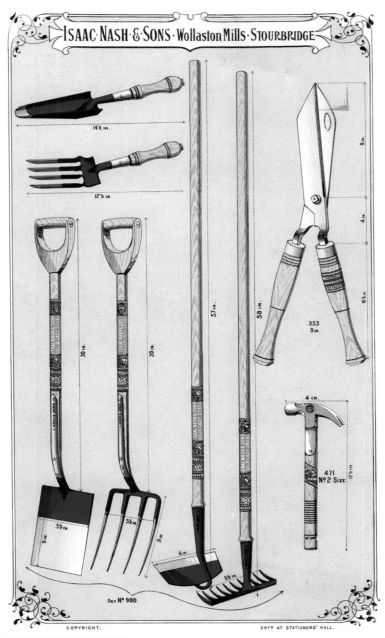

ISAAC·NASH·&·SONS·Wollaston Mills·STOURBRIDGE

SET Nº 900.

COPYRIGHT.

ENTD AT STATIONERS' HALL.

Paper labels like this example were applied to the wooden handles of all the tools and implements Isaac Nash made at his Wollaston Mills. This one was for his warranted hammer.

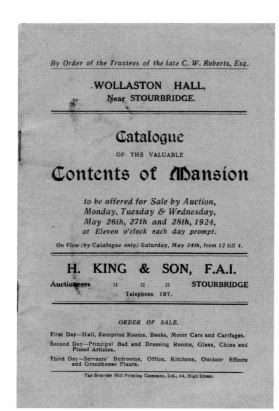

Wollaston Hall having failed to sell earlier in the month did not prevent the Roberts family from pressing ahead with sale of its contents over the three days 26-28 May 1924. This is the cover of the catalogue for that sale. In the event many lots failed to reach the prices hoped for them, and family members bought quite a lot of them.

A tile recovered from Wollaston Hall. It was made by Minton, and is of a pattern produced by them in the 1850s, which would suggest that William Blow Collis had it laid as part of the improvements he made to the Hall during that decade.

Edsel and Eleanor Ford commissioned Detroit architect Albert Kahn to design their new house at Grosse Point Shores, Michigan. Both Edsel, and his father Henry Ford, were no strangers to England, and this may explain how they came to learn about the dismantling of Wollaston Hall in late 1926.

Right: The panelling and fireplace in The Gallery at the Edsel & Eleanor Ford House, seen here, came from Wollaston Hall. *Edsel & Eleanor Ford House Museum*

Below: This panelling came from Wollaston Hall. It was transported to the USA and fitted in place by C Roberson & Co Ltd, a London-based firm of fine art dealers. *Josephine Shea/Edsel & Eleanor Ford House Museum*

Right: Another section of panelling in the Edsel & Eleanor Ford House that came originally from Wollaston Hall. The dentiled top is probably indicative of the original room's ceiling height, and the rooms in the Ford home were designed specifically to accommodate each panel's size and shape. *Josephine Shea/Edsel & Eleanor Ford House Museum*

Above: A detail of the cast-iron fireback in the fireplace from Wollaston Hall that is also now in The Gallery of the Edsel & Eleanor Ford House. It is dated '1605' and bears the initials 'C' and 'T'. It is not known if this fireback was also from Wollaston Hall, but if it was it predates the hall's rebuilding in 1617. *Josephine Shea/Edsel & Eleanor Ford House Museum*

In addition to its dairies, Wollaston once had an ice cream factory, built by Ashford's, who relocated to Lowndes Road from Bowling Green Road in the late 1960s. This tub of their ice cream will bring back many memories to those lucky enough to have tasted it. *Peter Ashford*

A milk order book provided to his customers by Thomas Fisher from his Bridle Road dairy, from where he traded until 1934. Inside they would indicate their requirements for milk, cream and eggs, which the rounds man would fulfil either there and then or on the next delivery.

The first milk bottles had card tops rather than the now more familiar metal foil ones. This is an unused surviving example used by Thomas Fisher. Pressing on the weakened centre button aided its removal.

On 6 March 1998 the Princess Royal opened the new Sunrise Medical factory in High Street, Wollaston. This has been developed from the former BSR works, which itself had been based upon Isaac Nash's Wollaston Mills.

The start of the new Millennium was also the 140th year of St James's Church, something the congregation marked by the installation of this specially designed window.

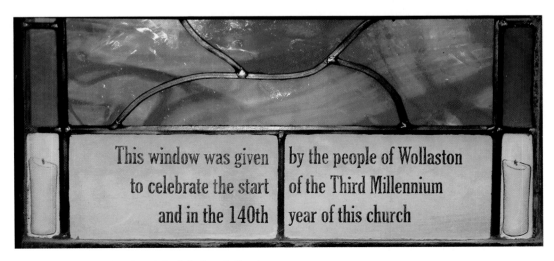

The inscription on the Millennium window in St James's Church.

The Leonard Road Christmas Lights have become a regional institution, and there are even scheduled coach trips to see them. These were part of the display in 2002.

From modest beginnings in 1974 the Leonard Road Christmas Lights have become a major event that takes all year to plan. In 1999 the organisers also began to collect for the West Midlands Air Ambulance, and in just four years they raised £155,000!

This book was brought to you by ... HOW, some of whom are seen here in Stepalong Shoes. Standing, left to right are: Don Price, Jean Hand, Geoff Hand, Muriel Raybould, Ian Williams, Dr Paul Collins (Chairman), Peter Hodnett, Pat Burrage, Peter Skidmore, Mike Powell, Sandra Hodnett, Stan Wakeman and Jack Goldney. Seated, left to right are: Tom Chapman, Betty Ginifer, Hylma Douglas, Cllr June Collins with Toby, and Janet Byard-Jones. *Graham Beckley*

Chapter Six

WOLLASTON AT PRAYER

The creation of the parish

At the beginning of the 19th century the Church of England recognised that there was an acute shortage of churches in the new industrial areas where the population was increasing rapidly. To remedy this deficiency the Church of England embarked on a massive church-building programme. Each decade of the period 1800-1870 saw an increase on the previous decade in the number of churches built, reaching a peak in the period 1861-1870 when 791 churches were built nationwide. This building programme was speeded up by the New Parishes Act of 1843 which made it possible to create a new parish without a separate Act of Parliament, and even before a church was built. Additionally the Ecclesiastical Commissioners, who were in charge of the church's finances, were empowered to divide large parishes into a number of smaller parishes. Wherever possible they endeavoured to augment the church's financial resources by encouraging substantial benefactors to become patrons of new churches. These legislative and administrative changes facilitated the establishment of the new parish of Wollaston.

What became the parish of Wollaston was once part of the ancient parish of Oldswinford. In the mid-19th century as the population of Stourbridge and district grew, churches were built to provide for the spiritual needs of the communities that were developing on the outskirts of the town. Christ Church in Lye was built in 1813 and consecrated in 1839, whilst Holy Trinity at Amblecote was completed in 1842 and consecrated in 1844. The latter church being relatively near to Wollaston served the needs of the village until 1860 when St James's Church was opened. Like its predecessors at Lye and Amblecote the parish of St James was carved out of the sprawling parish of St Mary's, Oldswinford.

The role of William Orme Foster

James Foster, the head of John Bradley & Co, died at his home, Stourton Castle, on 12 April 1853. He was a bachelor, and left the bulk of his substantial estate, approximately £700,000, to his nephew William Orme Foster. In the 1850s, as the 1851 census shows, a large number of Wollaston's male workforce was employed at Bradley's (48%). Predominantly, they lived in King Street and Withy Bank, near to the ironworks, in what are Lowndes Road and Bradley Road in 2003.

W O Foster's motive for giving land and money for the building of a church, school, schoolmaster's house and vicarage are unknown. However, in the 19th century, it was by no means unusual for a wealthy industrialist, such as a factory, mill or mine owner, to provide for the housing, education and spiritual needs of their workforce. It may therefore have been sheer altruism on the part of W O Foster, or more simply the down-to-earth enlightened self-interest of an entrepreneur who recognised that a contented workforce would be more likely to be cooperative, hardworking and productive. Perhaps he also saw the building of the church, dedicated to St James, as a means of commemorating the achievements of his uncle James Foster; or, perhaps, it was simply a desire to emulate his uncle who had contributed generously to the building of Holy Trinity Church, Amblecote. However, irrespective of the motives that can be ascribed to W O Foster, the inescapable fact is that Wollaston had, and still has, reason to be grateful for his considerable generosity.

The building of the church

Exactly when building work began on St James's Church is not known, but as the school was officially opened on 28 February 1859, it is highly likely that by this date work had already started on the construction of the church. Comparison with the nearby Church of The Holy Trinity, Amblecote, gives a likely timescale for the construction of Wollaston's church. Holy Trinity was opened almost 12 months to the day (on 6 August 1842) that its foundation stone had been laid (7 August 1841). On this basis and given the overriding national concern to increase the number of churches, as quickly as possible, it is not unreasonable to assume that the building of St James's Church had a similar timescale. Given that the three buildings, school, schoolmaster's house and church, exhibit a uniformity in terms of their style, construction and material, the likelihood is that brick, stone, and timber for all the buildings were delivered and stockpiled on the site, thus enabling work either to proceed on all three simultaneously, or for the builders to move on seamlessly from one to the other without delay.

The first legal step towards the creation of the parish, even though building work had already commenced, was

Left: There have been many images of St James's Church, Wollaston over the years, but few more beautiful than this one engraved on the side of a glass tankard.

Right: The first legal step towards the creation of the Parish of Wollaston was its authorisation by the Ecclesiastical Commissioners on 10 November 1859. This is the map they produced delineating the parish. To the north and east the boundary was the River Stour, to the west it was a 'line of hedge' along The Ridge, but the southern boundary was an 'imaginary line' which cuts across what is Dunsley Road, High Park Avenue and Swan Pool Park in 2003. *Dudley Archives*

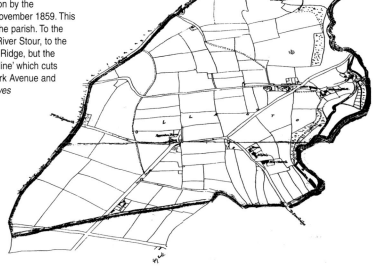

the authorisation by the Ecclesiastical Commissioners on 10 November 1859 of a new parish. Once the church authorities had given the go-ahead for a new church W O Foster stepped in to transfer to the Ecclesiastical Commissioners by a deed of conveyance, dated 27 March 1860, the following piece of land:

'… *comprising 3 closes or fields … (namely) Middle Piece, Mount Carmel, and Lower Little Triangle, south west of the highway from Enville to Stourbridge … as a site for a church to be called Saint James Church, Wollaston.*'

The opening of the church

The formal opening of the church on 15 April 1860 was described in the *Brierley Hill Advertiser* of 21 April as follows:

'*On Sunday this Church, erected at the expense of W O Foster, Esq, MP, was opened for divine service, but it will not be consecrated for the next two months. … The Church will accommodate about 650 persons, and on Sunday at both services it was quite full, in the afternoon several hundreds being unable to obtain admittance. At the afternoon service the infant daughter of W O Foster, Esq was christened, and at the same time the ceremony was performed on a child of the schoolmaster, Mr Hackwood. … The church, the school and schoolmaster's house, which are on a line with it, fronting the Bridgnorth Road are uniform. In front of the buildings there is an ornamental palisade of iron and six handsome lamps lighting the two entrances to the Church and the principal one to the school. … The Church is surrounded by grounds beautifully laid out. This has been the work of Mr Wallace, late head gardener to Mr Foster.*'

On a more technical level *The Builder* (a prestigious national journal for architects and builders) reported on 5 May 1860 that:

'*W O Foster, Esq, MP for South Staffordshire, has erected and presented to the neighbourhood of Wollaston a church, school and master's house, at a cost of nearly £10,000. The church consists of nave, side aisles, transepts, chancel, sacristy, south porch, and organ chamber (adjoining the*

chancel), and tower at the northwest angle of the building. The materials used for the walls of the whole of the building are blue brick and dressings of Bath stone. The style adopted by the architect is that of the fourteenth century Gothic. The church has a tower surmounted with trefoiled battlements and pinnacles. The interior woodwork of roof, seats, reading desk, screen to sacristy, and children's gallery at the west end, are of deal and stained; the roof and stalls in the chancel being more elaborate, and containing appropriate tracery. The organ has been supplied by Mr Walker of London. The east and west windows were painted by Messrs Clayton & Bell; and the building was heated by Messrs Haden of Trowbridge. The whole of the buildings were designed and carried out under the superintendence of Mr G Bidlake of Bidlake and Lovatt, architects of Wolverhampton; Mr Elliott, of the same town being the builder.'

A unique feature of the new church was that pipes carrying steam from John Bradley & Co heated it. This made St James's a very popular church!

On 17 September 1860 the Bishop of Lichfield duly consecrated the church in the absence of the Bishop of Worcester due to illness, and on 5 December 1860 the Ecclesiastical Commissioners formally approved the new church. Despite this, it took several years for all of the usual facilities to be provided. For instance, the vicarage was not built until about 1864, and the bells were not installed until 1865, being rung for the first time on 29 May that year.

Changes and developments in the 20th century

The legal and religious formalities having been completed, St James's Church was now ready to play an important role not only in the spiritual, but also in the social life of the village. The subsequent changes, over the next 140 years, to the fabric of the building, whether structural or ornamental, reflect not only important events in the life of the church, but also show that the church is responsive to the changing needs and demands of society.

Nine months after the death of W O Foster the village expressed its gratitude to him on an inscribed brass memorial tablet, which was fixed to the east wall of the nave and officially unveiled on 27 May 1900. Another memorial with even greater symbolic and lasting significance was installed in 1920. An oak tablet bearing the names of the Wollaston men who had died in the Great War was unveiled and dedicated on St James's Day, 25 July 1920, in the presence of a very large congregation.

The work of Wollaston's second vicar, Hugh Wanstall, was commemorated by the addition of a vestry to the church. This was consecrated on 27 October 1935.

Although the maintenance of the fabric of the building is an on-going concern for the Parochial Church Council (PCC), it was faced in 1939 by a problem that was unusual in its rarity. On 7 February the vicar reported to a meeting of the PCC that the bells had been inspected and pronounced unsafe to ring. He explained that five of the six bells had been hung incorrectly when they were installed in 1865. With the full support of the PCC the vicar launched an appeal for funds to have the bells overhauled. Within a week £350 was raised to pay for not only the repairs to bells, but also for extensive repairs to the church clock. By the middle of August the bells were back in Wollaston having been recast in Loughborough and on 1 October 1939 a large congregation witnessed the re-dedication of the bells.

As the 20th century progressed St James's Church embraced the technological changes that were beginning to have a profound effect on the daily life of its parishioners. In the autumn of 1924 to the obvious delight of church members electricity was installed, prompting the *Church Magazine* to describe the installation as: '*a great success*' and commenting, '*We are now able to read even small print and the cheering effect of having good light is very marked.*'

In 1956 a nationwide trend away from the burning of coal was reflected in the conversion of the church's heating system from coal to oil, whilst the fuel crisis of 1979 prompted a change to gas. In 1990 a sound amplification system was installed.

The Church Hall

As the 20th century drew to a close, work began on the building of a much needed and long overdue church hall, almost a hundred years after it had first been proposed. The *County Express* of 11 July 1908 reported that:

'*A representative meeting of the congregation of St James' Church, Wollaston, was held at the school yesterday week, to consider what steps could be taken towards providing a parish room in connection with the church. It was generally thought that such an institution would be a boon to the parish, and that immediate action should be taken to raise funds for the purpose.*'

Above: The land for Wollaston Church and Schools was formally conveyed to the Ecclesiastical Commissioners on 27 March 1860, by which time the building, designed by George Bidlake, of Bidlake & Lovatt, architects of Wolverhampton, and built by Mr Elliott, also of Wolverhampton, was nearing completion. It was formally opened on 15 April 1860, but not consecrated until 17 September 1860, by the Bishop of Lichfield. This is one of the earliest known photographs of the church. It's 14:05 if the clock is to be believed! *Stourbridge Library*

Right: W O Foster also paid for a vicarage to accompany the living at St James's Church, Wollaston. This was built about 1864 in what became Vicarage Road in 1890. The building, seen here in a detail from a commercial postcard, was identical in style to the church and schools, faced with engineering brick and with limestone detailing.

Above: St James's Church did not get any bells until 1865. These were rung for the first time on 29 May 1865. In 1939 the vicar launched an appeal for funds to have the bells overhauled. They were sent away to Loughborough to be recast, and arrived back in Wollaston in August 1939. Here they can be seen being unloaded on their return. On 1 October 1939 a large congregation witnessed the re-dedication of the bells.

Below: Bells are no use without people to ring them, and Wollaston has benefited from generations of dedicated ringers. Here, Fred Handley, Sid Thompson, Vic Cooper and Sam Thompson practise on something a little lighter in the bell tower.

◄ Wollaston ►
Parish Magazine.

FEBRUARY, 1936.

Vicar—Rev. J. R. BAMBER, M.A.

Churchwardens—Messrs. H. HUSSELBEE and J. F. PEARSON.

Organist and Choirmaster—Mr. E. T. HILL.

Verger and Sexton—Mr. J. H. WORTON 103, King Street.

SERVICES, Etc.

	Holy Communion.	Morning Prayer	Evensong.	
First & Third Sundays	8 & 12	11 a.m.	6-30	Sunday School—10 a.m.
Last Sunday	8 & 7-45	11 a.m.	6-30	Children's Service every Sunday at 2-45 p.m.
Other Sundays	8 a.m.	11 a.m.	6-30	Girls' Bible Class—Every Sunday in the Schools at 4 p.m. (Miss. Sharp)
Holy Days	10 a.m.			Women's Bible Class—Every Sunday in the Schools at 3-30 p.m.

Holy Baptism—Second and last Sundays in the month, 3-30 p.m. (Choral on last Sunday)

Boys' Bible Class—Every Sunday at the Schools at 2-30 p.m. (Mr. K. Haywood.)

Girls' Friendly Society—7-30 p.m., in the Schools, 2nd Thursday in the month
Mothers' Union—7-0 p.m. in Church, 2nd Monday in the month (Mrs. Bamber.)
Fellowship of Marriage.—7 p.m. (Schools) 1st Mon. in Month (Mrs. Battrum, Mrs. Hand, Mrs. Badger).

Above: As the 20th century progressed St James's Church embraced its technological advances. Electricity was installed in the autumn of 1924. Parishioners were kept informed of these advances by the *Church Magazine*, which described the installation of electricity as: *'a great success'* and commented that: *'We are now able to read even small print and the cheering effect of having good light is very marked.'*

Above: A church hall was first mooted in 1908, but it took almost 90 years to become a reality. Following closure of the school, the sale of land in 1898 made funds available for the building of a purpose-designed Hall. Construction work finally began on 28 July 1994, the hall was officially opened on 24 June 1995. Cynthia Powell was its first caretaker and warden.

Although some money was raised, the project was abandoned as the village gave its support to a multi-purpose secular public hall that was eventually opened in 1920 and then closed in 1930. The idea of a church hall was revived in the mid-1950s, but was again abandoned because of a lack of money. However, following the closure of the school, the sale of land in 1989 meant that at last funds were available for the construction of a purpose-designed Church Hall. Building work began on 28 July 1994, enabling the hall to be officially opened on 24 June 1995. The Hall's first caretaker and warden was Cynthia Powell.

The vicars

Since its foundation in 1860 St James's Church has had only six vicars:

- 1860-1913 Rev George Gilbanks
- 1913-1933 Rev Hugh Wanstall
- 1933-1948 Rev Reginald Bamber
- 1939-1945 Rev Oswald Craze (curate-in-charge)
- 1948-1955 Rev Frederic Cox
- 1955-1988 Rev Fred Honey
- 1988- Rev Michael Willows

George Gilbanks

George Gilbanks was born in 1826, and was the fourth generation of his family to enter the priesthood. Originally from Cumberland, he went to school in Penrith before studying at Clare College, Cambridge and was ordained deacon at Carlisle in 1849 and priest at Lichfield two years later. He came to the Midlands as a curate at St Mary's, Kingswinford, where he remained for four years. It was there that he met his future wife, Laura Addenbrooke, who was a descendant of the Addenbrooke family who had

Right: Wollaston has only had six vicars since the parish was formed in 1859. The first incumbent was George Gilbanks, who was formerly curate at St Mary's, Kingswinford. The growing village could not have had a better servant, as Gilbanks threw himself enthusiastically into all aspects of life there, spiritual and parochial. There were few developments and initiatives of the day in which he did not either take the lead or have a guiding hand. There was a great sense of loss when he died in January 1913.

Above: Wollaston Vicarage was home to the first five of the village's vicars. Built around 1864, it occupied the site of the village's windmill. The similarity of its architecture to that of the Church and Schools is very apparent in this view taken in 1964, immediately before its demolition. *Harry Cartwright/Stourbridge Library*

Above: George Gilbanks was also a family man. He and his wife Laura, who was a member of the Addenbrooke family, had seven children. Here he is seen at the wedding of one of his daughters. His eldest son, also George, is on the extreme right.

lived at Wollaston Hall. They were married in 1858. From 1855 to 1859 he was vicar of St Matthew's, Smethwick and during this time the parish of Wollaston was created.

He had met W O Foster while acting as chaplain at Himley Hall and was subsequently offered the living of St James. He came to work in the parish before the church and vicarage were completed, living for a time in Stourbridge.

He took a keen interest in the schools where he was chairman of the managers and, with the help of Edward Hackwood, headmaster of the Boys' School, ran a savings club for the people of the village.

His interests in other parts of Stourbridge were many, including Oldswinford Hospital School, the Corbett Hospital and the Stourbridge Savings Bank. He acted as chaplain to the Company of Stourbridge Volunteers of the 1st Battalion of the Worcestershire Regiment. He was a keen sportsman and until 1894 he conducted the parish affairs single-handed.

Mrs Gilbanks died in 1903. In September 1910 the parish celebrated the 50th Anniversary of the church and the incumbency of Rev Gilbanks. His death occurred on 4 January 1913 after a short illness.

Hugh Cotterill Wanstall

Hugh Wanstall, the son of the vicar of Dawley Magna in Shropshire, attended Rugby School and Keble College,

Oxford. He graduated in 1899 and in 1904 was ordained deacon. In 1905, in Worcester, he became a priest and for the following four years he taught at Rugby School. He was senior curate at Rugby Parish Church from 1907 until he came to Wollaston in 1913.

When a student at Oxford he played both rugby and association football for both his college and the university teams. While living at Rugby he was, for three years, captain of the Rugby Town RFC and a member of the Midland Counties team. His playing career ended in 1905 after an injury.

During his 20 years at Wollaston he forged links with the Non-conformists and was chairman of the Old Folks' Reunion Committee. His death took place in Wollaston on 29 April 1933 at the age of 56.

John Reginald Bamber

Reg Bamber was born in 1900 at Crowle Vicarage in Worcestershire where his father was the vicar. A move to Manchester enabled him to attend Manchester Grammar School from 1912 to 1917. After a short time serving in H M Forces he went to St John's College, Cambridge where

Left: George Gilbank's successor was Hugh Wanstall. A keen sportsman, until an injury ended his career in 1905, he continued his predecessor's keen involvement in parochial matters. Charlie Smalley, the village newsagent, produced this card when Hugh Wanstall was inducted at St James's Church on 22 June 1913.

Right: Reg Bamber came to Wollaston from Crowle in Worcestershire, where he had succeeded his father as vicar in 1927. Succeeding to Gilbanks and Wanstall's mantle, he made the *Parish Magazine* into an effective organ for putting forward his views, and he was not beyond doing this forcibly at times.

Left: During his 20 years at Wollaston Hugh Wanstall forged links with Non-conformists. He was also chairman of the Old Folks' Reunion Committee and instrumental in establishing the tennis club. His health began to fail in the late 1920s, and he died on 29 April 1933 at the age of 56.

Right: An accomplished artist, Reg Bamber drew this sketch of St James's Church in 1935. In September 1939 he joined the forces as army chaplain to the Gloucestershire Regiment. His artistic skills helped to sustain him when he became a prisoner of war early in 1940. After release in 1945 he returned to Wollaston, but left in 1948 to go to Holy Trinity, Malvern. Reg Bamber died on 9 February 1979.

he was awarded his BA in 1921. He spent 18 months at Ridley Hall Theological College, Cambridge and was ordained deacon in 1923 at Manchester Cathedral and priest in 1924. His first post was as curate of Christ Church, Salford from 1923 to 1926. After spending a year at Stretford he returned to Crowle as vicar from 1927 until 1933, when he came to Wollaston with his wife and two young children.

In September 1939 he joined the forces as an army chaplain and was in the Gloucestershire Regiment. He was taken a prisoner early in 1940. In a talk about his time as a POW, given to Brierley Hill Rotarians in 1945, he said that the first six months and the last six months of captivity were the worst times. The prisoners were always hungry. In a report of his talk in the *County Express* of 22 September he said: '*The four years between those two periods were better thanks to the Red Cross as they had a Red Cross parcel, or part of one, every week...and it made all the difference in the world.*'

After his release in 1945 he returned home. In 1946 he was awarded the military MBE. He left Wollaston in 1948

to go to Holy Trinity, Malvern. In 1956 he was made an Honorary Canon of Worcester Cathedral, and upon his retirement in 1970 he was made a Canon Emeritus. Reg Bamber died on 9 February 1979.

Oswald Romilly Craze

Romilly Craze was born in Yorkshire in 1911. The family moved to Worcestershire when he was 6 and he was educated at Worcester Choir School and, from 1921, King's School, Worcester, before going up to Hertford College, Oxford in 1931. In 1934 he left Oxford to study at Wells Theological College and was ordained deacon in 1937 and priest at Worcester in 1938. He came to Wollaston as curate in 1937, residing at 138 Bridgnorth Road, and when Reg Bamber enlisted, he became curate-in-charge of the parish, a post he held until the vicar returned.

He then joined the RAF as a chaplain leaving Wollaston in October 1945. After his time in the forces he returned to Worcester where he held a number of posts in the city and diocese of Worcester until his retirement in 1977.

Left: On 23 May 1937, Romilly Craze was licensed as Wollaston's first curate for 30 years. Blind in one eye, this prevented him from going on active service during World War II. Instead he acted as Wollaston's vicar in Reg Bamber's absence. He then joined the RAF as a chaplain and left Wollaston in October 1945. Here he is seen in his RAF uniform.

Above: The 'team' of Bamber and Craze were only reunited for a few months after World War II, during which time this photograph was taken. Romilly Craze was much admired in Wollaston, and his 'demonic' cycling was something to behold! After his time in the forces he returned to Worcester before his retirement in 1977.

Frederic Ingram Cox

Ingram Cox was an undergraduate at Jesus College, Oxford, graduating in 1932 when he entered Wycliffe Hall, Oxford to study for the priesthood. In 1933 he was ordained deacon in Birmingham and priest a year later. Following his ordination he spent three years as curate of Christ Church, Summerfield before going to Knowle in Warwickshire in 1936, where he was curate-in-charge of St Philip's, Dorridge for seven years.

His next post was in Douglas, Isle of Man, as vicar of St Thomas's until 1948. His induction as vicar of Wollaston was held in June 1948. He was rural dean of Swinford from 1951 until he left St James's in 1955 when he moved to Earl's Croome. He spent some years in rural parishes in south Worcestershire until he retired to Malvern.

Frederick Bernard Honey

Fred Honey was born in Surrey in 1922 and was educated at Bedford Grammar School and Selwyn College, Cambridge where he was awarded his BA in 1948. From Cambridge he went to Wells Theological College and was ordained deacon in 1950 and priest in 1951 at Southwark. His first post as curate was at St George the Martyr, Southwark where he remained for two years before moving to Claines near Worcester in 1952. In 1955 he came to Wollaston where he was to remain until his retirement 32 years later.

In 1972 he became rural dean of Stourbridge and a honorary canon of Worcester Cathedral in 1975. Canon and Mrs Honey retired to live in Bourton-on-the-Water in 1987.

Michael John Willows

Michael Willows was born in London in 1935, and attended Ashmore Secondary Modern School, leaving in 1951. It was not until 1970 that Michael began his training for the priesthood at Wells Theological College. Having completed his course in 1972 he became a curate at Pershore where he remained for two years. From 1975 to

Left: Frederic Ingram Cox came to Wollaston from Douglas, Isle of Man. His induction as vicar of Wollaston was held in June 1948. He was rural dean of Swinford from 1951 until he left St James's in 1955 when he moved to Earl's Croome. He spent some years in rural parishes in south Worcestershire, until retiring to Malvern.

Left: Fred Honey came to Wollaston from Claines, near Worcester in 1955. He was to remain in the village until his retirement 32 years later. In 1972 he became rural dean of Stourbridge, and an honorary canon of Worcester Cathedral in 1975. Canon Honey retired to live in Bourton-on-the-Water in 1987.

1981 he was priest in charge at Astley until moving to Hallow where he was vicar until 1988.

He came to Wollaston the year after Fred Honey retired and his induction was in April 1988.

Swan Street Mission Church

A mission church is shown on the 1st edition of the 25-inch OS map of 1885, set back off Swan Street, roughly opposite to the entrance to Swan Pool Park in 2003. This is also shown on a map of Stourbridge published in the mid-1890s. Nothing is known about its origins, denomination or fate. It is believed that the building was only used as a mission church for about ten years, and that later it became a glass cutting shop.

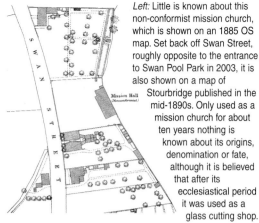

Left: Little is known about this non-conformist mission church, which is shown on an 1885 OS map. Set back off Swan Street, roughly opposite to the entrance to Swan Pool Park in 2003, it is also shown on a map of Stourbridge published in the mid-1890s. Only used as a mission church for about ten years nothing is known about its origins, denomination or fate, although it is believed that after its ecclesiastical period it was used as a glass cutting shop.

Bright Street Methodist Church

The credit for the construction of a Methodist church in Wollaston is due mainly to the efforts of one man, Henry Richards. He had attended a chapel in Stourbridge and had been inspired to build one in Wollaston. Until this was possible he had used his own house, Windmill Cottage in Vicarage Road, as a meeting place.

It was not until 1891 that efforts were made to collect money for this project. In July land was purchased in Bright Street; foundation stones were laid in August; by the end of September the church was ready for the opening services held on 4 October. The total cost was £390 10s 0d.

The Sunday School

A Sunday school was soon established and by 1902 it was reported that 200 children had been taken on the annual treat – an outing to Kinver by tramcar.

Above: Michael Willows was born in London in 1935, but it was not until 1970 that he began his training for the priesthood at Wells Theological College. In 1972 he became a curate at Pershore, where he remained for two years. From 1975 to 1981 he was priest-in-charge at Astley until moving to Hallow where he was vicar until 1988.

Below: Michael Willows came to Wollaston the year after Fred Honey retired, and his induction was in April 1988. He has become involved in all aspects of parochial life, and has maintained and developed a strong congregation at St James's Church.

Right: The land for Bright Street Methodist Church was purchased in July 1891, and the foundation stones, seen here, were laid that August. It was ready for opening by the end of September and the opening services were held on 4 October 1891. The total cost was £390 10s 0d. *Harry Cartwright/ Stourbridge Library*

Repairs, decorations and renovations to the building took place in 1902, 1914 and again in 1926. By 1931 it was proposed that extensions to the classrooms would be necessary. *The Herald*, a local quarterly Methodist magazine reported:

'*It makes a splendid addition to the premises and provides a fine room for teas, socials etc and also for Sunday School work. ... The opening took place on 21 May in the presence of a large asse*mbly.'

Above: A Sunday School was soon established at Bright Street. The gable of this can be seen on the extreme right. Repairs, decorations and renovations to this and to the main building took place in 1902, 1914 and again in 1926.

Youth Club

In 1944 a youth club was formed and became a full member of the Methodist Association of Youth Clubs the following year. Its members raised funds to replace the church's noisy gas lighting with electricity, and this was completed by September 1945. The youth club continued for over 40 years and finally closed in 1986.

Another renovation costing £196 2s 0d was carried out in 1949 and included the purchase of pews. A new fund was opened in 1950, to be used to extend the Sunday School. By 1952 this extension had developed into a new kitchen, toilets and a wash place. The opening of the new facilities took place in 1959 and cost £1,100.

Cobden Street Church

In 1960 a sum of money from a Trust Fund became available. This enabled the trustees of the church to demolish the old building where the entrance had been in Bright Street, and replace it with a new one in which the main entrance facing Cobden Street. Work began at the end of 1960 and the new church was opened on 15 July 1961. A memorial window was set above the entrance porch, dedicated to the founders of the trust and inscribed: '*In affectionate memory of Frank Ingham and Kate Whitehouse Payne, who gave this house to the Glory of God.*'

The organ, which was obtained from Kinver, was dedicated on 10 September, and the total cost came to about £7,500.

The morning Sunday School closed in 1968 and by the end of 1970 the afternoon school had only 52 pupils, down from about 80. In October 1983 first discussions were

Above: Bright Street Methodist Church's 1914 renovations were in part funded by the proceeds from this concert held on 5 March. The foot of this poster shows that Cobden Street once boasted a printer. *Trevor Raybould*

held on replacing the school building. Funds were raised and a rebuilding programme began in August 1987. The old schoolroom was knocked down and by July 1988 the new one was completed in time for its opening in October.

Above: In 1960 a sum of money from a Trust Fund became available, which enabled the trustees of Wollaston Methodist Church to demolish the old building and replace it with a new one facing Cobden Street. This is seen here shortly after opening. *Harry Cartwright/Stourbridge Library*

Above: Work began on rebuilding Wollaston Methodist Church at the end of 1960, and the new church was opened on 15 July 1961. A memorial window was set above the entrance, dedicated to the founders of the trust that funded the rebuilding. This is inscribed: '*In affectionate memory of Frank Ingham and Kate Whitehouse Payne, who gave this house to the Glory of God.*' *Harry Cartwright/Stourbridge Library*

Above: After losing the use of the Gospel Hall in Union Street, Stourbridge, the religious society known as the Open Brethren built a new church on the corner of Eggington Road. It was completed and opened in early September 1926, and was at first known as the Assembly Rooms. In 1950 its name was changed to the Wollaston Gospel Hall, and again in the 1970s to Wollaston Evangelical Church.

In April 1992 six old wooden window frames were replaced with uPVC double-glazed units at a cost of £2,765. In 1997 the church was decorated, and one of the front steps was replaced with a ramp to allow disabled access. At the same time elements of the porch window were replaced by stained-glass panels especially designed by church stalwart Robert Foley.

Open Brethren (Evangelical) Church

A new local church was reported in the *County Express* for 14 August 1926:

'*Some months ago the religious society known as the Open Brethren lost the use of the Gospel Hall in Union Street when it was acquired as a meeting place for the members of the Nationalist Spiritualist Church and a scheme for building a new church was launched. It is situated in Eggington Road and is nearing completion. It is larger than the Gospel Hall and will seat about 150 people. Built of patented corrugated asbestos, it makes a well-designed structure and in addition to the large assembly hall there is an anteroom, kitchen etc. The building is to be electrically lighted and heated by hot water radiators.*'

The building was completed and opened in early September, and was at first known as the Assembly Rooms. In 1950 its name was changed to the Wollaston Gospel Hall, and again in the 1970s to Wollaston Evangelical Church. Administration is undertaken and funded by local church members, but the Midland Evangelisation Trust owns the building.

The appearance of the building has changed very little since its construction, but late in 1979, an arson attack caused significant damage to the side rooms and extensive smoke damage in the main hall. The rebuilding of the western side enabled a kitchen to be added at the rear.

The Breaking of Bread (communion) is held on Sunday mornings and in the evening the Gospel is preached by visiting or local brethren. During term time children's meetings are held on Monday evenings; prayer and bible study meetings are held on Wednesday evenings and an annual conference takes place in July.

Wollaston Free Church

After taking over the former clubhouse of Stourbridge Rugby Football Club in Somerset Drive, members of South Street Baptist Church and their pastor held their first service as a new church on Wollaston Farm at Pentecost 1967. Developments have transformed the building over the years as social areas have been added to the worship area. A lift has been installed and in the 1970s a spire, which is illuminated every evening, was built. To non-worshipers the church's presence in Wollaston was most clearly declared by its bus, which tours the village collecting worshipers.

In the 1990s the church became a partner in Project Ruth, which aims to provide life chances to disadvantaged children, mainly from Roma (Gypsy) communities in Romania, by providing: activities, education, extra tuition, humanitarian aid, hygiene support and education, literacy training, meals and medical help. Project Ruth began in 1992, and by 2003 over 250 children were benefiting from the project, with 140 children enrolled at Grades I–V at the Ruth School in Bucharest, and over 100 children involved in smaller projects elsewhere.

A new foyer was opened at the Free Church in Wollaston in December 1985. Major alterations took place during the spring of 2000, when the worship area's low ceiling was replaced with a new roof, giving it a heightened interior with new lighting and an improved sound system.

This new look church, which is a member of the South Staffordshire Federation of Baptist Churches, was dedicated at Pentecost 2000 with a large congregation present.

Word of Life Church

Wollaston also has a developing church, whose growth echoes that of the Methodists in the late 19th century by being based in a house. The vision for the work of Cephas began in the early 1980s in Edgbaston, Birmingham and it was officially launched as a registered charity in 1991. The core of the vision is to provide a Christian retreat centre. Cephas moved to Stourbridge from its Halesowen Office in 1993, renting a house in the Lye area. Eight years of ministry and counselling to those within the church and the local community was conducted from these premises.

In order for the work to increase, and due to lack of space, a more permanent and larger house was needed. Faith House in High Park Avenue became available, and this now hosts the Word of Life Church. This meets on Sunday mornings and on Thursday evenings there is a midweek life group of fellowship and study. A short-term residential place is available as well as counselling facilities. The future vision of Cephas not only includes a much larger retreat facility, but also an outreach centre for the community of Wollaston and Stourbridge. This will include a coffee shop, with facilities for those with special needs.

Below: Members of South Street Baptist Church took over the former clubhouse of Stourbridge Rugby Football Club in Somerset Drive, and held their first service there at Pentecost 1967. Over the years social areas have been added, and in the 1970s a spire was built, which is illuminated at night. A new foyer was opened in December 1985, and during spring 2000 a new roof was built, giving a heightened interior.

Above: It is hard to believe that this former clubhouse of Stourbridge Rugby Football Club lies at the heart of Wollaston Free Church. This is how the building looked when the church took it over in February 1967. The front of the present church was built on the end of the building seen on the left of this photograph. Wollaston Free Church

Right: Wollaston Free Church's most visible presence in Wollaston is its illuminated spire, which was added to the building in the 1970s. Wollaston Free Church

Chapter Seven

WOLLASTON AT PLAY

An examination of village life over the past 150 years reveals that Wollaston's recreational opportunities and outlets have varied from generation to generation, reflecting changing social and economic conditions. During these years its pubs have played a major role in the social life of the village, not just as a place to drink, but also in providing a meeting place for a number of organisations, and as a venue for concerts and for a wide range of sporting activities.

Wollaston's public houses

There have been public houses in Wollaston since the early 19th century. A total of 15 pubs have existed, although not all at the same time. The Swan in Mamble Road, and the Bridge Inn in Enville Street, opposite Katie Fitzgerald's (formerly the Golden Lion and Stourbridge Lion), can possibly be numbered as Wollaston pubs, although they do not appear in any of the census returns for Wollaston, as the boundary between the village and Stourbridge was the Withy Brook. The Bridge Inn was first mentioned in an 1855 commercial directory, when it was named as a beer house. It was still in existence in 1912, but by 1916 had become a shop, known for many years as Cross's. The Swan Inn first appears under Joseph Walley, beer seller, Mombell (sic) Square, in 1841. It was named The Swan in an 1855 directory, and the premises, Nos 5 & 7 Mamble Road, were still in use as a pub in 1961.

Above: A little further down Mamble Road stood The Swan Inn. Again, although not a Wollaston pub precisely, it was extensively patronised by Wollaston people. It first appears in 1841 listed under Joseph Walley, beer seller, Mombell (sic) Square, and was still in use as a pub in 1961. *Harry Cartwright/Stourbridge Library*

In the 1901 census 15 inns, taverns or licensed premises were recorded, and in 2003 there were still 11 of these in use. Of the 15, three have been demolished and one is now a private house; three have changed their names; another three have been completely rebuilt, and all have had extensions or been altered and modernised. Where once there were gardens and bowling greens there are now car parks.

Labouring in the glassworks or ironworks was thirsty work and the need for refreshment by the employees must have contributed to the number of beer and spirit outlets in Victorian times. Some of these consisted of just a room in a house where beer or cider could be bought to be consumed on the premises or taken home. In the early days, most of the customers would have walked to their local, where much of the beer was home brewed. In King Street and Withy Bank there were a number of pubs near to the houses of the men employed at John Bradley's Ironworks. The old village also had three pubs, near to the rows of cottages in Firmstone Street, Vicarage Road and High Street, within walking distance of the spade works and glassworks.

Many records give dates when there were inns or pubs, and the earliest confirmed public houses are The Barley Mow and The Gate Hangs Well, both of which are marked on the 1827 Oldswinford Parish map. Local directories and the census of 1841 name The Waterloo Inn, and The Albion. In the 1850s the Britannia Inn, The Bull's

Above: Strictly speaking, the Bridge Inn was not a Wollaston pub at all as it stood outside the village boundary. It was first mentioned in an 1855 commercial directory, when it was listed as a beer house. It was still in existence in 1912, but by 1916 had become a shop, known for many years as Cross's. *Harry Cartwright/Stourbridge Library*

Head, The Eagle and The Plough appeared, and six more are named in the 1860s: The Alexandra, Cottage Spring, The Forester's Arms, The Golden Lion, The Rifleman's Arms and The Unicorn. By 1865 all but one of Wollaston's 15 pubs were in use. The only later addition was the New Inn, which was built in the mid-1930s and demolished in April 1991 to make way for new housing.

Census returns and local directories suggest that in Victorian times the job of a publican was often combined with other employment. For example, between 1851 and

Above: There were a number of pubs in King Street and Withy Bank, near to where those employed at John Bradley's Ironworks lived. The Albion is named in the 1841 census. It closed on 31 January 1921. Here, the redoubtable Mary Kendrick glowers out at the camera.

Below: Following its closure in 1921 The Albion become a private house, 23 Bridgnorth Road, which was not demolished until 1975. In 2003, the replacement 23 Bridgnorth Road stands in exactly the same spot.

Above: The Eagle Tavern stood in King Street, and first appeared in the 1850s. It was always a friendly little pub, with a bowling green at the rear. The last licensees' daughters, seen here, also kept horses there. It was demolished in the mid-1970s to make way for new housing.

Below: The Golden Lion is another of Wollaston's 'fringe' pubs. Wollaston's boundary with Stourbridge runs to the right of the building, but like The Swan and Bridge inns it was so heavily patronised by Wollaston people that it was regarded as one of the village pubs. It first appears in directories in the 1860s, and, like The Eagle Tavern, had a bowling green at the rear. Seen here in the early 1900s, the pub became The Stourbridge Lion in 1989 and in 2003 is called Katie Fitzgeralds. 'NWB' stood for North Worcestershire Breweries, which went bankrupt in 1908.

Above: Wollaston's last 'fringe' pub was the New Inn, on the corner of Dunsley Road and Sandy Lane, which was built in the mid-1930s and demolished in April 1991 to make way for new housing. *Harry Cartwright/Stourbridge Library*

were labourers. After 1901 there are no references to publicans holding down second jobs.

A snapshot of the value of some of Wollaston's licensed premises is found in sale notices from 1929. On 14 October, at auction in Birmingham, Atkinsons Brewery Ltd sold 45 licensed properties, among which were four in Wollaston. Lots 37-40 were: The Gate Hangs Well, which was sold for £5,000; the Cottage Spring, sold for £1,500; The Waterloo Inn, sold for £1,900, and The Bull's Head, sold for £650. All were described as freehold and fully licensed. The property descriptions give details of the buildings, accommodation, gardens and the surrounding outbuildings.

Many of Wollaston's licensees stayed for only a short time, but mention must be made of the Billingham family who kept The Unicorn. James Billingham took over in 1912 and was succeeded by his son, Horace James in 1929. He remained there for over 40 years when his son, Eric, followed him. The family connection came to an end in 1992 with Eric's death, thus ending an unbroken 80 years of one family in the same public house.

Other long-serving licensees were: Daniel Bagnall, who was at The Alexandra for 32 years from 1930; James Thomason, who kept The Britannia Inn between 1922 and 1946; and Fred Raybould, licensee of The Forester's Arms for 22 years from 1953; each of them had more than 20 years in the same premises.

Six of Wollaston's pubs closed in the 20th century.

1901, two pubs, The Alexandra and The Bull's Head, had adjoining butcher's shops. Other joint occupations included carpenter, coalman, coal merchant, contractor, farmer, flour dealer, gardener, gravel pit proprietor, sawyer, shopkeeper, and warehouseman; three others worked in the ironworks, while two each worked in the glass trade, tool making or

Wollaston Pubs Name	Address	Type of licence	Earliest record	First owner	First known landlord
The Albion	23 Withy Bank		Bentley's Directory 1841	Job Short 1861 census	John Porter, beer seller, 1841 Bentley's Directory 1841
The Alexandra	115 Bridgnorth Rd	Beer & cider 1943	1861 census	Bents Brewery	Samuel Rock 1861 census
The Barley Mow	129 High Street	Alehouse 1943	Oldswinford parish map 1827	Thos Siviter 1827 schedule	Richard Clark 1827 schedule
Britannia Inn	High Street	Alehouse 1943	Deeds of 1839	Samuel Bullus 1851 census	Samuel Bullus, Melville's Directory
The Bull's Head	62 High Street	Alehouse 1943	Melville's Directory 1852	Benjamin Brazier 1851 census	Benjamin Brazier, 1852 Melville's Directory & 1861 census
Cottage Spring	Enville Rd (1861) Withy Bank (1871)	Alehouse 1943	1861 census	William Bristow 1851 census	George Hill, 1861 census
Eagle Tavern	Lower King Street	Alehouse	Melville's Directory 1852	James Mogg 1851 census	James Mogg, beerseller, 1852 Melville's Directory 1852
The Forester's Arms	Bridgnorth Road & The Ridge	Beer, cider & wine 1943	Opened 1852	Thomas Cooper 1852 built house	Thomas Cooper, 1861 census
The Gate Hangs Well	1 High Park Avenue	Alehouse 1943	Oldswinford parish map 1827	Richard Clark 1827 schedule	James Giles, 1827 schedule Thomas Pardoe, Pigot's Directory, 1835
The Golden Lion	97 & 187 Enville St		Jones's Directory 1865	Bents N W Breweries	Thomas Whiston, 1873
New Inn	Dunsley Road		c1930	Bents M & B	Harold Hinton
The Plough Inn	127 & 154 Bridgnorth Rd	Alehouse 1943	Francis White Directory 1851		Jasper Mogg, 1855 Directory
The Rifleman's Arms	9 Wood St (named before 1867)	Alehouse 1943	Deeds 1856	Edward Moore	Edward Moore, 1861 census; house built 1860, from deeds
The Unicorn	145 Bridgnorth Road	Beer & cider 1943, billiards 1929	Jones's Directory 1865	Joseph Lakin	Built by J Lakin, 1859, 1 room opened as beer house after 1861
The Waterloo Inn	Withy Bank, Enville Sreet (1861), Bridgnorth Rd (1871)	Alehouse 1943	Oldswinford parish map 1827	John Hampton 1841 Bentley's Directory	Thomas Church, 1841 Bentley's Directory, Mary Cox 1861 census

Below: Two of Wollaston's pubs, The Alexandra and The Bull's Head, had adjoining butcher's shops. The 'Alex' appeared in the 1860s, and it had one of the village's longer serving landlords, Daniel Bagnall, who was there for 32 years from 1930. The pub was renamed 'The Princess' in September 1997.

Above: The longest association between any family and one of Wollaston's pubs was that of the Billinghams who kept The Unicorn. James Billingham took over in 1912 and was succeeded by his son, Horace James in 1929, who remained there for over 40 years; then his son, Eric, followed him. Eric's death in 1992 ended the family's 80-year long connection with the pub. Here The Unicorn is seen before it was remodelled in the mid-1990s.

Home brew	Name changes	Alterations
Yes	None	Closed 31.01.1921
No	October 1997 The Princess	Enlarged 1907
No	None	2nd rebuild c1965
To 1975	None	One cottage extended to 3
No	1871 census Triangle Inn	Garden at rear now car park
No	None	Bowling green & garden at rear
No	Eagle Inn	Bowling green at rear - closed 1980s
To 1935	None	Extended, date unknown
No	None	Bowling green & garden
Yes	Stourbridge Lion Katie Fitzgeralds	Bowling green at rear Demolished April 1991
No	1901 census Plough Hotel	Rebuilt c1905
No	None	Closed 1978, a house 2003
To 1963	None	Extension built in 1990s
No	None	Moved from opposite side of the road

The first was the Bridge Inn, which closed c.1914, as mentioned above, followed by the Albion, which closed on 31 January 1921, becoming a house, 23 Bridgnorth Road, which was demolished in 1975. Both the Swan Inn and the Eagle Tavern were closed and knocked down to make way for housing improvements, in the 1960s and 1970s respectively, as was the New Inn, which was demolished in April 1991. Still standing in 2003 is the former Rifleman's Arms, which served its last pint in 1978 before becoming a private house.

Buffalo Bill's Wild West & Congress of Rough Riders of the World

One of the most indelible memories formed in the minds of people living in Wollaston in the early part of the 20th century was the visit of Buffalo Bill's Wild West & Congress of Rough Riders of the World, which took place on 28 April 1904. Two shows were staged, in a field that formed part of Eggington Farm. In 2003 this is the area enclosed by Bridgnorth Road, Bridle Road and Meriden Avenue. This land had been sold by private treaty on 22 August 1903, but clearly nothing had been done with it by the following spring.

The visit by Buffalo Bill was part of his '*Last and Final Farewell Tour of England, Wales & Scotland*', so-called because he had already made a final tour of Europe, including the UK, in 1903! It opened in Stoke-on-Trent on 24 April 1904 and visited 130 other towns and cities, before completing its final engagement back in Hanley on 21 October 1904. During the course of this show travelled 4,114 miles by rail, and a further 441 miles from railway sidings to showgrounds and back again.

The shows, and the tour, were masterpieces of what today is called logistics. They had been masterminded by none other than the late Phineas Taylor Barnum, the famous circus promoter, and managed by Barnum's partner James Bailey. Showgrounds were scouted and secured by an advanceman, and advance publicity was provided by 'Major' John M Burke, the General Manager and PR man, who gave out copious press releases. Following the tour, the Wild West Show sailed back to New York from Liverpool, having covering some 10,000 miles in seven months.

Wollaston was the fourth venue on the tour, which had already called at Nuneaton and Walsall after Stoke, and went on to perform at Wellington in Shropshire on 29 April.

In the build-up to the shows the *County Express* became almost breathless with excitement over the forthcoming spectacle:

'Buffalo Bill's Wild West Show and Congress of Rough Riders of the World will visit Stourbridge for one day on Thursday week, April 28th. The show will be accommodated in the spacious field at the junction of Bridgnorth Road and High Street, Wollaston. Two performances will be given, the grounds being illuminated for the evening by the special electric apparatus, which Buffalo Bill brings with

Above: Buffalo Bill, photographed in 1903, the year before he visited Wollaston with his touring Wild West & Congress of Rough Riders of the World show.

him. The ground is very conveniently situated, being at the junction of the Stourbridge and Kinver tram routes, and is easily accessible by tram from all parts of the district.'

This intensity was maintained in their coverage of the preparation for the shows:

'The Wild West Show arrived via the GWR in three special trains consisting of 16, 19 and 20 cars respectively. Each of the cars is 54ft long by 8ft wide, and is fitted with American automatic couplings at one end and British couplings at the other, as well as Westinghouse and vacuum brakes. Seventeen of the cars were laden with the horses, 22 were laden with the great road wagons, and nine sleeping cars contained 'warriors of all nations', workmen, etc. The work of unloading the railway cars was accompanied without a hitch, and the road wagons conveyed the paraphernalia to the show ground at Wollaston. Here… an immense canvas town had been erected for the temporary accommodation of men and horses, and an army of workmen were busily engaged in the erection of a huge quadrangular tent for the reception of visitors to the show. This structure provides for the seating of 13,000 spectators, leaving the centre an immense area for the performance. The stables are a model of neatness, cleanliness and multum-in-parvo, which is essential in a travelling concern. The tepees of the Indians were visited and the Indian Chief – Two-Elk – greeted us good-humouredly with his impassive 'How!''

Two shows were staged at 2:00pm and at 8:00pm, with over 8,000 people seeing them in total. The evening performance was lit by electricity, which was almost as impressive to many of those attending as anything that took

Below: The Rifleman's Arms in Wood Street first appeared in the 1860s. It went on to play an important role in fostering the development of football in Wollaston, but served its last pint in 1978, becoming a private house.

place during the performances. The programme for both shows was the same:

- Overture – The Star Spangled Banner
- General Review – Col Cody introduces the Congress of Rough Riders of the World to the audience
- Exhibition of various methods of riding: Cowboy, Cossack, Mexican, Arab, North American Indian
- Artillery Drill – Veterans of the US Artillery with muzzle-loading cannon
- Life Saving – The mortar carrying lifeline and breeches-buoy
- Col W F Cody – Feats of shooting from horseback

- Pony Express Riding – Post and telegram delivery in the days before the transcontinental railway
- A Prairie Emigrant Train – Crossing the Plains, with Indian attack!
- Military Exercises by Veteran English Cavalrymen
- Riding Exhibition – American Girls from the Frontier

Above: Buffalo Bill's shows and tours were masterpieces of what is called logistics today. The late Phineas Taylor Barnum, the famous circus promoter, had masterminded them. One of his innovations was 'generic' posters like this one, which is contemporary to the Wollaston shows.

Left: This standard block advert appeared in the County Express in the build up to Buffalo Bill's shows on 28 April 1904. It was accompanied by almost 'breathless' editorial, which helped to build up anticipation for the day.

Above: Both of Buffalo Bill's shows were staged on one of Eggington Farm's fields, at the junction of Bridgnorth Road and High Street. So that his entourage could get on to the field, panels of the fencing seen in the foreground here had to be removed. Behind this, a breakfast party is about to set out from The Unicorn. The wooden building was the pub's brewery.
Heather Billingham

- The Horse Thief – Justice in Frontier Days
- Mexicans – Lasso skills
- Johnny Baker – Young American Marksman
- Custer's Last Fight – A re-enactment of the events in Montana on 25th June 1876
- Arab and Japanese Horsemen – Native sports
- Cowboy Fun – Severe tests of horsemanship
- Cossacks – Feats of horsemanship from Russia
- Military Exercises – Veterans from the US 6th Cavalry
- Indian Attack on the Deadwood Stagecoach
- Bareback Horse Racing by Indian Boys
- Carter, The Cowboy Cyclist – Jumping a 56ft chasm in a 171ft plunge!
- Ranch Life in the West – Indian Attack on a Settler's Cabin
- A Parting Salute – Col W F Cody and the entire company

The evening show was marred by the collapse and subsequent death of one of the audience: David Wright aged 56 of 11 Vicarage Road. He went out to see the show at 7:00pm, but at 7:30pm collapsed near to the ticket office and was found by PC Halford, who took him home. Sadly David Wright died at 11:00pm the same night.

Memories of Buffalo Bill

Buffalo Bill may only have been in Wollaston for less than one day, but his visit clearly left an indelible memory in everyone who experienced it in some way. Many recalled the evening performance, which was lit by electricity. This would have been the first such outdoors lighting most would have seen.

In connection with the screening of the musical film *Annie Get Your Gun* at the Savoy Cinema in Stourbridge in January 1951, the *County Express* asked for readers' memories of Buffalo Bill's Wild West Show 47 years earlier. Mr C Pratt of 8 Whitmore Road recalled being commissioned by Buffalo Bill to remove railings around the field so that 'a grand entry' could be effected, and to re-erect them later. For this work he received £1 from Buffalo Bill, payment being made personally in his elaborate caravan.

Mr C H Smith of 'Jesmond', Stourbridge, said:

'I well remember the great trek of the show from the Stourbridge Junction station to the Wollaston field opposite Cobden Street and Duncombe Street, via Brook Street and Swan Street. It was magnificent – thrilling, especially to us boys who had read every Buffalo Bill book. I can still picture Col. Cody riding round the great arena on a beautiful white horse, with his gun, accompanied by another rider with a basket of white clay balls, which were thrown or shot into the air for Buffalo Bill to shoot at. It was a clever performance – he never missed.'

Joe Burrows of Cross Walks, Lye, helped to shoe the horses, and added: *'Buffalo Bill was served with lunch at the Plough Inn, Wollaston.'*

The event also recurred in the events recalled in the *County Express* by Wollaston couples celebrating Golden Wedding Anniversaries. In March 1967, Mr & Mrs Hamblet of Lady Grey's Walk, remembered when Buffalo

Bill came to Wollaston and most of the estates were fields, and, in August 1973, Mary and Norman Rabey put Buffalo Bill's visit at the top of the list of many memorable events they had seen in the village.

Above: Most of the stupendous things seen by those who attended either of Buffalo Bill's shows in Wollaston are mentioned in this newspaper advert. Fifty years later, it was the electric light that illuminated the evening performance that most people remembered. It would be another 20 years before a public electricity supply would be available in the village.

BUFFALO BILL
(Hon. W. F. CODY).

Above: An illustration that appeared on the cover of the souvenir programme sold at Buffalo Bill's shows.

Below: The right-hand portion is almost half of a ticket for the 8.00pm night performance of Buffalo Bill's Wild West & Congress of Rough Riders of the World in Wollaston on 28 April 1904. An impression of how the whole ticket looked is given by pairing this up with a generous half of a ticket from his 1903 tour for another evening show at Aston Pleasure Grounds.

Fetes and carnivals

Like many communities Wollaston people enjoyed an opportunity to let their hair down and to dress up. Before the motorcar was accessible to all, and when holidays away from home were rare, a carnival or fete was a very popular and well-attended event. Invariably they were held to raise money for some worthwhile cause. At the end of the 19th century fetes in aid of the Corbett Hospital were hugely popular, one held on 7 August 1893 in fields off High Park Avenue was estimated to have attracted a crowd in excess of 4,000, or twice the population of Wollaston at that time:

HIGH PARK, WOLLASTON

BANK HOLIDAY, AUGUST 7TH 1893.
(IN AID OF THE CORBETT HOSPITAL)

GRAND FETE & ILLUMINATION.

BAND of the 1st V.B. WORCES. REGIMENT
and the
AUBER ORCHESTRAL BAND.

MONS. VOLA

and

MDLLE. VERA
In their celebrated Flying Trapeze and Mid-air Performances.

CLIFFORD & CLARKE.
Knockabout Negro Comedians, Stump Orators, Step Dancers, &c.

PROFESSOR BATE,
the gifted Ventriloquist, in his Popular Entertainment "FUNNY FOLKS,"
introducing his High-class Mechanical Figures.

PROMENADE CONCERTS.

Mr. HOWARD BENTLEY, Zither Banjoist; Mr. WILL GUEST, London Mandoline Expert; Mr. CHARLES BREEZE, Tenor; Mr. HOMER, Baritone; Mr. DAVIES, Bass.

THE ORPHEUS GLEE SINGERS.

DANCING, BALLOON ASCENTS, concluding with a GRAND DISPLAY OF FIREWORKS.

Refreshments will be provided.

**ADMISSION, SIXPENCE
GATES OPEN AT TWO O'CLOCK**

ALF. DOODY}
W. SEARLE } Joint Secs.

In 1913 and 1914, fetes were held in the grounds of Wollaston Hall to raise funds for the proposed Public Hall, and were adjudged to have been a great success. Twenty years later, in 1932, the programme for Carnival Week (11-18 June) included the novel idea of an open-air dance on The Crescent, whilst on 3 October 1931 the *County Express* carried a report on:

'*Grass Track Motoring. In aid of Wollaston's efforts for the Corbett Hospital an open rally and grass track meeting was held by the Wollaston Carnival Committee in conjunction with the Stourbridge Motor, Motor-cycle and Aero Club. It was held in a field off High Park Avenue and a good-sized track had been roped off. – Among the chief features was the driving of Mr Frank Hallam, chairman of Stourbridge Motoring Club and the well-known Ariel rider, of a Lagonda 14hp car in which he had raced at Brooklands at Whitsuntide.*'

In the 1960s successful events were staged to raise money for the Wollaston Old Folks' Building fund for a proposed Senior Citizens' Centre. The *County Express* of 4

June 1966 reporting on Wollaston's Gala and Gymkhana held on the 'Rec' said:

'*In the past the two events have been several weeks apart, but it was decided to save money on tentage by following Saturday's Gala with the gymkhana on Whit Tuesday. The main event in the horse show and gymkhana was The Daily Express National Foxhunter competition.*'

These events, with a wide-range of sideshows, displays and competitions, were popular with people of all ages. This is shown by the huge crowds that attended the fetes organised by Stourbridge Rugby Club, between 1961 and 1964 on their ground off Vicarage Road. At least 12,000 are estimated to have attended the final fete.

The ironworks reading room

Important though the role of the pubs was, not all sporting and social activities were pub-based. At the beginning of the 20th century there was effectively a working-men's club, which provided a range of sporting, cultural and recreational facilities. The *County Express* of 19 October 1901 reported the:

'***Opening of Stourbridge Ironworks Reading Room***. *On Saturday the winter session at the reading room in connection with Messrs Bradley and Co's Stourbridge Ironworks, was commenced by a social evening and concert. There was a crowded attendance, including Mr R Lowndes and Mr C Cole. In opening the proceedings Mr Lowndes said it was a great gratification to them to see so many present to show their interest in the institute. It had rather been allowed to lapse recently, but they all hoped in the future it would be a very potent influence for good. What was especially wished was that in one way or another every working-man on the ground should become interested. They now had a bowling club, and next year hoped to have a cricket club; and a book would be placed in the reading room for suggestions from the members as to what forms of amusement or recreation they would wish. All such suggestions would receive the committee's earnest consideration, and if any were found practicable, be quite sure the necessary steps would be taken to carry the suggestions out. ... During the interval selections were given on the gramophone. Light refreshments were served during the evening and were greatly appreciated by all.*'

Air-gunnery

Another popular pub-based sport in the early years of the 20th century was air-gunnery. Many pubs had an air gun club with an indoor range. The *County Express* regularly published match results along with the Air Gun League table. This sport was very popular in the years following the ending of the Boer War in 1902. That war had revealed deficiencies in the marksmanship of the British soldier. Consequently the government unofficially encouraged air gun clubs as they were seen as a way of improving the overall standard of marksmanship. A typical report of this period was that in the *County Express* of 6 June 1908 entitled:

'***Air gun supper at The Rifleman's Arms***. *On Monday, at the conclusion of the season, the annual supper was held at The Rifleman's Arms, Wollaston, in connection with the air gun club. Upwards of 30 members enjoyed the excellent fare provided by the host, Mr Whittaker.*'

Bowls

At the beginning of the 20th century at least five pubs (the Cottage Spring, The Eagle, The Gate Hangs Well, The Golden Lion and The Unicorn) had a bowling green, and in all probability other pubs had one as well. The *County Express* of 11 April 1903 carried this report on The Eagle Inn Bowling Club:

'*The opening meeting of this club was held on Monday last when over 30 members were enrolled. The host, Mr F Millinchamp, (landlord) has unfortunately had great trouble with the green, but it is now in very fair condition and the season's prospects are very rosy.*'

Three years later the *County Express* reported the opening of The Gate Hangs Well Club on 21 April 1906:

'*The formal opening of the Gate Hangs Well Bowling Club took place today, a good muster being present. Mr T Edkins, president, performed the ceremony, expressing the pleasure of being present, and offering good prizes to be bowled for during the season. ... A word of praise is due to the host, Mr T Higgins, (landlord) for the manner in which he has prepared the greens, which are in excellent condition.*'

The role of the church and the schools

The church and the schools also played an important part in promoting recreational activities and in providing a meeting place for group activities. In October 1921 the

Above: At the beginning of the 20th century at least five Wollaston pubs (the Cottage Spring, The Eagle, The Gate Hangs Well, The Golden Lion and The Unicorn) had a bowling green. This is the club that met at The Golden Lion, photographed on the green there before the Great War. Who the man and the little boy are, lurking in the shrubs behind, may never be known.

Above: The Eagle Inn Bowling Club held its inaugural meeting on 11 April 1903. Here the pub's landlord enjoys a game of bowls. The houses in the background are in King Street.

Below: The inaugural meeting of The Gate Hangs Well Bowling Club was held on 21 April 1906. Praise was lavished upon the landlord, Mr T Higgins, for the greens, which were said to be in excellent condition. Although not confirmed, this photograph may well record that first meeting. Certainly the variety of headgear is noteworthy.

Above: The Church promoted many activities for young people, including football. Here curate-in-charge, Romilly Craze, stands proudly with the Wollaston Boys Club team who had just won the Molineux Shield in 1940. The photograph was taken by the pavilion at Stuarts glassworks in Wordsley. Holding the shield is Reg Thatcher, who would play a leading role in forming Wollaston Wanderers FC after World War II.

Below: Sunday Schools also provided activities for young people. This smartly turned out bunch are a group of Sunday School teachers and pupils at Bright Street Methodist Church in the 1930s. They include members of the Martin family, who ran a dairy in Duncombe Street.

Wollaston Athletic Club was formed. It was to be run in conjunction with the existing St James's cricket and tennis teams. The Chairman was Hugh Wanstall and the vice-chairman was Joe Pearson. The *County Express* of 23 February 1924 had a report on the AGM of St James's Cricket Club, and contains details of the fixtures already arranged for the coming season. Matches against Belbroughton, Chaddesley Corbett, Enville and Hagley, possibly indicate that Wollastonians of this period saw themselves as living in a semi-rural village.

In February 1920 a meeting was held in Wollaston Schools to form an orchestral society. By May weekly Friday night practices were taking place in the school. How often the orchestra performed in public is not known, but there is record of a concert given in the Public Hall on 3 November 1921, as part of a social evening.

Cross-country running

Intriguingly, in the 1920s The Plough Inn appears to have been used as the base for a branch of Birchfield Harriers, as there were a number of reports in the *County Express* in 1921-22 of cross-country runs, organised by Birchfield Harriers, starting and finishing at The Plough.

Clubs and societies

Over the last 100 years Wollastonians have organised a wide variety of clubs and societies to cater for their leisure-time needs. Whilst most clubs have been of a sporting nature there have been others, such as cage birds or quilting, which have had a more limited or specialist appeal. Some have had a very short life, whilst others have lasted longer, albeit with fluctuating fortunes in terms of both achievement and membership. Regrettably in the second half of the 20th century the number of clubs and societies in Wollaston has declined as people have become affluent and lifestyles have changed. Consequently, many people now look beyond the village for their leisure and recreational activities. Equally regrettable is that few records, if any, have survived of the many clubs which are known to have existed; this is particularly true of soccer and cricket clubs, some of which lasted for one or two generations only.

Rugby in Wollaston

Stourbridge Rugby Club was founded in 1876. In its early years the club had a chequered history during which it played on a number of different grounds, struggled to raise a team, and on two separate occasions folded. It was revived in 1921, playing first at Clent before moving to Chawn Hill. Neither of these locations was satisfactory and so in 1923 the club moved to Wollaston to begin a long and happy association with the village.

The new ground was in Vicarage Road on land that not only adjoined the old Vicarage, but also belonged to the Church. This land, which drained extremely well, was considered to be a great improvement on the Chawn Hill quagmire. The only snag seemed to be the possible loss of revenue as it was possible to watch a game without even entering the ground since there were only iron railings between the pitch and the road. A possible solution, which was considered and then dismissed, was the erection of a canvas screen barrier!

The very first game at Vicarage Road was on 29 September 1923 when Stourbridge lost narrowly, by 4 points to 6, to Bournville, a team dubbed, inevitably in those days, the 'Cocoamen.' As for those perimeter iron railings, they reappear briefly in the later annals of the club. With ten minutes to go, in a match against Walsall, the ball was punctured on the spiked railings. Unfortunately the grounds man had already left with the spare ball and since it was getting dark the referee was left with no alternative but to blow the final whistle. Fortunately Stourbridge were leading!

In the Rugby Club's first four seasons at Vicarage Road teams changed in the Public Hall opposite The Crescent. However, in 1927 the club negotiated changing facilities at the Cottage Spring, even though it was an even longer walk to the ground for the players! Nevertheless, there were considerable advantages in this move. On match days, in the Club Room upstairs, five tin baths full of refreshing hot water awaited the players returning from Vicarage Road, and, moreover the baths were refilled as the water-cooled and muddied – such luxury! As the Cottage Spring was a public house the players refreshed themselves in other ways after the game, but as the games didn't finish

Above: In 1923, at the instigation of Hugh Wanstall, a former Rugby player, Stourbridge Rugby Club moved to a field next to the vicarage in Wollaston. The very first game was played there on 29 September 1923. The vicarage can be seen in the background of this post-war home match photograph. Between 1961 and 1964 the field was also the venue for highly popular August Bank Holiday fetes, held to raise funds for the Corbett Hospital. On 4 February 1964 the club announced that it had bought land at High Park Farm, Stourton, a site that would allow it to develop. Rugby Road occupies the Wollaston site in 2003.

until 4:00pm, and the licensing laws did not permit the serving of drinks after 3:00pm, a post-match pint was illegal. In the mid-1930s the local constabulary, determined to enforce the law, carried out a raid that led to the team and the landlord being prosecuted for drinking out of hours. They were defended, by the Captain, Harry Parkinson, who had just qualified as a solicitor; nevertheless all the players were fined 2s 6d each, whilst the landlord had to pay 5s.

In the early seasons at Vicarage Road the lease was negotiated on an annual basis. In 1931-32, for example, the rent was £10, an increase of £3 on the previous season. The reason for this swingeing increase was that the hay that year was of no use to the farmer when it was cut. This suggests that the church had an arrangement with a local farmer who paid the Church for the summer growth, which he harvested and, in doing so, he did the club a favour by keeping the grass short.

Throughout the 1930s most local clubs were improving their facilities and Stourbridge felt that they were falling behind so much, that at the AGM on 26 July 1937 the idea for the construction of a pavilion with changing rooms was aired. It was quickly built and was opened by the Mayor, Councillor J A Mobberley, on 15 January 1938 before a game against Old Yardleians, which Stourbridge won 5-3. The pavilion was a small wooden construction with only two gas-heated showers, and yet it must have seemed heavenly compared with the tin baths of the Cottage Spring.

The Rugby Club like its neighbour, Wollaston Tennis Club, was put into mothballs during World War II. Playing resumed in the 1945-46 season, with the Old Edwardian Club in Stourbridge acting as the social and administrative headquarters, whilst the players continued to change in the wooden pavilion. In 1949 a corrugated iron extension was added to this pavilion, but the inadequacy of these arrangements was obvious to all. A new clubhouse actually on the Wollaston site was needed but since, almost by definition, it would contain a bar selling alcoholic drinks, it could not be built on the land leased from the Church. Moreover the building of a major permanent structure required much more careful planning and money raising activities than the wooden pavilion of the 1930s had necessitated, so it was almost a decade before the brick clubhouse was completed. It was opened on 25 April 1957 on land adjoining the rugby field that had been purchased by the club for £350. It was a great success and served the club well until it became obvious that the huge increase in membership and the resulting extra teams fielded, cried out for a much larger playing area.

One of the major sources of income for the club at this time was the annual fete held on the ground on the August Bank Holiday. The first was held in 1961 and by 1964 a profit of £800 was made thanks to the support not only of members and their families, but also of the wider local community. The first fete attracted a crowd of 3,000 and was so successful that the range of attractions was extended and attendances increased so much so that the final fete in 1964 attracted a record crowd.

On 4 February 1964 the club announced that it had bought 11 acres of land at High Park Farm, Stourton; this was a site that would enable it to develop for the foreseeable future. It was an expensive move, but wisely some years previously the annual lease of the Wollaston ground had been converted by the club into a 25-year tenancy. Selling the remaining period of the lease back to the Church, which was keen to sell the land for building, raised some welcome money. Further money was raised through the sale of the clubhouse.

Although Wollaston was forsaken at the end of the 1964-65 season for the open pastures of Stourton, all is not forgotten. A permanent reminder of those 43 eventful 'rugby' years is the aptly named Rugby Road that runs parallel to Vicarage Road and through the old playing area; whilst the clubhouse has been transformed into Wollaston Free Church.

Cricket

Wollaston has had a number of cricket clubs. One of the earliest on record played in the 1880s and 1890s in a local league that also included: Coseley, Dudley Priory, Hart's Hill, Old Hill Trinity, Quarry Bank, Rowley Regis and Sedgeley. Accounts of their matches appear in the *County Express*. Their fortunes seem to have been mixed in the extreme. A report of a match against Old Hill printed in the paper of 27 June 1885 said of Wollaston that: '*a little fresh bowling blood would do good if it were infused into the team.*' Things were little better in the same fixture seven years later, as the *County Express* of 25 June 1892 reported:

'*Wollaston were badly beaten in this league game, which was played at Old Hill on Saturday (18 June), thought it must not be forgotten that they took a very weak team. Still it was an eleven which ought to have made more than a paltry 19, especially as the second wicket fell at 14. Still, there it is.*'

A St James's club, associated with the church, was active in the 1920s, whilst Wollaston Old Boys, linked to both church and school, was active in the 1930s. The club that survived the longest was the one formed in 1964 by members, or former members, of the Youth Club run by the Methodist Church in Cobden Street, hence it was originally known as Wollaston Methodist Cricket Club. The lead in creating this was taken by Wollaston-born Keith Brookes, who became its first captain and secretary. His great friend Trevor Worton, and his brother-in-law Edwin Gentry, became joint fixture secretaries, and were immediately faced with the near impossible task of trying to persuade well-established clubs to include a newly formed side in their fixture lists. The first season yielded just 13 fixtures and at the end of that season the Treasurer Alan Tomkins reported a credit balance of just one penny. Despite these very modest beginnings the members were determined to persevere in developing the club, hence its successes in later years were a fitting reward for all the players, officers, wives and girlfriends who had worked hard in establishing it.

The club began its playing life at Wollescote Park, because, unfortunately, there was no suitable ground in Wollaston. However, as the club was founded and run by Wollastonians (by birth or by residence), considerable efforts were made in the early seasons to find a home in Wollaston; the council, farmers and landowners were all approached without success. For a number of seasons matches were played on Handrahan's sports ground at Wall Heath, and then in 1989 the club relocated to the grounds of Lea Castle Hospital. Finally in 1995, faced with further ground problems and a declining membership, the club merged with the Amblecote Club to form Amblecote & Wollaston Cricket Club who played their home matches on the Dudley-Kingswinford Rugby Club ground at Wall Heath.

A key figure in the early years of the club's history was Jim Perry, Chairman from 1964 to 1974. Whatever the weather, Jim and his wife Nellie were to be seen on the boundary keenly watching the team in action. Unfortunately ill health forced Jim to stand down, but the club recognised his long years of hard work and dedication by making him President. Sadly the club's first and only President died in 1976. John Sage was the club's second Chairman, taking office in 1975, the year in which the word 'Methodist' was dropped from the its name. Allen Perry, who succeeded him in 1981, remained in office until 1995, when the club amalgamated with Amblecote.

In the first 25 years of the club's existence most fixtures were on a 'friendly' basis; the only competition in which the club was involved was the West Midlands midweek evening league. However, the move to Lea Castle in 1989 coincided with the club's entry into the Morganite Village League, a Saturday competition set in the heart of rural Worcestershire, entailing visits to villages such as Birlingham, Broadwas, Elmley Castle, Fladbury and Hallow. The first season was a testing time with Wollaston finishing ninth out of 12, but the following season saw the club finishing a very creditable fifth. This improvement was maintained in 1991 when Wollaston were runners-up to Bretforton, a performance repeated in 1992 when the club ended the season as runners-up to Elmley Castle. The climax to this fine run of successful seasons was the winning of the league championship in 1993.

The club was fortunate in being served by a number of dedicated players who formed the core of the side for many years, in many cases turning out both on Saturday and Sunday every week throughout the season. The distinction of making the highest number of appearances goes to Ken Worton with 509, followed by Steve Perry with 347, Roger Perry 326, John Foley 307, Alan Tomkins 296, and Norman Guest 295. To Ken Worton also goes the distinction of serving as captain for more seasons than any other player, skippering the team from 1973 to 1981, with the exception of 1976, and then a further two years 1991 and 1992 when the club was playing in the Morganite League. In terms of individual performances the club's batting record is held by Simon Barnett with 176 not out, followed by Alan Edwards with 143 not out, whilst the bowling honours are shared by Tony Ollis, Barry Lacey and Steve Perry who each took nine wickets in an innings. John Foley was the club's star all-rounder in the early years, opening the batting and bowling numerous overs. In later years Jon Masefield and Simon Perkins ably filled the all-rounder role.

Stourbridge (Wollaston) Standard FC

In the 1880s, the decade that saw the birth of professional football, the leading soccer club in the Stourbridge area was Stourbridge Standard FC. Despite its name it was a Wollaston-based club, run by Wollaston men. The exact date when the club was formed is not known, but there is a report in the *County Express* of Standard playing Brierley Hill at Moor Lane on 2 March 1878. The Rifleman's Arms in Wood Street were used as the team's headquarters and it also provided accommodation for teams to change.

Home matches were played on a field at the back of the pub (Eggington Road had not yet been built). The Standard's existence is also recorded in the *Stourbridge Almanack & Directory* for 1885; the club's officers are listed as:

- Patron – Sir H F Lambert
- President – Rev George Gilbanks
- Vice-Presidents – Charles Webb, Henry Turney
- Secretary – G H Smith (address – *'near the Church'*)
- Match Secretary – F Rogers (address – *'High Street'*)
- Treasurer – A Price.

The committee comprised H Price, W Noke, J Simpson, H Kelly and W Pratt. The Captain of the first team was A Price, and S Smith captained the seconds. The annual subscription was four shillings, a figure that remained unaltered for the remaining years of the club's existence as Stourbridge Standard.

At this time clubs lacked resources, whilst public transport and communications were in their infancy (no cars! no telephones!); consequently there were no league competitions. Stourbridge Standard, like all their neighbours, had to content themselves with friendly matches and cup competitions. Involvement in the latter brought them opponents such as West Bromwich Albion, Walsall Town and Kidderminster Harriers, whilst the 'friendlies', as the *County Express* match reports reveal, were often keenly

contested physical encounters in which the referee's decisions were as fiercely disputed as they are in 2003.

Standard's most successful season was 1887-8 when they entered or were invited to compete in four cup competitions: the Kidderminster Cup, the Kidderminster Weavers' Challenge Cup, the Worcester Charity Cup and the Birmingham Junior Cup. In the final of the Worcester Charity Cup Standard beat St Paul's, Worcester 2-1 at Worcester. The final of the Kidderminster Cup pitted Standard against their local rivals, Wordsley Harriers, who had secured their place in the final by beating Kidderminster Harriers in the semi-final at Wollaston on 14 January 1888. Standard entered the final after beating Brierley Hill Alliance 1-0 in a second replay of the semifinal. Thus on 31 March, on Stourbridge Cricket Ground at Amblecote, a crowd of around 3,000 saw the final end in a 2-2 draw. The replay on 14 April, also at Amblecote, attracted between 3,000 and 4,000 spectators. The result was a 2-1 victory for the Wollaston team (most teams were made up of local men). The winning line-up was: A Price (goalkeeper), J Jones, W Vaughan; H Price, Noke, Perry, Thorns, Collins, Parton (centre forward), W Jones, T Jones.

Unfortunately for Wollaston the Standard Club's success in the spring of 1888 led to it severing its links with the village. In view of the increasing number of spectators attracted to its matches it became imperative to find a larger ground, so the club moved at the start of the 1888-89 season to Amblecote to become known simply as Stourbridge FC.

Above: Stourbridge Standard FC was formed in the late 1870s. The earliest match report identified is that against Brierley Hill at Moor Lane on 2 March 1878, but clearly if they were playing a full season, the club must have been in existence in 1877. They used The Rifleman's Arms in Wood Street as their headquarters, and it also provided changing accommodation. Home matches were played on a field at the back of the pub, where this photograph was taken, Eggington Road not having been built yet. The club moved to Amblecote in 1888. *Stourbridge Library*

The Vics and the Wanderers – The golden years of Wollaston soccer

In the 20th century two soccer clubs that stand out from the many who played their home matches in Wollaston, or used one of the local pubs as their headquarters, were Wollaston Vics and Wollaston Wanderers. Both played on 'the Rec' (Wollaston's recreational field) and were members of the Brierley Hill League.

Above: Wollaston Old Boys football team for the 1910-11 season, plus their coach and his assistants. Little is known about this club, which, presumably, was made up of ex-pupils of Wollaston Schools. Their kit is very smart though, and the dog may have been their mascot!

The Wanderers, founded in 1938, originally played in the Stourbridge & District League as Wollaston St James, and then in the 1940s, when Romilly Craze ran them, they were known as Wollaston Boys Club. They were a very successful club, winning the league championship twice and the Molineux Shield three times. They were reformed after World War II in 1947, largely due to the initiative of Reg Thatcher, a former St James player. As most of the players had just been demobbed after the war in which they had 'wandered' far and wide, they called themselves the 'Wanderers' and entered the first division of the Brierley Hill League, no doubt on the strength of their previous successes as teenagers in the Stourbridge League. An influential figure in the life of the club was Fred Lloyd, licensee of The Eagle Inn. For most of their existence the Wanderers changed into their strip of white shirts and black shorts at The Barley Mow, before playing on the nearby 'Rec'. When the club folded at the end of the 1961-62 season it was the oldest serving member of the Brierley Hill League. Wollaston Wanderers' principal achievements were:

- 1947-48 Victory Cup losing finalists
- 1951-52 League Cup losing finalists
- 1952-53 West Bromwich Albion Shield losing semi-finalists
- 1952-53 Corbett Hospital Cup losing semi-finalists
- 1954-55 West Bromwich Albion Shield losing semi-finalists

There is photographic evidence of a Vics team in existence in the early 1930s, but no records of its foundation or demise have been discovered. **The Vics**, who were formed in 1947, had initially to play under the name of John Hall Juniors to enable them to use the pitch belonging to John Hall & Co (firebrick makers) in Vicarage Road, Amblecote, but they were simply known as the 'Vics.' When a pitch became available on Wollaston 'Rec' in 1948 they moved there and changed their name to Wollaston Vics. In their early days of playing on the 'Rec' their changing room was at the Cottage Spring on Bridgnorth Road; subsequently they changed at The Queen's Head in Enville Street. At first their strip was in the style and colours of Aston Villa, but subsequently a Wolves look was adopted. Throughout the whole of the club's 13-year existence its business was in the hands of George Foxall, who combined the roles of secretary and manager. Eventually, in the 1959-60 season, after playing only nine league games, the club folded because of the difficulty in raising a team. Although the Vics had a short life, it was one in which they achieved many successes, as the following record shows:

- 1949-50 Div III League Cup – joint holders
- 1950-51 Div III League – runners up
  League Cup – winners
  Coronation Cup – winners
  Auxiliary Cup – winners
- 1951-52 Div I B League – Champions
  League Cup – winners
  Victory Cup – runners up
  Corbett Hospital Cup – semi-finalists
- 1952-53 Div I Coronation Cup – winners
  West Bromwich Albion Shield – winners
  Corbett Hospital Cup – runners up
- 1953-54 Div I League Cup – winners
  West Bromwich Albion Shield – winners
  Coronation Cup – runners up
  Birmingham Junior Cup – reached the 4th round

Below: Wollaston Vics FC with their trophies from the 1931-32 season. The photograph was taken on Tooby's field at the top of Meriden Avenue. The team changed at The Forester's Arms, and played their home matches on a pitch close to the later Stourbridge Rugby ground, just over The Ridge in Stourton. The team reformed in 1947, but folded during the 1959-60 season.

- 1954-55 Div I League – Champions
  West Bromwich Albion Shield – runners up
- 1955-56 Div I League – runners up
  League Cup – semi-finalists
  West Bromwich Albion Shield – runners up
- 1956-57 Div I West Bromwich Albion Shield – runners up

The Vic's other achievements
1951-52 Centre forward Dennis Poole was the league's leading goal scorer with a tally of 73 goals in 35 games. Ernie While, another team member, scored an impressive 34 goals in 32 games. In 1952 centre-half Lawrence 'Lol' Tibbetts signed for Bristol City, then playing in the Third Division (South). The Vics received the princely sum of £5 from the Football League club!

1953-54 The Vics created a league record in defeating Weldall & Assembly FC by the improbable score of 22-1. Dennis Poole scored 12 goals, whilst Ron Mobberley and Harold 'Brit' Payne each scored a hat trick.

1954-55 As a consequence of the club's involvement and success in a number of competitions its players were faced with 14 matches in the last 21 days. In this same season the club had five players in the representative Brierley Hill League team, which beat the very strong Birmingham Works League in the final of the prestigious Campbell Orr (inter-league) Shield. The five Vics were Jim Brooks, Pat Nightingale, David Poole, Dennis Poole and Bill Swingewood who captained the team, and for good measure Don Brooks and Pat Cook were named as reserves.

1955-56 The Vics had to play 11 matches in the last 12 days of the season.

Tennis
Although tennis has been played competitively in Wollaston for over a century as the advert from the front page of the *County Express* of 23 May 1896 shows, the early clubs were short-lived and had a very restricted membership:

A TENNIS TOURNAMENT
(Mixed Doubles)
To be held at the Vicarage on July 2nd
Entrance fee (Tournament) 2 shillings per player
Admission (Spectator) 6d each
Family ticket to admit 5 (2 shillings)
Prizes £1 to each of the winning pair
10 shillings to each of the losing pair

The *County Express* of 9 November 1912 carried a report of a whist drive in aid of Wollaston Tennis Club. As the President was George Gilbanks, the probability is that the club played on the Vicarage lawn, as there were no public courts. George Gilbanks' successor, Hugh Wanstall, was also a tennis enthusiast, and it was his interest in the game that led to the establishment of a new Wollaston tennis club in 1930. Wanstall had his own grass court in the grounds of the vicarage, where he regularly played with his brother Archie, Richard Lowndes, manager of John Bradley & Co, and Joe 'Pecker' Pearson.

Although in 2003 Wollaston Tennis Club is situated in Stourton, its roots, both in terms of its membership and location, are unquestionably in Wollaston. Before 1930 tennis was played only on private courts in the gardens of some of the bigger houses in Wollaston, such as the Vicarage (as mentioned above), and that of Herbert Husselbee at No 3 High Park Avenue. The group of friends who played on Husselbee's court decided to form themselves into a club with a membership limited to 25 playing members, paying an annual subscription of £1.

On 29 April 1930 Hugh Wanstall was elected the club's first President. Its first matches were against Marsh & Baxter's Social Club (Brierley Hill). Wollaston won 14-1 at home and 8-1 away. At the end of the first season a balance of 6s 3d was reported at the AGM by the Treasurer, George Perry, of High Park Avenue.

If the club was lacking in money at this time, its members were not short of enthusiasm. Their playing activities produced so much wear and tear on Husselbee's court that the club soon had to look for somewhere else to play. To the rescue again came its President, Hugh Wanstall, who offered the use of his own court at a rent of £5 per year. The club accepted, and thus moved to Vicarage Road in 1931. In 1932 a hard court was laid alongside the grass one, at a cost of £25. The next year saw the replacement of the grass court by a second shale hard court, and the conversion of the vicar's summerhouses into a clubhouse. Wollaston Tennis Club had been established.

Hugh Wanstall's premature death in 1933 was a potential setback for the club, but fortunately his successor, Reg Bamber, was also a tennis fan; thus he succeeded Hugh Wanstall not only as the spiritual leader of the community, but also as President of Wollaston Tennis Club. By 1934 the club had 50 members and was beginning to prosper, so

Above: In addition to championing Rugby in Wollaston in the 1920s, Hugh Wanstall was also an enthusiastic tennis player. It was his interest in the game that led to the establishment of a Wollaston Tennis Club in 1930, which played on Wanstall's own grass court in the grounds of the vicarage. Some of the larger houses in High Park Avenue, such as No 3, the home of Herbert Husselbee, also had private tennis courts, and this a likely location for this photograph.

much so that it spent money on a floodlighting system – gaslights! This ambitious experiment was not a success. Unfortunately the gaslights attracted all the moths and flying insects in the neighbourhood, with the result that players found not only was their playing style disturbed by insects flying in their faces, but also, periodically, as they raced panting across the courts, they inadvertently swallowed some of the intruders!

The outbreak of World War II led to several members joining the forces and as a result, by 1943, the club had effectively ceased to exist. It was revived in 1946 when former members were demobbed. At first there were few members, but after the courts were restored to good order, and clubhouse facilities had been improved, numbers began to increase steadily, so that by 1954 there were 49 playing members. Further improvements to the courts took place in 1956 and 1959, and by 1960 serious consideration was being given to the building of a new clubhouse. Unfortunately this project had to be abandoned when it became clear that the Worcester Diocesan authorities, who owned both the tennis courts and the adjoining Stourbridge Rugby Club ground, were determined to sell the land for housing. Therefore in 1965 the club severed its physical link with Wollaston and moved to Stourton.

Boy Scouts

The 1st Wollaston St James troop is reputed to have been registered shortly after the Boy Scouts movement was founded in 1908, which would make it one of the oldest in the country, but there is no documentary evidence to suggest that there was a scout group in existence in Wollaston before February 1912.

The troop's first recorded meeting place was a room above the coach house of 'The Hollies' in Cobden Street. 'The Hollies' (later known as The Beeches, 28 Cobden Street) was the home of the Hammond family. The troop used this room at the invitation of Miss Annie Hammond, who proved to be a life-long supporter of the scouts. She was the Group Treasurer for a number of years until her death in 1944. The first scoutmaster was E E Wilson, a lay reader at St James's Church. Shortly after its formation this fledgling troop was involved in the house-to-house collections for the 'Titanic Relief Fund' in June 1912, raising £6 7s. E E Wilson left Wollaston in September 1912, and the name of his successor is unknown.

In April 1913 the 1st Wollaston St James troop had the honour of being inspected by General Sir Robert Baden-Powell, founder of the Boy Scout movement. For a number of years the Wollaston troop met in the village schools. The early 1920s was a difficult period for the scouts, and the troop nearly folded. George Layland, of 3 Bright Street, revived the troop in February 1926, and registered the Wollaston St James (No.15007) with the Boy Scouts Association on 21 May 1926. They continued to meet in the schools until 1928 when they acquired a new meeting place in a loft over stables belonging to Joe Forrest, a coal merchant in Gladstone Road. These new premises, which were officially opened on 21 February 1928, were far from satisfactory however, as the following extract from the scout's logbook for 1930 shows:

'On Tuesday April 21 a start was made to dismantle the interior of our clubroom. Although the place had served its purpose for three years, it had never been satisfactory. Due to the decay of the roof and the floor through old age, the place was always dirty, despite our efforts to keep it clean; but worse even than this; the one end of the room was attached to the bedroom of the adjoining house. Mr Forrest had received complaints from his neighbours of our noise, so he had asked us to try to find other accommodation. ... And the final straw – The smell from the pigs, which were being kept below us, helped to speed up our efforts!'

The troop returned reluctantly to its former base in Wollaston Schools from 28 April 1931. However, good fortune was at hand, when the Public Hall Committee decided to disband their organisation. At a public meeting held in Wollaston Schools on 16 October 1930, to discuss the disposal of the of the defunct Public Hall's assets, it was proposed that the money (£59) should be given to the scouts and guides towards the cost of purchasing a hut. Consequently, the logbook of 1932 records that:

'Shortly after the August holidays the material arrived for the building of our new headquarters. This was to be a sectional wooden structure measuring 30ft by 20ft. The majority of the woodwork for the building had already been done; it now remained for it to be assembled.'

The new headquarters, which was behind the schools, was first officially opened on 19 November 1932 and served the scouts until 1970, when they took an opportunity to move into larger premises in Birch Drive, by Lowndes Road, off Enville Street. These had been temporary offices erected for the Inland Revenue whilst their new offices

Left: Wollaston St James Scout Troop was registered with the Boy Scouts Association on 21 May 1926. They met in the schools until 1928 when the moved to a new meeting place in a loft over stables belonging to Joe Forrest, the coal merchant in Gladstone Road. These new premises were in fact part of the old Novelty Glassworks, and were officially opened on 21 February 1928, but they proved far from satisfactory, being dirty and smelly, due to the pigs kept below! *Wollaston Scouts*

were built in Lower High Street. The Birch Drive land belonged to Severn Trent, who leased the building to the scouts on 1 November 1970. Two further leases extended this for a total of 17 years, the scouts finally vacating Birch Drive in November 1987. Since then they have met in the Senior Citizens' Centre/Village Hall.

Many people have contributed to the development of scouting in Wollaston. Special mention must be made of the contribution of Chris Layland, who revived scouting in the village. He took charge in August 1928, and in 1932 supervised the erection and fitting-out of the new headquarters. Chris Layland remained active in Wollaston scouting for the next 25 years, even though he resigned as Scoutmaster in 1942. Dave Guest became scout leader in 1967, and Margaret Bradley became the group treasurer in 1969, and both were still fulfilling these roles in 2003.

Girl Guides

Guiding activities began in Wollaston with the formation in 1926 of the 6th company of Stourbridge Guides. Their captain was Nancy Hill who also ran the Brownies. By 1975 the 6th Stourbridge Company had grown so big that it was considered necessary to split it into two companies, the new company was to become the 13th company of Stourbridge Guides. Sadly, in March 1982, the Guide hut was burned to the ground in an arson attack. This also destroyed all the company's camping equipment, its records and photographs. The hut's loss prompted a huge fund raising effort to provide a new meeting place for Guides and Brownies. The new headquarters, on the Rec', were officially opened in 1985. In 1996 the 6th company celebrated its 70 years of existence, and in the same year Lou Chambers died aged 77. She had been appointed Captain in June 1951, and gave leadership and service for the next 33 years, until she retired in December 1984.

Below: This line up of Wollaston St James Scout Troop in October 1948 includes Chris Layland (front row, centre), who revived scouting in the village. He took charge in August 1928, and in 1932 supervised the erection and fitting-out of new headquarters behind the schools. Chris Layland remained active in Wollaston scouting for the next 25 years, even though he resigned as Scoutmaster in 1942. *Wollaston Scouts*

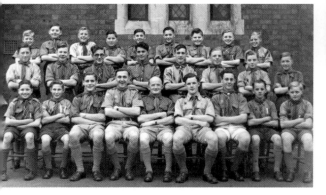

Above: Guiding began in Wollaston in 1926 with the formation of the 6th company of Stourbridge Guides, who are seen here in 1955. *Wollaston Guides*

Below: No-one did more for guiding in Wollaston than Lou Chambers. She was appointed Guide Captain in June 1951, and she gave leadership and service for the next 33 years, until she retired in December 1984. Lou Chambers died in 1996, aged 77. *Wollaston Guides*

Boxing

Wollaston has a long association with boxing, something that comes largely through the work of the Davies family. Around 1939 Ben Davies began to train boys for boxing in the Toc H Club in Wollaston Street, Stourbridge. This stood to the rear of the old Savoy cinema in Lower High Street, which is the Fitness Academy in 2003. Amongst the trainee boxers were Ben's sons Eric and Ken, and, together with Jack Saunders, they also began to give

Above: Wollaston's former prominence in boxing is due to Ben Davies, and the success of his two sons, Ken and Eric. Ben began to train boys for boxing in the Toc H Club in Wollaston Street, Stourbridge, around 1939. In 1942 they moved to a large shed at the rear of The Forester's Arms pub, which was fitted out as a gymnasium. There Wollaston Boxing Club was established. The club continued until Eric Davies became a professional in 1950. Here Ben looks proudly over the trophies won by his sons Ken (left) and Eric (right). *Eric Davies*

exhibition bouts at Prestwood Sanatorium and the Corbett Hospital Fetes.

Interest grew and larger premises were sought. In 1941 the training was moved to Brook Street School (Stourbridge College's Art & Design Annexe in 2003), where it was held two or three times a week. The following year Joseph Tromans, licensee of The Forester's Arms, offered the use of a large shed at the rear of the pub. This was fitted out as a boxing gymnasium, and many local boys joined, including Boyd Davies, Horace Dudley, John Knight, and Paddy and Roy Garrington.

With a suitable and more permanent home, Ben Davies set things up on a formal basis. Wollaston Boxing Club was established, which was affiliated to the Amateur Boxing Association (ABA), and a management committee was formed. Its members included Horace Billingham, Charlie Chapman, Harry Chapman, Bill and Sam Porter, and Darky Stinton. The committee met at The Unicorn.

When Joseph Tromans died in 1946 the boxing club moved again, this time to the canteen at Stourbridge Rolling Mills, courtesy of the Standish family. There the club continued until Eric Davies became a professional boxer in 1950. Thereafter Eric continued to use the canteen for training, sparring with ex-marine commando Eric Parker and a number of local policemen.

Wollaston Gardeners' Guild

The Gardeners' Guild was formed in 1942. Allotment holders, and those who merely tended their domestic

'patch', joined forces to respond to the government's 'Dig for Victory' appeal. This campaign was aimed at producing food, at a time when there were increasing shortages as a result of the German U-boat offensive, which was threatening to cut off Britain's food supplies from overseas. The Guild's first management committee consisted of a representative from each of the then seven Wollaston allotments (Bridgnorth Road, High Park Avenue, Lady Grey's Walk, Park Road West, South Road, Wollaston Hall and Wollaston Playing Fields), together with representatives of those gardeners resident in Wollaston.

The first AGM was held in Bright Street Methodist Church on 16 September 1943. Since then a variety of venues: The Unicorn Inn, New Inn, The Gig Mill Inn, The Longlands Tavern, Norton Community Centre and St Michael's (Norton) Church Hall have hosted the monthly meetings, the shows and the AGMs. Currently the monthly meetings are held in the Conservative Club in New Road, Stourbridge, and since 1998 the annual show and presentation supper has been held in St James's Church Hall in the heart of Wollaston.

During the war years the Guild was concerned exclusively with the growing of vegetables and with maximising the yield of each allotment or garden. After the end of the

Above: Wollaston Gardeners' Guild was formed in 1942. Its first management committee consisted of a representative from each of Wollaston's seven allotments: Bridgnorth Road, High Park Avenue (seen here), Lady Grey's Walk, Park Road West, South Road, Wollaston Hall and Wollaston Playing Fields. The old bus body at the rear served as a shelter.

war in 1945, and the end of food rationing in July 1954, the pressure to concentrate on vegetables was relaxed, and through competitions the Guild began to encourage the growing of flowers and recreational gardening. Over the past 50 years its regular programme of monthly meetings, competitive shows and visits to parks and country houses, has engendered a greater awareness of plant varieties and growing techniques in members and their friends.

In 1984 the Guild assumed responsibility for the allotments in Wollaston, but in the following year it was felt that only allotment holders should be responsible for the management of allotments and so the Wollaston Allotments Society was formed to look after the interests of the four remaining plots, namely those off Charles Road, South Road, High Park Avenue and Lady Grey's Walk. The two organisations work together amicably and many gardeners are members of both organisations.

Of the many members who have given considerable service to the Guild some of the most notable are:

- Bill Niblett – Secretary for 25 years
- Reg Gardener – who, in recognition of 40 years' service, including 21 years as Secretary and 15 years as President, was made the first Grand President in 1998
- W Hinton – a founder member who was made the first life member in 1970
- Walter Jackson – the longest serving allotment holder in Stourbridge, who was presented with a special achievement award in 1992. He took over his father's allotment in 1931
- Tom Hadgkiss – Treasurer for 33 years

Wollaston Angling Society

Ken Davies founded the Angling Society in 1955 when he was the new licensee of The Waterloo Inn. In 1958 the society moved its headquarters from The Waterloo to the British Legion Club in Enville Street. In its early years it was a thriving club with nine trophies, plus prize money, to be won each season. By 1962 it had a full complement of 45 members and in 1966, at the AGM held at The White Horse Inn, Norton, it was announced that the membership waiting list had had to be closed, even though there were still 12 would-be members waiting to fill vacancies as and when they occurred. An important factor governing the size of the club was the number of persons who could be carried in coaches such as those operated by Sammy Johnson's 'Supreme' Coaches. As few people owned cars in the 1950s and early 1960s, a club coach outing made it possible to fish in waters other than the local canal. Furthermore, one of the attractions of Wollaston Angling Society was the camaraderie and the sense of belonging that sprang from all travelling together to and from the fishing places. Wollaston Angling Society was affiliated both to the Birmingham Anglers Association and the Kidderminster & District Anglers Association, and mainly fished stretches of the rivers Severn and Avon. Unfortunately its separate existence came to an end in 1990 when, because of dwindling membership, it merged with the Colley Gate Angling Club.

Darts

Even without documentary evidence, almost certainly every pub, at some time in its existence, has had a darts team, which had competed in a local league. In 1960 there was a Wollaston Darts League. The league table for that November, published in the *County Express*, shows that whilst most of the teams were Wollaston based, there were a few 'foreigners' from Stourbridge! The Wollaston teams were from The Gate Hangs Well, The Swan, The Barley Mow, New Inn, The Alexandra, The Plough and The Waterloo.

Right: Every Wollaston pub almost certainly had a darts team, which had competed in local leagues. Here is The Bull's Head Darts Team in 1938-39, displaying a somewhat modest cup.

Above: Ex-boxer Ken Davies founded Wollaston Angling Society in 1955, when he was the new licensee of The Waterloo Inn. In 1958 the society moved its headquarters to the British Legion Club in Enville Street. Here are members of the society on an outing on one of Samuel 'Sammy' Johnson's coaches in 1959. Because of dwindling membership, the society's separate existence ended in 1990 when it merged with the Colley Gate Angling Club.

Wollaston Townswomen's Guild

The Wollaston branch of the Townswomen's Guild was established on 9 November 1965. At this inaugural meeting, held in the canteen of the old junior school, the Chair was taken by Beryl Grant, with Vi Morgan as Vice-Chairman and Mrs B Wood as Registrar. The Townswomen's Guild is a nationwide organisation with the aims of advancing the education of women and also of providing recreational and leisure activities for them. The Wollaston Guild is affiliated to the West Midlands Federation of Townswomen's Guilds. Each federation is represented at the annual National Council, when issues concerning women and other topical matters are debated. HRH The Princess Royal is the organisation's national Patron in 2003.

In 1965 when the Wollaston Guild was founded a member's annual subscription was 7s 6d, and there were over 100 members. By 2003 the subscription has risen to £12, whilst membership has stabilised at just over 80. The Guild has met in a number of venues in its 35-year existence: after its initial meetings in the junior school canteen, it moved a short distance into the school hall, and when the school moved to The Kingsway the Guild did likewise, meeting in the school hall there. However, when the new Church Hall was opened in 1995, the Guild returned to the heart of the village to hold its meetings.

In 2003 the main meeting was held on the second Tuesday of each month. This may be a slide presentation, quiz, demonstration, film or talk. In addition the Guild has a number of other regular activities catering for a wide-range of interests, such as Arts & Crafts, Bowls, Drama, Floral Art and Rambling. The AGM is held in March when officers for the coming year are elected. The Chairman for 2002-03 was Ann McKenzie.

Above: Wollaston Townswomen's Guild was established on 9 November 1965. Amongst their most successful activities was the drama group. In October 1970 they won the West Midlands Federation of Townswomen's Guild Drama Cup with their presentation of 'They Made Her Wild.' Here, standing, are: Joyce Aston, Ruth Bashforth, Marion Clarke, Margaret Willetts, and kneeling are: Irene Johnson, Vi Morgan and Margaret Hickie.

Wollaston Tappers

This tap dance group started in 1981 as an offshoot of Wollaston School PTA. The group's original aim was to raise money for the school. Kaye Millichip was the founder member of the group. An advert placed in a local newspaper attracted ten members to the first meeting in the school hall. The teachers were Kaye Millichip and Margaret De Saulles and the pianist was Gwen Ebert. Although the emphasis was on a 'fun night', a strict British Ballet Organisation syllabus was followed.

In the early days of their existence the Tappers' shows were on a small-scale and were held in the school before audiences comprising mainly parents and elderly groups. In addition to the entertainment the Tappers provided a free after show supper. Latterly the shows have become more adventurous with proceeds going to charitable organisations such as the Roy Castle 'Cause For Hope' appeal.

In November 1999, a Millennium show was held at Ridgewood High School raising over £1,300 for local charities. Although some Tappers have hung up their tap shoes, the group is young at heart and weekly practices are held in St James's School.

Wollaston Community Association

Stourbridge Youth & Community Worker Percy Oakley was largely instrumental in the formation of Wollaston Community Association (WCA). A Steering Committee was formed at a public meeting held in Wollaston Junior School on 13 September 1982. This produced a constitution for the organisation, which came into being at a second public meeting held in Bright Street Methodist Church on 29 November 1982. Here more people were recruited to the committee, and, after a series of meetings, WCA embarked upon a highly successful series of events and activities. These began with a social event held in the hall at Wollaston Junior School on 14 January 1983, which over 100 members attended.

Much momentum was put behind the growth and development of WCA by the election of John Ginnifer as Chairman on 22 February 1983. Under his direction and enthusiasm, WCA embarked upon its most successful year. The events organised included a series of barn dances, regular dancing classes, a Halloween party, and, most successful of all, a Thanksgiving Supper, held on 25 November 1983.

These successes were built upon in 1984, but a social event held in the school hall on 13 April was the last use WCA was able to make of the building following the school's closure, and, despite the best efforts of all concerned, without this focus the association began to struggle.

Events were held in the new St James's School, and elsewhere, such as a pig roast held on Kent Road field on 18 August 1984. A series of meetings was held between May and August 1985 to try to secure use of the old school hall, which stood empty and prey to vandals, but to no avail. That summer WCA organised a weeklong Summer Play Scheme on Kent Road Field from 12-16 August. By the autumn some of the Committee had become disheartened over the failure to persuade the authorities to allow them to use the old school hall, and a number resigned over this issue at a committee meeting held on 14 October 1985.

The following year, again largely due to the efforts of Percy Oakley, WCA secured a pair of temporary buildings, which were erected at the rear of the Senior Citizens Centre. Here WCA continued to organise events and serve the village, but persistent vandalism and waning interest led to the WCA's closure in 1988.

Crystal Quilters

As a result of a small group of Wollaston ladies visiting a quilting exhibition it was decided to form a quilting group in Wollaston. The original members were all members of St James's Church and included Shirley Horne, Alex Quinn, Eunice Horton and Betty Harper. The first meeting of Crystal Quilters took place on 8 March 1989. The name Crystal Quilters was chosen partly because of the area's strong links with the glass industry and partly because of a desire to attract members from a wide area. It was thought that the name Wollaston Quilters might give the impression that membership was confined to Wollaston residents only. Since its formation the group has attracted members from Amblecote, Oldswinford and Stourton. At first members met in one member's home, but this became impracticable when the membership increased, so the group moved to St James's School to hold its meetings. A group quilt, made and exhibited in 1990 in Stourbridge Library, aroused much interest and as a result there was an increase in membership. This quilt was raffled in March 1992 and raised £900 for The Mary Stevens Hospice Appeal. In 1994 the Third Eye Film Co filmed the group for a programme called 'Scrimpens' which was shown on Channel 4 later that year.

By 1997 group meetings were attracting an average attendance of 20 members and it was felt that a more spacious venue was essential, consequently the group moved its meetings to St James's Church Hall. On moving to the church hall the group decided to stage an exhibition, and to finance it they successfully applied for a Lottery grant of £500. In 1998 the group was asked by Mary Stevens Hospice to make a wall hanging for the reception area of the new residential unit. This was made as a group effort, with smaller wall hangings made by individual members to hang in some of the corridors.

In addition to raising money for good causes the group also encourages pupils in local schools to learn and enjoy their craft.

Indoor Bowls

Founded by Percy Oakley, following the opening of the Church Hall in 1995, the Indoor Bowls Club meets there every Tuesday and Friday afternoon to play short mat bowls.

And finally …

… for those who wanted to get away from Wollaston, to relax and let their hair down when they got to Weston or Blackpool, the following, from the *County Express* of 10 May 1947, is typical of many adverts which appeared in the immediate post-war period (1945-1950) – a time of crowded trains, few cars, and petrol shortages:

WESTON-super-MARE. Seats vacant to and from Weston on May 24, 31 and June 14; also for Blackpool on May 31, June 7, 14 and 21. Book now with Chance Private Hire Cars Service, 79 Bridgnorth Road, Wollaston (opposite the church).

In view of the demand for seats it might be necessary to share a car with someone else, so it was essential to book early!

Above: The election of John Ginnifer as Chairman of Wollaston Community Association on 22 February 1983 put much momentum behind the growth and development of the organisation. Under his direction and enthusiasm the Community Association embarked upon its most successful year, organising events that included barn dances, regular dancing classes, a Halloween party and a Thanksgiving Supper held on 25 November 1983. John is seen here with his wife Betty and one of their grandchildren. *Betty Ginnifer*

Right: If more local journeys were required in the car-less days immediately following World War II, Wollaston also boasted its own taxi service, run by the Abbisses, who also ran a plumbing business from their home in Bridgnorth Road.

Chapter Eight

WOLLASTON AT WAR

Wollaston people have undoubtedly become involved in many wars and other conflicts since settlement first began there. However, the first war in which the involvement of someone from Wollaston can be confirmed is, perhaps, a bit of a surprise.

The American Civil War (1861-1865)

Curiously, the earliest record of military service involving someone from Wollaston is contained in a letter from **Frank** (Francis) **Millward** to his father in which he described his experience as a Prisoner of War during the American Civil War. The *Brierley Hill Advertiser* of 28 January 1865 carried the following headline:

'*Letter from a Stourbridge Man Engaged in the American Civil War. The following graphic account has been received from Mr Francis Millward, son of Mr Wm Millward, of Stourbridge, engineer for Mr W O Foster, MP, and handed to us for publication. Mr F Millward is a senior captain in the Federal Service: Cincinnati, Ohio, January 1st 1865*'

The Millward family lived on Withy Bank, and later moved to Wood Street. Frank Millward was born in 1834 and like many young men of his time 'went west' in the mid 1850s to seek his fortune in the rapidly developing USA. When the American Civil War began in 1861 he joined the Union (or Federal) army of the northern states as an engineer. He rose through the ranks attaining the rank of Captain. He was captured by the Confederates (soldiers in the army of the southern states) on returning unescorted from a visit to divisional headquarters in Maryland. For a while he was a prisoner in the 'Libby' prison in Virginia, which housed over 1,100 Union officers. He was subsequently moved to another prison camp in Charleston. His letter describes his capture, his daring escape and recapture, as well as the grim conditions of life in a Confederate POW camp. Frank Millward died in Cincinnati in 1878.

20th century conflicts

Although Wollaston emerged unscathed from the three major wars of the 20th century, its people were actively engaged in each of them, both on the battlefields and in many war-related activities at home. By the end of World War II, Wollaston had lost around 100 men whose potential contribution to the life of the village and beyond can only be speculated upon.

The Boer War

Britain entered the 20th century at war with the Boers in South Africa. Whilst this far off conflict involved only a handful of regular and reservist soldiers from Wollaston, newspaper reports and the school logbook show that the war was very much at the forefront of people's lives.

War was declared on 11 October 1899 and on 20 January 1900 the *County Express* published a list of local men serving in South Africa. One of these was **Jessen Parkes** of Mamble Square, who was a member of the Duke of Cornwall's Light Infantry.

The school logbook records the following war related events:

- '*The school closed early on 15 January 1900 to allow the room to be prepared for a lecture on the Transvaal crisis.*
- *News of the relief of Kimberley was received on 16 February 1900. After school the same day the vicar opened the new playing field behind the schools, which was named the Kimberley recreation ground in celebration.*
- *The pupils were given a half-day holiday on 1 March 1900 to celebrate the relief of Ladysmith on the previous day.*'

The *County Express* of 10 March 1900 noted the departure for South Africa of four Wollaston reservists: Corporal **Hill** (Police Constable), Private **John Rabey**, Private **T Lees** and Private **David Skelding**.

The news of the relief of Mafeking on 22 May 1900 was celebrated with cheers for Baden-Powell and the soldiers of the Queen, and after school the boys paraded through the village singing patriotic songs. The 24 May 1900 was a school holiday to commemorate Victoria's birthday and the relief of Mafeking.

During the more exciting periods of the war, Messrs Turney & Co put their steam bull (hooter) at the disposal of the *County Express*, to communicate the receipt of important war news to the general public. The sounding of the bull indicated that the latest war news had been posted outside the *County Express*' offices. News of the peace settlement at Vereeniging, the end of the Boer War, was received in Stourbridge on 1 June 1902, by telephone from Birmingham. The *County Express* of 7 June 1902 reported:

'*Messrs Turney's bull was heard on Sunday night, and the steam hooter of Messrs Isaac Nash & Sons at Wollaston Mills gave the same joyful news to the inhabitants of Wollaston. At Wollaston, upon definite confirmation that peace had been signed, a number of school boys asked their master's permission to ring the school bell. This was given, and they commenced to clang it vigorously, an example which the bellringers of the church soon followed upon the church peal. The village was astir until midnight. On Monday morning the streets were made gay with flags and bunting, and very little work was done that day. The children assembled at school in the morning as usual, and the terms of the peace were explained to them, following which ringing cheers were given for the King, the soldiers at the front, and finally for the 'brave enemy.' The lads' excitement was so great that work was out of the question, and the schools were closed for the rest of the day. Among other flags hoisted was the old church flag, which has signalled the reliefs of Kimberley, Ladysmith, and Mafeking; on Monday it waved over the church probably for the last time, as a new flag has been purchased with which to celebrate the coronation.'*

The Great War

1914

The United Kingdom declared war on Germany on 4 August 1914, and on Austria a few days later. Britain's small standing army was mobilised and reservists were called up. The *County Express* of 15 August 1914 reported that First-class Stoker **Thomas Harper** of Bridle Road, Wollaston had been saved after HMS Amphion had been sunk when it struck a German mine. He was in hospital suffering from the effects of the explosion, but recovering well. There was a sad sequel to this story, when the *County Express* of 25 October 1919 recorded that the same Thomas Harper had committed suicide, in a gas filled house.

For three years prior to the war, Rev Hugh Wanstall's sister had been governess to the children of Princess Stolberg of Wernigerode, whose husband was a German diplomat stationed in Vienna. Concern was raised, by the *County Express* of 3 September 1914, about her safety and whereabouts, as Austria was Germany's ally in the war. However, news was received in the middle of October that Kathleen Wanstall was safe and well in Vienna.

The *County Express* of 24 October reported the arrival of 11 Belgian refugees under the heading '*Wollaston's Belgian Guests.*' They were installed in a house at the corner of Laburnum Street, which had been furnished for them by residents of the parish. A committee had been formed to provide food.

The first battle of Ypres, in October/November 1914, brought the first Wollaston casualty, Private **Samuel Firmstone**, who was killed on 5 November, although the *County Express* did not report his death until January 1915.

1915

The experiences of a '*Wounded Wollaston Soldier*', Private **Wilfred Johns**, were related by the *County Express* of 13 February 1915. Private Johns had been in all the campaigns from the Battle of Mons in late August 1914, and had been wounded in the foot at La Bassée, while trying to rescue a comrade. At the point that he related his experiences, he had recovered from this wound and was about to rejoin his depot.

The spring of 1915 saw renewed fighting on the western front around Neuve Chapelle and also the second battle of Ypres. This brought a crop of casualties with Wollaston connections:

- Private **Walter Burrows**, 37, died 12 March and had been a blacksmith's striker before the war. He left a wife, Annie Elizabeth, and three daughters.
- Private **Richard Jones** died 7 May, was 22 and single.

- Private **Claude Douglas Hammond** was just 19 when he died 24 May. His grandparents lived in Cobden Street.
- Private **John Clarke** died 31 May. He was also 19 and a former pupil of Wollaston Schools.
- Lance Corporal **Harry Stevens**, an ex-pupil of Wollaston Schools and King Edward VI Grammar School, Stourbridge, died 23 June aged 22.

All of the above together with Corporal **Claude Arthur Gordon Rutter**, who died 25 May in the fighting at

Right: Harry Stevens, a Lance Corporal with the 1st 8th Royal Warwickshire Regiment, was amongst the first Wollaston casualties of the Great War. Held in high esteem by his colleagues, Harry, from Duncombe Street, was an ex-pupil of Wollaston Schools, and King Edward VI Grammar School, Stourbridge, He died on 23 June 1915 aged 22 and was buried in Ploegsteert Wood, Belgium. This is how the *County Express* reported his funeral.

The War.
"Salute the Dead!"
Wollaston Old Edwardian's Funeral.

A simple and touching account of the funeral of Lance-Corpl. H. Stevens, 8th Warwicks, a Stourbridge Old Edwardian, has been sent to his parents, Mr. and Mrs. H. Stevens, "High View," Duncombe Street, Wollaston, by Pte. R. W. Stanton, a comrade of the deceased soldier. Pte. Stanton writes:—"I thought you would like to hear an account of Harry's funeral. It was on the evening of June 24th, and we took his body to a soldiers' cemetery which has been made in Ploegsteert Wood, just behind the firing line. Ploegsteert is just over the Belgian frontier from Armentieres, and I think in the direction of Messines.

THE LATE LANCE-CORPL. H. STEVENS.

The service was read by Lieut. Colonel Innes, of the 8th Warwicks, and I can assure you it was a most impressive and solemn occasion. Besides the colonel there were present Lieut. Whitehill, Capt. Morten, of A Company, all the members of Harry's year in Saltley College who are out here with us, and several of his juniors. At the end of the service the colonel called upon us all to salute Harry, with the words 'Officers, non-commissioned officers, and men, salute the dead. Honour to whom honour is due.' Later on we put a wooden cross painted white at the head of the grave, with this inscription in black lettering 'In memory of 1393, Lance-Corpl. H. Stevens, 1st 8th Royal Warwickshire Regiment (T.F.) killed in action 23rd June, 1915.' Round the grave too, we placed a border of white painted wood. Since this we have been moved to another part of the line."

Gallipoli, and **Arthur Jones**, were commemorated at a memorial service held in St James's Church on 6 July.

There was a further casualty from the fighting around Ypres when Private **Harry John Payne** was killed in action on 28 July. He was 23 years of age.

On 7 August, the *County Express* published a long letter written by Corporal **C R Gittins**, B Company, 1st/7th Worcesters, formerly secretary of Wollaston Cricket Club. The letter describes in reassuring terms the living conditions of, and activities undertaken by, English soldiers in France who were awaiting front line service camped in a forest:

'*In another part of the forest you descry a Sgt J Loxton, of Wollaston, and his men busy repairing boots, while you can see parties of men stripped to the waist, making the roadway, or track better for the transport. Still going on, you come to the transport lines where the men are busily engaged tending to their horses. Elsewhere you will find the 'Red Cross', where Surgeon Major Addenbrooke can be seen dispensing various remedies to ailing Tommies, while on the other side of the way are the headquarters of the regiment. While on your travels you will have met parties of men with towels on their arms, on their way to wash in the stream.*'

He then goes on to describe a little of what they had seen and done on the way towards the front:

'*Practically the whole of the old Wollaston cricket eleven are either at the front or in training. Brown, Foxall, and myself are out here, while Pagett is training in the 2nd/7th, and Hawkins with the South Staffords, and Davis and Oliver are serving with the ASC in the Dardanelles. Not bad for a local cricket eleven? I met Sid Allchurch, the Stourbridge cricketer, while he was at the rest village, and he said he was fit and well. It was he who informed me of the death of Harry Stevens, of Wollaston, and I must have passed within a few yards of his grave. I saw in the County Express Major Dan Taylor's reference to the cemetery we left behind at our last trenches. Soldier cemeteries are nearly always to be found in the vicinity of the trenches, and are always looked after by the regiment that is holding the position.*'

He adds as a postscript: '*Since writing the above letter I learn that among the new officers, which have arrived from England, is Second-Lieut E Cookson, Wollaston. We were one of the divisions which Lord Kitchener and Asquith inspected when they visited the 1st Army.*'

On 25 September, as a prelude to a successful attack on the small mining town of Loos, the British used chlorine gas for the first time. A casualty of this offensive was Private **Sylvanuss Bourne**, who died on 26 September, aged 24. He had been born in Kingswinford, and was living there in 1901, but was probably related to one of the Bourne families living in Wollaston.

The *County Express* of 30 October reported that Private **Allan Stanier** had been wounded again at Gallipoli, and printed a reassuring letter to his mother who lived in Bridgnorth Road. Allan's brother, Percy, was also in the army.

1916

In contrast to the reports of casualties, there were numerous articles in the newspapers, which were designed to encourage men to volunteer for the army. One example appeared in the *County Express* of 15 January 1916 under the title '*Patriotic Stourbridge Family. Five Soldier Brothers.*' It reported that Mr and Mrs T Garland, of 15 Wood Street, had the proud record that their five sons were all serving with the colours, three with the army, one in the navy and one with the Canadians. Another form of encouragement to enlist was the publishing of Rolls of Honour for various schools showing those former pupils who were serving in the armed forces. The Wollaston Schools Roll of Honour appeared in the *County Express* of 12 February 1916. It gave the names of 171 old boys and the units with which they were serving.

The County Express of 18 March 1916 reported the death of Lance Corporal **Charles William Dockerill**. He was killed on 5 March in the Somme area, aged 24. He had formerly been employed by W J Turney & Co and had married in October 1914.

Although there were no major battles around Ypres in the spring of 1916, there were some casualties as result of shelling and minor skirmishes:

- Private **Frederick Dennis Howells** died on 31 March as a result of a sniper's bullet. He was 23, single, and had been gardener to Frank Palfrey of Wood Street.
- Private **Charles Richard Robins** was reported as missing on 24 April. He was 32, had emigrated to Canada before the war and returned to fight with the Alberta Regiment of the Canadian Infantry. The family home was in High Street. It was not until November that his mother was notified that he was presumed dead.
- Private **Leonard Herbert Garland** also fought in the Canadian Infantry with the Quebec Regiment. One of the five brothers referred to above, he died on 24 May at The Duchess of Connaught Canadian Hospital in Taplow as a result of wounds received at St Eloi. He was buried at Cliveden, Berkshire. He had been born in Wollaston in 1889 and emigrated in 1912. He had written to the recruiting officer in Stourbridge on several occasions offering his services to the British Army, and having been refused, joined the Canadian Infantry.
- Sapper **Benjamin Burford** of the Royal Engineers died of 'spotted fever' in hospital in Henley-on-Thames on 12 May. He had been a carpenter. He was 40 and left a wife and seven children all under the age of 16. The family lived in Cobden Street.

There were three further deaths in May:
- Corporal **John Dennis Bill** was killed on 22 May near Ypres. He had emigrated to Canada and served with the Manitoba Regiment of the Canadian Infantry. He was a farmer and his parents lived in Park Lane, Wollaston.
- Private **Charles Morgan Harris** died on 25 May in the campaign against the Turks in Iraq. His parents

Shot by Sniper

Mr. T. Howells, Scotts Rd., Stourbridge, who recently lost a son in action on the Continent, has received a sympathetic letter from a sergeant of the Worcestershire Regiment, in which his son was serving. Having explained that the young soldier was shot dead by an enemy sniper, the sergeant states: "He had been acting as section leader for some time, under very trying times and I am very happy to say he proved to be hard working, thorough, and willing. You can be sure you have every reason to be proud of him for his conduct over here."

Having remarked that he was one of the most reliable men and that his loss was felt by the whole platoon, the sergeant says: "We managed to fix him up quite a decent grave together with five other lads from his own company, and the spot is exactly where he fell, overlooking quite a nice valley and not in a position to be disturbed or overlooked. He has his own grave complete with cross."

Above: Frederick Howells died on 31 March 1916 as a result of sniper fire. Aged 23, he was single and had been a pattern maker, and also gardener to Frank Palfrey of Wood Street. Accounts like this would become increasingly common in the *County Express. Stourbridge Library*

Above: The attestation papers of Corporal John Dennis Bill, who had been born in Wollaston, had worked as a grocer's porter, but had emigrated to Canada, and served with the Manitoba Regiment of the Canadian Infantry. He was a farmer, and had possibly gone to Canada in response to the many newspaper adverts calling for people with farming and industrial skills to emigrate there. His parents lived in Park Lane (later Road), Wollaston. John Bill was killed on 22 May 1916 near Ypres; he was 23.

Right: Older men were also lost in the Great War. Before the war, Ben Burford had been a carpenter and joiner, and lived with his wife and their seven children, all under the age of 16, in Cobden Street. A sapper in the Royal Engineers, he died of 'spotted fever' in hospital in Henley-on-Thames on 12 May 1916, aged 40.

lived in Brook Street, Wordsley, but were buried in Wollaston churchyard, where he is also commemorated.

• Private **Alfred Ernest Fryer** was wounded in the leg near Arras on 28 May and died as a result of his wounds. He was 35, unmarried, the youngest of a family of six and previously worked as a carter and labourer.

The Battle of the Somme began on 1 July 1916, and continued until November. Inevitably this brought a new crop of casualties:

- Private **Harry Male** died on 15 July aged 33. He was formerly employed as a blacksmith.
- Private **George Newton** died on 16 July aged 26. Under the heading '*Wollaston Territorial Killed*', the *County Express* of 12 August reported his death. They also reproduced an extract from a letter, from Corporal W S Lee to his father, which explained the circumstances of his death, together with a tribute from his lieutenant and an extract from the last letter to his father in which he sought to reassure him that all was well.
- Corporal **Adrian Vernon Scott Wakeman** was wounded on 8 July and died on 17 July aged 22. On 29 July the *County Express* contained a report of his funeral, which had taken place at Wollaston on 22 July. This was said to have attracted a crowd of between 3,000 and 4,000 people, when all of those lining the route taken by the cortège from Vicarage Road were included. This massive interest was a reflection of the fact that Adrain Wakeman was the first of the Wollaston fallen to be buried in the village. Adrian had previously been wounded at Gallipoli, had recovered and was then posted to France in 1916. He was married to Harriet, and had one son, Albert Adrian, who was baptised after his father's death. He had formerly been employed as a blacksmith. Ironically Adrian's older brother, Hubert, served with the Manchester Regiment and survived the war, but died in November 1919 from injuries caused by the explosion of a firework.
- Lance Corporal **Albert Charles Hitchings** was killed in action near High Wood on 23 July. He was just 21, and prior to the war had a promising career ahead of him as a building surveyor. He was the youngest son of Mr J P Hitchings who was a director of Edward Webb & Sons Ltd (the seed merchants) of Wordsley.

The *County Express* of 30 September 1916, under the heading '*Patriotic Wollaston Family*', reported that two of the 11 sons of Mr and Mrs J Jenkins of Vicarage Road had recently been killed. All 11 brothers were of military age and had all enlisted or attested. Private **Frederick H Jenkins** was killed at Delville Wood on 19 July, aged 24 and Private **Joseph Jenkins** fell in action on 26 August aged 36.

Private **Douglas Bethell**, the 19-year-old son of Thomas Bethell (a County Court cashier), was killed in action on 3 September.

In the area south of Ypres, Lance Corporal **William Pagett** was killed on 4 July aged 20. He is not mentioned on the Roll of Honour in the church, but is commemorated on his parents' gravestone in the churchyard. His father had died in 1904 and his mother in 1922.

On the 29 July the *County Express* reported the death of Private **Walter Nightingale** in the campaign in Mesopotamia. He had died on 13 July aged 31. He was formerly a steam hammer driver at Samuel Taylor & Sons.

The *County Express* of 12 August reported that **Caleb William Roberts Jr** had been awarded the French Cross of Honour and had been recommended for the Distinguished Conduct Medal (DCM). Caleb Roberts was the second son of Mr & Mrs Caleb William Roberts of Wollaston Hall.

Patriotic Wollaston Family.

Two Sons Fall in Action.

Mr. and Mrs. J. Jenkins, 4, Vicarage Road, Wollaston, have lost in action two of their 11. sons. All the 11 were of military age, and all enlisted or attested. Tidings reached them recently that their son, Pte. Joe Jenkins, of the Worcesters. fell in action on August 26th. He was 36 years old, enlisted April 1st, 1916, and was drafted to France last July. It has only been six weeks since his brother, Pte. F. H. Jenkins, was killed at Delville Wood. Pte. F. H. Jenkins was 24 years years old, enlisted on February

LATE PTE. F. H. JENKINS. LATE PTE. J. JENKINS.

DRIVER F. JENKINS, R.Q.M.S. A. JENKINS.

12th, 1916, in a Gloucester Battalion. went to France on June 22nd, and fell in action on July 19th. A younger son, Driver Frank Jenkins, has sent word that he has received his first letter and parcel since he went in January to Mesopotamia. He enlisted in February, 1915, at the age of 17 and went to France in August, 1915, but was invalided home with foot trouble in December. After treatment he went in January to the Eastern war zone. and while the life is very rigorous, he is keeping very fit. Another son, Reg. Quartermaster-Sergt. Alfred Jenkins, is in the Canadian Expeditionary Force . Of the remaining brothers, one, Sidney, has been rejected four times, having offered for both the Army and Navy. Two others expect to be called up shortly.

Above: Later in 1916 a terrible tragedy befell the Jenkins family of 4 Vicarage Road, Wollaston. They had 11 sons, all of whom were either enlisted or attested. The *County Express* of 30 September 1916 (seen here) reported that two of them had recently been killed. Frederick Jenkins, a former baker, aged 24, died at Delville Wood on 19 July, and Joseph Jenkins, aged 36, fell in action on 26 August.

A casualty in another peripheral campaign was Private **Harold George Farley** who died of wounds sustained in Greece on 25 August aged 21.

A report of a memorial service held at Wollaston Church in memory of Douglas Bethell, Harold Farley, Frederick Jenkins, Joseph Jenkins and George Newton was carried in the *County Express* of 14 October. Rev Hugh Wanstall conducted the service.

On 2 December the *County Express* reported that Lance Sergeant **Thomas James Howells** had been awarded the DCM for rescuing a comrade from No-Man's-Land. Second only to the Victoria Cross in prestige, the DCM was a means of recognising acts of gallantry performed by non-commissioned officers.

Above: In its 2 December 1916 issue, the *County Express* reported that Lance Sergeant Thomas James Howells of King Street, Wollaston, had been awarded the DCM for rescuing a comrade from No-Man's-Land. He is pictured here on the left, with two colleagues. This medal was a means of recognising acts of gallantry performed by non-commissioned officers, and was second only to the Victoria Cross in prestige.

1917

The year began with two further casualties from the campaign in Mesopotamia:

- Private **Reginald Frank De Saulles** who died 25 January aged 26, and Sapper **George William Attwood** who died 1 April aged 20. George Attwood had only been in the Army about six months. He had formerly been employed at Wollaston Mills. His mother was a widow and his brother was serving in France with the Royal Field Artillery.

- Private **Frank Kelly** of the Royal Warwickshire Regiment died near Arras on 16 April aged 23. His death is commemorated on his parents' grave in Wollaston churchyard.
- Private **Edward Benjamin Smith** of the Royal Army Medical Corps also died on 16 April from wounds received during the battle of Arras. He was 39, single, and worked as a gardener.
- Later in the battle, Private **William Ward**, who was born in Herefordshire but came to live and work in Wollaston, sustained wounds from which he succumbed on 7 June, aged 21.
- Private **Albert Welch** also died of wounds on the same date aged 22.

The third battle of Ypres (Passchendaele) began at the end of July 1917 and continued until November. This produced the largest number of casualties from Wollaston to date. They were:

- Private **Albert George Morley** who died on 16 August, aged 32, was married and formerly employed as a parchment maker.
- Warrant Officer **Frederick Thomas Dakin** had risen from the rank of Private in 1914 to become Deputy Assistant Director of Ordnance Supplies Staff at the time of his death on 17 August. He was 23 and prior to the war he had been employed in the office of Thomas Webb & Sons.
- Private **Edward Bowen** of the Machine Gun Corps was wounded in a secondary action associated with the Ypres offensive. He died from his wounds on 8 September. Edward was 36, single, and had previously been employed at W J Turney & Sons as a leather dresser.
- Second Lieutenant **Dudley Marshall** had only been transferred from the training battalion for a few months before he was killed on 26 September. He was 23 years old and had previously worked at Lloyds Bank, Cradley Heath. His father, James Marshall, had been the manager of the Novelty Glassworks in Gladstone Road.

Left: Second Lieutenant Dudley Marshall's father James had been the manager of the Novelty Glassworks in Gladstone Road. Dudley, who had worked at Lloyds Bank, Cradley Heath, had only been transferred from his training battalion a few months before he was killed on 26 September 1917. He was 23 years old.

- There were two deaths on 9 October 1917: Private **Charles Thomas Pagett** aged 22, the son of an ironworker; and Lance Corporal **Arthur Timmins**, age 21, who was hit by a shell.
- Private **Norman Harper** of the Royal Marine Light Infantry died 26 October aged 23.
- Private **William Henry Bristow** of the Canadian Mounted Rifles was killed in action on 30 October. He was 27, unmarried, and had emigrated to British Columbia in 1911 where he worked as a carpenter. His death was reported in the *County Express* of 24 November.

L8663

Ecclesiastical Insurance Office, Ltd.

11, NORFOLK STREET, STRAND, W.C.

GOVERNMENT INSURANCE AGAINST WAR RISKS.

The Managers of the Church of England Schools, Wollaston, having paid the undermentioned premium for the insurance of the property specified in fire policy number _130224_____against damage by aerial craft, the said insurance is hereby held in force, subject to the conditions endorsed hereon, pending the issue of the policy.

Sum Insured £ *3000*

For His Majesty's Government.

Robert Love

Premium £ *3 : 10 : -*
COUNT 50%   £ *1 : 10 : -*
.T PREMIUM.   £ *1 : 10 : -*

Above: Zeppelin raids over parts of the Black Country in 1916 may have motivated the Managers of Wollaston Schools to take out Government Insurance Against War Risks. Whatever the reason, the schools were insured for £3,000 with the Ecclesiastical Insurance Office Ltd on 19 April 1917. *St James's School PTA*

The following appeared in the *County Express* of 28 August under the title '*Wollaston Driver loses Right Arm*':

'*Driver Maurice Hull, RE, son of Mrs F Hull, Ivydene, Cobden Street, Wollaston, was home on leave only a few weeks ago. He is now in England again, recovering from serious injuries, having lost his right arm. It is only a few days since his mother received a field postcard stating the young soldier was all right. Then came a card addressed from Brook War Hospital at Woolwich, intimating that he had arrived there. Yesterday, a letter written by him, but with his left hand, reached his home. It read: "Dear Mother, a few lines to let you know I am in Blighty again. Jerry put four iron foundries into us, and made a mess of things. The first three missed me, but the next blew me over the hedge. I expect you would rather see me as I am than not at all, so for god's sake don't worry. I feel all right myself, only weak from loss of blood. Jerry smashed my wrist and elbow, and I had to have my arm off. I am getting well looked after and the best of food. I think I shall be all right when I am well again; with a light job and a bit of a pension I shall have enough to keep me going.' So recently as June, Driver Hull was specially complimented. The Major-General*

commanding an Irish Division wrote to him: "I have read with much pleasure the reports of your regimental commander and brigade commander regarding your gallant conduct and devotion to duty in the field in June 1917, and have ordered your name and deed to be entered into the record of the Irish Division." '

On 17 November the *County Express* reported that Private **Maurice Hall** of King Street, had been awarded the Military Medal. He was 28, single, and had been in the army for nine years.

Private **Harry Perks** and his wife had run a drapery and ladies-outfitters business in High Street Wollaston before he joined the army early in 1917. He had been in France about a month and in the trenches only a few days before he was killed on 22 November. He was 40 and left his wife with two children.

1918

The *County Express* of 5 January 1918 contained an advertisement that invited people to register the names of war casualties, presumably with the intention of producing a roll of honour at a later date. It is not known what happened to any information that was collected as a result of this appeal.

On 26 January the *County Express* contained an article headed '*Late Wollaston Bandsman – His Bandmaster's Tribute*.' The bandsman in question was Private **Arthur George Dickins** who was 21 when he was killed in action at Cambrai on 30 November 1917. He played the trombone and violin, and had been a member of a number of local bands. He had joined the Territorials and become a first-class bandsman before being sent to France. His parents had a grocery shop in High Street, Wollaston.

Charles Garland, brother of Leonard, who was killed in 1916, was awarded the Military Medal and a commission in 1918 for gallantry in the field. He was a former employee of London, City & Midland Bank at Smithfields, Birmingham. He had enlisted in January 1915 and went to France in November that year. While serving as an Acting-Sergeant in October 1917 he captured a German pillbox and was wounded, for which he was recommended for a commission by his Captain.

Under the title '*Stourbridge Highlander Sergt*' the *County Express* of 23 February reported the award of the DCM to Sergeant **Charles Haywood** of the Argyll & Sutherland Highlanders. The report stated:

'*Although wounded in both legs, he refused to leave the firing line, and went on to the second and third enemy line. There he organised the men, setting them a splendid example of coolness and devotion to duty. Immediately afterwards he was hit by bomb splinters in sixteen places. His fearlessness on this occasion is typical of the courage invariably displayed by him. Sergt. Haywood is the son of PC Haywood, night reserve constable at Brierley Hill, who had completed his service in the Staffordshire Constabulary, but has returned to duty since the outbreak of war to assist the depleted ranks of the county force. His home is at Wollaston.*'

Sadly **Charles Haywood** died in Greece on 19 September at the age of 23.

The early part of 1918 was characterised by German offensives around Ypres and Armentières in the north and the Somme and Aisne areas further south. Casualties in the area around Ypres were:

- 19-year-old Private **Joseph Sydney Rabone**, died 10 April.
- Lance Corporal **William Yates**, aged 30, died 14 April. William was born in Wollaston but married before the war and lived in Coventry where he was a master painter.
- 19-year-old Private **George Samuel Dakin** died 25 April.
- 19-year-old Lewis gunner Private **Victor Donald Pratt**, a victim of the Aisne offensive, was killed on 7 June.

'*Wollaston Corporal Awarded Military Medal*' was the title of the following article published in the *County Express* on 13 April:

Above: In addition to being commemorated on the village war memorial inside St James's Church, the names of some Wollaston soldiers are also inscribed on memorials abroad. Victor Donald Pratt's name is on the Soissons Memorial in Aisne, France, seen here. He lived in Cobden Street, and had been a telegraph boy. A victim of the Aisne offensive, 19-year-old Victor was killed on 7 June 1918. *Avril Williams*

'*Corpl **Thomas Punfield**, who married the daughter of Mr and Mrs George Thomason of the "Britannia" Inn, Wollaston, formerly resided at Wordsley, but some years ago journeyed to Canada where he carried on a successful business. At the outbreak of war in 1914 he volunteered his services, and was attached to the 20th Canadian Battalion. Sent to this country, and subsequently to France, he took part in many engagements, and went over the parapet 11 times, only once being seriously wounded. He enlisted as a private, and was later promoted to Corporal for his gallantry. His daughter, Miss Margaret Punfield, of the*

Britannia Inn has recently received a communication from the "Overseas Military Forces of Canada" enclosing a silver Military Medal, awarded to her father for conspicuous bravery in the field. It was on August 15th 1916, that he took charge of the carrying party, and brought ammunition to the Stokes guns in the face of severe enemy gunfire. The original party comprised 20 men, and on the third trip the deadly barrage of the German guns wiped out all but five of the heroic little party. Corpl Punfield was severely wounded and it was necessary for the other four men to carry him back to safety. On the recommendation of his captain he was awarded the Military Medal. Corpl Punfield has since been in hospital in this country, and has now been transferred to Canada to recuperate with a view to obtaining his discharge.'

Private **Richard Henry Ward** aged 19 was killed in Italy on 16 June. His older brother William had died a year earlier.

A further article in the *County Express* of 13 July reported that:

'*Private **Walter Unitt** of the Worcestershire Regiment, who joined up about two years ago, has seen much hard service*

A Wollaston Family's Record.

The three sons of Mr. and Mrs. T. Arnold, Victoria Terrace, Duncombe Street, Wollaston, are all serving with his Majesty's forces, Corpl. W. J. Arnold, R.G.A., Gunner J. B. Arnold, R.F.A., and G. S. Arnold, O.S., R.N.V.R., wireless operator. They were all choristers at Wollaston Church, in the choir of of which the father has been conne ted for 24 years. Corpl. Arnold enlisted with the first batch of Kitchener's Army, and has been in France 2½ years. He was a promising footballer, and was formerly apprentice to glass engraving at Messrs. Webb and Corbett's. Gunner Arnold, an Army reservist, was working on the Midland Railway at Whitchurch, when he was called up in August 1914. He was in the retreat from Mons, and his 28 engagements include St. Quentin, Aisne, Marne, Sossoins, Hill 60, Ypres, Vimy Ridge, Arras, Festubert, Richeburg, Somme, Mametz, Fricourt, Monteban, Luzanne, Bray, Neuve Eglise, Kemmel and Ypres. He was wounded on October 2nd, 1917. G. S. Arnold was working in the accountant's office at Messrs. Chance and Hunt's before joining the wireless at the Crystal Palace in December 1917 and passed out as an operator on April 25th this year. He was secretary to the Wollaston Sports Club.

Left: Another Wollaston family with all their sons serving in the forces was the Arnolds of Victoria Terrace, Duncombe Street, as the *County Express* reported in May 1918. All three had been choirboys at St James's Church. *Stourbridge Library*

in France, has won the Military Medal for conspicuous bravery on the field. Previous to enlisting, he was a glass blower at Dennis Glass Works. He was also an enthusiastic footballer and good all round sport. His home is at King Street, Wollaston.'

On 20 July 1918 the County Express reported that around 300 wounded soldiers from Studley Court (later Mary Stevens Park) and the Southern General (later Wordsley) hospitals had been entertained on the previous Saturday at The Croft, Wollaston, the home of Mr & Mrs A H Guest. Stourbridge and District Wounded Soldiers Entertainment Committee organized the event that comprised a picnic tea followed by a concert.

The allied counter-offensive on the Western Front began in mid-July and continued until the armistice on 11 November. This resulted in quite a number of casualties in Northern France in the autumn in addition to a few from the other fronts:

- On 23 August, 19 year-old **Harold Edward Grace** was killed near Bapaume. Harold had been born in Wolverhampton but the family moved to Wollaston before the war. His father was a railway worker.
- Private **Walter Timmins**, 25, was killed near Arras on 18 September. His younger brother Arthur had been killed at Ypres the previous October.
- On 19 September Private **William Boulton** of the Essex Regiment died near Peronne aged 19. His death is commemorated on his parents' grave in Wollaston churchyard. The family had lived at Newtown, Prestwood.
- Private **Horace Moore** was killed in action near Cambrai on 28 September at the age of 21.

On 12 October 1918 the County Express, reported Sergeant **George David Wainwright** as missing. In fact he had been killed in Iran on 14 September. George was 24 and prior to his war service had been employed as a gas fitter at Stourbridge gas works. The family lived in Ridge Street and he had two brothers. Also recorded in the same issue was the death of Lance Corporal **Bert Lee** on 22 September aged 19. He had previously worked as an iron moulder.

Under the heading 'Wollaston Military Medallist Wounded' the 19 October issue of the County Express printed part of a letter from Private **H Turner** to his brother in law in which he described how he had been shot through the thigh by a sniper while taking ammunition to a forward position. He then described how he won the Military Medal in Italy:

'We went over on a raid on the Asiago Plateau. The sergeant and I took the right of the trench ourselves, capturing 13 prisoners and a machine gun, besides doing several in. The General, when he gave me the ribbon, said he was proud to do so.'

The County Express of 2 November reported that Private **George Henry Cookson** had been killed in action on 26 September. He was 21 and had been employed at Thomas Webb & Sons, Dennis Glassworks. He had only been in France for about three weeks.

Driver **Frederick William Parker**, of the Royal Field Artillery, died of wounds near Cambrai on 23 October aged 20. Meanwhile in Turkey, Private **Wilfred Henry Johns** died on 24 October. He had previously been wounded in France early in 1915.

On 4 November Gunner **Cyril William Priest** died near Cambrai as a result of a shrapnel wound to the neck, he was just 20. He had been employed by the GWR before joining the army.

The armistice was signed on 11 November, but the County Express of 30 November reported the death of Driver **Frederick Thomas Lee** at Salonica on 6 November. He was 22 and died from pneumonia. His younger brother, Bert, had been killed in September 1918.

1919

In the 25 January issue of the County Express it was reported that Sergeant **Thomas James Howells**, son of Mr G Howells of King Street, had been awarded the Military Medal for his part in operations in Italy from the Asiago Plateau to the Trentino in early November 1918. Sergeant Howells had been wounded twice, once in the Battle of the Somme and again at Ypres.

A report in the County Express of 19 July 1919 records that on the previous Saturday about 200 returned soldiers and sailors were entertained at The Croft. A

Above: The County Express of 25 January 1919 reported that Sergeant Thomas James Howells, seen here standing proudly, had been awarded the Military Medal for his part in operations in Italy from the Asiago Plateau to the Trentino Valley in early November 1918. Thomas Howells had been wounded twice, once in the Battle of the Somme, and again at Ypres, and had also been awarded the DCM in November 1916.

committee set up to welcome home those of the parish who had served in the war organized the event. Those who had won gallantry awards were each presented with an inscribed silver cigarette case. The recipients were: Sergeant **J T Davis** DCM, Lieutenant **S T Handley** MM, Lieutenant **G H Garland** MM, Sergeant **T J Howells** MM, Sergeant **E Southall** MM, Corporal **M Hull** MM, Private **H Turner** MM, Private **J Richards** MM.

The *County Express* of 22 November 1919 reported that a military funeral had taken place at Wollaston on the previous Wednesday. The deceased was Private **Harry Moore** who died 13 November aged 31. He was the older brother of Horace Moore who had been killed in September 1918.

Above: Sapper Benjamin Burford of the Royal Engineers died of 'spotted fever' in hospital in Henley-on-Thames on 12 May 1916. Ben was aged 40 and lived in Cobden Street with his wife and seven children all under the age of 16. He was buried in a special portion of Botley Cemetry, Oxford, seen here, which was reserved for those who died at the local hospital. *Avril Williams*

1920

The dedication of Wollaston Church War Memorial was reported in the *County Express* of 31 July 1920, the event having taken place the previous Sunday, 25 July. The memorial was described thus:

'*The memorial is a beautiful oak tablet, placed immediately under the Gilbanks' stained glass window in the south transept. On it the names of upwards of 50 Wollaston men who fell in the war are printed in bold black and gold letters. The words "Pro Patria" are inscribed at the top of the memorial, and "Roll of Honour, 1914-1919," at the foot: a beautiful carved figure of the Angel of Victory adorns the centre. Voluntary subscriptions from members of*

Above: The St James's Church War Memorial was dedicated on 25 July 1920. It is an oak tablet, and had been placed immediately under the stained glass window dedicated to George Gilbanks in the south transept. Relatives and friends who had lost loved ones had submitted the 53 names on the memorial.

the congregation only have met the cost of the memorial, which the vicar aptly describes as "Beautifully simple and simply beautiful." '

The 53 names on the memorial were submitted by relatives and friends who had lost loved ones which may explain why not all those who lost their lives, and had Wollaston connections, are included. Only one of the names has not been positively connected to Wollaston, that of **Alex Cumming**. There are several casualties of that name but no connection with Wollaston has been found for any of them. One more name was added to the memorial at a later date, that of **William Arnold**. The lettering used is slightly different to that for the other names. Second Lieutenant William Joseph Arnold died on 18 April 1923, aged 28, after a long and painful illness following exposure to poisonous gas during his war service. He is buried in Wollaston Churchyard. Pre-war he had been a promising footballer and had been a member of the choir with his father and four brothers. Messrs Webb Corbett had employed him as a glass engraver.

World War II

Preparations

Air Raid Precaution (ARP) areas for Stourbridge were published in the *County Express* of 17 September 1938. Wollaston was to be divided between groups A and B; the dividing line was Bridgnorth Road. Preparations were clearly well in hand as the April 1939 edition of the parish magazine published a list of Wollaston's ARP wardens. The *County Express* of 3 June 1939 stated that the distribution of gas masks to the residents of Wollaston would take place the following week. Nominated collection points were: Wollaston Schools, Bright Street Methodist Church and St Thomas's Mission Church, South Road.

The mobilisation of Anti-Aircraft Command was ordered for the last week of August 1939 and the Royal Engineers set up an anti-aircraft and listening station on Swan Pool Park, Studley Gate. It comprised a spotter chair, listening dish and binoculars mounted on a trailer, a generator and an anti-aircraft gun, all of which were towed around by three lorries. A battery of searchlights was also provided. Local scouts were used as messengers. The operators were under the command of a Corporal and initially housed in a tented camp, but later in wooden huts.

On 2 September the *County Express* reported that five communal air raid shelters had been completed in the town's open spaces. One of those shelters was under the playing fields on Studley Gate, at the Park Road end, and could accommodate 230 people. A similar shelter was constructed beneath Wollaston Rec., and beneath three other open spaces in Stourbridge.

Local people recall that there was an air raid decoy at Brooks' Farm, Whittington. This was staffed by MoD civilians and was intended to draw German bombers away

MILITARY FUNERAL. — Second Lieut. W. J. Arnold, R.G.A., eldest son of Mr. and Mrs. T Arnold, of Duncombe Street, Wollaston, died on Wednesday week after a long and painful illness following his war service. The funeral in St. James's Churchyard on Saturday was conducted by the Rev. H. U. Wanstall and was attended by many demonstrations of regret and regard. Full military honours were accorded by a gun team of the 268th Battery R.F.A., Dudley, and men of the 7th Worcesters (Stourbridge Company) who formed a firing party. The mourners were T: Arnold (father), Messrs. Arthur, George, and Fred (brothers), Messrs. George and Arthur Shenton (uncles), and Messrs. P. Bland, J. Piper and M. Hall.—There were no flowers by request.—The service cap of the deceased was buried with him in accordance with his last wish.—The funeral arrangements were carried out by Mr. C. H. Cook, South Road, Stourbridge.

Left: One more name was added to the war memorial later, that of William Arnold. He died aged 28 on 18 April 1923 after a long and painful illness following exposure to poisonous gas during his war service. He was buried in Wollaston Churchyard. Before the war he had been a promising footballer and had worked at Webb Corbett as a glass engraver.

Above: Anti-Aircraft Command was mobilised during the last week of August 1939. The Royal Engineers set up an anti-aircraft and listening station on Swan Pool Park, Studley Gate, at the Park Road end. It comprised a spotter chair, listening dish and binoculars mounted on a trailer, like the one seen here, plus a generator and an anti-aircraft gun, all of which were towed around by three lorries. *Imperial War Museum*

Below: A battery of searchlights, like this one, was also provided on Swan Pool Park. Local scouts were used as messengers to pass the intelligence collected to Anti-Aircraft Command. *Imperial War Museum*

Above: Six Wollaston soldiers are commemorated on the great Thiepval Memorial on the Somme in France, seen here. They are: Douglas Bethell, Albert Hitchings, Frederick Jenkins, Joseph Jenkins, Harry Male and George Newton. *Avril Williams*

from ammunition factories in the area. In the event, only two bombs fell locally, one on the Roman Road and one on Stourbridge golf course, where a large gun was stationed.

In the issue of 30 September, the *County Express* reported that Rev Reg Bamber had been appointed Chaplain to the Gloucestershire Regiment. The curate, Rev Romilly Craze, had been one of the first clergymen in the diocese to be called up, but was later turned down because he was blind in one eye. He was left as curate in charge of the parish. In the same issue it was stated that the windows in the church had been blacked out as an air raid precaution so that evening services could carry on as normal.

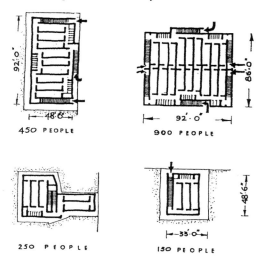

450 PEOPLE

900 PEOPLE

250 PEOPLE

150 PEOPLE

PLANS SHOWING DIFFERENT
SIZES AND ARRANGEMENTS

Above: On 2 September 1939, the day before war was declared, the *County Express* reported that five communal air raid shelters had been completed on the town's open spaces. One of those shelters was under the Swan Pool Park playing fields on Studley Gate, at the Park Road end, and could accommodate 230 people. These are some of the various designs of communal shelter constructed in the country at that time. *Imperial War Museum*

Below: The communal air raid shelter beneath Swan Pool Park is still there. The buried walls of the shelter below cause this unnatural looking ridge.

Above: Local people recall that there was an air raid decoy at Brooks' Farm, Whittington. This was staffed by MoD civilians and was intended to draw German bombs away from Birmingham. Only two bombs fell locally during World War II, one on the Roman Road and one on Stourbridge golf course, where a large gun was stationed. This is the control room to the QL decoy at Whittington.

1940

In the February edition of the *Parish Magazine* Romilly Craze reported that Reg Bamber had been moved from his Battalion and had been attached to a Casualty Clearing Station, which was under orders to leave for France in the near future.

In a radio broadcast on 14 May, the Rt Hon Anthony Eden, Secretary of State for War, called for: '*men of all ages who are for one reason or another not at present engaged in military service and who wish to do something for the defence of the country*' to come forward and join the Local Defence Volunteers which was envisaged as an anti-parachutist force. The name of the force was changed to the more familiar Home Guard with effect from 31 July. The Wollaston Home Guard was D Company of the 10th Worcestershire Battalion, commanded by Major Frank Hejl. He was born in 1898 and served in the Great War in the

Below: The Home Guard was formed following a radio broadcast by Anthony Eden, Secretary of State for War, on 14 May 1940. Wollaston Home Guard was D Company of the 10th Worcestershire Battalion, commanded by Major Frank Hejl. He ran a tailors and furriers business at 149 Bridgnorth Road, on the corner of Duncombe Street. The company trained in the old Eggington Farm buildings, as seen here, and their 232 members included one Chris Gittins, later to find fame as Walter Gabriel in *The Archers*.

Duke of Lancaster's Own Yeomanry. He ran a tailors and furriers business at 149 Bridgnorth Road, on the corner of Duncombe Street.

Soon after the outbreak of World War II, as part of Civil Defence measures, a static water tank was erected in Meriden Avenue. This would provide water if it was needed to extinguish fires caused by bombing. Meriden Avenue had only a few houses at the village end of the road in 1939. Stourbridge builder, Edward R R Tooby, had purchased about 16 acres of land in November 1924, which had been part of Eggington Farm, but house building proceeded at a slow pace. The council had not adopted the road, but one pair of semi-detached houses (Nos 86 and 88 in 2003), had been built before the war. They stand where the avenue turns left, and it was next to these, on land that was requisitioned, that the water tank was installed. Its size was about equal to a pair of houses. At the end of the war, after the tank's demolition, more properties were built, and another pair of semis, Nos 90 and 92, occupy the land where the tank once stood. It is probable that most of the inhabitants of Meriden Avenue are unaware that such a large structure once existed in their locality.

On 20 May Sergeant **Kenneth Victor Thrift** of the RAF became the first casualty whose name is recorded on the Roll of Honour in Wollaston Church. He was 20 and his parents lived in Kinver. He was buried in The Netherlands.

Private **Joseph William Chapman** died near Lille in northern France on 21 May. He was 21 and his family lived in Harmon Road. Private **George Taylor** also died near Lille

Above: Wollaston's Home Guard also had a band, whose members are seen here, again at Eggington Farm. Seated by their cups on the left is Norman Rabey, a barber who had a distinguished record of service from the Great War.

on 26 May. He was married, aged 21, and his parents lived in King Street. Both the above died on the retreat to Dunkirk and Private **James Conrad Smith** was taken prisoner in the same retreat. He died at Cambrai on 10 June aged 19. According to the *Parish Magazine* he had joined the armed forces under age. In its July edition the *Parish Magazine* reported that the Reg Bamber was missing and had probably been taken prisoner. It was later confirmed that he was a

POW, together with seven other Wollaston men. The November issue of the magazine reported that **Victor Yates** had been awarded the OBE *'for gallantry at Dunkirk.'*

In December the Wollaston platoon of the Home Guard marked the opening of their base in buildings at Eggington Farm with a supper and entertainment. The Battalion Commander Major Laughton Goodwin performed the formal opening ceremony.

At a meeting of the Stourbridge Branch of the Red Cross Penny-a-Week Fund, in early December, it was decided to adopt Reg Bamber, now a POW in Germany. Under this scheme he would receive a weekly Red Cross parcel to the value of 10s. Such parcels could contain food, soap, a postcard, cigarettes or tobacco.

Driver **Joseph Edward Fletcher** died of meningitis on 8 December. A member of the Royal Army Service Corps, he was 21, married and lived at Whittington.

1941

The January edition of the *Parish Magazine* reported that Lance Bombardier **Gilbert Garrington** had been mentioned in despatches on 20 December 1940. In the same issue, a letter from Reg Bamber, written in a POW camp, was reproduced. This described church life within the camp, which housed around 1,400 officers and men, including 30 chaplains. In February it was reported that he had been moved to a nearby camp in a medieval castle containing only 150 officers. As a non-combatant Reg Bamber was officially being held in protective custody pending repatriation.

In the *County Express* of 8 February it was recorded that the Military Medal had been awarded to Lance Bombardier **J P Haskew**, Royal Artillery, whose father lived in Fir Grove.

The *County Express* of 8 March stated that Wollaston Schools were to be used as the headquarters of the Lower Bridgnorth Road firewatchers.

Gunner **Thomas Henry Hill**, who served with an anti-aircraft battery of the Royal Artillery, died in hospital on 21 March as the result of an unspecified accident. He was 34 and married.

Youth organisations in Wollaston Parish were reported to have arranged the billeting of evacuee children from Coventry, according to the *County Express* of 12 April. In the same issue it stated that approximately 250 men from Wollaston were on active service.

In May 1941 **Emmie Harrison** of Ridge Street started a National Savings Scheme. The initial aim was to target 40 streets and by August 28 groups had been formed comprising 531 people and raising an average of 6s per person. By October the whole village had been covered and a 'thermometer' was erected outside the schools to record the monthly and total savings.

Ordinary Seaman **Graham Creed** of HMS Fiji was killed aged 25 on 23 May in fighting off Crete.

Sergeant **William Henry Lewis** of the RAF Volunteer Reserve was killed in a flying accident on 1 June. He was 26 and his family lived in Mamble Road. He had attended Wollaston Schools and later King Edward VI Grammar School, Stourbridge. He was buried with full military honours in Wollaston churchyard.

Private **Edmund Wadley** was killed in action near Karachi in Pakistan on 4 June. He was 22 and had attended Wollaston Schools. The logbook records that in September 1927 he and others had been playing hide and seek with Wilfred Weaver, who was run over and killed by a Midland Red bus.

On 16 June Gunner **Howard Ernest Bullock** died in Israel aged 26. The school admissions register notes that he left to become an electrician.

The *County Express* of 21 June reported that Sergeant **Leslie Owen Hodnett**, a wireless operator/air gunner in the RAF Volunteer Reserve had been killed in a flying accident on 19 June, just over a week after his 19th birthday. He had been a Sunday school teacher, cub master, church sides man, a member of the YPS and had been employed in the fitting shop of Bailey, Pegg & Co. When the war broke out he was also an ARP messenger. He was buried with full military honours in Wollaston churchyard.

In July 1941 the first Italian POWs arrived in the UK. At some point after this, the wooden huts at the searchlight battery at Studley Gate were demolished and replaced by three Nissen huts to house POWs. A high chain link fence surrounded the huts. Local people recall that the Italians worked at Ashford's Dairy and also on farms in Kinver and Enville, to which they were transported each day by lorry. Apart from working, they gave the impression of being scruffy, lounging about and chasing the local girls. They earned a small income by selling sandals, which they had made from rope. Kenneth Woodward recollects that there were about 30 POWs who were guarded by three soldiers, although they were never a threat to anyone. They were good at making toys and rings from sixpenny coins, which they did in exchange for cigarettes.

Private **Samuel Eggington** died on 13 August aged 33. He was buried in Kidderminster where he had lived with his wife Marion.

The *County Express* of 27 September recorded that High Park Estate fire-watching scheme, one of the largest in the borough, had organised a women's First Aid section, and that 150 women had volunteered to attend instruction at Wollaston Schools.

Sergeant **Arthur Dexter Southall** was a wireless operator/air gunner in the RAF Volunteer Reserve who had married Eileen Marjorie Dimmock at Wollaston Church on the 16 August. He was killed in a raid over Europe on 29 November aged 23.

1942

A letter from Reg Bamber, dated 11 December 1941, was reproduced in the March edition of the *Parish Magazine*. He had been moved from Germany to Rouen with the seriously wounded and Royal Army Medical Corps personnel pending negotiations about repatriation, however negotiations broke down and he was transferred as padre to

Above: The death of Leslie Hodnett shocked Wollaston. A wireless operator/air gunner in the RAF Volunteer Reserve, he was killed in a flying accident on 19 June 1941, one week after his 19th birthday. Most people in the village knew Leslie. He lived at 7 Firmstone Street and had been a Sunday School teacher, a cub master, church sidesman, a member of the YPS, and had worked in the fitting shop of Bailey, Pegg & Co. When war broke out he was also an ARP messenger.

Below: Five months after Leslie Hodnett's death, a second Wollaston wireless operator/air gunner in the RAF Volunteer Reserve, Sergeant Arthur Dexter Southall, was killed in a raid over Europe on 29 November 1941, aged 23. He had married Eileen Dimmock at Wollaston Church on the 16 August 1941.

a men's prison camp. News of the death of the vicar's father, Rev John Bamber was reported in the April edition with sympathy expressed by Romilly Craze to the vicar and his family. Further postcards/letters from the vicar were reported, usually at Easter and Christmas until the end of 1943 when there is no further comment in the magazine until the vicar's return in April 1945.

The death of Bombardier **Geoffrey Worrall** was reported in the May edition of the *Parish Magazine*. He died in Malta on 8 April aged 20. His four brothers and father had all been on active service. His father, who had been awarded the Military Medal in the Great War, had also served in the war until he was invalided out in 1941.

Guardsman **George Williams** was drowned on 4 June 1942 aged 26. According to the *Parish Magazine* his parents had only recently moved to Wollaston.

On 22 July the battle of El Alamein claimed the life of Trooper **Walter Hickman** of the Royal Tank Regiment. He was 21.

Sergeant **Austen Douglas (Bill) Evans** of the RAF died in Germany on 1 August. He was a married man aged 30, whose parents lived in Hyperion Road. Another RAF man, Sergeant Pilot **Albert J R (Jackie) Millman** died in France on 7 September aged 21.

Flying Officer **Alan Norman** was awarded the DFM for operations on 6 August while serving with 408 Squadron of Royal Canadian Air Force. He went on to serve throughout the six years of the war and was promoted to Pilot Officer while serving with 196 Squadron. Most of his flying was done in Hampden bombers.

On 1 November, Leading Seaman **Charles H D Rowberry** of HMS President III was lost in the sinking of the SS Mendoza, which had rescued him. He was 29 and the son of Charles Rowberry, deputy head teacher of Wollaston Schools. November also saw the death of Pilot Officer **Harold Otho Male** of the RAF who died in Nova Scotia, Canada, on 20 November aged 23.

December 1942 also saw the formation of a Wollaston Knitting Party, which produced gloves, scarves and socks

Above: In addition to the protection afforded to the Coalbournbrook water pumping station by the Home Guard, the workers there organised themselves into their own, small, civil defence unit. Messrs Bridge, Cozel, Gibbs and White posed proudly for the camera ready to repel all comers!

for allied POWs. Their prodigious output was regularly reported in the parish magazine.

1943

Lance Bombardier **Michael McHale** died of wounds on 8 March in Tripoli, North Africa. He was a married man aged 31.

In March 1943 the Women's Home Guard Auxiliary was formed, later better known as 'Mum's Army.' Here the intention was for women to work as clerks, cooks, messengers and typists, to free up men from these duties. In practice they took on most of the tasks performed by the Auxiliary Training Service (ATS) in the regular Army, and nationally their strength grew to 32,000. Wollaston's Mum's Army comprised just four: **Sheila Burroughs**, **Betty Davis**, **Dot Davis** and **Margaret White**.

Private **Arthur Taylor** died in Thailand on 12 June aged 23.

In September the *Parish Magazine* recorded that Leading Airman **W H Aston** had been mentioned in dispatches and the December issue reported that a Roll of Honour had been started at the rear of the church.

The death of Sergeant **Gordon Alec Worrall**, aged 24, occurred on 27 September in Italy, but as late as January 1944 the *Parish Magazine* still recorded him as missing, possibly a POW. In the same issue, Gunner **Leonard Harwood** was reported to be a Japanese POW, however he actually died in Thailand on 6 November aged 28.

1944

In January, a concert was held in Wollaston Schools in aid of the Red Cross Prisoner of War Fund. The school was packed to overflowing and many people had to be turned away. The *County Express* of 29 January, under the heading 'Saved by Regimental Badge,' reported the experiences of

Above: One of the Home Guard's main duties was to protect important installations in the area, such as the water pumping station at Coalbournbrook, seen above just before it was demolished.

Above: The Women's Home Guard Auxiliary, later better known as 'Mum's Army', was formed in March 1943. They were intended to work as clerks, cooks, messengers and typists, to free up men from these duties. Wollaston's Mum's Army comprised just four: Betty Davis, Dot Davis, Margaret White, and Sheila Burroughs.

Raymond Taylor of the Worcestershire Regiment in the invasion of Sicily. He had been wounded by shrapnel when a shell hit his landing craft, but the regimental badge on his belt had deflected a piece of this, which might otherwise have shattered his spine.

The *County Express* of 4 March reported the death of Private **Edward Arthur Cunningham** on 8 February at Anzio in Italy. Sergeant Flight Engineer **Charles Harry Marsh** died over Germany on 21 February aged 27.

The May edition of the *Parish Magazine* recorded the deaths of:

- Leading Airman **Frederick Harry White** of the Royal Navy Fleet Air Arm, HMS Shrike, as a result of a flying accident on 23 April.
- Flight Lieutenant **Walter Roy Hare** DFC, an air gunner with the RAF, died in Belgium on 11 May aged 23.
- Corporal **Ernest Richard Page** was killed in action at Anzio, Italy on 27 May aged 23.

The death of Flight Sergeant **John Douglas Hadlington** occurred on 25 June in northern France. He was 31 years of age and married. Sergeant **Ronald Ernest Woodus**, a married man of 25, died in northern France on 18 July. On 27 July, Flying Officer **William Hoskins** was killed in Corsica; he was 27. He married Joyce Jarvis in Wollaston, but previously he had lived in Meddins Lane, Kinver.

Private **Kenneth Howells** of King Street died in Normandy on 9 August. He was the 19-year-old son of Thomas J Howells, who gained the Military Medal in the Great War, and nephew of Frederick Dennis Howells who was killed in 1916.

Following the signing of the Italian Armistice on 8 September 1943, Italian POWs were gradually repatriated

and the first German POWs arrived in local camps about September 1944. Local inhabitants recall the Studley Gate camp being empty for about a fortnight between the Italians leaving and the first Germans arriving. The impression made by the German POWs was that they were hard workers. They laid out the camp with gardens and earned a few shillings by digging gardens for local people. They worked at the local glassworks, on the railways, and on Wollaston Farm, and referred to the camp as 'Studley Gate Hostel.' In the winter they also helped to clear the snow. They made friends with local people; particularly the children for whom they made dolls, and Mrs Bamber took some of them to church. Local people laid in electricity to the camp so that the prisoners could have Christmas decorations. After Bergen Belsen Concentration camp was liberated in April 1945 they were taken to local cinemas to see newsreels of what was found there. It was said that none of them could believe what their fellow countrymen had done.

With the immediate threat of invasion receding due to the progress of the war, the need for the Home Guard

Above: A Prisoner of War camp, to house Italian prisoners, was built on Swan Pool Park, on the site of the former listening station there. Following the Italian Armistice on 8 September 1943, their POWs were gradually repatriated, and were replaced by German POWs about September 1944. Five German POWs pose in a relaxed way outside the Swan Pool POW Camp after the war.

diminished and operational Home Guard duties were suspended from 6 September 1944. After this date parades could continue on a voluntary basis. The official stand down of the Home Guard was announced in mid-December to take effect from 31 December. In its four years' existence, Wollaston Home Guard had a total of 232 members! A log recording the home address of each member and the equipment with which they were issued is preserved in Stourbridge Library.

Merchant Navy Week in Wollaston was from 4-11 September. Various fund raising events were organised including; Church collections, a variety concert, a garden fete at The Croft and a Gala Day on Wollaston Crescent. These events raised £665.

Fusilier **James Walter Harris**, a married man of 24 was killed in Italy on 6 September. Both he and his wife

MAJOR F. A. HEJL.
OFFICER COMMANDING "D" COMPANY 10TH WORCS. BN., HOME GUARD.
HIS FELLOW-OFFICERS AND COMPANY CHAPLAIN
CORDIALLY INVITE YOU AND YOUR FAMILY TO ATTEND

A SERVICE OF THANKSGIVING

FOR WORK DONE AND DANGERS AVERTED.

AT WOLLASTON PARISH CHURCH

ON SUNDAY, DECEMBER 3RD. 1944. AT 18.30 HRS.

DRESS; UNIFORM   SEATS RESERVED UNTIL 18.25 HRS.

Above: With the war going the Allies way, Home Guard duties were suspended from 6 September 1944. After this parades could continue on a voluntary basis. The Home Guard official stand down was announced in mid-December, to take effect from 31 December. In most places, stand-down parades and thanksgiving services were held. Wollaston was no exception.

Below: Major Frank Hejl takes the salute at the Wollaston Home Guard stand-down parade on 3 December 1944 as he leads his troops past the end of King Street.

were from Beauty Bank Crescent. On 21 September, Sergeant **Frank Tomkins** was killed in action in the Netherlands aged 32. He was married and had lived in Lye, although his parents lived in Wollaston. On 24 September, Sergeant **Kenneth Victor Lowe** also died in the Netherlands aged 30. He was a Wordsley man, but married Elsie Louisa Sutton from Bridle Road on 9 December 1939.

Left: Whilst the threat at home may have subsided, Wollaston soldiers were still at risk overseas. Fusilier James Walter Harris, a married man of 24, was killed in Italy on 6 September 1944. He lived at 93 High Street, but both he and his wife were from Beauty Bank Crescent. He posed for this photograph on 12 March 1944.

1945

On 10 February, the *County Express* reported on a meeting of the Wollaston Street Groups Committee: 28 collectors covering 38 streets had collected £54,289 0s 6d worth of National Savings.

In April the Vicar was repatriated and returned to Wollaston on 42-days' leave. He was demobilised on 2 July and gradually took over the responsibilities of the parish. Romilly Craze officially handed over responsibility on 26 July. Reg Bamber was later awarded the MBE for his services during the war.

The May edition of the *Parish Magazine* contained news of the death of Company Sergeant Major **Albert Edward Chapman** in Burma on 8 February aged 30. He was the cousin of Joseph Chapman who was killed in 1940.

Left: The death of Company Sergeant Major Albert Edward Chapman, in Burma on 8 February aged 30, was reported in the May edition of the *Parish Magazine*. He lived at 3 Unwin Passage, at the heart of the old village.

Private **Ernest Veal**, who was married and lived in Lye, was killed in action on 27 March in the Reichswald forest in Germany aged 35.

At the beginning of May, after the announcement of the German surrender, the church bells were rung to celebrate the end of the war. The *County Express* reported that further celebrations took place on 19 May. The children of High Street, Vicarage Road, Wood Street, Firmstone Street and Apley Road celebrated victory with a procession, sports and picnic tea on Wollaston Playing Field. The day concluded with a bonfire and the burning of an effigy of Adolf Hitler.

The *County Express* reported that a large gathering

Above: VE celebrations took place in Wollaston on 19 May 1945. Children in High Street, Vicarage Road, Wood Street, Firmstone Street and Apley Road celebrated with a procession, sports and picnic tea on Wollaston Playing Field. The day's events concluded with a bonfire and the burning of an effigy of Adolf Hitler. Various street parties, like this one, were also held.

Below: The German POWs on Swan Pool Park remained for over two years after the war ended. They struck up good relations with local people and were allowed considerable freedom. Here one of the prisoners (right, rear) enjoys an afternoon in a garden in Bright Street.

had assembled in the Wollaston School canteen on 8 September to bid farewell to Romilly Craze, who for the previous eight years had been Curate at St James's Church. There was a short musical programme and tributes were paid to him. On behalf of the parishioners Reg Bamber presented him with a cheque and expressed gratitude for the excellent work he had done especially during his enforced absence. He also wished him well in his new career as an RAF Chaplain. Romilly Craze received many other farewell gifts and expressed his gratitude to everyone for their kindness. He preached his final sermon at Wollaston the next evening, to a crowded congregation.

On 29 September the *County Express* reported that **Frank Grainger** of Gladstone Road, a Petty Officer Air Gunner of the Fleet Air Arm had been awarded the DCM for gallantry, skill and devotion to duty. He had joined the Fleet Air Arm in September 1939, aged 18 and had completed six years service.

1946

Fusilier **Roland Edgar Ellis**, aged 22, died near Udine in Italy on 9 February.

Left: As with the POWs, the troops on active service abroad did not return home immediately after the war. Sadly, Fusilier Roland Edgar Ellis, aged 22, of 21 Vicarage Road Wollaston, died near Udine in Italy on 9 February 1946.

1947

A letter was published in the *County Express* of 5 July, which suggested the building of a community centre on Park Road playing fields. It was said that: *'At present German POWs are using the buildings, which after they are vacated would be admirable for conversion.'*

The POW camp was closed on 16 August 1947, but the buildings remained. At first the were used as a depot by the Post Office Telephones, and in the early 1960s they became the barracks of the local Territorial Army unit, until their new premises opened in Oldswinford in 1965.

Thirty-five of the names mentioned above appear on the Roll of Honour in Wollaston Church, the remaining three casualties being connected to Wollaston by newspaper reports or personal memories.

Left: The last German POWs remained at the Swan Pool Camp until the summer of 1947. One of the last to leave was Bernhard Schnittkamp, pictured here.

Northern Ireland

Trooper **Simon Tipper** of the Blues & Royals was killed when an IRA bomb exploded on 20 July 1982 near Hyde Park. He was 19 years old, the son of Donald Tipper of 5 Dorset Road. After attending Meadow Park Infants' School between 1967 and 1970, he transferred to Wollaston Junior School, which he left in 1974. Simon then attended Longlands School, and joined the Household Cavalry in 1979. After a year's training at Pirbright, he was posted to Knightsbridge Barracks. A funeral service took place at St Mary's Church, Oldswinford. Simon Tipper was buried in Brierley Hill Churchyard, near to his grandfather's grave.

Below: This letter from Rolf Schmidt pins the closure date of the POW camp on Studley Gate down precisely to 16 August 1947. He writes in gratitude for all the kindnesses shown him during his stay there, and seems truly sorry to be leaving.

Saturday night. August 16th.   Studley Gate Hostel

Dear

THIS LETTER IS WRITTEN TO EXPRESS MY APPRECIATION FOR ALL THAT YOU HAVE DONE FOR ME. I AM DEEPLY GRATEFULL. YOU ALL GAVE ME SO MUCH AND I KNEW I COULD COME TO YOU, AS IF WERE, MY OWN HOME. THE HARD LIFE OF MY PRISONER OF WAR TIME MADE YOU MUCH EASIER FOR ME; SO EASY THAT I WISH SOMETIMES, I COULD STAY HERE. BUT YOU KNEW, MY PARENTS AND SISTER ARE WAITING FOR ME AND IT WOULD NOT BE FAIR TO THEM TO STAY AWAY.

I HOPE THE FRIENDSHIP WILL CONTINUE, WHEN I AM BACK IN GERMANY — I SHALL WRITE TO YOU! IF YOU WISH TO WRITE ME AN ANSWERLETTER HERE IS MY ADDRESS. HERRN ROLF SCHMIDT (23) OLDENBURG i/O. PHILOSOPHENWEG 8 GERMANY / BRITISH ZONE

Chapter Nine

MODERN WOLLASTON

1. The Centre of the Village

Road developments

One of the biggest differences between the Wollaston of the 1940s and 1950s and that of the 21st century has been the growth of traffic. Car ownership was limited to a small number of people in the immediate post-war years, when walking, cycling or using public transport were more common. As recently as 1971 only 58.5% of households owned a car but by 1991 the number had risen to 69%, while the number of households with two or more cars was 25.8% in 1991, a rise of 8.6% since 1981. In 2003 more inhabitants own at least one car, and many households have two. This has necessitated many changes in the layout of the roads and parking in the area around Bridgnorth Road and its junction with High Street where most of the shops are to be found.

Above: Interspersed throughout this chapter is a series of photographs that take the reader on a tour of Wollaston, mainly in the 1950s and 1960s. The tour begins in Bridgnorth Road, on the occasion of a carnival. A pipe band precedes the floats, which are pulling up level with the school. There's also a small crowd gathered outside Harrison & Sons, a grocery store which is Fletcher's Drinks Cabinet in 2003.

The first car park

The first parking spaces were provided on what had been the public space of The Crescent at the junction of Meriden Avenue and Bridgnorth Road. In January 1955 a plan for highway alterations at Wollaston to improve traffic arrangements and safety at The Crescent was proposed by the council. These changes included the realignment of Meriden Avenue; the installation of a keep-left bollard and a loading bay for buses in Bridgnorth Road; a reduction of the island at the junction of High Street and Bridgnorth Road; a widening of the road in front of the shops, and the surfacing of The Crescent, which was to become a car park. For many years shoppers often had to park in neighbouring roads when this small car park was full.

Above: The first parking spaces in Wollaston were provided on The Crescent at the junction of Meriden Avenue and Bridgnorth Road. In January 1955 the council proposed a plan for highway improvements. These included surfacing of The Crescent, which was to become a car park.

One-way system

By August 1963 the volume of commercial traffic using Cobden Street was the subject of a letter and petition to Stourbridge Council. In May of the following year the three-month trial of a one-way system was introduced for traffic using Cobden Street and Duncombe Street. This scheme was extended until November and again until June 1965. On 28 June the one-way system was confirmed and became permanent.

Above: By August 1963 the volume of traffic using Cobden Street was the subject of a petition to Stourbridge Council. In May 1964 a three-month trial of a one-way system was introduced for traffic using Cobden Street and Duncombe Street. This scheme was extended until November and again until June 1965. On 28 June 1965 the one-way system was confirmed and became permanent. Thereafter, turning right up Cobden Street from this point was illegal. The gas lamp on the island was of the Webb's Sewer Ventilation kind, and appears to be burning. *Harry Cartwright/Stourbridge Library*

Car park plans

By 1967 the need for more parking in Wollaston for visitors to some of the public houses and for shoppers, became a subject for Stourbridge Council's meeting in September. The Borough Engineer was asked to write to the residents of 2 to 18 Cobden Street with regard to the possible purchase of part of their rear gardens for a car park. However this scheme was abandoned at the next council meeting, and an alternative site in Bridgnorth Road was suggested. This suggestion was not pursued.

It was not until 1972 that notices of compulsory purchase were served on land behind the shops in Bridgnorth Road, between Cobden Street and Duncombe Street. Some objections were received and considered at the April council meeting and a public enquiry was held on 24 May to hear these objections. The Council's evidence was that off-road parking behind the premises would considerably ease the problems caused by delivery vehicles parking in front of the Bridgnorth Road shops. A traffic survey revealed that the road carried approximately 8,750 vehicles every weekday and at peak times up to 840 vehicles an hour. The car park would provide spaces for 55 cars.

Above: The tour of Wollaston continues with this 1958 shot of Wollaston Junction viewed from outside Wollaston Garage. Meriden Avenue runs plumb straight away from the camera and to this day occasionally fools the odd motorist into thinking that it comes out into Vicarage Road. This was indeed the original intention, but it was never proceeded with. *Harry Cartwright/Stourbridge Library*

Above: Parking remained a problem in Wollaston throughout the 1960s. Partly to ease this, and partly to make movement between Cobden and Duncombe streets easier, a service road and car park was constructed in 1972. The car park, seen here, would provide spaces for 55 cars.

In September 1972 the proposition to build the car park and an access road between Cobden Street and Duncombe Street was given the go-ahead, with building due to start in the next financial year. There was space left at the rear of the shops to allow for parking and unloading. Since its completion this road has remained un-named, and in 2003 is still known simply as 'the service road.'

The proposed dual carriageway

Readers of the *County Express* in the autumn of 1970 were confronted with the following headlines.

- *'Dual road at Wollaston sacrifices people and property to traffic'* (16 October)
- *'Stop this horror' say dual road objectors, as 300 pack into Wollaston Protest Meeting'* (25 November)

What was it that aroused the anger of normally even-tempered Wollastonians and led to talk of the heart of the village being ripped out, and of gloomy predictions of the death of the community? The cause was the proposed construction of a dual carriageway to run from the Stourbridge Ring Road (opened in October 1969) to the county boundary at The Ridge Top. The proposal was to construct a 70ft wide dual carriageway with a central reservation and a huge traffic island at the junction of High Street and Bridgnorth Road, measuring 300ft by 230ft. In Wollaston alone this would necessitate the demolition of 148 houses, 11 shops, two pubs, two men's hairdressers, the launderette, and the post office in High Street. A detailed description of what would have been destroyed shows that the anger and fear of the village was fully justified.

Entering Wollaston from Enville Street the proposed dual carriageway would have first cut a swathe through properties on the left-hand or south side of Bridgnorth Road, starting with the Golden Lion Inn (Katie Fitzgerald's in 2003), and old houses on the eastern corner of King Street, one of which is dated 1837. Continuing up the old 'Withy Bank', the road would have required the demolition of the terraced houses on the same side of Bridgnorth Road as far as, but not including, the Cottage Spring (these houses were demolished in 1975). The road's width would have been increased by taking land from the frontages of properties on the right hand or north side of the road, including the site for the proposed Senior Citizens' Centre (opened in 1972 and known as the Wollaston Village Hall in 2003), the Church, the School and the Schoolmaster's House.

The devastation proposed for the centre of the village was huge. The construction of the traffic island would have seen the loss of all buildings on the school side of the road past the Master's House, including The Waterloo Inn, and round the corner, along High Street, as far as, and including, the launderette. All the buildings on the opposite side of

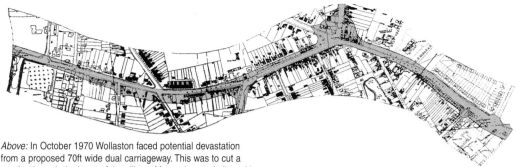

Above: In October 1970 Wollaston faced potential devastation from a proposed 70ft wide dual carriageway. This was to cut a swathe through the heart of the village. Most ruinous of all would have been a huge traffic island at the junction of High Street and Bridgnorth Road, measuring 300ft by 230ft. In Wollaston alone construction of this road would have necessitated the demolition of 148 houses, 11 shops, two pubs, two men's hairdressers, the launderette, and the post office in High Street, as this plan shows.

Below: The dual carriageway devastation proposed for the centre of Wollaston was huge. Construction of the traffic island would have seen the loss of all buildings on the school side of the road past the Master's House, including The Waterloo Inn, and round the corner, along High Street, as far as, and including, the launderette. All the buildings on the opposite side of High Street would have been demolished, as far as the corner of Wood Street.

taking the frontage off the properties on both sides of Bridgnorth Road.

The origins of the dual carriageway scheme can be traced back to 1964 when the District Road Engineer submitted a plan to Stourbridge Council on '*Traffic in Towns*', followed by a detailed study of Stourbridge's roads. In October 1966 a report was presented to the council's Planning and Development Committee. This report contained plans for 'road improvements', and on 18 October the committee recommended that the proposed highway improvement lines be approved, adopted and submitted to the Worcestershire County Surveyor and the Divisional Road Engineer. On 31 October Stourbridge Borough Council accepted their committee's recommendation.

Above: On the tour of Wollaston the view is now back towards the church. Prominent on the right is the 'Mazawattee Tea' shop, as it was known. Once a grocery store run by Ambrose Lugg, and later by the Hadlington family, it had born this conspicuous advertisement for many decades, long, indeed, after the tea in question has ceased to be made. The view also shows the area of the disputed dual carriageway island as everyone hoped it would remain.

High Street would have been demolished, as far as the corner of Wood Street.

Continuing up towards The Ridge the new road would then have required the demolition of the Edwardian shops on the right hand side of the road, including Wollaston Bakery, plus the loss of the bus stop and a large part of The Crescent car park. Next the road would have taken off most of the gardens of the houses that lie between the bakery and Hamilton Avenue.

The shops and properties on the left-hand side of Bridgnorth Road, from the Cottage Spring to The Gate Hangs Well would have remained. Beyond The Gate Hangs Well the destruction would have switched sides, claiming all the properties fronting the left hand side of Bridgnorth Road to a point opposite the entrance to Ridge Street. Thereafter the road's width would have been achieved by

At this time no one in Wollaston, including its councillors, had any real idea what these 'improvement lines' were, because they were cloaked in bureaucratic anonymity. The council minutes merely show that there had been a resolution: '*to recommend that proposals for a* primary distributor road shown on plans Nos 2157/1-35 now submitted be approved and adopted.' Following the council's decision in October 1966 there was no public discussion of the scheme until 1970 when, on a visit to the Borough Engineer's Department, Molly Harrison of Ridge Street accidentally saw detailed plans and grasped the implications of what they entailed. She was understandably horrified, and equally determined to make public what she had seen. On her own initiative she organised a petition opposing the scheme. This was reported in the *County Express* of 16 October 1970 and the resulting publicity it received led to a group of concerned residents and business people forming the **Wollaston Village Association** (WVA) to fight the dual carriageway.

The chairman of the WVA was Derek Rudd of Meriden Avenue and its Secretary was Rosemary Taylor of Bridgnorth Road. The association organised a protest meeting on 25 November 1970 in Wollaston school, which was attended by council officials, the three Wollaston councillors, Dot Topliss, Fred Allport and Ken Ison, and 300 angry Wollastonians. The committee of the association decided to hold a referendum on the question: '*Are you in favour of a dual carriageway through the centre of Wollaston?*' The vote was held on Saturday 12 June 1971 and the result was a huge majority against the proposed road. In total, 69% of the inhabitants of Wollaston voted. Of these only 592 voted 'Yes' in favour of the road, whilst 4,001 voted 'No' against it. The result of the referendum was sent to Stourbridge Borough Council, Worcestershire County Council, and Peter Walker MP, Minister for the Environment.

Although work on the dual carriageway had not been envisaged before 1985, it soon became clear after the referendum that the scheme had been abandoned. Confirmation came in 1975 when the *County Express* of 14 March carried the front-page headline '**Wollaston Road Scheme is Axed.**' This article explained that: '*County Council officers had recommended in the light of the*

attitude of the Secretary of State that the road improvement line should be rescinded.'

The exact reasons for the abandonment of the scheme are not known, but in all probability it was a combination of the following factors:
- the strength of the opposition in Wollaston
- the construction costs together with the huge bill for compensation to property owners
- the reluctance of Staffordshire County Council to continue the dual carriageway beyond the Ridge Top down to the Stewponey
- the reorganisation of local government in 1974 which had seen Stourbridge merge with Halesowen and Dudley, raised the question of whether the new Dudley authority would be willing to pick up the bill of a scheme created by one of its predecessors?

New shops open

When new shops opened in 1969, on land between Duncombe Street and High Park Avenue, there was enough room on the frontages to allow some more parking for shoppers. The land behind the buildings included space for garages for the occupants of flats above the shops and parking spaces for shopkeepers.

Above: New shops were built fronting to Bridgnorth Road, on land between Duncombe Street and High Park Avenue, in 1969. This photograph, taken to capture a traction engine passing through the village, also recorded the shops and houses that were demolished to make way for this new development. The engine is passing the tailors and furriers business of Frank Hejl, formerly Captain of Wollaston's Home Guard.

Below: The new shops development on Bridgnorth Road allowed sufficient room on the frontages to provide some more parking for shoppers. Land behind the buildings included space for garages for the occupants of flats above the shops, and parking spaces for the shopkeepers.

WOLLASTON VILLAGE ASSOCIATION

June Referendum

VOTING SLIP

Are you in favour of a dual carriageway through the centre of Wollaston ?

Yes ☐   No ☐

(Please tick one box)

No person may vote more than once.
Poll closes at 6 pm on Saturday, 12th June, 1971

Above: To fight the proposed dual carriageway, a group of concerned residents and business people formed the Wollaston Village Association (WVA). They organised a referendum on the topic, from which this is a voting slip. In all, 69% of Wollaston's inhabitants voted. Of these only 592 voted 'Yes' in favour of the road, whilst 4,001 voted 'No' against it. The result was sent to Stourbridge Borough Council, Worcestershire County Council, and the Minister for the Environment, Peter Walker MP.

Traffic island

1972, to prevent pedestrians using it when crossing the road, large pebbles replaced the grass and Rose beds on the traffic island at the junction of High Street and Bridgnorth Road. Subsequently elevated by the installation of large stone blocks, this island was reduced in size to improve the traffic flow and give better visibility for vehicles in May 2003.

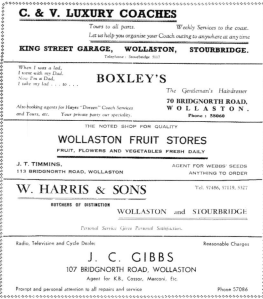

Above: In 1972, to prevent pedestrians using it to cross the road, large pebbles replaced the grass and rose beds on the traffic island at the junction of High Street and Bridgnorth Road. Subsequently elevated by the installation of large stone blocks, in May 2003 this was again reduced in size to improve the traffic flow and give better visibility for vehicles.

Above: These advertisements recall some of the best known shops and businesses in Wollaston during the 1950s and 1960s.

Parking ban

In August 1978 a 24-hour parking ban was introduced at the traffic island and a 12-hour ban on its approaches was extended to 24 hours.

Wollaston bus services

'Midland Red' buses served Wollaston from 9 February 1930, the day after the closure of the Kinver Light Railway. More services followed from Sunday 2 March 1930, the day after the last tram ran between Dudley and Stourbridge. The following list of Wollaston Midland Red services was compiled from their summer timetable for 1957, which came into force on 1 June that year:

- 250 Stourbridge–Kinver via Wollaston and Stewponey
- First 04:55, last 22:33, every 20 minutes to 09:03, $^1/_2$-hourly thereafter, 24 minute journey
- S41 Stourbridge–Wollaston–New Wood (via Enville Street, Wollaston Junction, High Street, Vicarage Road to Junction Hyperion Road) first 07:32, last 20:32, hourly, 10 minute journey
- S42 Stourbridge–Wollaston Farm Estate via Amblecote (Fish Inn) (via Wollaston Road, High Street, Vicarage Road, Gerald Road, Kingsway to junction Norfolk Road) first 07:02, last 20:02, hourly, 9 minute journey

- S50 Stourbridge–High Park Estate (Brook Street, Swan Street, Park Road, High Park Avenue to Junction South Road New Inns) first 06:06, last 20:33, $^1/_2$-hourly to 18:33, hourly thereafter, 10 minute journey
- S51 Stourbridge–Wollaston (Ridge Street) (Bridgnorth Road, Wollaston Junction, Bridgnorth Road to junction Ridge Street) first 06:00, last 22:00, $^1/_2$-hourly to 14:18, hourly thereafter, 8 minute journey
- X93 Birmingham–Church Stretton (Sundays only) via Stourbridge, Kinver, Enville, Bridgnorth, Much Wenlock and Longville 1 daily, Wollaston 11:14, return 20:53, 1hr 57min journey
- 190 Birmingham–Stourbridge–Bridgnorth–Ludlow, via Wollaston and Enville to Ludlow 11:09, 15:09, 17:09, 21:09 journey time 2hr 11min; To Bridgnorth only 13:09, 19:09, 51 minute journey

The last two services, in particular, show that Wollaston was far from isolated in the 1950s, and that those Wollastonians without a car still had a wide choice of destinations at their disposal.

On 3 December 1973, 413 Midland Red vehicles, six depots and a number of staff, were transferred to the West Midlands Passenger Transport Executive (WMPTE). By 1976 Wollaston was one of their 'Black Country Services', which included some familiar Midland Red route numbers:

- S50 STOURBRIDGE–HIGH PARK via Brook Street
- S52 STOURBRIDGE–WOLLASTON FARM (circular) via Amblecote

Above: The tour pauses for an unusual view through the 'Mazawattee Tea' shop, which was being demolished to create an open air car sales area for Wollaston Garage.

Below: Continuing the tour of Wollaston, this is back to 1958, when The Crescent car park was still comparatively new and, on this occasion, under used.

- S53 STOURBRIDGE–WOLLASTON FARM (circular) via Wollaston
- 250 STOURBRIDGE–KINVER via Wollaston and Bridle Road
- 251 STOURBRIDGE–KINVER via Wollaston

Following the privatisation of buses in 1986, Wollaston has been served by services operated on behalf of WMPTE by West Midlands Travel (WMT) and Hansons. In 2003 these included:
- 227 Stourbridge–Kinver via Wollaston Junction: Kinver–Bridgnorth Road, Wollaston Road, Vicarage Road, Bridle Road, Bridgnorth Road, Enville Street–Stourbridge (WMT/Hansons)
- 228 Kinver–Stourbridge–Merry Hill–Brockmoor: Kinver–Bridgnorth Road, Wollaston Road, Vicarage Road, Bridle Road, Bridgnorth Road, Enville Street, Bath Road–Stourbridge (Hansons)
- 289/290 Stourbridge–Norton–Wollaston Farm circular (Hansons)
- 291 Stourbridge–Merry Hill–Brierley Hill–Wollaston Village–Norton–Stourbridge (Hansons)
- 291E As 291 terminates Brettell Lane (mornings) and High Park Avenue (evenings) (Hansons)

- 292 Stourbridge-Merry Hill via Norton, Wollaston & Brierley Hill: Stourbridge–Norton–High Park Avenue–Bridgnorth Road–Meriden Avenue–Eggington Road–Vicarage Road–Somerset Drive–Kingsway–Gerald Road–Vicarage Road–Merry Hill–Stourbridge (Hansons)
- 293 Stourbridge–Stourbridge–Wollaston Farm–Stourbridge, via Wollaston Junction, Kingsway and Bridle Road (WMT)
- 294 Stourbridge–Wollaston Junction–High Park–Norton–Stourbridge anti-clockwise circular (WMT).

The Midland Bank

For 42 years Wollaston enjoyed banking facilities. On 21 March 1949 a sub-branch of the Midland Bank was opened at 125 Bridgnorth Road. Initially it had very limited opening hours, of 10.15am to 11.45am each Monday, Wednesday and Friday. Nevertheless in the days in which few people had their own transport, it was a facility that was greatly appreciated by both the business community and the private investor. Its closure on 22 March 1991 was brought about by changes in the banking system (such as credit cards and cash points) and the increased mobility of the population.

Above: On 21 March 1949 the Midland Bank opened a sub-branch at 125 Bridgnorth Road. Initially it had limited opening hours, of 10:15am to 11:45am each Monday, Wednesday and Friday. The facility was greatly appreciated by both local businesses and residents. The bank closed on 22 March 1991, and is the premises of a security firm in 2003. The patch of lighter brickwork to the right is where the night safe was removed. Above Dulson's is Wollaston's perennial Christmas decoration!

The Post Office

After extensive modernisation the Post Office, which occupied premises in High Street, almost opposite the junction with Wood Street, re-opened on 23 January 1960.

Above: Wollaston Post Office in High Street underwent extensive modernisation, reopening on 23 January 1960. It moved to its present site, at 159 Bridgnorth Road, opening there on 28 March 1971, a move occasioned by of the threat of demolition of the existing premises for the proposed dual carriageway. In 2003 the old Post Office is a delicatessen called Deli-shus.

In 1971 it moved to its present site at 159 Bridgnorth Road, opening there on 28 March. The move was made because of the threat of the demolition of the existing premises to enable the proposed dual carriageway to be built.

Food outlets in the village

A change in eating habits in the late 20th century is shown in the number of places where it is possible to eat out or to buy ready cooked food to take home. In 2003 most of Wollaston's pubs offer bar snacks or have a restaurant menu. This widespread availability of ready cooked food contrasts sharply with the first half of the 20th century when the fish and chip shop was the only source of ready cooked meals. For many years Wollaston Bakery has offered for sale filled rolls, sandwiches, cakes and drinks that prove to be very popular, especially with the pupils of Ridgewood High School.

Below: Looking back along Bridgnorth Road on a very wet day c.1960, the tour of the village pauses to take shelter. A van has been parked on the wrong side of the road outside Cooper's Toy Shop, where several generations of Wollaston schoolchildren parted with their pocket money.

Janet Harris ran the first restaurant, The Gallery, which was above Harris's Butcher's Shop in Bridgnorth Road. It opened in 1972, was sold in 1983 and then again in 1985, this time to Charles Ashton, who was chef/proprietor, but still traded under The Gallery name. Another change of ownership came in 1996 when the new owner, Robbie Fitzgerald, redecorated the restaurant with an Irish theme and changed its name to Fitzgerald's. In November 2001 it was sold again, this time to Mr Lulu Miah and, following a major refit and refurbishment of the kitchens, it was re-opened in February 2002 as an Indian restaurant called East One.

Above: Janet Harris opened Wollaston's first restaurant, The Gallery, in 1972, above Harris's Butcher's Shop in Bridgnorth Road. It was sold in 1983, and again in 1985, but continued to trade as The Gallery until 1996, when another new owner, Robbie Fitzgerald, redecorated with an Irish theme and changed its name to Fitzgerald's. In November 2001 it was sold to Mr Lulu Miah, who re-opened it in February 2002 as an Indian restaurant called East One.

On the opposite side of Bridgnorth Road an Indian take-away, Red Forte, opened in 1990. At the top of High Street is the Neel Akash Balti and Tandoori restaurant, which also sells take-away meals. This has been open since 1985 and came under new management in 1994. On 19 November 1990 the Red Forte was the scene of an explosion, for which there was an appeal for witnesses in the *County Express*.

Wollaston's two Chinese takeaways are Happy House on Bridgnorth Road and San Wu House on the corner of Meriden Avenue and High Street. The latter opened in 1982, changed hands in 1987 and was completely refurbished in 2003.

Above: The Red Forte Indian take-away opened on Bridgnorth Road in 1990. This was the scene of an explosion on 19 November 1990, for which there was an appeal for witnesses in the *County Express*, as well as coverage on radio and television. Although extensively damaged, the building was carefully restored.

Above: Wollaston's first Chinese takeaway was San Wu House, on the corner of Meriden Avenue and High Street. It opened in 1982, changed hands in 1987 and was completely refurbished in 2003. The shop itself has had a varied career, once being a fish & chip shop and later a dry cleaners.

Left: At the top of High Street is the Neel Akash Balti and Tandoori restaurant, which also sells take-away meals. This has been open since 1985 and came under new management in 1994.

Another recently opened outlet is the sandwich bar in High Street, which occupies the old post office and trades under the name of Deli-shus.

The Luncheon Club

The 'Luncheon Club' provides an opportunity for people to meet and relax in a friendly atmosphere whilst having a meal. Although the lunches take place in the Church Hall under the auspices of the Church Hall Committee, chaired by Shirley Horne, the club is not strictly a church activity and moreover the word club is a misnomer as there is no official organisational structure or constitution.

The idea of providing a community lunch began in 1995 when a celebration lunch was held to mark the opening of the new Church Hall and to demonstrate its facilities. This lunch was such a success that a decision was

Left: Wollaston's other Chinese takeaway, is the Happy House on Bridgnorth Road, housed in a shop formerly run by Allen Decorators, whose clock can still be seen above the façade.

Below: One of the events to mark the opening of the new Church Hall and to demonstrate its facilities was that of providing a celebration lunch. This was such a success that a decision was made to continue lunches on a weekly basis, although the frequency later became monthly.

made to continue providing lunches on a weekly basis, although the frequency later became monthly. From the outset it was made clear that all are welcome, irrespective of age or religious affiliation, 'membership' is not confined to members of the congregation.

At first the meals were cooked and supervised by Val Radford who had long experience of large-scale catering at both St James's and High Park schools. Pauline Devereux ably assisted her. When Val reluctantly retired from the kitchen because of health problems Pauline and Eve Ibbs stepped in to continue the good work.

This highly successful community activity is entirely dependent on an army of volunteers who undertake all the tasks involved in preparing and serving a meal. The rota of helpers, organised by Megan Baxter, includes stalwarts such as Elsie Chambers, Lorna Singleton, and many others who are ever present. The combination of an informal friendly atmosphere and a well-cooked lunch consistently attracts around 60 friends to each month's 'get together', whilst the Christmas lunch regularly attracts a sitting in excess of 100.

Above: The last point on the tour afforded a view of Cooper's Toy Shop. Many relieved parents watched the transformation of this into the Crescent Arcade, which opened on 13 March 1989.

2. Away from the village centre

Senior Citizens' Centre

From the late 1940s there was talk of a community centre being built in Wollaston. A plea for a centre in Wollaston was made to Stourbridge Council and in October 1949 a sub-committee was set up to investigate community centres in Norton and Wollaston. As far as Wollaston was concerned nothing came of this and it was 1954 before the matter was again raised in a council meeting when it was shelved because there was talk of the church building a parish hall. Indeed in May, there was a firm proposal to build one within 12 months. In spite of this, the council decided to build a community centre on land between the church and Foster Place. Again this plan was abandoned and it was left to the residents of Wollaston to raise the necessary money themselves if they were to be successful in their efforts to provide a centre for the village.

A committee was set up and during the 1960s and 1970s many fund raising events were held to raise enough money to build the Senior Citizens' Centre.

Above: Ten years of fundraising between 1962 and 1972 raised £12,000 towards the building of a Senior Citizens' Centre, which was built set back from Bridgnorth Road, next to St James's Church, on Wollaston Rec'.

The earliest events ran over six days and were very popular with the people of Wollaston and visitors from neighbouring areas. The carnivals included talent and variety shows, sports days, flower fetes and, most successful of all, horse shows and gymkhanas. These were held annually for many years and drew crowds of between 2,000 and 3,000. In 1972 the £12,000 raised over ten years went towards the construction of the building. In February the foundations were dug and at the ceremony were five members of the original committee who had worked hard to see their efforts achieved. They were: Bert Potts-Perkins, president, Mr & Mrs Arthur Smith, Lily Vale and Councillor Fred Allport.

In August 1972 there were reports in the *County Express* of vandalism and over £200 worth of damage was done both to the outside and inside of the still unfinished building.

After its completion money was still needed to help with running costs and fund raising events were frequently held. In 1973 BSR employees gave £400 to the centre and

Below: The tour resumes as a carnival procession comes up Cobden Street in its two-way days. To the right is the Alexandra Inn, behind which the service road and car park were built in 1972.

in November of the same year a toy fair raised £256. One source of funds was the ongoing collection and re-sale of 'nearly-new' household items, which could be offered for sale or repaired and given a new lease of life at the centre or donated to needy pensioners. A continuous collection and storage system was operated between the sales, which were held regularly at the centre, and by these methods as much as £1,000 could be raised in a year.

Although its use was intended primarily for the older members of the village, and indeed all Stourbridge pensioners were welcome, a pre-school playgroup was held there for many years and it also served as the headquarters of the Wollaston Scouts. Bingo, handicraft classes and Christmas parties were among the activities, which, for many years, were held at the centre for the senior members of the community.

Wollaston Village Hall

The Senior Citizens' Centre was originally envisaged as a recreational and social centre for retired people, but at the beginning of the 21st century it took on a new role. A decision was made to widen its activities and to make it accessible to all age ranges, and so the name was changed to Wollaston Village Hall. Unfortunately, as noted above, the building had suffered from persistent vandalism, and broken windows and a leaking roof were just two of the many problems facing the new management committee.

However, in the three years since 2000 the management committee has received two grants from the Heritage Lottery Fund, which have been used to buy new curtains, provide staging and completely replace the flooring in the hall. With a further grant from the Stourbridge Area Committee the roof has been repaired. Security cameras have been installed, the kitchen has been refurbished and, with help from Wollaston PCC, a new central heating boiler has replaced the original system.

A committee of eight members, under the chairmanship of Val Radford, is responsible for organising the activities and raising money to cover maintenance, running costs and insurance. Occasional events, such as Christmas fairs and fashion shows, are held to help fund these expenses.

In 2003 the hall is used regularly for a wide-range of activities. Weekly classes are held for bingo, computing, dog training, keep-fit, slimming, watercolour painting, and a variety of handicrafts.

Above: By the 1990s declining use and almost perpetual vandalism resulted in a change of purpose for Wollaston Senior Citizens' Centre. In form it is like many of the community centres built in the 1960s, and thus in 2000 the centre was renamed Wollaston Village Hall.

Wollaston Farm Estate

The original plans for a development on the 140 acres of Wollaston Farm date back to 1935, when tenders were invited for the layout of the site and the construction of roads and sewers etc. In 1936 there were negotiations for the purchase of a ten-acre plot for the building of a new infants' school. These schemes were all delayed by the outbreak of war in 1939 and it was not until 1949 that Stourbridge Council agreed in principle to a scheme to build 156 houses on the estate and 14.3 acres were purchased for this development.

At the end of 1951 Stourbridge Borough Council decided to name the main road on the estate Meadow Way, but at the first council meeting of 1952 this decision was revoked, and the name The Kingsway was chosen instead to correspond with Norton Estate's The Broadway.

Above: Back on the tour of Wollaston the view is now along Bridgnorth Road towards High Park Avenue, in 1958. Prominent on the skyline is the long barn from Eggington Farm, formerly used by the Home Guard during World War II. At this date the site was still the home of Wollaston Motor Spares, run by Don Despres.

In August 1952 it was announced that £1,000,000 was to be spent on housing at Wollaston Farm and Pedmore Fields. The two schemes were due to be completed by 1954/55. The building schedule had been planned so that the work could be subdivided, a section being completed before the next was started. Already 157 houses were being built and due for completion in two months. Plans had been made for a further 470 dwellings to be constructed over the next two years.

Some of the first residents on the new estate had to face the danger from a working sandmine. The problem was reported in the *Evening Despatch*:

'*Within a few feet of the estate's boundaries running parallel with the gardens of the houses is a 50ft sheer drop down a sandstone face to the bottom of a busy sandmine. There is not one piece of fencing to protect the growing numbers of children coming to the estate. Families are warned by the 'old hands' of the danger as the frequent rumbling noises of blasting operations add a constant*

Above: Although purchased for housing in 1935, Wollaston Farm was not developed until after World War II. In 1949 Stourbridge Borough Council agreed in principle to a scheme to build 156 houses on the estate and 14.3 acres were purchased for this. Work began in 1953, and this shows some of the first houses completed along the Wentworth Road end of the main spine road, which was named The Kingsway in January 1952, to correspond with Norton Estate's The Broadway.

Below: Some of the first residents on the new Wollaston Farm Estate had to face danger from a working sandmine. There was a 50ft sheer drop, down a sandstone face to the bottom of the busy mine, illustrated here. The mine was owned by local firm J Fletcher and Co, and produced some of the finest foundry sand in the country, but the company were reluctant to do anything to prevent children from being injured. Eventually the Borough Surveyor agreed to fence the Council's property as soon as possible. *Stourbridge Library*

reminder. ... *Many parents are asking 'why allow the mining to continue. Every week as more sand is taken out, the position gets worse.' Mr J F Sutton, who is in charge of the mine owned by the local firm of J Fletcher & Co, supplied the answer: 'This mine produces some of the finest foundry sand in the country. This is no ordinary sand. It is sent for from as far away as South Wales to meet the special need of the works there. There is enough here to last us 50 years. ... He looked up at the sheer wall of sand towering above him and said: 'A fence is needed, and needed quickly. It is all right while I am here to scare them off, but I should hate to come to work and find some poor kiddies dead.' Mr G N Maynard, the Borough Surveyor, said: 'We*

shall be fencing our property as soon as possible, but the edge of the quarry is a matter for the owners.'

By 1954 Stourbridge Council had acquired the whole of the land they required at Wollaston Farm, and two shops and flats were nearing completion by that May.

There was controversy in 1956 when residents of Wentworth Road objected to the building of a public house in their road on the grounds that it would reduce the value of their homes. They claimed that if the pub was to serve the people who lived on Wollaston Farm, it should be built there. In a tied vote on the matter, the casting vote of the mayor was against the proposal.

Above: There is something strangely magical about ironmonger's shops, and Wollaston once had Griffiths's in Bridgnorth Road, where the village tour now pauses. It was the kind of shop where things could be bought in small quantities, or by weight, e.g. ½ lb of nails. The adverts on the window also serve as a reminder of just how dependant everyone used to be on flashlights.

Later in 1956, plans were put forward for the erection of a further 104 dwellings which included a block of six shops, six maisonettes and nine flats. Suggestions were made for the use of a plot of land at the junction of Norfolk Road and Kent Road either for a public house or a doctor's house and surgery or a house for a district nurse, all of which were rejected.

In January 1957 plans for an infants' school were to be drawn up by the Worcestershire County Council architect.

By February of that year the council made an application to the Ministry of Housing for a loan of £154,600 for 104 dwellings on the estate. A playing field was to be included in the development between Kent Road and Devon Road and was to be open to the public.

March 1958 saw the opening of Stourbridge's 2,000th post-war council home. This was 24 Kingsway. By 1959 the block of shops, flats and maisonettes was completed and during a visit by the mayor and councillors of Stourbridge, the keys were handed over to the new tenants.

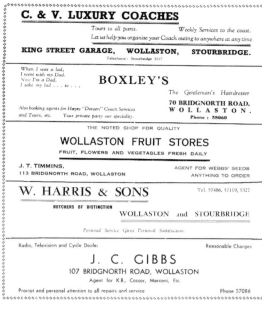

Above: A second selection of advertisements recalling some of Wollaston's best known shops and businesses during the 1950s and 1960s.

Below: March 1958 saw the opening of Stourbridge's 2,000th post-war council house, at 24 Kingsway. By 1959 the block of shops, flats and maisonettes on the estate was completed, and during a visit by the mayor and councillors of Stourbridge, the keys were handed over to the new tenants.

A final group of buildings was another block of 17 bungalows for old people together with a warden's flat, which were erected in Kent Road in 1962.

Specifications for house building have changed over the last 50 years. Looking back from the 21st century, where central heating and electricity are the norm, the houses being built in the 1950s were to have fireplaces in the bedrooms and connections to the gas supply. In a council meeting in the early years of the development, the question of electric power points was raised. It was stated that no provision had been made for them and some of the bedrooms had no fireplaces. In a reply quoted in the *County Express* it was stated that: '*In the interests of economy, the Housing Committee had decided in favour of gas, but there would be no objection to tenants providing electric points at their own expense.*'

The Dell

The land where The Dell was developed in the 1960s covered an area of approximately 16,580 sq yds and, since 1902, had belonged to William Edward Edkins, the owner of Edkins' Repository. This building still stands in 2003 as part of Wollaston Garage. Once used as a sandpit, the deep hole left behind had remained largely undeveloped after Edkins' death in 1942, although tipping, particularly of hot ashes from ironworks, had gone on since the 1930s, and continued until at least 1952. Periodically too the sandpit used to flood, and on 22 February 1930 it was the scene of a tragedy. Cyril Joseph Fletcher, aged 7¼, and John Joseph Wood, aged 6, fell through thin ice on water collected in the sandpit and drowned. The scene of the tragedy was described in the *County Express* of 1 March 1930:

Below: The land where The Dell was developed in the 1960s covered an area of approximately 16,580 sq yds. Since 1902 it had belonged to William Edward Edkins, owner of Edkins' Repository. Once used as a sandpit, the deep hole left behind had remained largely undeveloped after Edkins' death in 1942. Periodically too it used to flood, and on 22 February 1930 it was the scene of a tragedy. Cyril Joseph Fletcher, aged 7¼, and John Joseph Wood, aged 6, fell through thin ice on water collected in the sandpit and drowned.

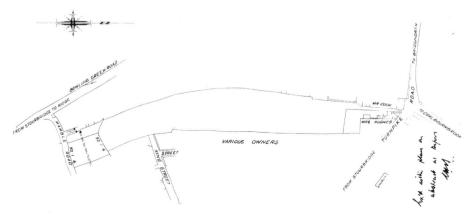

'*The sandpit ... is in a field between the lower part of Upper King Street and Cobden Street. For some years, up to nearly two years ago, the sand hole was worked, and the excavations had produced a cavity of very considerable size and depth; most of the sides are steep, and upon one side, adjacent to some King Street gardens there is a cliff face, high and almost perpendicular. In recent times, and especially during the abnormal rains which fell in the closing three months of last year, the sandpit had become filled with water, and it is computed that in parts of its area, some 20yds wide and 30 to 40yds long, the depth of the water was ten to 12ft or even more. Since the sand mining ceased the only use to which the surrounding field had been put would seem to be the accommodation of a shed for housing motor lorries of a Wollaston haulier, and it was stated at the inquest that the fence enclosing the land was in disrepair at one point, and that the gates giving access to the field were often left open.*'

In 1944 George Alfred Cooper and Reginald Bayes Victor, trading as C & V Luxury Coaches, purchased the land for £1,000, and both they, and John Bradley & Co, used buildings on the site as garages.

In 1952 C & V Luxury Coaches became a limited company and, in December of that year, 16,157 sq yds of the land was conveyed to Messrs Cooper & Victor Ltd for £6,850.

In an edition of the *County Express* in February 1962, it was reported that:

'*Stourbridge Council's Planning Committee had refused an outline planning application by C & V Coaches for permission to use the deserted sand mines off King Street as an industrial estate. The grounds of refusal are that the site is allocated for residential development and it also considered that the proposed development would be likely to affect adversely the amenities of neighbouring houses especially by reason of the noise.*'

In August 1964 another sale of 11,000 sq yds was made to James F Long, an estate agent, for £13,100 and the land was developed by the builders, John McLean & Sons Ltd who purchased it in December of the same year. A total of 19 pairs of semi-detached houses were built there and Stourbridge Borough Council adopted the name The Dell on 2 April 1968.

Below: The acquisition of a further 11,000 sq yds of land in August 1964 enabled the sandpit off King Street to be developed. The builders, John McLean & Sons Ltd purchased it in December 1964.

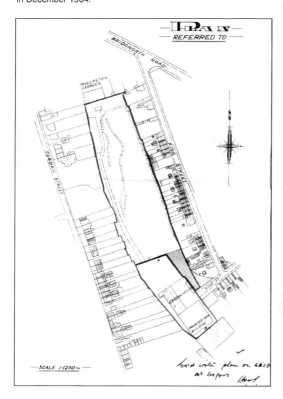

Above: John McLean & Sons Ltd built 19 pairs of semi-detached houses on the infilled sandpit off King Street. This photograph shows their construction. The large white house is The Beeches in Cobden Street. Stourbridge Borough Council adopted the name The Dell for this development on 2 April 1968.

Below: Back on the tour of Wollaston, another carnival procession is heading down Bridgnorth Road. Here the large brick barn from Eggington Farm mentioned above is even more prominent.

Gladstone Drive (Meriden House)

Meriden House used to stand in Gladstone Road. It was an imposing five-bedroom Victorian house with large bay windows on either side of the main entrance, and stood in three-and-a-half acres of land. When it was offered for sale in 1926 it was described as: '*being built of the best red bricks with a slate roof and approached by a circular carriage drive.*' Its date of construction is not known, nor is it clear exactly when it acquired its name.

Census returns for 1861 and 1871 reveal that John Thomas then occupied it. He was described as an ironworks' clerk, but given the size of the house he was probably what is called an office administrator or manager in the 21st century. The 1881 census shows that it was the home of Charles Skelding and his family. He was described as a brick manufacturer and colliery proprietor, employing 50 men, 20 women and six boys. Ten years' later the 1891 census shows that John Todd, a farmer, occupied Meriden House. He was born near Meriden in Warwickshire, and in all probability it is he who gave it the name 'Meriden House.' The first document to mention the 'Meriden' name is *Mark & Moody's Stourbridge Almanack & Directory* for 1889. On John Todd's death in 1895 his property, including the Eggington Farm estate, passed to his nephew, Thomas Rawson Vickers. He sold off the Eggington Farm land for building purposes in 1903. This sale led to the development of Eggington Road, Meriden Avenue, and subsequently of Meriden Close.

Thomas Penn, ironmaster, of Penn Bros, Cradley Heath, acquired Meriden House following John Todd's death. When Penn died in 1926 the house was bought by William Arthur Stuart of the Wordsley glass manufacturing company Stuart Crystal. His wife Elinor was the daughter of Richard Lowndes of Beauty Bank House, who was the manager of John Bradley & Co. In 1929 Elinor Stuart was the successful candidate in a council by-election and became Wollaston's first lady councillor. She died in 1962. Her husband, who died on 17 September 1965, was instrumental in securing the name 'Stuart' as the registered trademark of the Wordsley glass company. After William Stuart died, Meriden House was demolished, and in 1966 the site was redeveloped as Gladstone Drive.

Tyrol Close (Tyrol House)

The builder Percy Cox Ltd of Quarry Bank developed Tyrol Close, a cul-de-sac off High Park Avenue, in the late 1960s. To enable this development to take place two substantial houses fronting High Park Avenue had to be demolished. They were No 3, the home of Herbert and Gertrude Husselbee for over 50 years, and No 5, or 'Tyrol House', which stood on an adjoining plot of land and gave its name to the new development. Around 1909 these two houses were built on land that had formerly belonged to Henry Nickless of Hodge Hill Farm Kidderminster. After

Below: The sites of a number of Wollaston's larger houses were redeveloped for housing in the 1960s and 1970s. One example was Meriden House in Gladstone Road, seen here in sales particulars from 1926. It was formerly the home of the ironmaster, Thomas Penn, whose death occasioned this sale. William Stuart of the Wordsley glass manufacturing company Stuart Crystal bought the house. In 1929, his wife, Elinor, became Wollaston's first lady councillor. After William Stuart died, Meriden House was demolished, and the site was redeveloped as Gladstone Drive in 1966.

PARTICULARS.

WOLLASTON, nr. STOURBRIDGE.

Pleasantly situated in a good residential neighbourhood, between the Bridgnorth Road and High Park Avenue, about one mile from the Town and Station G.W.R.

LOT 1.

The Attractive and Well Built Moderate Sized Freehold Residence

known as

"MERIDEN HOUSE"

standing in its own well matured grounds, with GARDENER'S COTTAGE fronting Gladstone Road, the whole containing an area of about

6,420 SQUARE YARDS.

Left: The tour of Wollaston has leapt to Swan Pool Park, seen here in the late 1950s. The culverted Withy Brook fed the eponymous pool, which was formed into a small boating lake. In the distance, between the trees, the rounded roofs of the former POW camp can be discerned.

Nickless' death in 1908 his executors sold the land.

Herbert Husselbee was instrumental in the foundation of Wollaston tennis club. It was begun, in the late 1920s, by a group of his friends who played on his court in the large garden of No 3. He died in 1950. His widow, Gertrude, sold the property to Percy Cox Ltd in October 1967.

The first occupants of No 5, or Tyrol House as it later came to be known, were James Disher Marshall and his wife Catherine. James Marshall had a long association with the glass trade, and in the 1890s owned the Novelty Glassworks in Gladstone Road. James Marshall died in 1916, and the ownership of Tyrol House changed many times in the ensuing 51 years. The last owners, Mr and Mrs

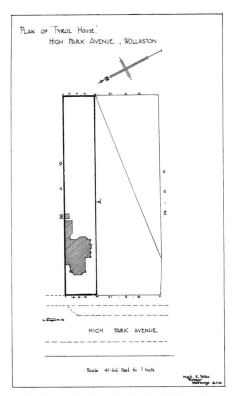

HIGH   PARK   AVENUE.

Scale   41·66 Feet to 1 Inch

Above Another road developed on the site of a large house is Tyrol Close, off High Park Avenue. Formerly No 5 High Park Avenue, Tyrol House was the home of James Disher Marshall, owner of the Novelty Glassworks in Gladstone Road. Percy Cox Ltd bought Tyrol House in October 1967, together with No 3 High Park Avenue, the former home of Herbert Husselbee, who helped to found Wollaston tennis club. The first houses were built by 1968, and Stourbridge Borough Council adopted the name Tyrol Close for this development in October 1971.

Above: Wollaston has grown considerably since the 1950s, but few developments are more conspicuous than Firmstone Court, seen here from the Rec', rising above The Britannia Inn and houses in High Street.

Below: The visual impact made by the construction of Firmstone Court is emphasised in this view of the flats from High Street, behind older houses. Stourbridge Borough Council built Firmstone Court's 77 flats in 1963-64.

Fred Taylor, also sold it to Percy Cox Ltd in October 1967.

In October 1971 Stourbridge Council adopted Tyrol Close, the first houses of this development having been completed in 1968.

Further building development

The village has grown considerably since the 1950s; many new roads have been built and small open spaces used for housing. Some of the major developments are:

- Wyre Road, first discussed by the council in 1957 but held in abeyance
- Fir Grove extensions in 1951 and 1962
- Gregory Road, named in 1955
- Firmstone Street 77 flats built in 1963-64
- Wolverley Avenue began in 1961 when a plan for the demolition of a house, Ridge Leigh, opposite Ridge Street was proposed. This would allow access to the land which was built on in 1963/64

- Fairfield Rise, name adopted 26 October 1964
- Richmond Grove, name adopted 23 March 1964
- Wildacres, name adopted 27 September 1967
- Blakeney, Hamilton and Whitney avenues, names adopted 24 May 1967
- Meriden Close, name adopted 11 July 1967
- Rugby Road, name adopted 5 March 1968
- Wyre Road 75 houses, flats and bungalows built by the council in 1969/70
- Ridgewood Avenue 1972
- Falcon Rise, name adopted 27 November 1973
- Twickenham Court 1982, and
- Lydiate Court 1992/1993 – 89 apartments for retired people, plus a home for a manager, built on land formerly part of Wollaston School.

Population figures

The increase in the population in Wollaston is shown when comparing the number of inhabitants given in the 1931 census with the number in 1951. There were 4,456 people living in the village in 1931. As there was no census in 1941, it was not until the 1951 census figures were

Above: Leaving Swan Pool Park on the tour of Wollaston, this is Swan Street in the late 1950s. The notice and fencing on the right-hand side were another entrance to the Durbar Works of Stourbridge Engineers & Ironfounders (see Chapter Seven). This was subsequently developed for housing and became Tudor Close. *Harry Cartwright/Stourbridge Library*

published that the scale of Wollaston's growth over the previous 20 years became clear. In 1951 the total was 7,603 people, of whom 3,623 (48%) were male and 3,980 (52%) were female, living in 2,361 households.

Unfortunately it is not possible to ascertain the growth between 1951 and 1981 or 1991 as figures given in documents published by Dudley Council are based upon the electoral ward of Wollaston & Stourbridge West. This area excludes part of Wollaston, namely the properties from Park Road West and the south side of Park Road, which for electoral purposes are regarded as part of Norton Ward. Wollaston & Stourbridge West Ward also includes the area bounded by Mamble Road, Swan Street, South Road and Worcester Street and reaching to the centre of Stourbridge. However some of the statistics aid understanding of Wollaston's development.

In 1989 Dudley's Planning & Architecture Department produced a document, which set out to provide basic information about the character of the area, to identify

Below: Looking back along Swan Street in the late 1950s. The large house on the left was demolished when Tudor Close was developed.

local issues and opportunities and to indicate development proposals for Stourbridge, Amblecote and Lye.

The statistics for Wollaston & Stourbridge West Ward produced in this document are summarised below:

Land Use	Percentage
Residential	58.8%
Highways & other	22.6%
Industrial	5.1%
Leisure spaces	3.9%
Retail & offices	3.6%
Vacant	3.5%
Agriculture	2.4%

The area of the ward was 250.38 hectares, which showed that it was the smallest of the wards but had the largest concentration of housing. There was a list of six areas in Wollaston, totalling 7.7 hectares, which were named as uncommitted vacant land and as possible areas for residential or industrial development. Nearly 63% of houses were owner-occupied and nearly 30% were council rented accommodation.

Figures from a document produced by the Research & Information Group provide a picture of Wollaston & Stourbridge West Ward based on the census returns for 1971, 1981 and 1991. These are summarised below:

	1971	1981	1991
Unemployment	3.2%	10.1%	7.3%
Pensioners		16.0%	20.4%
Houses with children			5,023
Total inhabitants	13,928	12,334	11,861

Retirement and residential homes

The first retirement home to open in Wollaston was the conversion of Dr Mitchelson's house in Vicarage Road. It is Rosemary Retirement Home, which opened on 1 June 1984. Strad House, in Eggington Road, built and named by J H Taylor, a local violinist and violin teacher, was extended and converted into Strad House Residential Home in 1985. The Woodlands in Bridle Road opened for business in January 1986, and later the house next door was added and linked to the original house by a conservatory. Two other homes are Caxton House in High Street and Beechlawns

Left: Apart from being demolished, some of Wollaston's larger houses have also been turned into retirement or care homes. The first such conversion was that of Dr Mitchelson's house in Vicarage Road into Rosemary Retirement Home, which opened on 1 June 1984.

Above: Strad House Residential Home in Eggington Road opened in 1985. It had been built and named by J H Taylor, a local violinist and violin teacher.

Residential Home in Wood Street.

Leonard Road Christmas Lights

The annual Christmas Lights display in Leonard Road began in 1974 on a very modest scale when Sheila Littlewood and Harry and Glenis Shaw began to decorate the outside of their houses for the benefit of their respective daughters. The practice began to spread when Harry gave a spare set of lights to neighbour Colin Hutton, followed soon afterwards by fellow resident Cliff Buckley. Within a couple of years many other families had begun to join in, and by the 1990s the whole venture had grown enormously, with an added element of competition between households.

In 1999 the residents decided to hold a collection in aid of the West Midlands Air Ambulance. Even though the collection did not start until three weeks after the 'switch-on', £22,000 was collected. The following year the collection began on 1 December and produced an impressive total of £42,000,whilst in 2001 a staggering £52,045 was collected. In 2002, when the lights were ceremonially switched on by Coronation Street star Johnny Briggs, £38,000 was collected, making a total of £155,000 raised in four years.

Bad weather does not seem to deter people, some of whom travel long distances to see the display, which has achieved national status through its coverage in the press and on television. People have travelled specifically to see the lights from as far away as Bournemouth, Eastbourne and Cornwall, and in 2001 a Kidderminster coach firm advertised trips to the 'Leonard Road Lights.' It was estimated that well over 250,000 people visited the street to see the lights over the six-week period from 1 December 2000 to 6 January 2001.

In April 2003 the fund raising efforts of the residents of Leonard Road were officially recognised when they were all invited to attend the Mayor's Parlour in the Council House, Dudley, to receive an award from the Mayor, Councillor Margaret Wilson. The award came about as a result of a plea by Stourbridge MP Debra Shipley that their efforts should receive public recognition.

Right: The sign above the shop on the corner of Swan Street and Park Road seemed to give signwriters a problem. When Jones Corner Stores were taken over by Fred Rutter, the 'F' and the 'R' were painted so close together that many people took to calling the shop 'Frutters', or simply 'Frutts.'

Above: In recent years the Leonard Road Christmas Lights have given Wollaston a celebrity far beyond the locality. They began in a modest way in 1974, but by the late 1990s they had become a major seasonal attraction. In 1999 it was decided to hold a collection in aid of the West Midlands Air Ambulance. By 2002 this had raised the staggering total of £155,000, in just four years.

Right: Corner shops were once a feature of many parts of Wollaston. The tour stops here, outside Jones' Supply Stores (curiously spelled Jone's), which was on the corner of Swan Street and Park Road. In addition to groceries, they were agents for Stourbridge Model Laundry, and both bus and cinema times could be obtained from notice boards outside the shop.

Chapter Ten

EVENTS and PEOPLE

1857 – William Millward

The column of the Stourbridge Clock, which stands in High Street outside the Crown Centre, was designed and built in Wollaston. It was made in 1857 at John Bradley & Co. Its designer was William Millward, who lived on Withy Bank and was employed as an engineer at the ironworks.

Above: The Stourbridge Clock, which stands outside the Crown Centre in High Street, was designed and built in Wollaston. Its column was made at John Bradley & Co in 1857, and the designer was William Millward, who lived on Withy Bank, and was employed at the ironworks as an engineer.

Below: William Millward's contribution to the design of the Town Clock in Stourbridge is recorded on a plate cast into the base. How many people have ever noticed this?

1861 – George Mark

Although born in Stourbridge, George Mark grew up in Wollaston. In 1851 he was aged seven, living with his parents, George, a glasscutter, and Ann. In 1861, by now 17, he was working as a bookseller's apprentice and it was from this position that he eventually became a partner in the firm of Mark & Moody, well known in Stourbridge for over 100 years as booksellers, printers, publishers and owners of the *County Express* newspaper.

Above: George Mark grew up in Wollaston. In 1861, aged 17, he was working as a bookseller's apprentice. It was from this that he eventually became a partner in the firm of Mark & Moody, well known in Stourbridge for over 100 years as booksellers, printers, publishers and owners of the *County Express* newspaper. This was their shop in High Street, which was called Paperway in 2003.

1867 – William Henry Foster

On 9 April 1867 an address was written to congratulate William Henry Foster on his coming of age:

'*We the undersigned inhabitants of Wollaston in the County of Worcestershire desire most heartily to congratulate you on the attainment of your 21st birthday. We beg you to accept the assurance of our deep interest in your welfare and happiness and our hearty good wishes for the prosperity of your future career. It is to few that so brilliant a prospect is opened. In addition to being heir to ample wealth, you will succeed to the still better inheritance of a name respected and beloved for the sake of the good deeds and admirable qualities of those who have borne it before*

you. We sincerely hope and trust that the same sentiments of honour, the same integrity of purpose, and the same noble liberality which have so pre-eminently characterised those who have preceded you will continue to make that name more honoured and beloved.

On our affectionate gratitude you have an especial claim as the son of one to whose bounty we owe our beautiful church and spacious schools.'

The address went on to praise his parents and concluded with every good wish for his future happiness and prosperity. It was signed by George Gilbanks, Edward Elcock, Joseph Hammond (churchwarden), Robert Bill, Edward Hackwood, John Thomas, William Shakespeare, John Cook, H O Firmstone and William Lewes.

PHOTOGRAPH TAKEN ON THE OCCASION OF
3000 WORKMEN IN THE EMPLOY OF W. O. FOSTER, ESQ., M.P.
MEETING AT STOURTON CASTLE, APRIL 23RD, 1867,
TO PRESENT AN ADDRESS TO WILLIAM HENRY FOSTER, ESQ.,
ON HIS COMING OF AGE.

G. H. POPE, Photo.   STOURBRIDGE.

Above Such was the esteem in which the Foster family were held in Wollaston that on the occasion of William Henry Foster's coming of age on 9 April 1867, an illuminated address was produced to congratulate him. Stourbridge photographer, G H Pope, also thought the occasion momentous enough to produce this souvenir, which shows W O Foster standing to the left of his son.
H Jack Haden

1874 – A raid upon Ridge cock-fighters

The following report appeared in the *County Express* of 27 June 1874:

'On Monday afternoon about four o'clock, some 150 of the genus 'Black Country Rough' arrived at a place called Ridge Top, two miles from Stourbridge. They had a number of bags, which turned out to contain a number of gamecocks, and the ostensible object of the party's 'outing' was to enjoy the cruel sport, which is technically termed 'fighting a main.' They fixed on a plot of ground near to the public house, and two of the birds were set to. In the meantime information had been sent to Superintendent Freeman at Stourbridge, and by the time the first battle was over Sgt Jones and three other officers appeared on the scene. Several of those present were caught, but were immediately rescued by their companions and the police, being stoned and roughly handled, deemed it discretion to withdraw. A number of the roughs were recognised as denizens of Woodside and Quarry Bank, and although none of them have been captured at the present, in all probability some of their number will be identified, and we trust, deservedly punished.'

1874 – A walking champion

The following advertisement appeared on the front page of the County Express on several occasions in June and July 1874:

RIDGE TOP PLEASURE GROUNDS, WOLLASTON, NEAR STOURBRIDGE.

FORESTERS' ARMS,
PROPRIETER - - - J. COOPER·

1000 MILES IN 1000 HOURS!

COME and see the WALKING LADY, the Champion Female Walker of the World, who astonishes all creation with her splendid walking. The Lady commences this extraordinary feat

THIS DAY (SATURDAY), JULY 4TH, 1874,

At a Quarter to Six o'clock in the Morning.

Walking Hours :—5.45, 7.45, 9.45, 11,45, and so on.

Tuesdays :—String Band. Saturdays and Mondays — Brass Band.

The Lady carries her Child at the finish.

Admission :—Saturdays and Mondays, 3d., other days 2d. Gates open Night and Day for Six Weeks.

Refreshments of the best quality.

N.B.—No Dogs or Disorderly Persons Admitted.

It is possible that the Running Grounds referred to were where Wolverley Avenue is. This is a fairly level piece of land towards Ridge Top.

1887 – Wollaston Fete

A fete was held in Wollaston on 8 September and it recorded takings of £67 16s 7d. The audited balance sheet listed expenditure on: brass & string bands, a platform, a bandstand, a ticket box, chairs, illuminations, fireworks & balloons, tents, plants and the hire of scenery. The cost of these was £36 12s 4d giving a profit of £31 4s 3d.

1892 – Charles Hackwood

Charles Hackwood was born in February 1870, the youngest child of Edward Hackwood and his wife Jane. After attending the Infants' School, he moved up to the Boys' School in April 1877. He was already showing an aptitude for arithmetic when he was awarded a prize in the following April. In 1882 he was acting as a monitor and in December of that year he left Wollaston school to attend Stourbridge Grammar School. His father wrote in the logbook:

'Jan 1883, Of all the candidates from all the various schools in the neighbourhood for the Grammar School Exhibition Chas Hackwood stands first.'

His successes continued and in March 1886 the Vicar brought the news to Edward that his son had gained first class honours in the 'Cambridge Local' examinations. In July 1888, when his father was not well enough to carry out his duties: *'Charles very efficiently took my place.'*

On 4 October 1889 Edward recorded in the school logbook:

'This week my son Charles, a former scholar, gained a sizarship at St John's College, Cambridge: in July he won a Walker Exhibition at Stourbridge Grammar School.'

A sizarship was an award at Cambridge University. The holder received a college allowance towards his expenses.

The *County Express* of 18 June 1892 reported that:

'We are pleased to notice that Mr Charles Hackwood, of Wollaston, is classed among those 'deserving of honours', and that he stands first in line of Junior Optimes in the Mathematical Tripos at Cambridge University. He will take his BA degree on Tuesday week.'

The term 'Junior Optime' is an old Cambridge classification of those students taking their final examination in mathematics.

During the time following his graduation, Charles often helped with teaching at Wollaston Boys' School and on one occasion in 1894, it was noted that he was one of the masters at Dean Close School, Cheltenham.

In the 1901 census he was living in Handsworth but his occupation was now a commercial traveller. He was still single and his father, Edward, was living with him.

1892 – Fire at the Novelty Glassworks

'At 11.30pm on Saturday night (18 June) the local fire brigade received a call to the premises of James Marshall, glassmaker, of Bridle Road, Wollaston. It was discovered that the beams and rafters of his glasshouse were glowing and smouldering. The outbreak is supposed to be due to a spark out of the chimney. The damage is estimated at about £5, though a considerable amount of property was at risk.'

1892 – Liberal rally at Wollaston

On 4 July Richard Biddulph Martin, Liberal candidate for Mid-Worcestershire, addressed an open-air meeting at Wollaston, and there was a large attendance. The report of this rally in the *County Express* however failed to mention the whereabouts of the meeting!

1893 – Wollaston fetes

On 7 August, 4,000 people were present at the fetes held at High Park. The *County Express* reported that the attendance was not as high as anticipated. Trapeze artists, musicians, singers, a choir, a band and a ventriloquist entertained the crowd. The evening ended with a firework display.

In the *County Express* of 12 August an account read:

'*The grounds were illuminated with fairy lights and Japanese lanterns, and High Park Avenue was also lit up ... The front of The Gate Hangs Well was also set off ... the tout ensemble was one to excite admiration.*'

1893 – A collection of soap wrappers

In the Logbook of the Boys' School, dated 28 October, there is mention of a collection of soap wrappers, which had resulted in a gift of two footballs. In order to qualify for this they had collected between 4,000 and 5,000 wrappers, which had been sent to the firm of Messrs Watson of Leeds. Nothing new under the sun then!

1897 – An entertainment

An entertainment to raise money for Wollaston Parish Funds was held on 17 February at Union Hall, Stourbridge. Admission charges were 2s, 1s or 6d. The showman, Sidney Dudley, introduced the waxworks, which were exhibited, and Mrs Frank Grazebrook and Company performed a farce. One of the players was Miss Mabel Gilbanks, the daughter of Wollaston's vicar.

1897 – Mr Smith's Handicap

An advertisement in the *County Express* of 8 May was for a race:

'*Ridge Top Running Grounds, Wollaston. Entries for Mr Smith's Handicap will close on Wednesday May 19th 1897. First heats run on Saturday, May 22nd; Finals on Saturday, May 29th at 3.30 o'clock each day. Entrance 6d each, to be made at the above, or Mr A Garrington's, Heath, Stourbridge.*'

1897 – Diamond Jubilee celebrations

The *County Express* of 19 June carried a report that £245 was to be spent throughout Stourbridge UDC to celebrate Victoria's Diamond Jubilee. All poor people aged over 60 were to

be given a dinner costing 2s 3d per head; 80 qualified in Wollaston. All children under 14 were to be entertained to tea (which cost 4d each); 630 children took part in this event. The logbooks for the schools record that they were to be closed for three days, 21 to 23 June, and Edward Hackwood wrote: '*Distributed to the Boys tickets for refreshments (tea etc.) on Tuesday next.*'

Each child also received a commemorative medal and after parading around the village, tea was served, followed by games in a nearby field.

1899 – Death of W O Foster

The ironmaster William Orme Foster was an important figure in the lives of Wollaston people for over 50 years.

He was born in 1814 at Oldswinford, the elder son of William Foster. His father was of the third generation of ironmasters. He had been a partner in the family firm of John Bradley & Co until he sold out to his brother James and his half brother John Bradley in 1813.

W O Foster was an agent for his

Above: Wollaston owes a lot to William Orme Foster, seen here. He built and endowed the church, vicarage and schools and made regular grants to schools in places where he had business interests. He died on 29 September 1899 and was buried at Stockton, near to his home at Apley Park. There is a memorial to him in St James's Church and he is remembered in the street names Foster Place and Apley Road.

uncle James before 1850, and presumably in effective charge of the 30 or so separate mining, iron working and engineering works in which James had an interest.

In 1853 he inherited the bulk of James's fortune of £700,000 and in 1860, on the death of his father, he inherited a further £60,000.

He had married Isabella Grazebrook in 1843 and they lived at Himley House before moving to Stourton Castle in 1853, which had been his uncle James's home, and then to Apley Park, near Bridgnorth, in 1867. They had two sons and four daughters, born between 1844 and 1860.

When W O Foster took over sole charge of the businesses in 1853 he continued his uncle's system of agents and managers. The Stourbridge Ironworks was the operational centre for his Black Country enterprises. He kept direct control, even into his 70s, with the managers reporting directly to him. From 1870 onwards his elder son, William Henry, took some part in the running of the various works.

In 1857 he was elected as a Liberal MP for South Staffordshire, but lost his seat in the 1868 general election. He served as High Sheriff of County Wexford in 1876 and of Shropshire in 1883. He was also Deputy Lieutenant of Shropshire, a JP and hunted regularly with the Albrighton Hunt.

He enjoyed a reputation as a good and thoughtful, if demanding employer; for example he gave sick pay and pensions to his clerks and agents, and donated a library and reading room for the use of his workpeople in Stourbridge.

He built and endowed the church, vicarage and schools in Wollaston, and made regular grants to schools in places where he had business interests.

On his death his personal fortune, invested mainly in land and stocks and shares, was valued at £3 million. He died on 29 September 1899 and was buried at Stockton near his home at Apley Park. There is a memorial to him in St James's Church and he is remembered in the street names of Foster Place and Apley Road.

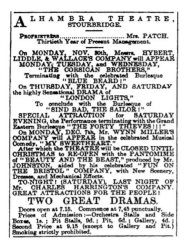

Above: Wollaston Churchyard is the final resting place of William Patch and his wife Eliza. Born Eliza Bennett in Dudley in 1824, she married William Patch in 1844 and they set up a permanent theatre, the Alhambra, in Barlow's Yard off Stourbridge High Street in 1869. This advertisement is from 1899, the 30th year of Eliza Patch's management of the theatre.

1900 – Eliza Patch

In Wollaston Churchyard there are the graves of William Patch and his wife Eliza. Neither of them appeared to have had any other connection with Wollaston, unless they attended church there, but they were both well-known figures in Stourbridge from 1855 onwards. However the deeds to Nos 5 & 6 Wood Street, dated May 1866, recite that William Patch bought the two houses from Edward Moore who had built them six years earlier. These became The Rifleman's Arms, but were resold in March of the following year. Whether William and Eliza ever lived there is not clear.

Eliza Bennett was born in Dudley in 1824, into a family of actors and proprietors of a travelling theatre. The company moved around the Black Country regularly performing in many venues, including Stourbridge.

She married William Patch in 1844 and he became a partner in Bennett & Patch's Travelling Theatre. Eliza and William set up a permanent theatre, the Alhambra, in Barlow's

Alhambra Theatre, STOURBRIDGE.
With Miss Maude Lynton's (Mrs. Douglas C. Phelps) Compliments.

Above: The Alhambra was a wooden theatre, but nonetheless quite a smart venue. Eliza Patch was once also a performer, but she gave up acting regularly in the early 1880s. William died in March 1895, not long after their Golden Wedding Anniversary, and his funeral was held at St James's Church. When Eliza died in November 1900, she too was buried in Wollaston. *Brian Standish*

Yard off Stourbridge High Street in 1869.

Eliza gave up acting regularly in the early 1880s, and William died in March 1895, not long after their Golden Wedding Anniversary. His funeral was held at St James's Church and when Eliza died in November 1900, she too was buried in Wollaston.

1902 – Coronation Dinner

To celebrate the coronation of Edward VII, 113 old people were entertained to a dinner on 4 July, after which they were presented with gifts, tobacco for the men, and a packet of tea and an orange for each of the women.

On 3 July 650 children were given tea in the schoolyard and afterwards played games on the Kimberley Recreation Ground.

1905 – A W Foster

Arthur W Foster, the grandson of W O Foster, was 21 in February 1905. Stourbridge Council moved a resolution to send congratulations to him. At the Council meeting Isaac Nash Jr, one of Wollaston's councillors, proposed:

'That we, the Urban District Council of Stourbridge, do, on behalf of the inhabitants offer to Mr A W Foster our sincere congratulations on his attaining his majority, and express our

earnest wishes that he may be favoured with long life, health and happiness.'

Councillor Arthur T Spiers supported the resolution, and said that:

'As one who had been somewhat connected with the family of Foster for something like 35 years, through the Wollaston School Foundation, I know perhaps as much as a number of other councillors of the great and good work which the present members of the family had done, not only for Wollaston, but for the whole of the neighbourhood. The late Mr W O Foster spent, they know, something like £20,000 in building a church and schools for Wollaston and likewise spent a considerable sum of money in supporting churches and schools throughout the district of the Urban Council.'

1908 – Death of Isaac Nash Jr

Isaac Nash Jr played an important part in the growth and development of Wollaston from the 1880s until his death on 12 July 1908.

Above: Isaac Nash Jr played an important role in Wollaston's development both before and after it became part of Stourbridge. He was a Wollaston Councillor until his death on 16 January 1908, and his 14 years of service included five years as Chairman of Stourbridge UDC, followed by three years as Deputy Chairman.

He was born in 1845, the eldest child of Isaac Nash Sr. He began his working life with his father in Belbroughton, but in 1880 he bought Stourbridge Forge from Firmstone & McEwan. In 1887 on the death of his father, he took over the running of the mills in and around Belbroughton where a workforce of 105 men and six boys were employed in the manufacture of scythes. In the same year he purchased a spade works known as Wollaston Mills, from Alexander Norris.

His brother, William, took over responsibility for the Belbroughton site, and Isaac concentrated on expanding his business in Wollaston. By the time of his death 250 men and boys worked for him, producing a wide range of tools used in agriculture and industry.

He had two daughters, the elder of whom married Frederick James Boulton, a solicitor from Wollaston. He had been articled as a solicitor to his uncle Harry Mills. In 1900 he went into partnership with his father-in-law and when Isaac died, the business became a private limited company with F J Boulton as the managing director. On his death in 1934, Isaac Nash's grandson, Charles Boulton, succeeded him and remained in charge until the factory closed in the late 1950s.

In addition to his role as a major employer, Isaac Nash was elected in 1894 as one of the first councillors to represent Wollaston on Stourbridge UDC. For a number of years before Wollaston became part of Stourbridge, he had served both as a member and chairman of Stourbridge Improvement Commissioners, which was a forerunner of the UDC. This experience of local government enabled him to play a leading part in the discussions on Wollaston's future. He judged it would be advantageous for Wollaston to join Stourbridge. He was to remain a councillor until his death in 1908. His 14 years of service included five years as Chairman of Stourbridge UDC, followed by three years as Deputy Chairman. His life and work was commemorated by the erection of the Isaac Nash Memorial Tower, which stands in Hagley Road, at the rear of the old library (The Living Gallery in 2003), next to The Swan Hotel.

1908 – Gerald Mills

Gerald Rusgrove Mills was born in Wollaston in 1877. He was the son of a solicitor, Harry Mills, and his wife Jane, a younger sister of Isaac Nash Jr. They were living in High Park in 1881 but there is no record of their whereabouts in Wollaston in the 1891 census.

Harry Mills died in February 1897 and by 1901 his widow and two other children, Olive and Kenneth, had moved to Guildford. Gerald was then living in Chelsea, single, and employed by a book publisher where he was described as '*Manager, Educational.*'

The firm he worked for was Methuens, and it was here that he met Charles Boon. In 1908 they founded their own publishing house, Mills & Boon. At first they published books of general interest and among their early authors were P G Wodehouse, Jack London and Georgette Heyer.

During the Great War they both served in the forces, leaving Charles's sister, Margaret, to run the business. By their return in 1918 it had nearly collapsed and as a result they decided to concentrate on commercial lending libraries. Sometimes large companies such as W H Smith or Boots ran these, but there were also many small shops, which would have a few shelves of popular novels, which could be borrowed for 2d a week. Their clientele was wide but appealed mainly to women who could not afford to buy books but could just manage a small amount weekly to borrow them. It was at this time that they took the decision to concentrate on short romantic stories and attention was focused on marketing and promotions.

Since the death of Gerald Mills in 1928, the firm has become one of the best-known publishers, not just in the UK, but worldwide, and most famous for their romantic novels.

1910 – Election of B F Mason

In 1910 Benjamin Francis (Frank) Mason stood as a candidate at Wollaston in the local elections for Stourbridge UDC. His notice to the electors of Wollaston stated,

'*TO THE ELECTORS OF WOLLAS-TON WARD.*
Ladies and gentlemen, Having been

Above: Isaac Nash Jr's life and works were commemorated by the erection of the Isaac Nash Memorial Tower, seen here, which stands in Hagley Road, at the rear of the old library (The Living Gallery in 2003), next to The Swan Hotel.

Below: Another important figure in Wollaston's development was Frank Mason, who was a Wollaston Councillor on Stourbridge UDC from 1910, and on Stourbridge Borough Council from 1914. He was Chairman of the Town Council Highways and Improvements Committee, and acted as Treasurer of Wollaston Public Hall committee; president of Wollaston Benevolent Committee from 1912; and both a People's Warden and Vicar's Warden at St James's Church. He died on 5 August 1925.

requested by a number of Electors to offer myself as a Candidate for the Urban District Council, I have much pleasure in stating that I have decided to do so.

One main reason for my standing is, that I consider that local elections should be altogether OUTSIDE THE RANGE OF PARTY AND IMPERIAL POLITICS.

The chief qualifications necessary surely are business and administrative capacity, and not one's opinions on national and imperial questions.

My policy, if elected, will be to keep down the Rates at the lowest point consistent with efficiency, and to aid the town's advancement, to watch particularly the interests of our own Ward, in which I've been A RESIDENT OVER 15 YEARS. Your interests are, therefore, identical with my own, and these, I take it, are to secure for Wollaston Ward its proper benefits as an important and growing residential suburb.

Should you honour me with your support and vote for me on these grounds, I would do my best to act in the best interests of the whole district.

I beg to remain,
Yours obediently.'

He was duly elected and represented Wollaston for the next 15 years.

Frank Mason was born in 1860 in Dudley. He attended Holly Hall School and was a pupil teacher there from 1871 to 1876. After two years at Saltley College, he began his teaching career in a school in Birmingham. After six months he was appointed second master at a Brierley Hill school, a position he held for three years. In 1882 he became head teacher of Wordsley School and when the new building in Brook Street, Wordsley was opened, he moved there as its first headmaster, a post he held for 40 years until his retirement in 1922.

He moved to live in Wollaston, and in the 1901 census he was living with his wife, mother, two daughters and one son at 73 High Street.

As a councillor Frank Mason served on both Stourbridge UDC from 1910 and Stourbridge Borough Council from 1914; he was chairman of the Town Council Highways and Improvements Committee; he acted as Treasurer of Wollaston Public Hall

committee; he was president of Wollaston Benevolent Committee from 1912; he was People's Warden and Vicar's Warden at St James's Church and a trustee of the Richardson Hall in Wordsley.

During the Great War he served in the Worcestershire Volunteers from October 1914 to May 1919. He was a member of Stourbridge War Memorial Committee and a vice-president of the Stourbridge Brotherhood.

Frank Mason died on 5 August 1925, whilst on holiday in Eastbourne.

1911 – T W Watson

Thomas William Watson had a distinguished academic and military career, followed by 29 years in the teaching profession.

He was born in March 1889 and his early education was at Wollaston schools. He won a scholarship to King Edward VI Grammar School in 1900.

In the 1901 census he was living with his parents and an older sister at 61 High Street. He was the only member of the family to be born in Wollaston. His father, a glassmaker, came from Tutbury in Staffordshire, and his mother was born in Derby.

His mathematical ability was recognised whilst at King Edward's when he came first in all England for two successive years in arithmetic examinations. A scholarship to St John's College, Cambridge where he read maths, followed in 1908.

In 1911 he achieved a first class pass in both parts of the final examinations in mathematics. The *County Express* had a headline on 1 July: '*Stourbridge Wrangler.*'

The term wrangler was a Cambridge title conferred on someone who gained a double first in maths. The village schools decided to mark the occasion and it was recorded in the Boys' School logbook:

'*July 13 1911 – Tomorrow there is a holiday partly for attendance and partly to celebrate Mr Watson's success. Advantage is being taken to use the holiday for the annual outing of the upper children. 70 boys and 51 girls are going by brake to Habberley Valley.*'

In 1912 after leaving Cambridge he began his teaching career in

Above: Thomas William Watson was born in Wollaston and educated at Wollaston Schools. He won a scholarship to King Edward VI Grammar School in 1900, and after a distinguished military and academic career, he returned there in 1934 as headmaster. When he retired in 1951 it was recognised that in the period under his stewardship the school's reputation had been considerably enhanced. Tommy Watson, seen here in the gown, second left, died in London in January 1957. *Stourbridge Library*

London. This ended when war broke out in 1914 and in September he enlisted in the Artists' Rifles. He was commissioned in March 1915 as a 2nd Lieutenant in the Royal Field Artillery. Promotion followed rapidly: Lieutenant in 1915; Captain in 1915; Acting Major in 1916-1917. In France he was mentioned in dispatches and on 1 January 1918 he was awarded the Military Cross.

On being demobbed in 1919 he worked for three years at the Ministry of Munitions before resuming his teaching career. From 1922 to 1925 he taught maths in Pocklington, East Yorkshire, before returning to the Midlands when he was appointed head of King Edward's School, Camp Hill in Birmingham. In 1931 he moved to Dudley to become headmaster of the Grammar School, and three years later he became headmaster of King Edward VI Grammar School in Stourbridge.

When he retired in 1951 it was recognised that, in the period under his stewardship, the school's reputation had been considerably enhanced.

Tommy Watson died in London in January 1957.

1913 – A Wollaston winner

Albert Charles Hitchings was

one of four winners who shared a 20-guinea prize in a national newspaper competition in April. This was for 19 year olds and under, and comprised the re-writing of advertisements.

Albert Hitchings was born in 1895, the youngest son of Mr J P Hitchings. He had attended King Edward VI's Grammar School and had recently been awarded a certificate in the Surveyors' Institute examinations. He was killed in 1916 while on active service.

1917 – Daisy Druller

In 1917 Daisy Druller joined the staff of King Edward's School in Stourbridge. She was born in October 1894 and had attended Stourbridge Girls' School from 1908 to 1913 before going to Birmingham University. She taught English and Latin full-time at King Edward's from 1916 to 1959, and continued part-time until 1974.

She had moved to Wollaston when her parents bought a house in Vicarage Road in 1929, and she spent the rest of her life in the same house. She was a well-known figure in Stourbridge and Wollaston and over a long period, taught many of the boys who attended the Grammar School. She died in 1978.

1918 – Chance's fire-cone

On 26 September there was an advertisement in the *Daily News* for a 'Patent Incandescent FIRE-CONE' placed by G B Chance & Co, Wollaston, Stourbridge. A fire-cone (right) was a shaped firebrick placed in a grate before the coal was built up. It had three effects: saving coal by taking up space, allowing air to circulate through the fire, and keeping the fire going due to its incandescent properties.

In 1921 G B Chance was living at 17 Wood Street and had moved to Eggington Road by 1925.

1921 – Death of Job Til Short

Job Til Short was born in February 1832, the only son of Job Short of High Park. After attending Mr Wright's Commercial School in Union Street, he joined his father in the building trade.

In 1854 he married Emma, the daughter of William Millward who

How to use Less Coal.

Put a Patent

Incandescent FIRE-CONE

(Firebrick)

in the Centre of your Grate, as shown above, with the Fire over it.

It will save 50% of your Coal.

Don't be misled by poor substitutes. See you get the article you want.

Ironmongers and Stores can get supplies from

G. B. CHANCE & CO., Wollaston, Stourbridge.

London District and Home Counties apply to:

BLAKES, 159, Victoria St., S.W.1.

Above: One of Wollaston's odder products was Chance's Fire Cone. The shaped firebrick fire-cone was placed in a grate and the coal built up on top of it. The cone saved coal by taking up space, allowed air to circulate through the fire, and its incandescent properties kept the fire going. G B Chance lived at 17 Wood Street in 1921, but had moved to Eggington Road by 1925.

was superintending engineer at John Bradley & Co. They had three daughters and one son, Sir Frank Short.

In the census returns for 1851 and 1861 Job Short is described as a

Above: Job Til Short, who was born in Wollaston in 1832, began work as a builder, but his interest in engineering led to him becoming one of the country's most respected inspectors of steam boilers. His many interests in Stourbridge included the waterworks and the Stourbridge Institute, of which he was treasurer for 40 years. He also served as a manager of the Penny Bank. The father of the Wollaston artist Sir Frank Short, Job died at home in Gladstone Road on 21 February 1921.

bricklayer, but by 1871 he had become an inspector of steam boilers and by 1891 a boiler inspector for an insurance company. His upwardly mobile career was undoubtedly due to his innate ability and determination, but his father-in-law, William Millward, may have helped him. As steam power drove machinery in all late 19th century factories, regular maintenance and inspection of boilers was essential, as boilers were prone to explode with devastating consequences. He was later employed by the Midland Steam Boiler Inspection & Insurance Company and his work took him to many parts of the UK.

His many interests in Stourbridge included the waterworks and the Stourbridge Institute, of which he was treasurer for 40 years. He also served as a manager of the Penny Bank.

In politics he was a radical Liberal and in religion he was a Unitarian and lived to become the oldest member of the Stourbridge Presbyterian Church.

He died at home in Gladstone Road on 21 February 1921.

1923 – Wollaston's health

In the Wollaston Parish

Magazine for 10 October there was a tribute to the healthiness of Wollaston by Hugh Wanstall. He wrote that:

'there had not been a death since 25 June and on that date the death had been a suicide. Since the building of the church there had not been such a long interval. The average death rate for Wollaston was about one per week. A resident who had moved from Stourbridge jocularly said his household expenses had nearly doubled as the air produced such an increase in appetite.'

1925 – Emanuel Cookson

The *County Express* of 25 July reported that Mrs Cookson, the widow of Emanuel, was going to present a reredos (an altar screen) to St James's Church in memory of her late husband. He and his father had both been churchwardens.

1926 – Death of W H Foster

William Henry Foster, who was born at Himley House in 1846, was the older son of William Orme Foster. He worked in the family concerns and from 1870 onwards he was allowed by his father to take some part in the management of their many business enterprises. From 1874 there was a decline in the Midland iron industries, and although a recovery was made in the 1890s, the result was the closure of some of the works. From 1874 to 1895 no profits were made.

On his father's death in 1899 W H Foster succeeded to the much-reduced family businesses, disposing of the last of them in 1919, by which time the family, over five generations, had been connected with the iron industries for almost 175 years.

1926 – Earthquake tremors

On 15 August an earthquake had been felt in King Street; a woman lying ill in bed had been greatly upset by the shock. There had been a low rumbling noise followed by the rattling of a window; the sash cord of a partially opened window in the bedroom had broken and the window had fallen and been smashed. So the Gornal earthquake on 23 September 2002 was not the only tremor felt in the area!

1927 – Bricklaying record

Fred Hawthorne, of Roseville, Eggington Road, laid 1,000 paving bricks in 21 minutes. He wrote to the *County Express* of 17 December asking if this was a record.

1928 – H J Guest

H J Guest, a native of Wollaston, was appointed Goods Commercial Manager of the LMS railway company in May. He was born in 1870, the son of Thomas Guest and started work at the age of 16 for LNWR at Wolverhampton and worked in a number of posts including a spell at Euston. He gained promotion when the LNWR merged with the L&YR in 1922.

He was the younger brother of the wife of Alderman Frank Taylor.

1929 – A quiet(er) fair

At the Stourbridge Council meeting in March Councillor Pearson mentioned that the quietude of Wollaston had been disturbed when a fair had been held in the village. He asked whether the council had any power to prevent this happening in such a quiet spot. When the Town Clerk replied that fairs had been held in Stourbridge from time immemorial Councillor Wright said: *'But not in Wollaston.'*

1929 – Election of Elinor Stuart

In the Wollaston by-election held in December to elect a successor to Councillor Samuel Wright who had been elevated to the rank of alderman; there were only two candidates. They were Frank B Bellamy (Labour), a locomotive driver of Firmstone Street and Mrs W A Stuart (Independent) of Meriden House, Gladstone Road. 1,649 voters went to the three polling stations, and the result was announced one hour after the polls closed. Mrs Elinor Stuart was elected with 953 votes against 695 for Mr Bellamy. She was Wollaston's first lady councillor.

1929 – Prince Rainier

Kathleen Wanstall, the sister of the vicar, became nanny to Prince Rainier of Monaco and his sister Princess Antoinette. When the prince was six years old he visited the village, staying at the vicarage and The Croft, the home of Mrs A H Guest. who was

a friend of the Wanstalls and had visited Monte Carlo on a number of occasions.

Kathleen Wanstall remained with the family for many years, later taking charge of Princess Antoinette's children. In 1949 Prince Rainier came to the throne and in 1950 Miss Wanstall was awarded the honour Chevalier de l'Ordre de St Charles.

1930 – Four generations

In October the *County Express* published a photograph of four generations of the Worton family of Yardley's Row, off High Street. Mrs Worton, aged 84, was the grand daughter of Major Thomas Brooke who fought at the Battle of Waterloo.

1931 – The Hammond family

Joseph Hammond Jr, who died in 1931, was born in 1854. His father, also Joseph, and his sisters were to play an important and influential role in the life of the church and the wider community in the second half of the 19th century and, more importantly, the first half of the 20th century.

Their home, The Hollies, in Cobden Street, has long since been converted into two homes. Exactly when the family moved in is not known but they were certainly living there by the time of the 1861 census. Joseph and his sister Annie, were born in Amblecote in 1856, but their three younger siblings, George, Frances and Arthur were born in Wollaston, almost certainly at The Hollies.

Their father, **Joseph Hammond**, 1821-1882, had a sister, Jane, who married Joseph Webb, the glass manufacturer of Coalbournbrook, Amblecote. When Joseph Webb died in 1869 his will entrusted the management of the glassworks to his brother-in-law, Joseph Hammond Sr, at a salary of £300 plus 10% of the annual profits. With this financial security Joseph and his family were able to live in style at the Hollies. There is anecdotal evidence of the family being driven in their horse drawn carriage to St James's Church, where he was a churchwarden.

Joseph Hammond Jr, known locally as Captain Hammond, worked initially in the glass trade and then went into business on his own account as an iron and steel merchant. In 1871, at the age of 17, he joined the Stourbridge Volunteers as a private. The Stourbridge Volunteer Company was one of hundreds of volunteer infantry companies that were founded in the 1860s in response to prompting and encouragement by the War Office. They were the 19th century equivalent of today's territorial army. Eventually the Stourbridge Volunteers became the 9th Company of the Worcestershire Rifle Corps, which, in turn, became part of The Worcestershire Regiment. Joseph Hammond served in the company for about 20 years, being promoted through the ranks, firstly to ensign, then lieutenant, eventually attaining the rank of captain in 1879. Then, because of the demands of his business interests, he resigned from the Volunteers, but on the outbreak of war in 1914, he volunteered, at the age of 60, for service abroad. Although he was rejected for service in France, he saw wartime service as a Captain in the Home Defence Volunteer Corps guarding bridges and railway installations in Devon. Throughout his life he was keenly interested in rifle shooting. During his service with the Rifle Volunteers he represented his battalion in competition shooting, and at the time of his death in 1931, he was vice-president of the Stourbridge Rifle Club. Although not at the forefront of village activities he served as vice-president of the Parochial Church Council, as a manager of Wollaston Schools and was secretary of the St James's Church Free Will Offering.

His spinster sisters **Frances**, born 1860, and especially **Annie**, had a much greater involvement in village life, particularly church activities. In 1952 their work for the church was commemorated by the installation of a brass plaque above the vestry door in the church. Indications in the Parish Magazine in the months immediately following Annie's death in January 1944, were that a more substantial memorial was envisaged. This was to be the erection of an altar in the War Memorial Chapel in her memory and accordingly the 'Hammond Memorial Fund' was established. Unfortunately this proposal was never executed, but the fact that a memorial of this kind was thought appropriate is testament to her work for the church. The

County Express report on her death and funeral said:

'*For more than half a century Miss Hammond was one of the most active workers as well as being one of the most beloved and respected members of the village. For many years she was the Superintendent of the boys' Sunday School, local secretary of the Society for the Propagation of the Gospel, a keen supporter of the church overseas, a member of the Deanery Missionary Association, a member of the PCC since its inception, joint secretary of the Free Will offering at the time of her death and responsible for the care of the church's linen and silver. In many parts of the church there is visible evidence of hours of work and devotion in hand made furnishings which will live in her memory for many years.*'

In addition to her work for the church, 'Miss Annie', as she was known, was also a life long supporter of the Boy Scouts and for a number of years was treasurer of the local association.

Miss Annie's death in January was followed in December by the death of her younger sister, Frances. The Hollies was subsequently sold. The house still stands in 2003 but it is called The Beeches. Its grounds once extended along half of one side of Cobden Street, but they were sold off in sections, in the 1930s, 1950s and 1970s, and developed for housing. Fragments of the wall that once edged the grounds survive outside Tree Tops and Kinley.

1931 – Open rally

On 26 September an open rally and grass track meeting was held in a field off High Park Avenue. The field belonged to John Roberts of Lawn Street and the event was part of Wollaston's effort to raise money for the Corbett Hospital Fund. Before the creation of the NHS in 1948, hospitals were dependent on funds raised by the local community.

The *County Express* of 3 October carried the following report:

'*A good-sized track had been roped off. The going was rather bumpy and difficulty was experienced at the cor-*

ners, but there was some good riding, and the spectators, of whom there was a fair assembly, were provided with thrills which kept them interested throughout the proceedings which lasted about three hours.'

Other attractions included a 14hp Lagonda car driven by Frank Hallam in which he had raced at Brooklands.

There were classes for motor cycles, light cars and three-wheelers. A few spills occurred but none of the competitors was injured. A serious accident involved a boy who was run over by a motorcyclist riding outside the course after the end of a race. The injuries were a severe cut on his leg and after receiving attention at the course, he was taken to Dr Simkiss's surgery where his wound was stitched.

In February 1932 a court action was brought claiming damages for the boy's injuries. The case for compensation was dismissed.

1932 – Flying circus

On 21 August there was a visit from '*Britain's Greatest All British Flying Circus*' to The Ridge Top at Wollaston. Two separate displays were held at 3:00pm and 7:00pm and the gates opened an hour before the displays began.

The programme included:

Above: On 21 August 1932 there was a visit from '*Britain's Greatest All British Flying Circus*' to The Ridge Top, Wollaston. Two separate displays were held at 3:00pm and 7:00pm and the gates opened an hour before the displays began. Unfortunately, there was bad weather on the day, which greatly interfered with the flying. Here crowds have gathered around one of the aircraft, a Bleriot Experimental BE 2E, which was built in 1916.

'1 – Formation flight
2 – Tommy Bateman, the Lincolnshire Grass Track rider issues a challenge to all-comers for a three-circuit race
3 – Wing Walking, Jack Harris, the Human Fly
4 – Aerobatic Display by the Dare-Devil Major
5 – Special event for ladies – Ankle competition - 1st Prize a 10-minute free flight, 2nd Prize a 5-minute free flight
6 – Race – Aeroplane v. Grass Track Riders
7 – Special demonstration of the latest model CIERVA AUTO-GIRO (the Windmill Plane). This machine rises and descends vertically
8 – Dual Parachute descent by A W Fairlie (Britain's foremost parachutist)
Adults 1s; Children 6d; Cars 6d; Motorcycles 3d; Cycles 2d.
PASSENGER FLIGHTS ALL DAY'

However there was bad weather on the day, which greatly interfered with the flying displays. There was some stunt flying as well as grass track riding but because of the weather there was not a very large crowd.

1933 – Wollaston sensation

There was a shocking discovery in St James's Church in February, which caused a sensation in the district. About 2.00pm, shortly after a wedding ceremony, a 65-year-old man, Alfred J Holloway, was found lying on the floor of a back pew. He was bleeding profusely from a wound in his throat and an open razor was found nearby. He was an unemployed bachelor who lodged with the verger. He was taken to Sandfield House, (Wordsley Workhouse), where his condition was said to be serious.

1933 – Birth of triplets

On 18 February there was an article in the *County Express* about the birth of triplets, all girls, to Kate and Wilfred Capewell of 9 Bridgnorth Road.

1934 – Election apathy

There was a poor turnout at the County Council elections held in March. Joseph Wooldridge (Independent) edge tool manufacturer of Duncombe Street polled 403 votes;

Above: Alexander Francis (Frank) Taylor lived in High Park Avenue for over 40 years, until his death on 15 December 1935. He was elected a councillor for Wollaston on Stourbridge UDC in 1899, and, except for a three-year period, he represented Wollaston until his resignation on health grounds in November 1935, a month before he died. He always spoke up for Wollaston, and it was due to his efforts that the village gained an extra councillor in 1910. He is seen here during his time as Mayor of Stourbridge in 1914. *Stourbridge Library*

Thomas Edward Walton (Labour) retired postman of Enville Street polled 343 votes.

1935 – Death of Frank Taylor

Alexander Francis (Frank) Taylor lived in High Park Avenue for over 40 years, until his death on 15 December 1935.

He was at the forefront of decision-making concerning developments affecting Wollaston in the formative years of the 20th century.

Born in Kidderminster in 1858, he was living in Halifax in 1881, where his father, also born in Kidderminster, was working as a carpet weaver. In the 1881 census Frank was unmarried and working as a schoolmaster. He came to Stourbridge in 1883 as headmaster of Scott's Charity School in Wollaston Road, near to the Quaker Meeting House. He stayed there until it closed in 1912, when he became the first head of Valley Road School, Lye, remaining there until he retired.

In 1894 Frank Taylor stood unsuccessfully as a Liberal candidate for Wollaston on the newly created Stourbridge UDC, and he had been actively involved earlier that year in the parish discussions on the future of Wollaston, the momentous question was: *'Should Wollaston join Stourbridge?'* He was elected a councillor for Wollaston on Stourbridge UDC in 1899; this was the start of a long commitment and involvement in local government. Except for a three-year period he was to represent Wollaston until his resignation on health grounds in November 1935, a month before he died.

In 1907, as a Wollaston councillor, he initiated the debate on the level of Wollaston's representation on Stourbridge Council, arguing that Wollaston was under-represented and ought to have more councillors; as a consequence Wollaston gained an extra councillor in 1910.

In 1908 he proposed that the council should purchase the land now occupied by The Crescent car park, on the grounds that: *'the land would be valuable for any future public building.'* Sometime earlier there had been talk of a branch library opening there.

His integrity and ability were recognised by his fellow councillors when they invited him to become Chairman of Stourbridge UDC in 1913. That was the last year of the UDC's existence, as the town acquired borough status, with a mayor, in 1914.

The first mayor was Sir Henry Foley Grey of Enville Hall and he invited Frank Taylor to become his deputy. Sir Henry was essentially a figurehead for the new borough and he recognised the wealth of experience that Frank Taylor had as a councillor, as chairman of the Finance Committee for many years and, most recently, as the last chairman of the UDC. Sir Henry died six weeks after accepting the office of mayor, and so Frank Taylor became acting mayor for the rest of that year. He continued as deputy mayor in the following year and in 1916 was unanimously elected mayor. By now he was an alderman, a rank to which he was elevated in 1914.

During the Great War he was responsible for food control and recruitment. In his mayoral year

Worcestershire recruited more soldiers than any other county, and Stourbridge more than any other town in the county.

In the remaining 20 years of his life, Frank Taylor was to hold many important positions in the fields of local government in both Stourbridge and at county level. In 1921 he was involved in the negotiations to dispose of council-owned land at The Ridge in exchange for what was to become the Recreation Ground off High Street. When the Public Hall Committee was formed in 1913 he was elected chairman and when the hall was opened in 1920 he became chairman of the trustees, a position he held until it was sold in 1930. He served as a governor of several local schools and was chairman of the Stourbridge Higher Education Committee.

Although not a native of Wollaston, it is clear that Frank Taylor cared deeply for the community that he lived in and represented for 40 years.

1937 – Coronation honours

In April a Wollaston boy, Thomas Taylor of Leonard Road, was chosen to represent Stourbridge to see the passing of the Royal procession on Coronation Day. He was an employee of Stourbridge Rolling Mills and was chosen at the Duke of York's annual holiday camp at Southwold in 1936.

1937 – Children's outing

On 12 August an outing to Rhyl was organised for 100 poor children from Wollaston. Mrs H Clark of The Waterloo Inn had collected the money to pay for three Midland Red coaches that left the village schools at 7:30am and travelled via Llangollen to Rhyl. On arrival the children were provided with lunch at a cafe and then proceeded to the sands for games and donkey rides. At 5:30pm they left the beach for tea and an hour later began their return journey and reached Wollaston at about 11:15pm.

It was hoped that this would be the first in a series of outings, and a committee was formed by Mrs Clark to make arrangements for the future and to prepare a balance sheet, which was to be distributed to those who had contributed to the cost of this outing.

Above: Sir Frank Short was the son of Job Till Short, and followed his father into engineering. However his artistic abilities, particularly in etching and engraving, soon came to the fore. He went on to direct the Engraving School of the Royal College of Art from 1891 until his retirement in 1924.

1945 – Sir Frank Short

Francis Job Short who died in April, was arguably Wollaston's most distinguished son. He was born on 19 June 1857, the son of Job Til Short and his wife Emma, and lived in Bridle Lane (now Gladstone Road), in the house built by his father.

As the only son, he was educated at a private school, Prospect House in Oldswinford, which was run by Henry Newnam, a friend of his father. He left school to learn engineering at the office of his uncle, John Millward, in Birmingham. He also attended evening classes at Stourbridge School of Art and studied maths and chem-

istry at the Stourbridge Institute, where, in 1876, he won a prize for chemistry - a book with the title *'Sketching from Nature.'* Many years later he wrote of his early education:

'I was at school till I was fourteen and learned little of any value. Then my father, meaning me to be a Civil Engineer, wisely sent me to carry mortar to a bricklayer till I had learned much of his craft. Then through many kinds of engineering works till I acquired the title of AMICE which I take some satisfaction in, for it was not got without hard and earnest work.'

In 1874 he left his uncle's employment and for a short time he worked for his brother-in-law, E B Marten, in Stourbridge.

When he was about 20 Frank Short set up in business in Stourbridge as a consulting engineer, but failing to make a success of it, he moved to London in 1881. Two years later he abandoned his career in civil engineering and enrolled at the National Art Training School (later the Royal College of Art) in South Kensington. He also attended a life drawing class in Westminster.

While still a student he won high approval from a number of distinguished critics. Although interested in painting, producing a number of watercolours, his main interest was in etching and engraving, and it is on his wide-ranging contributions to this

Above: Frank Short is seated centre front in this group of artists. In 1906 he was elected an Associate of the Royal Academy, becoming a full member in 1911, the same year in which he received a knighthood. In 1910 he was elected President of the Royal Society of Painter-Etchers & Engravers, holding this office until 1939. He also served as treasurer of the Royal Academy from 1919 to 1932. Sir Frank Short died at Ditchling, Sussex, on 22 April 1945.

artistic medium that his reputation stands. Perhaps it was his early training in science and engineering which enabled him to make his own tools and invent new ones, to experiment with existing processes and develop new techniques.

In 1885 he was elected a fellow of the Royal Society of Painter-Etchers and in 1891 was appointed as teacher in charge of etching at South Kensington. He was to direct the Engraving School of the Royal College of Art from 1891 until his retirement in 1924.

In 1906 he was elected an Associate of the Royal Academy, becoming a full member in 1911, the same year in which he received his knighthood.

In 1910 he was elected President of the Royal Society of Painter - Etchers and Engravers, holding this office until 1939. He served as treasurer of the Royal Academy from 1919 to 1932. International recognition of his work came in the shape of four medals, which are shown in the colour section:

- 1889 République Française Exposition Universelle
- 1900 République Française Exposition Universelle
- 1908 Franco-British exhibition
- 1923 Art institute of Chicago - Frank C Logan medal

Sir Frank Short's works are to be found in many galleries, including Dudley Art Gallery. In Stourbridge he has been honoured by three exhibitions, in 1887, 1957 and 1986. He died at Ditchling, Sussex, on 22 April 1945.

1946 – Death of Joe Pearson

Joseph Francis Pearson, born in Pensnett in 1880, played a leading role in the educational, social and political life of Wollaston for almost 30 years. He is probably best remembered for his sporting achievements.

When he came to Wollaston in 1919 to take up his appointment as headmaster of the Boys' School, he was already a well-known sporting personality having won a number of local tennis tournaments in South Staffordshire and North Worcestershire and, more famously, an F A Cup

Above: Like Franks Mason and Taylor, Joe Pearson, seen here in his Mayoral robes, was another local teacher who also devoted himself to Wollaston's affairs. When he came to Wollaston in 1919 as headmaster of the Boys' School, he was already a well-known sporting personality, having won a number of local tennis tournaments in South Staffordshire and North Worcestershire and, most notably, an F A Cup Winner's Medal with Aston Villa FC in 1905. *Stourbridge Library*

Winner's Medal with Aston Villa FC.

Educated at Pensnett Church of England School and Dudley Grammar School, he went on to serve as a pupil teacher at Wolverhampton Street School, Dudley before entering St Peter's College, Saltley, Birmingham, a Church of England teacher training college. On qualifying as a teacher he taught at Bromley School where he combined teaching with professional soccer.

His football career had begun earlier when, as a teenager, he had captained Dudley Town in the Birmingham League from 1898 to 1900. In the 1899-1900 season they had finished third behind Wolves Reserves and Villa Reserves. It was here that his ability as a centre half attracted the attention of the Villa scouts. He signed for Villa in 1900 and remained with them until a knee injury forced him to retire in 1908. He made many first team appearances including playing in the FA Cup Final against Newcastle United at Crystal Palace in 1905. The match that Villa won 2-0 was in front of a crowd of 101,117 spectators!

When his playing days were over he became a referee and for ten years took charge of First Division games. The highlight of his refereeing career was when he was a linesman in

In 1947, the "Birmingham Evening Despatch" published a pictorial history of Aston Villa F.C., by Norman Edwards. This cartoon, featuring former Saltley College personalities, was one of the series.

Above: This cartoon which appeared in the Birmingham Evening Despatch in 1947, neatly summarises what Joe Pearson achieved in his lifetime. *Birmingham Post & Mail*

the England v Scotland match at Villa Park in 1922.

In 1916 he enlisted in the army, serving for three and a half years in the Army Ordnance Corps, before being demobilised with the rank of acting sergeant major.

On his arrival in Wollaston Joe Pearson soon took an active role in the life of the village. At Easter 1922 he became a churchwarden at St James's Church and continued in that office for the next 24 years. In the same year he was elected as an Independent councillor for Wollaston on Stourbridge Borough Council and he continued to represent Wollaston until his death in 1946.

His work for Wollaston was recognised when he was elected Mayor of the Borough of Stourbridge in 1941 and again in 1942. He received a further civic honour when he was raised to the rank of alderman during his second year as mayor. He served for a further two years as deputy mayor.

His greatest achievements as a councillor came when he chaired the Estates Committee, responsible for public buildings and undertakings. It was while serving in this capacity that the improvement to the Council House in Mary Stevens' Park and the improvement and extension of the swimming baths were carried out.

His sudden death on 26 April 1946, only six days after his retirement presentation at Wollaston School, was a great blow and loss to the village.

1946 – Geoffrey Beard

The booklet *A History of Wollaston* by Geoffrey W Beard is published. To date this is the only published historical account of the development of Wollaston. At the time Geoffrey Beard had just left King Edward VI Grammar School, Stourbridge. He went on to become a leading historian of furniture and interior decoration. Between 1965-1974 he assumed the position of editor of the journal *Furniture History*, focusing on the craftsmen involved. He was the Director of the Visual Arts Centre at the University of Lancaster between 1972-1982; and co-founder of the Furniture History Society, holding the position of Chairman between 1984-

Above: Prior to the publication of this book, the booklet *A History of Wollaston* by Geoffrey W Beard, published in 1946, was the only historical account of the development of Wollaston. At the time Geoffrey Beard had just left King Edward VI Grammar School, Stourbridge. He went on to become one of the country's leading historians of furniture and interior decoration. *H Jack Haden*

1991. In this period Geoffrey Beard established an international reputation as one of the best-known scholars working in the related fields of conservation and the decorative arts, with a reputation for sound archival research and the kind of single-mindedness that has transformed knowledge of plasterwork and furniture.

His book Decorative *Plasterwork in Great Britain* (1975) revolutionised understanding of that field, and his *Upholsterers and interior furnishing in England, 1530-1840* did the same for upholsterers in 1997. Geoffrey Beard also made his mark as a museum director and teacher, and in practical conservation through his passionate commitment to the Attingham and Idlewild Trusts, holding the position of President of the Attingham Trust since 1996.

On 3 September 2002 Geoffrey Beard received an Honorary Degree of Doctor of Arts from the University of Wolverhampton's School of Art & Design in recognition of his scholarship and contribution to the understanding of the Applied Arts. His books include: *English Abbeys* (1949); *Nineteenth Century Cameo Glass*

(1956); *Georgian Craftsmen and their work* (1966); *Decorative Plasterwork in Great Britain* (1975); *International modern glass* (1976); *The work of John Adam* (1978); *Craftsmen and interior decoration in England, 1620-1820* (1981); *Stucco and decorative plasterwork in Europe* (1983); *Dictionary of English furniture makers, 1660-1840* (1986); *The National Trust Book of English Furniture* (1986); *The work of John Vanbrugh* (1986); *English Furniture, 1500-1840* (1987); *The work of Christopher Wren* (1987); *The work of Grinling Gibbons* (1989); *The Compleat Gentleman: Five centuries of aristocratic life* (1993); *Upholsterers and interior furnishing in England, 1530-1840* (1997).

1948-1953 – Wollaston on Air

There have been a number of times when life and events in Wollaston have been broadcast on radio.

On 5 January 1948 Wollaston OAPs were interviewed at New Road Methodist Hall, by the BBC for their 'Around and About' programme. The interviewees included Elizabeth Haden, 75, of Yardley's Row, a brickyard worker; Frank Richards, 74, who was still working as a chain maker at E Baylie & Co of Stourbridge; George Horton, 92, of Harmon Road and William Horton of Palfrey Road who between them had 100 years' service with the GWR.

In October 1949, there was a broadcast of a service from St James's Church on the BBC Midland Home Service. Unfortunately the lights failed during the service but the congregation managed by using matches, lighters and torches. Power was restored at the end of the second hymn. Many messages were received about the excellence of the reception from as far away as the Isle of Man.

After another broadcast from St James's Church on 13 June 1953 on the BBC overseas service, letters were received from India, Turkey, Persia, Egypt, Uganda, Oklahoma and Massachusetts, all saying the reception was very good.

1950 – Death of Herbert Husselbee

Herbert Husselbee died on 22 May aged 77. Although born in Wordsley, the son of a glassmaker, for most of his adult life he was resident in Wollaston, where he lived in High Park Avenue. Educated at Oldswinford Hospital School, he started working for Edward Webb & Sons, the Wordsley seed merchants, at the age of 13. He was promoted to become a commercial traveller, or sales representative, after 20 years service. In that capacity he worked for the next 40 years. By the time of his retirement at the age of 73 in 1946 he had completed 60 years unbroken service for the company and, in doing so, had become a well-known figure in Midland farming circles, and an acknowledged expert on many aspects of horticulture.

Throughout his life he was involved in a wide-range of community affairs, and he never lost contact with Wordsley, where for many years he was active in running the Boys' Brigade. In Wollaston he was a founder member of the tennis club, a member of the Board of Managers of Wollaston Schools, and the Vicar's Warden at St James's Church from 1932 to 1942.

1953 – Coronation duties

Graham Holton, the 19-year-old son of Mr & Mrs T H Holton of Gilbanks Road, was chosen to be on duty at the Coronation. He was serving in the RAF.

Above: The Coronation of Elizabeth II was celebrated in Wollaston by the distribution of special mugs to all the pupils at the school. Here Cllr E R R Tooby presents the mugs, ably assisted by Cllr Eric Heynes, whilst the Vicar, Rev Ingram Cox, looks on amused.

1957 – Ken & Eric Davies

The Davies brothers were both boxers, and although they weren't born in Wollaston, they belonged to

Above: Wollaston boxer Ken Davies' first win was in the Midland Counties Boys' Clubs Championships. His professional debut was in May 1949, with a win, but in his next fight he was knocked out after only two minutes 55 seconds. Despite this defeat he made a good start to his career with three wins and one draw. After his boxing career was over, Ken was licensee of The Waterloo Inn from 1955 to 1957.

Wollaston Amateur Boxing Club, where their father, Ben Davies, was the coach. Wollaston ABC was based at The Forester's Arms.

Ken Davies' first win was in the Midland Counties Boys' Clubs Championships. He joined the Royal Navy where, in 1946, he won the Portsmouth Command Boxing Championship. His professional debut was in May 1949, with a win, but in his next fight he was knocked out after only two minutes 55 seconds. Despite this defeat he made a good start to his career with three wins and one draw. After his boxing career was over, Ken Davies was the licensee of The Waterloo Inn from 1955 to 1957.

Eric Davies' professional boxing career began in August 1950. He was a welterweight and had over 200 victories and very few defeats before retiring in 1957. As an amateur he became RAF champion in 1949 and won the Imperial Services title the same year. He also represented England a number of times.

His first professional fight was in Wolverhampton on 27 September 1950. After a run of ten unbeaten contests, he lost a fight in December and this affected his confidence. On 22 January 1951 Eric had the singular

honour of boxing on the same programme as up-and-coming British heavyweight Randolph Turpin of Leamington Spa, something he repeated on 14th July 1951 at Halesowen, where Turpin gave a three-round workout just four days after becoming World Heavyweight Champion.

Over the next three years he had nine wins, six losses and one draw, and succeeded in winning the British Lightweight title, which caused one reporter to comment that Eric: '*had put Wollaston on the Boxing World Map.*' His last bout was on 2 September 1957 in Birmingham when he out pointed his opponent, Ken Barley, over six rounds.

Ken's brother Eric Davies began his professional boxing career in August 1950. His first professional fight was in Wolverhampton on 27 September 1950. As seen here, on 22 January 1951 Eric had the singular honour of boxing on the same programme as up-and-coming British heavyweight Randolph Turpin of Leamington Spa. Over the next three years Eric had nine wins, six losses and one draw, and succeeded in winning the British Lightweight title. His last bout was on 2 September 1957 in Birmingham, when he out pointed his opponent over six rounds.

1958 – Weather records

Ever since January 1958 Gerald Langley of High Park Avenue has been taking daily weather recordings. Thanks to Gerald's efforts over the years it is known that the coldest day he has recorded was 8 February 1969, when the temperature fell to −10.6°C (13°F), and that the hottest day in this period was 3 August 1990, when the temperature soared to 36.6°C (96°F), a range of 46°C (83°F). The previous local record high temperature was recorded on 6 August 1911.

1960 – Gift to museum

On 25 February the old pumping equipment from Enville Street pumping station was given to Birmingham Science Museum.

1960 – Post Office robbery

On 13 December there was a robbery at Wollaston Post Office. It took place between 6:45pm on Monday and 8:05am on the following day, £31,300 was missing. There were two puzzling features about the robbery: how the thieves got into the post office, and how they managed to open the safe?

1961 – Blood transfusion

In August the life of a patient who was critically ill in a Paris hospital was saved by a transfusion from a Wollaston woman. Dorothy Ellis of 128 High Street was found to be the only person in Europe with a matching blood type. Her rare blood group, which has no name or symbol, was discovered whilst she and her husband were living in Canada. She said that she was pleased to help and would have travelled to Paris if it had been necessary.

1967 – Frank A Hejl

In April the retirement of Frank Hejl was announced. He had lived in Bridgnorth Road and retired to Hampshire.

He first arrived in 1926, when he came to work at a tailor's in Stourbridge. Four years later he set up on his own in Wollaston and later bought a men's tailoring business in Birmingham

In 1939, because he was too old to join up, he joined the Home Guard, serving from its first day until the force was stood down. By then held the rank of Major and commanded D Company, Wollaston.

He was an active member in a number of societies; he joined the Merchant Tailors' Society and was vice-chairman in 1951. From 1948 to 1953 he was chairman of the Central Midlands organisation of the National Federation of Master Tailors & Cutters.

Among some of his other activities he was a founder member of the Stourbridge Rifle Club; a member of the Stourbridge Chamber of Trade;

founder-treasurer of Stourbridge Civic Society; and chairman of the Exhibition Committee to celebrate the centenary of the Great Exhibition of 1851.

1967 – Death of E A Heynes

Eric Arthur Heynes was a well-known figure in Wollaston from the time when he first established his business here in 1924.

Eric, born in 1897 in Harborne, was the son of an engineer who produced engine-turning machines for the Birmingham jewellery trade. During the Great War he served as a despatch rider in the 51st Highland Division. On his return to civilian life he joined a motor trade business in Sherborne, Dorset.

Above: Eric Haynes, seen here serving as a despatch rider in the 51st Highland Division during the Great War, established Wollaston Garage at 91 Bridgnorth Road in 1924. He was a Wollaston councillor for 25 years, being first elected as an independent in 1938. He became an alderman in 1952. In the early 1940s he was also appointed a magistrate, a position he held for 25 years, eventually becoming Chairman of the Stourbridge Magistrates' Bench.

In 1924 he established Wollaston Garage at 91 Bridgnorth Road, which began trading as a vehicle repair shop and taxi service. In 1926 he married D D Lush, who came from Sherborne, and for ten years they lived over the shop, moving to Wood Street in 1936, into a house they called Sherborne House.

Eric was a Wollaston councillor for 25 years, being first elected as an independent in 1938. He became an alderman in 1952. In the early 1940s he was appointed a magistrate, a position he held for 25 years, eventually as

Above: Eric Heynes was both a governor and chairman of governors of Wollaston School, and chairman of the Stourbridge & District Water Board from 1946 to 1958. He is seen here speaking at the Coronation celebrations at Wollaston School in 1953. In later life Eric moved to live at Lawnswood in Wordsley, where he died, aged 70, in 1967.

Chairman of the Stourbridge Magistrates' Bench. He was both a governor and chairman of governors of Wollaston School and chairman of the Stourbridge & District Water Board from 1946 to 1958. In that year he was involved in the formation of the North West Worcestershire Water Board.

In later life Eric moved to live at Lawnswood in Wordsley, where he died, aged 70.

1973 – Last mayor of Stourbridge

The *County Express* of 13 April announced that the last mayor of Stourbridge was to be Councillor Alfred Allport who owned a butcher's shop in Bridgnorth Road Wollaston. Local government reorganisation, and a change in the county boundaries, meant that Stourbridge was to become part of Dudley MBC. Councillor Allport was a founder member of the Senior Citizens' Centre Building Fund and a governor of both High Park and The Ridge schools.

1973 – Golden wedding of Norman & Mary Rabey

In August Norman & Mary Rabey celebrated their golden wedding anniversary. Both were born in Wollaston and they could remember the visit of Buffalo Bill and his Wild West Show, and the first tram through the village in the early years of the 20th century.

Above: Councillor Alfred Allport, who owned a butcher's shop in Bridgnorth Road Wollaston, had the singular honour of being the last Mayor of Stourbridge in 1973-74, before the town became part of a larger Dudley MBC. He is seen here in an official photograph taken immediately prior to the last ever meeting of Stourbridge Borough Council. Seated bottom left is John Watteson, another much respected Wollaston Councillor, who was propelled into public life through his involvement with the campaign to stop the proposed dual carriageway in 1970.

Above: Norman Rabey served with the Worcestershire Regiment in Belgium, France and Italy during the Great War, achieving the rank of Company Sergeant Major. Whilst in Italy he won a special medal for his skills in bayonet fighting. In 1924 he established a ladies' and gentlemen's hairdressing business at 94 Bridgnorth Road, and in 1928 he moved this across the road to premises next to The Waterloo Inn, where he continued to work until his retirement in 1979.

Above: Outside business hours Norman Rabey was much in demand as an MC for dances and whist drives in Wollaston and throughout the Stourbridge area. Norman and his wife Mary, pictured on the left, with their son Ken, were keen ballroom dancers, and when most of the people of their age had retired, they were still teaching old-time dancing in Wollaston and Stourbridge well into their 80s. Norman Rabey died in 1980.

Norman Rabey was born in 1895 in Cobden Street, the son of Joseph, a foreman forge master at Isaac Nash's spade works. After attending Wollaston Schools he was apprenticed to a hairdresser in Stourbridge.

During the Great War he served with the Worcestershire Regiment in Belgium, France and Italy achieving the rank of Company Sergeant Major. Whilst in Italy he won a special medal for his skills in bayonet fighting in an inter-regimental tournament.

In 1924 he established a ladies' and gentlemen's hairdressing business at 94 Bridgnorth Road. In 1928 he moved across the road to premises next to The Waterloo Inn, where he continued to work until his retirement in 1979. In the 1930s, in addition to providing a hairdressing service in his shop, he also made home visits to some of his regular clients who lived in outlying districts. These weekly visits to Clent, Belbroughton, Kinver, Wordsley and Oldswinford were made by cycle, regardless of the weather! In the early 1930s he embarked on a business venture with Cecil Hawkeswood (the village chemist)

when they bought the fish and chip shop opposite the traffic island on Bridgnorth Road. When Cecil Hawkeswood withdrew from the partnership to concentrate on building up a chain of chemist shops, Norman took over as sole proprietor.

During World War II he joined Wollaston Home Guard and was in charge of the platoon that guarded Coalbournbrook pumping station.

After the war he continued to combine the management of both businesses until 1948, when he sold the fish & chip shop to Frank Eastwood. He did not retire however, but continued as the village barber until he was well into his 80s. Outside business hours Norman was much in demand as an MC for dances and whist drives, not only in Wollaston, but also throughout the Stourbridge area. The protocol of the ballroom was that after the MC had announced the dance, he and his partner would take the floor and lead off, effectively setting an example for other dancers to follow. Taking the lead was second nature for Norman and Mary, who were keen ballroom dancers, and when most of the people of their age had retired, they were actively teach-

ing old-time dancing in Wollaston and Stourbridge, and continued to dance well into their 80s. Norman died in 1980.

1973 – Ken Rabey & His Orchestra

Ken Rabey, son of Norman, was born in Wollaston in 1925. He probably inherited his musical talent from his mother, Mary, who was an accomplished pianist, and from his grandfather, Albert Lea, who played the flute and piccolo. In his early teens Ken became interested in the popular music of the day, the big band sound, swing and jazz. Although the piano was his first instrument, he played drums from the age of 15 with a number of dance bands in many venues around the area, sometimes fronting his own band.

In 1947 his musical career changed direction when he formed a five-piece dance orchestra, which enabled him to feature the vibraphone, an instrument on which he had begun to excel. This is a member of the percussion family and similar to a xylophone both in appearance and method of playing. Ken's orchestra comprised himself, a pianist, a drummer and two very versatile saxophonists who could also play clarinet and violin. Ken

Above: Norman and Mary Rabey's son Ken inherited his musical abilities from his mother, who was a pianist. In 1947 he formed a five-piece dance orchestra, which featured him on the vibraphone, seen here, an instrument on which he excelled. In 1950 Ken and his band moved to The Stewponey after a three-year spell as the resident dance band at The Old White Horse in Norton. They remained there for the next 23 years, providing music for Saturday night dinner dances, held there weekly. In 1973 Ken retired from the music scene.

believed that this combination would produce a melodious sound that would provide not only easy listening but also music with a beat for dancing the waltz, foxtrot and quickstep. The orchestra's signature tune 'Sweet and Lovely' invariably introduced a range of standard evergreens often featuring the music of Cole Porter and George Gershwin. After a three-year spell as the resident dance band at The Old White Horse in Norton, in 1950 Ken and his band moved to The Stewponey. For the next 23 years they provided the music for the weekly Saturday night dinner dance, which regularly attracted people from as far afield as Bridgnorth, Birmingham and Wolverhampton.

In 1973 Ken retired from the music scene because of the demands of his daytime job. In 1940 he had joined the drawing office of Samuel Taylor & Sons of Brierley Hill. The company originally produced steel chain, shackles and anchors, but in the 1920s switched to the manufacture of

life-saving appliances for ships. During the last 12 years of his 47-year association with the company, Ken worked as Technical Director, and in that capacity needed to travel abroad frequently; this ever-increasing demand on his time led him reluctantly to put down his conductor's baton.

1973 – E R R Tooby

Although he never lived in Wollaston, Reed Tooby's name is still remembered in the area. Born in October 1893, he was a pupil at Wollaston Infants' School until 1891 when he transferred to the Boys' School. He then lived in Beauty Bank where his father, also Reed, was a painter. He left school in April 1897 and he too became a painter.

For ten years he worked for his father but in 1907 he opened his own building business in Wheeler Street. The first houses he built were on the corner of Cathcart Road and Unwin Crescent.

He was a member of the Stourbridge Volunteer Corps and in 1917 joined the Durham Light Infantry, later transferring to a Royal

Above: For someone who only lived briefly in the village, Reed Tooby's name is very closely associated with Wollaston. In 1907 he opened his own building business in Wheeler Street; the first houses he built being on the corner of Cathcart Road and Unwin Crescent. In November 1924 he purchased about 16 acres of land, which consisted of most of Eggington Farm, and over the course of the next 30 years his building firm developed Meriden Avenue and Meriden Close. His policy of building only a small number of houses at any one time has meant that there is an interesting variety in both building styles and materials. Here is one of his houses going up in Ridge Street in the 1930s.

Engineers Field Regiment. He saw service in France, becoming a staff captain in 1919. In November 1924 he purchased about 16 acres of land, which consisted of most of Eggington Farm, and over the course of the next 30 years his building firm developed Meriden Avenue and Meriden Close. His policy of building only a small number of houses at any one time has meant that there is an interesting variety in both building styles and materials.

After 1945 his two sons, both residents of Meriden Avenue for many years, joined him in his business. His older son, Colonel E R W Tooby OBE, MC, TD moved to Churchill in 1973 and his younger son, G D Tooby, retired Regional Director of the National House Building Council, still lives there. Standing as an Independent candidate, he was elected a councillor for Stourbridge East, a position he held for 26 years, retiring in 1954. In 1949 and again in 1952 he was appointed Stourbridge Borough Council's Representative manager of Wollaston Schools. He held many other posts while a councillor and became Mayor of Stourbridge in 1952. He took an interest in establishing the Stourbridge Glass Collection, which was an outcome of the Festival of Britain exhibition held in the Town Hall.

He died at his home in Unwin Crescent in July 1973.

1976 – Wood Street

In January 1976, the BBC Schools Service broadcast a programme in its Art & Humanities Series, entitled 'Wood Street.' This was a broadcast commentary to accompany a filmstrip containing 37 photographs of the houses, showing many specific architectural features.

The programme had two commentators, one of whom was Gordon Boon, a Wood Street resident, writer and college lecturer, with a particular interest in suburban architecture and the built environment.

The houses were discussed in great detail with references to the different styles of building which had been developed since the first half of the 19th century.

The commentary made the point that there were no two houses the

Above: Reed Tooby stood as an Independent candidate in 1928, and was elected a councilor for Stourbridge East, a position he held for 26 years, retiring in 1954. He held many posts while a councillor, becoming Mayor of Stourbridge in 1952, and is seen here in his Mayoral robes. He died at his home in Unwin Crescent in July 1973.

same. Some of the older properties had been altered or modernised. One rather grand house, built in the 1890s, had been given a mock 'Tudor' appearance and, although originally the home to one family, in 1976 it was a set of four flats.

More recent developments were houses and bungalows that had been built on what were formerly gardens or

Above: In January 1976, the BBC Schools Service broadcast a programme in its Art & Humanities Series, entitled 'Wood Street.' This was a broadcast commentary to accompany a filmstrip containing photographs of the houses. One of the programme's commentators was Gordon Boon, a Wood Street resident with a particular interest in suburban architecture and the built environment. Photographed in 1906, this is one of the houses he talked about.

orchards of some of the large Victorian or Edwardian houses.

After drawing attention to the many different doors, windows, hedges, gates, chimney pots and building materials, Gordon Boon summed up the programme by saying: *'Each house has its own individual personality. And I think, too, that one of the great things about the street is that it is a street of many people and many occupations. ... It's a street with detail, it's a street with architecture.'*

In 1990, when the council approved a conservation area for Wollaston, the whole of Wood Street was included.

1980 – Death of oldest person

In September the *County Express* reported the death of Stourbridge's oldest resident: Mrs Sarah Hughes, of 74 Bridgnorth Road, who was 105.

1983 – The Wollaston 'Marathon'

The Wollaston Marathon was run annually for five years, from 1983 to 1987, and raised a total of over £6,000 for The League of Friends of Corbett Hospital. This 'fun race' was the brainchild of Frank Downes, then licensee of The Forester's Arms. It was conceived at a time when there was an upsurge of interest in marathon running nationally, and when opening hours at Sunday lunchtimes were restricted to 12 noon to 2:00pm. At noon the runners, each of whom had paid £1 to enter the marathon, gathered at The Forester's Arms, together with friends and well wishers. At 1.00pm, at the crack of the starter's gun, they began to dash down Bridgnorth Road to The Unicorn Inn, where its licensee, Eric Billingham, welcomed them. A unique feature of the event was that each runner received a free pint of beer both at the start and finish of the race, thanks to the generosity of the breweries that supplied the two pubs.

The first marathon was a very basic event in terms of its organisation, attracting only 60 runners. Nevertheless £200 was raised, and much publicity was gained from coverage in the *Stourbridge News* and *Express & Star*. In the following years, with more time for planning, the event was expanded to include a

raffle, the sale of 'Wollaston Marathon' T-shirts and a celebrity starter. In 1984 Geoff Boycott, the Yorkshire and England cricketer fulfilled this role, and in 1986 and 1987 the starter was Grant Baynham, a local resident, and then one of the presenters of the popular TV programme 'That's Life.' Moreover in 1986 the event attracted a runner of international standing, Ainsley Bennett, a Commonwealth Games silver medallist. He tied for first place with fellow Birchfield Harrier David Caro. However, despite the participation of trained runners the marathon's emphasis was on fun. Not just content with running downhill, many of the competitors teamed up with a friend to do a three-legged run, others ran with a dog, whilst Grant Baynham was pushed down the hill on a bed! This carnival approach was echoed by the fancy dress that many of the runners wore.

Above: The Wollaston 'Marathon', which was held between 1983 and 1987, was more of a fun run. The route was between The Forester's Arms and The Unicorn Inn. A fundraising event for The League of Friends of Corbett Hospital, each race had a celebrity starter, and in 1984 this was the Yorkshire and England cricketer Geoff Boycott, seen here on the steps of The Unicorn. *Heather Billingham*

From its modest beginning in 1983 the event grew in size and popularity, and accordingly the amount of money raised for the Corbett Hospital also increased; the last marathon in 1987 attracted 140 runners and raised £2,315. The event was revived in September 2003.

Above: A great success, The Wollaston 'Marathon' raised a lot of money for The League of Friends of Corbett Hospital. This is the cheque for the 1985 event, which is made out for £1,325. Eric Billingham, proprietor of The Unicorn Inn, looks proudly on, as he holds the real cheque! *Heather Billingham*

1984 – Cecil Hawkeswood

Stanley Cecil Hawkeswood, born in Quarry Bank in 1898, served an apprenticeship in a chemist's shop in Brierley Hill before qualifying as a pharmacist at Birmingham Technical College in 1921. In 1928 he opened his own chemist's shop in Bridgnorth Road, Wollaston. The original premises was single fronted, but in the 1960s it was enlarged by the acquisition of two adjoining shops to form one large shop facing Wollaston Junction bus stop. Interestingly a study of trade directories reveals that the premises he bought in 1928 had been in continuous use as a chemist's or druggist's since 1911.

From his Wollaston base Cecil Hawkeswood built up a chain of chemist shops, which served Stourbridge and district for over 50 years. In its heyday S C Hawkeswood & Son had six branches: Bridgnorth Road, Wollaston; Market Street and High Street, Stourbridge; Hagley Road, Oldswinford; Brettell Lane, Amblecote and the Broadway, Norton. In 1938 he and his family moved from living above the shop to a purpose built detached house in Meriden Avenue in sight of the shop. This house, built on the site of the former Public Hall, was called 'Galen', an appropriate name for the home of a pharmacist, as Galen was a Greek physician of the 2nd century AD, and for centuries regarded as the supreme authority in medicine and as the founding father of pharmacy.

Even when he had six shops to run, Cecil never forgot the need to maintain good customer relations and was to be found, well into his 70s, in his Wollaston shop, dignified in his appearance and courteous in his manner, serving customers alongside his counter assistants.

After Cecil's death in 1984 his son Bob carried on the business until he too, ceased trading in 1988.

1985 – Norman Whiting

Norman Harry Whiting was born in October 1920 in Wollaston where he lived in Bridgnorth Road, subsequently moving to Strad House, in Eggington Road.

As a teenager he played both cricket and football for Stourbridge, as an amateur. He served in the RAF for over five years during World War II, and from 1946 to 1952 he played cricket for Worcester. Norman Whiting became a professional in 1948 and in his first match he scored 155 not out. The only Wollaston born person to have been a professional cricketer, he was a middle order batsman and an off-break bowler and played in 59 first class matches.

After his playing days were over he continued to be closely associated with Worcestershire CCC, serving on

Above: Cecil Hawkeswood, seen with his son Bob, opened his own chemist's shop in Bridgnorth Road Wollaston in 1928. From this Wollaston base, Cecil Hawkeswood built up a chain of chemist shops, which served Stourbridge and district for over 50 years.

Above: In 1938 Cecil Hawkeswood moved to a purpose-built detached house in Meriden Avenue, on the site of the former Public Hall. Hawkeswood named the house 'Galen' after the 2nd century Greek physician, regarded as the founding father of pharmacy. This is Hawkeswood's Wollaston shop before enlargement in the 1960s. In its heyday S C Hawkeswood & Son had six branches. Cecil Hawkeswood died in 1984.

Above: Norman Whiting, seated front row, third from the right, is the only Wollaston-born person to become a professional cricketer, to date. He played for Worcestershire from 1946 to 1952. After his playing days he served on the club's committee for 30 years, and was President of the Worcestershire Old Players Association. To crown his lifetime involvement with Worcestershire, Norman was elected President of the club at its AGM in 2003 – a very rare distinction in the world of cricket.

the committee for 30 years, and also as President of the Worcestershire Old Players Association. In 1988 he was made a Vice-President of the county club. This honorary title is only conferred on someone who has shown commitment and loyalty to the club over many years. It is a lifetime award. The recipient holds the title until his death. To crown his lifetime involvement with Worcestershire Norman was elected President of the club at its AGM in 2003. To be elected President of a first-class county club is a very rare distinction in the world of cricket.

1990 – Conservation area

In December a report was produced by Dudley Planning & Architecture Department that designated a conservation area for Wollaston. The Planning (Listed Buildings & Conservation Areas) Act, 1990 required every local planning authority to determine which parts of their area were of special architectural or historic interest.

The original plan was submitted to the committee in May. After consultation with two local councillors, Mercia Fenton and Mike Vaughan, an amendment was proposed to include two more small areas in order to unite the three separate areas and simplify the boundary.

1993 – The Milk Race

On 8 June 1993 stage eight of The Milk Race, a 200km leg between Birmingham and Llandudno, passed through Wollaston. The Milk Race had begun in 1958 as the successor to the Daily Express Tour of Britain, which was held between 1951 and 1955. This was in fact the last time the Race was held owing to the break-up of the Milk Marketing Board, its sponsor. The stage was won by Australia's Patrick Jonker, in a time of 4hr 40m 55s, but Britain's Chris Lillywhite won the overall race in a combined time of 43hr 19m 38s.

1994 – Centenary exhibition

11 September 1994 was the 100th anniversary of Wollaston becoming part of Stourbridge. Local historian, Dr Paul Collins, was determined not to let this date pass unmarked. Assisted by his mother, Cllr June Collins, he put together an exhibition on Wollaston's history, which was displayed in the aisle of St James's Church for the week beginning 6 September 1994. So many local

Above: On 8 June 1993 stage eight of The Milk Race, a 200km leg between Birmingham and Llandudno, passed through Wollaston. Here, crowds at the end of High Park Avenue watch as stage leader Patrick Jonker passes by. The event was also televised, note the TV cameraman on the back of the motorcycle on the left. *Stan Wakeman*

people visited the exhibition and commented favourably upon it, that it was left in the church for a further week. The following September the exhibition was restaged in the new Church Hall. Researching its contents sparked an interest in Wollaston's history in Dr Collins, which led to his involvement in HOW, and to the production of this book.

1996 – The death of Don Kenyon

Although Don Kenyon was born in Wordsley in 1924, he lived most of his adult life in Wollaston. The first mention of him playing cricket was in the *County Express* on 26 July 1937: '*Kenyon was splendidly caught by Fradgley off the first ball sent down by Evans.*' The match was the Senior Schools' Shield final. However, in spite of this beginning, his ability was recognised by his headmaster who coached him and introduced him to the Stourbridge team, where he played in their second and third elevens in the Birmingham League in 1938. At the same time he was invited to the nets at Worcester's New Road ground but,

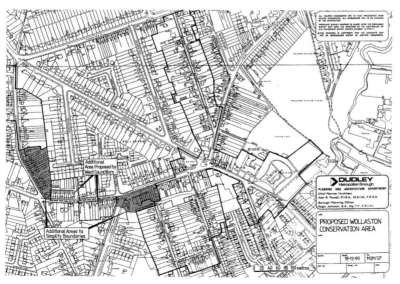

Above: A plan showing the Wollaston Conservation Area, which was adopted in 1990. Buildings within the black lines and shaded areas are protected by the Planning (Listed Buildings & Conservation Areas) Act, 1990, which aims to recognise and preserve its essential character. *Dudley MBC*

because he had been born in Staffordshire, he had wait for two seasons in order to qualify to play for Worcestershire. On 3 August 1939, while still under 16 years of age, he scored 103, the youngest batsman to reach a century in the Birmingham League.

Above: In 1961 Wollaston became the home of Worcestershire and England cricketer Don Kenyon. His career began in 1937, and on 3 August 1939, while still under 16 years of age, he scored 103, the youngest batsman to reach a century in the Birmingham League. Here is the young Kenyon in action. *Jean Kenyon*

Called up into the RAF in 1942, he was still able to play regular cricket for the RAF and the Combined Services. In December 1946 he joined Worcestershire and played in all the County Championship matches in 1947. Later the same year he married a local girl, Jean Corneloues, at St James's Church, and they came to live in Wollaston in 1961. In 1950 and 1951 Don scored over 2,000 first class runs and was selected for the England tour of 1951/52 to India, Pakistan and Ceylon. In 1953 he made two test appearances against Australia and in 1954 he came fourth in the first class averages when he scored 2,656 runs, with an average of 51.68.

In 1959 Don Kenyon was appointed captain of Worcester and in 1964 they won the County

Above: In 1950/51 Don Kenyon scored over 2,000 first class runs, and was selected for the England tour of 1951/52 to India, Pakistan and Ceylon. In 1953 he also made two test appearances against Australia. He wears the three lions on his jumper with obvious pride. *Jean Kenyon*

Championship, for the first time in their history, a feat repeated the following season. Don was appointed to the Test Selection Committee in 1964, a post he held until 1972.

He led Worcestershire on a World Tour in 1964/65 and retired at the end of the 1967 season, with a Worcester record of 34,490 runs, including 70 centuries, a record which has since only been broken twice, by Glenn Turner and Graeme Hick.

Don joined the WCC Committee in 1968, and in 1986 he became the first ex-professional player to be elected President of Worcester.

He died suddenly on 12 November 1996 whilst preparing to show his films of the 1964/65 Worcestershire Tour.

2000 – HOW exhibition

Two years into their research, the members of HOW felt it timely to share the fruits of this with the rest of the village. Accordingly an exhibition, featuring over 50 display panels, was put together. This was based upon the 1994/5 exhibition put together by Dr

Above: Kenyon led Worcestershire on a World Tour in 1964/65, and retired at the end of the 1967 season, with a Worcester record of 34,490 runs, including 70 centuries. He died suddenly at the Worcester cricket ground on 12 November 1996, whilst preparing to show his films of the 1964/65 Worcestershire Tour. *Jean Kenyon*

Paul Collins, and its staging was made possible by a Millennium Award of £500 from Dudley MBC, which helped to pay for mounting the exhibits and for display stands. The exhibition was staged in the Church Hall every weekend in September 2000, starting on 2 September and finishing on 1 October. Hundreds of people visited the exhibition, which brought forward a great deal of new material, and many leads, all of which had to be pursued before this book could be written.

2001 – HOW on Television

On 15 September 2001 the work of the HOW group was featured on an Open University programme, 'Well Connected', on BBC-2, on the use of the Internet. The programme featured members of the group, who were able to demonstrate how the Internet had been used to try to discover the whereabouts of Wollaston Hall, and to trace the history of the fallen of the two world wars.

Left: HOW staged an exhibition showing their research to date in Wollaston Church Hall every weekend in September 2000, starting on 2 September and finishing on 1 October. Hundreds of people visited the exhibition, which brought forward a great deal of new material, and many leads, all of which had to be pursued before this book could be written. *Graham Beckley*

Left: Members of HOW welcomed the visitors to their September 2000 Exhibition in Wollaston Church Hall. Among the meeters and greeters were: Tom Chapman, Janet Byard-Jones, Mike Powell, Stan Wakeman, Pat Burrage, Don Price and Peter Skidmore. *Graham Beckley*

Left: On 15 September 2001 the work of HOW was featured on an Open University programme, '*Well Connected*', on BBC-2, on the use of the Internet. It featured members of the group who demonstrated how the Internet had been used to try to discover the whereabouts of Wollaston Hall and to trace the history of the fallen of the two world wars. In this still from the programme the Chairman of HOW, Dr Paul Collins, is seen talking to presenter Mariella Frostrup.

Wollaston Trade Directory

One of the most useful sources of information available to researchers is a trade directory. Produced in increasing numbers, and with ever greater detail, until 1940, and then only occasionally thereafter, HOW decided to commemorate the Millennium by compiling a new trade directory of Wollaston in the year 2000. Preceding this are the Wollaston entries extracted from four 19th century Stourbridge trade directories.

Wollaston in 1841 (from *Bentley's Directory of Stourbridge*, 1841, pp.17-46)

Beersellers
Henry Cox
William Holloway, & farmer

Chair makers
Richard Jones, Withy Bank

Farmers
Charles Grazebrook
William Holloway, & beerseller

Spade & shovel manufacturers
Samuel Hodgson

Taverns
Thomas Barlow, Gate Hangs Well
George Taylor, Barley Mow

Wollaston in 1851 (from *White's Directory of Staffordshire*, 1851, p.805 et seq.)

Benjamin Brazier, butcher
Joseph Burton, chair maker
James Foster, iron master
Thomas Griffin, tailor, Withy Bank
Edward Kindon, boot & shoemaker, Withy Bank
William Merrington, boot & shoemaker
Edward Nash, maltster
Samuel Robinson, ironmaster
Isaac A. Savage, tailor
Job Short, bricklayer
Joseph Short, , bricklayer, Withy Bank

Wollaston in 1854 (from *The Post Office Directory of Stourbridge*, 1854, p.211 et seq.)

Richard Aston, butcher, Withy Bank
John Baker, Barley Mow
John Baker, beer retailer
John Bill, coachbuilder
Robert Bill, farmer
Benjamin Brazier, beer retailer & butcher

William Bristow, assistant overseer & collector
Samuel Bullus, Britannia
Thomas Cheese, shopkeeper, Withy Bank
John Cook, shopkeeper
Henry Cox, beer retailer
John Cutler, shopkeeper, Withy Bank
Thomas Dudley, beer retailer, Withy Bank
Charles Green, plumber, &c., Withy Bank
Thomas Griffin, tailor, Withy Bank
Mrs. Mary Hartshorne, shopkeeper, Withy Bank
Edward Kindon, boot & shoemaker, Withy Bank
Samuel Mees, Old Barley Mow
James Mogg, beer retailer, Withy Bank
Mrs. Mary Morgan, beer retailer, Withy Bank
Benjamin Rider, tailor, Withy Bank
James Ward, Gate Hangs Well
John Wood, shopkeeper
William Wyatt, grocer

Wollaston in 1864 (from *The Post Office Directory of Stourbridge*, 1864, p.1215 et seq.)

George Arey, beer retailer
Thomas Cheese, cider retailer
John Cook, grocer & provision dealer
Thomas Cooper, beer retailer & contractor
Henry Cox, beer retailer
Joseph Cutler, cow keeper
Alfred Davies, Britannia
Enoch Davis, beer retailer
John Elcock, Plough
George English, butcher
Edward Green, bootmaker
James Jordan, bootmaker
Edward Kindon, bootmaker
Richard Matty, Barley Mow
Edward Moore, beer retailer
Mrs. Mary Morgan, beer retailer
William Nickless, farmer
Benjamin Rider, tailor
Joseph Rock, flour dealer
Mrs Ann Snead, post office
John Ward, beer retailer
Joseph Whitmore, farmer
William Wyatt, shopkeeper

Wollaston Trade Directory 2000

Belfry Drive	
84	Allsafe (K. Stanley) – Central Heating Contractor
Bradley Road	
	Fitness Factory (Graham Webster) – Gymnasium
	H.V.C. Supplies (Stourbridge) Ltd – Heating, Ventilating & Cooling Supplies
Bridgnorth Road	
	Seymour Motor Co (Steve Hickman) – Car Sales
	Central Foams Ltd – Foam Supplies
	Stourbridge Upholstery Products Ltd – Furniture Mfrs & Upholsterers
	Hewitts of Stourbridge Ltd – Car Accident Repairs
	House of Beauty (Susan Lee Hewitt) – Beautician
65	J.R. Wadhams - Rover P4, P5 & P6 Products
73	The Cottage Spring (Helena Perrett) – Public House
79	A.K. Duncan – Veterinary Surgeon
83-85	O.W.S. Television Services (Jim O'Neill) – TV Rental, Sales & Service
91	Wollaston Garage Ltd – Vauxhall Dealer & Car Sales
	H.G. Scooters at Wollaston Garage – Motor Scooters
99	The Paper Shop (Andrew & Helen Smith) – Newsagents & Confectioners
101	Wollaston Fish Bar (Loucas Partali) – Fish & Chip Shop
103-105	Stourbridge Tile Studio (Linda Pugh) – Kitchen & Bathroom Tiles
107	Fotofinish (Andrew Smith) – Photographic Services
109-111 Crescent Arcade	
	S.A.S. Window Blinds (Anthony & Rachael Gardner) – Window Blinds
	Cottage Crafts (Jan Bates) – Gifts & Fancy Goods
	Sarah's Home & Garden (Sarah Thompson) – Home & Garden Supplies
	Pet's Paradise (June Darby) – Pet Shop
	Hair & Co (Pam Francis) – Hairdressers
113	Knockout Sports (M.P. & C. Richmond) – Leisurewear
115	The Princess (R. & K. Vines) – Public House
117	Vacant
119	Harris Butchers – Butchers
121	Fitzgerald's (Robbie Fitzgerald) – Restaurant
123	Vacant
125	Autoguard Alarms (Bernard Keightley) – Burglar Alarms
127	Dulson's (Clive Dulson) – Butchers
129	Allen Decorators (Dennis Allen) – Painters & Decorators
129	Happy House (K. Chan) – Chinese Takeaway
131	The Barbers Shop (Neil Price) – Hairdressers
133	Bright 'N' Beautiful (James Prior) – Dry Cleaners
135	Trueman Bros. (L. Trueman; Len Lowe) – Electrical Supplies
137	Daniel James (Jan Edwards) – Hairdressers
139	Home and Hardware (David Powis) – Hardware & Garden Supplies
141	Moss Pharmacy – Pharmacist
143-145	The Unicorn (John Freeman) – Public House
147	Spar Stores (A.F.B. Blakemore & Sons) – Supermarket
149	Elizabeth King (Ann McKenzie) – Ladies Fashions
151	Stepalong (Pat Burrage) – Shoes, Wool & Crafts
	C.E. Burrage Decorations (C.E. Burrage) – Decorator
153	Wollaston Beauty Clinic (Rachael Ward) – Beauticians
155	A.J.L. Design Ltd – Fitted Kitchen Specialists
157	Wollaston Post Office & Stores (R. & B. Hill) – Postal Services & Newsagents
159	Wine Rack (First Quench Group) – Wine & Spirit Retailers
161	Blockbuster Video – Video & DVD Rentals
163	William Hill (William Hill Organisation) – Bookmakers
	The Foresters Arms (Jean Rawson) – Public House
156	Chiselwicks (John Bate) – Furniture Maker
154	The Plough Inn (Margaret Hayward) – Public House
128a	Ken Griffiths – Painter & Decorator
84	Beach Insurance Brokers – Insurance Brokers
82	P.M.H. Accountants (Philip M. Hester) – Accountants
80	Three Villages Medical Practice (D.F. Powell; A.G. Wild; J.S. Issit; R.P. Higgins) – Medical Practice
72	Wollaston Bakery (Mr I. Balderston) – Bakers
70	The Redforte Asian Cuisine (Sean Hussain) – Indian Takeaway
68	Capital Design Partnership (G.J. Sidaway & A.W. Bray) – Architectural & Building Design Contractors
66	Stourbridge Travel (Kate Brazier) – Travel Agents
64	The Little Suite Shop (Lynne Boddis) – Furniture Supplies
62	Siviter Morgan & Co (Susan M. Morgan) – Surveyors, Estate Agents, Auctioneers & Valuers
	Morgan & Co (Susan M. Morgan) – Solicitors
62	Middleton Scriven Investment Ltd – House Builders & Renovations
60	L.A. Mayne – Optometrist
58-56	The Waterloo Inn (Martin Hartill) – Public House
50	Fletcher's Drinks Cabinet (K. Gora) – Wine, Spirits & Beer Retail
46	(Master's House) St James's Dental Centre (Dr Helen Christie) – Dental Surgeon
	(Master's House) Accessible Hire & Refrigeration Ltd – Refrigeration Suppliers
Unit 3,	St James's Court Hayburn Rock Associates Ltd – Independent Financial Advisors
Unit 4,	St James's Court Morley Haswell (S.R. Morley; R.E. Haswell) – Chartered Accountants & Auditors
Bridle Road	
66	Woodlands Retirement Home (Mrs S. Shroff & Mr J. Davies) – Residential Home
Bright Street	
11	Hughes Builders – Builder
Cobden Street	
	Acorn Catering Services (Mary & Helen Hubery) – Caterers
	Beech Haven Industrial History Services (Paul Collins) – Industrial Archaeology Surveys
66	Chris Davies – Art Ceramist/Tutor
Dorset Road	
11	Martin Hammond – Diving Instructor
30	Dorset Paving Specialists (John Watkins) – Block Paving Specialists

Duncombe Street

35	D.J. Ellis, FRCS - Surgeon

Eggington Road

1	Woodside Domestic Fuels (Joe Stackhouse) – Domestic Fuels
19	Geoff Tristram – Fine Artist, Cartoonist & Caricaturist
24	K.R.Preservation (K.M. & S.J. Rowley) – Damp & Dry Rot Specialists
12	Strad House (Karelink Ltd) – Residential Home

Enville Street

187	Katie Fitzgeralds (Petrina R. Keane) – Public House

Francis Road

18	Neil and Liz Meredith – Rod & Custom Car Club

Gerald Road

46	Jonathon P. Clay – Piano Technician

Gilbanks Road

21	John Hunter – Carpentry Services
51	Wollaston Education Services (Richard Wilkins) – Education Consultant

Hamilton Avenue

8	Graham Beckley - Photographer

High Park Avenue

1	The Gate Hangs Well (G. & L. Darby) – Public House
3	Jancraft (Julian Jankowski) – Printed Textiles & Leisure Products
12	P.J. Raden – Chiropodist/Podiatrist

High Street

1	Partybusters (Alyson Bate) – Party & Fancy Dress Supplies
2	Tiny Tots (Chris Carter) – Infants & Children's Wear
2b	Impressions (Nick Cosnett) – Ladies & Gents Hairdresser
2c	Tan-Tastic (Lynne Edwards) – Tanning Studio
2d	Vacant
2e	Fleurs de Vie (Joanna Wooldridge) – Florist
2f	Neel Akash – Balti & Tandoori Restaurant & Takeaway
3c	Images Photography – Photographer
4	Sugar and Spice – Cake Decorators
8	Wollaston Laundercentre (Irene Butler) – Laundrette
62	Bulls Head (P. Boyle) – Public House
90	Scizors Salon (Sue Easthope) – Hairdresser
146	Caxton House (Mrs Benbow & Campbell) – Private Rest Home
	Stourbridge Stockholders Ltd – Steel Trade Service
	Sunrise Medical Ltd – Wheelchairs & Mobility Aids
	Pre-Press (S. Sankey & G. Scriven) – Digital Reprographics
	Palace Furniture Ltd – Pub & Restaurant Furniture Mfrs.
155	Reliance Garage (Stourbridge) Ltd – Motor Engineers
	Midlands Auto Diagnostics – Auto Engine Specialists
	Kershaw Mechanical Services Ltd – Heating & Ventilation Engineers
133	Wollaston Mill – Antiques Centre
133	Chambermaids – Domestic Cleaning Services
133	SACS – Specialised Accounting & Computer Services
131	Barley Mow (Jennie Davies) – Public House
	Britannia Inn (Sandra Flavin) – Public House
17	Discordian Promotions
13	Websters (Marion's) – Greengrocers, Florists & Garden Supplies
9	Wollaston Bathroom Centre Ltd – Bathroom Specialists

9	Audnam Plumbing & Heating Co Ltd – Plumbing & Heating
3c	Kitchen Manor (Yvonne Pearce) – Kitchen Supplies
3a	Nailenvy (Khadine Coleman) Manicurist & Nail Specialist
1	San Wu House (F.S. Wong) – Chinese Takeaway

King Street

43	Pugh Ceramics (Dental) Ltd – Dental Ceramics
81a	Mike Goode Garage (Mike Goode) – Car Repairs
King's Court	Ellie Bears Day Nursery (Sharon Westwood) – Children's Nursery

Kingsway

4	Jill Hair Care (Mrs G. Payne) – Hairdresser
6	Kingsway Stores
41	Aimes Transport Services – Haulage Contractor
199	Maryna Wray – Floristry Designs & Preserved Flowers
201	Jet Set (Mrs F. Wheeler) – Hairdresser
203	Vacant?
205	Brian Palmer – Butcher
207	David Dunn – Foodstore
209	Stars News Shops Ltd (Mrs E. Malpass) – Newsagent & Confectioner

Lowndes Road

	Laser Claddings Ltd – Architectural Claddings
	Sidney Smith Castings Ltd – Iron Castings

Mamble Road

	A.T.C. (Tony Carter) – Moblie Auto-Electrical Services
	Invert Surveys (Matthew J. Newall) – CCTV & Drain Technology
	Landscape Excel Ltd - Landscapers

Meriden Avenue

1	Dr J. Firth – Medical Practitioner
20	S.J. Hamblin – Painter & Decorator
54	Pegg Bros. Builders (Colin Pegg) – Building Refurbishers

Norfolk Road

66	T. & A. Moreton – Building & Plastering Contractor

Park Road West

2	Wollaston Woodcraft (Jeremy Drew) – Carpenter & Furniture Maker

Richmond Grove

51	M.P. Worrall – Plastering Contractor
32	Brian Powell – Flooring Systems
82	P.D. Electrical Ltd – (Peter Dutfield) – Electrical Contractors

Rugby Road

13	PJW Associates (P.J. Williams) – Building Designs

Somerset Drive

14	Trinity Road Developments Ltd - Builders

Vicarage Road

64	Diamond School of Motoring (Ian Southall) – Motoring School
120	S. Pardoe & Sons (Lye) Ltd – Builders
134	Pro-Fit (Bill Watkins) – Machine Tool Repairs & Installations
136	Joyce & Michael Aston – Piano Tuition
141	R.A.Bate – Engineer
133a	Rolls-Royce Wedding Cars of Stourbridge (P.R. Guinness) – Wedding Cars
65	Rosemary Retirement Home (Mr & Mrs R. Smith) – Residential Home

Wild Acres
62   C & J Building Contractors Ltd (C.A. Cartwright) – Building Contractor

Wentworth Road
      G.R. Price Autos (Graham Price) – Car Repairs/Garage

Wood Street
20   Hands on Care – Community Home for Adults with Learning Difficulties

Trades

Accountants & Auditors
P.M.H. Accountants (Philip M. Hester) 82 Bridgnorth Road
Morley Haswell (S.R. Morley; R.E. Haswell) Unit 4, St James's Court Bridgnorth Road
SACS (& Computer Services) 133 High Street

Antiques
Wollaston Mill Antiques Centre 133 High Street

Archaeological Consultants
Industrial History Services (Paul Collins) Beech Haven, Cobden Street

Art Ceramists
Chris Davies 66 Cobden Street

Auctioneers & Valuers
Siviter Morgan & Co (Susan M. Morgan) 62 Bridgnorth Road

Architectural & Building Design Contractors
Capital Design Partnership (G. J. Sidaway & A.W. Bray) 68 Bridgnorth Road

Architectural Claddings
Laser Claddings Ltd Lowndes Road

Auto Engine Specialists
Midlands Auto Diagnostics 155 High Street

Bakers & Confectioners
Wollaston Bakery (Mr I. Balderston) 72 Bridgnorth Road

Bathroom Specialists
Wollaston Bathroom Centre Ltd 9 High Street

Beauticians
House of Beauty (Susan Lee Hewitt) Bridgnorth Road
Wollaston Beauty Clinic (Rachael Ward) 153 Bridgnorth Road

Block Paving Specialists
Dorset Paving Specialists (John Watkins) 30 Dorset Road

Bookmakers
William Hill (William Hill Organisation) 163 Bridgnorth Road

Building Contractors
C & J Building Contractors Ltd (C.A. Cartwright) 62 Wildacres
Hughes Builders 11 Bright Street
Middleton Scriven Investment Ltd (& renovators) 62 Bridgnorth Road
T. & A. Moreton 66 Norfolk Road
S. Pardoe & Sons (Lye) Ltd 120 Vicarage Road
Pegg Bros. Builders (Colin Pegg) 54 Meriden Avenue
Trinity Road Developments Ltd 14 Somerset Drive

Building Designs

PJW Associates (P.J. Williams) 13 Rugby Road

Burglar Alarms
Autoguard Alarms (Bernard Keightley) 125 Bridgnorth Road

Butchers
Dulson's (Clive Dulson) 127 Bridgnorth Road
Harris Butchers 119 Bridgnorth Road
Brian Palmer 205 Kingsway

Cake Decorators
Sugar and Spice 4 High Street

Car Accident Repairs
Hewitts of Stourbridge Ltd Bridgnorth Road

Car Dealers & Sales
Seymour Motor Co (Steve Hickman) Bridgnorth Road
Wollaston Garage Ltd 91 Bridgnorth Road

Car Repairs
Mike Goode Garage (Mike Goode) 81a King Street
G.R. Price Autos (Graham Price) Wentworth Road
Reliance Garage (Stourbridge) Ltd 155 High Street

Car Spares
J.R. Wadhams - Rover P4, P5 & P6 Products 65 Bridgnorth Road

Carpentry Services
John Hunter 21 Gilbanks Road

Cartoonists & Caricaturists
Geoff Tristram (& Fine Artist) 19 Eggington Road

Caterers
Acorn Catering Services (Mary & Helen Hubery) Cobden Street

Central Heating Contractors
Allsafe (K. Stanley) 84 Belfry Drive

Children's Nurseries
Ellie Bears Day Nursery (Sharon Westwood) King's Court, King Street

Chiropodists/Podiatrists
P.J. Raden 12 High Park Avenue

CCTV & Drain Technology
Invert Surveys (Matthew J. Newall) Mamble Road

Community Homes
Hands on Care 20 Wood Street

Damp & Dry Rot Specialists
K.R. Preservation (K.M. & S.J. Rowley) 24 Eggington Road

Dental Ceramics
Pugh Ceramics (Dental) Ltd 43 King Street

Dental Surgeons
(Master's House) St James's Dental Centre (Dr Helen Christie) 46 Bridgnorth Road

Digital Reprographics
Pre-Press (S. Sankey & G. Scriven) High Street

Diving Instructors
Diamond School of Motoring (Ian Southall) 64 Vicarage Road
Martin Hammond 11 Dorset Road

Domestic Cleaning Services
Chambermaids 133 High Street

Domestic Fuels
Woodside Domestic Fuels (Joe Stackhouse) 1 Eggington Road

Dry Cleaners
Bright 'N' Beautiful (James Prior) 133 Bridgnorth Road

Education Consultants
Wollaston Education Services (Richard Wilkins) 51 Gilbanks Road

Electrical Contractors
P.D. Electrical Ltd – (Peter Dutfield) 82 Richmond Grove

Electrical Supplies
Trueman Bros. (L. Trueman, Len Lowe) 135 Bridgnorth Road

Engineers
R.A. Bate 141 Vicarage Road

Fitted Kitchen Specialists
A.J.L. Design Ltd 155 Bridgnorth Road

Flooring Systems
Brian Powell 32 Richmond Grove

Florists
Fleurs de Vie (Joanna Wooldridge) 2e High Street
Websters (Marion's) 13 High Street
Maryna Wray (Floristry Designs & Preserved Flowers) 199 Kingsway

Foam Supplies
Central Foams Ltd Bridgnorth Road

Foodstores
David Dunn 207 Kingsway

Furniture Makers, Manufacturers, Supplies & Upholsterers
Chiselwicks (John Bate) 156 Bridgnorth Road
The Little Suite Shop (Lynne Boddis) 64 Bridgnorth Road
Palace Furniture Ltd (Pub & Restaurant Furniture) High Street
Stourbridge Upholstery Products Ltd Bridgnorth Road
Wollaston Woodcraft (& Carpenter – Jeremy Drew) 2 Park Road West

General Stores
Kingsway Stores 6 Kingsway

Gifts & Fancy Goods
Cottage Crafts (Jan Bates) Crescent Arcade 109-111 Bridgnorth Road

Greengrocers
Websters (Marion's) 13 High Street

Gymnasium
Fitness Factory (Graham Webster) Bradley Road

Hairdressers
The Barbers Shop (Neil Price) 131 Bridgnorth Road
Hair & Co (Pam Francis) Crescent Arcade 109-111 Bridgnorth Road
Impressions (Nick Cosnett) 2b High Street
Daniel James (Jan Edwards) 137 Bridgnorth Road
Jet Set 201 Kingsway
Jill Hair Care (Mrs G. Payne) 4 Kingsway
Scizors Salon (Sue Easthope) 90 High Street

Haulage Contractors
Aimes Transport Services 41 Kingsway

Heating, Ventilating & Cooling Supplies
H.V.C. Supplies (Stourbridge) Ltd Bradley Road
Kershaw Mechanical Services Ltd 155 High Street

Home, Hardware & Garden Supplies
Home and Hardware (David Powis) 139 Bridgnorth Road
Sarah's Home & Garden (Sarah Thompson) Crescent Arcade 109-111 Bridgnorth Road
Websters (Marion's) 13 High Street

Independent Financial Advisors
Hayburn Rock Associates Ltd Unit 3, St James's Court Bridgnorth Road

Infants & Children's Wear
Tiny Tots (Chris Carter) 2 High Street

Insurance Brokers
Beach Insurance Brokers 84 Bridgnorth Road

Iron Castings
Sidney Smith Castings Ltd Lowndes Road

Kitchen & Bathroom Tiles
Stourbridge Tile Studio (Linda Pugh) 103-105 Bridgnorth Road

Kitchen Supplies
Kitchen Manor (Yvonne Pearce) 3c High Street

Ladies Fashions
Elizabeth King (Ann McKenzie) 149 Bridgnorth Road

Landscapers
Landscape Excel Ltd Mamble Road

Laundrettes
Wollaston Laundercentre (Irene Butler) 8 High Street

Leisurewear
Knockout Sports (M.P. & C. Richmond) 113 Bridgnorth Road

Machine Tool Repairs & Installations
Pro-Fit (Bill Watkins) 134 Vicarage Road

Manicurists & Nail Specialists
Nailenvy (Khadine Coleman) 3a High Street

Medical Practices
Dr J. Firth 1 Meriden Avenue
Three Villages Medical Practice (D.F. Powell; A.G. Wild; J.S. Issit; R.P. Higgins) 80 Bridgnorth Road

Moblie Auto-Electrical Services
A.T.C. (Tony Carter) Mamble Road

Motor Scooters
H.G. Scooters at Wollaston Garage 91 Bridgnorth Road

Newsagents & Confectioners
The Paper Shop (Andrew & Helen Smith) 99 Bridgnorth Road
Stars News Shops Ltd (Mrs E. Malpass) 209 Kingsway
Wollaston Post Office & Stores (R. & B. Hill) 157 Bridgnorth Road

Optometrists
L.A. Mayne 60 Bridgnorth Road

Painters & Decorators
Allen Decorators (Dennis Allen) 129 Bridgnorth Road
C.E. Burrage Decorations (C.E. Burrage) 151 Bridgnorth Road
Ken Griffiths 128a Bridgnorth Road
S.J. Hamblin 20 Meriden Avenue

Party & Fancy Dress Supplies
Partybusters (Alyson Bate) 1 High Street

Pet Shops
Pet's Paradise (June Darby) Crescent Arcade 109-111 Bridgnorth Road

Pharmacists
Moss Pharmacy 141 Bridgnorth Road

Photographers & Photographic Services
Graham Beckley Hamilton Avenue
Fotofinish (Andrew Smith) 107 Bridgnorth Road
Images Photography 3c High Street

Piano Technicians
Jonathon P. Clay 46 Gerald Road

Piano Tuition
Joyce & Michael Aston 136 Vicarage Road

Plastering Contractors
T. & A. Moreton 66 Norfolk Road
M.P. Worrall 51 Richmond Grove

Plumbing & Heating
Audnam Plumbing & Heating Co Ltd 9 High Street

Postal Services
Wollaston Post Office & Stores (R. & B. Hill) 157 Bridgnorth Road

Printed Textiles & Leisure Products
Jancraft (Julian Jankowski) 3 High Park Avenue

Promotions
Discordian Promotions 17 High Street

Public Houses
The Barley Mow (Jennie Davies) 131 High Street
Britannia Inn (Sandra Flavin) High Street
The Bulls Head (P. Boyle) 62 High Street
The Cottage Spring (Helena Perrett) 73 Bridgnorth Road
The Foresters Arms (Jean Rawson) Bridgnorth Road
The Gate Hangs Well (G. & L. Darby) 1 High Park Avenue
Katie Fitzgeralds (Petrina R. Keane) 187 Enville Street
The Plough Inn (Margaret Hayward) 154 Bridgnorth Road
The Princess (R. & K. Vines) 115 Bridgnorth Road
The Unicorn (John Freeman) 143-145 Bridgnorth Road
The Waterloo Inn (Martin Hartill) 58-56 Bridgnorth Road

Refrigeration Suppliers
(Master's House) Accessible Hire & Refrigeration Ltd 46 Bridgnorth Road

Residential & Care Homes
Caxton House (Mrs Benbow & Campbell) 146 High Street
Rosemary Retirement Home (Mr & Mrs R. Smith) 65 Vicarage Road

Strad House (Karelink Ltd) 12 Eggington Road
Woodlands Retirement Home (Mrs S. Shroff & Mr J. Davies) 66 Bridle Road

Restaurants
Fitzgerald's (Robbie Fitzgerald) 121 Bridgnorth Road
Neel Akash (Balti & Tandoori) 2f High Street

Rod & Custom Car Club
Neil and Liz Meredith 18 Francis Road

Shoes, Wool & Crafts
Stepalong (Pat Burrage) 151 Bridgnorth Road

Solicitors
Morgan & Co (Susan M Morgan) 62 Bridgnorth Road

Steel Trade Services
Stourbridge Stockholders Ltd High Street

Supermarkets
Spar Stores (A F B Blakemore & Sons) 147 Bridgnorth Road

Surgeons
DJ Ellis, FRCS 35 Duncombe Street

Surveyors & Estate Agents
Siviter Morgan & Co (Susan M Morgan) 62 Bridgnorth Road

Takeaway Foodstores
Happy House (Chinese – K. Chan) 129 Bridgnorth Road
Neel Akash (Balti & Tandoori) 2f High Street
The Redforte Asian Cuisine (Sean Hussain) 70 Bridgnorth Road
San Wu House (Chinese – F.S. Wong) 1 High Street
Wollaston Fish Bar (Fish & Chips – Loucas Partali) 101 Bridgnorth Road

Tanning Studios
Tan-Tastic (Lynne Edwards) 2c High Street

TV Rental, Sales & Service
O W S Television Services (Jim O'Neill) 83-85 Bridgnorth Road

Travel Agents
Stourbridge Travel (Kate Brazier) 66 Bridgnorth Road

Veterinary Surgeon
A.K. Duncan 79 Bridgnorth Road

Video & DVD Rentals
Blockbuster Video 161 Bridgnorth Road

Wedding Cars
Rolls-Royce Wedding Cars of Stourbridge (P R Guiness) 133a Vicarage Road

Wheelchairs & Mobility Aids
Sunrise Medical Ltd High Street

Window Blinds
S A S Window Blinds (Anthony & Rachael Gardner) Crescent Arcade 109-111 Bridgnorth Road

Wine & Spirit Retailers
Fletcher's Drinks Cabinet (K. Gora) 50 Bridgnorth Road
Wine Rack (First Quench Group) 159 Bridgnorth Road

Acknowledgements

Acknowledgements

Everyone associated with HOW's research into the History of Wollaston is grateful to the following individuals and organisations for their kind assistance with this project. Without their help this book would not have been possible. HOW apologise to any who have been inadvertently left out of this list: Delia Allen, Aston Villa FC, the late Andrew Bassett-Spiers, Graham Beckley, Fred Beech, Heather Billingham, Birmingham Post & Mail (Ray Dunn), Black Country Bugle, Tim Booth, Dennis Bowen, Staff At Brierley Hill Library, Irene Brookes, Rebecca Burrage, Gerald Butler, Elsie Chambers, Mary Chance, Reg Cook, Alan Cox, David Cox, Corning Glass Museum, Eric Davies, Vernon Davies, Registrar of the Diocese of Worcester, Roger Dodsworth, Staff at Dudley Archives, Don Edwards, Brian Elliott, Jason Ellis, Marilyn Ferris, George Foxall, Margaret Gleiwitz, Dave Guest, H Jack Haden, Tom Hadgkiss, Ernest Hall, Brian Hardyman, Sue & Eric Harris, Mellanie Hartland, Liz Hathway, Hereford Record Office, David Hickman, Stan Hill, Tony Hitchmough, Shirley Horne, Eunice Horton, Hulbert Collection, Broadfield House, Stephen Hyde, Joe Jenkins, John Jenkins, Gavin Jones, Jean Kenyon, Harold Lamming, Herbert Langer, Gerald Langley, Robert Little, John Lloyd, John Mason, Pam Mackie, John Moreton, John Morton, National Monuments Record, Margaret Parkes, Anne Penn, Nigel Perry, George Prosser, Public Record Office, Val Radford, Jacque Randle, Trevor Raybould, Michael Reuter, Yvonne Richards, Bill Riley, Grahame Robertson, Keith Roden, Derek Rudd, John Saunders, Debra Shipley MP, Norman Simpson, Gloria Skidmore, Jane Spillman, Ann Sprague, Staff at Stourbridge Library, Kate Thomas, Lawrence (Lol) Tibbetts, Bill Tompkins, Don Tompkins, Dennis Tooby, John & Janet Tribbel, Philip Turner, David Tyler, Joan White, Michael Willows, Wollaston Garage, Kenneth Woodward, Bob Wooldridge, Worcester Record Office, Ken Worton, and Ted Wright.

American Acknowledgements

HOW's search for Wollaston Hall has been cast far wider than would have been possible a few years ago through use of e-mail and the Internet. We are grateful to the following individuals and organisations in the USA and Canada for their continuing help in our search: Eldred W. Atkinson (York, Pennsylvania), Kathleen Arnold, Barbara Ayars, Dorothy M. Bialek (Equinunk Historical Society), Garth Brackbill, Peggy Lumbard Brill, Eric Bryan (Frontier Culture Museum of Virginia), Sheila M. Campbell (Preservation Pennsylvania), Sharman Meck Carroll (Thorndale, Pennsylvania), Charles Connolly and Sharon (New Jersey), Mary Ellen Courtney (Los Angeles, California), Nadine Davis, Meredith De Hart (Pennsylvania), Denise (Western Pennsylvania), Robear Dyer (Elverson, Pennsylvania), Ranee Egee (Dublin, Pennsylvania), Tim Fisher, Kathy Flynn, Joan Sholl Francis, Jim Gilbert, Larry E Gundersen, Jo Gurney, Don Hazelton, Ray Hildenbrand, Sally Huntley, Kay Hutchinson (Salisbury, Maryland), Greg & Liz Lang, Peter Lapham (Chestnut Hill Historical Society, Pennsylvania), Jim Lenhart, Wendy LeVan, Evelyn Lowell, Sherry Luckenbaugh, Eric Lund, John MacFarland (Timber Framers Guild of the USA), Carol Potter Meadows, George M. Meiser, IX (President, Historical Society of Berks County, Pennsylvania), 'Tink' (Susan) Miller (Auburn, California), Beverley Montgomery (Berks County, Pennsylvania), Mike Murray, Rhonda Newton (Pennsylvania Federation of Museums), Cary Nickless-Leclaire (Westmount, Quebec, Canada), Paul Neis, Langley, Washington, Bill Patterson, Bobette Prell, John Roede, Jessica Rowcroft, Sara S. Sanders-Buell (National Gallery of Art), Wayne F. Seibert (Fairborn, Ohio), Dave Silcox Shillington (Pennsylvania), Smithsonian Institution (Washington, DC), Mary A. Sutphin, Boyce Thompson, Edwin G Troutman, MD (Fort Worth, Texas), Tom Weber (College of Agricultural Sciences, Penn State University, Pennsylvania), Gail Williams Susan Witter (Bellingham, Washington), Donna HELLER ZINN (Newville, Cumberland County, Pennsylvania), and Nathan Zipfel (Pennsylvania-Roots Webmaster).

Index

Generic postcards of this kind were very popular in the early 20th century. By the application of an overprint, or, as here, a rubber stamp, one could not have '*had a dull moment at ...*' or missed '*the last tram from ...*' anywhere. This apart, its the sentiment that counts here. Everyone involved in the production of this book hopes that all who read it have not had a dull moment, and that it will continue to provide everyone who does so with as much enjoyment and interest as it has given all of us in researching and writing it – The History of Wollaston Group – HOW.

**Research into the History of Wollaston continues.
Keep up with the latest discoveries by logging onto
HOW's website regularly.
Also, please let us know if you have any photographs
or memories of Wollaston you would like to share:
www.communigate.co.uk/bc/historyofwollaston/index.phtml
or type 'history of wollaston' into a search engine.
Alternately you can write to HOW c/o Stepalong Shoes,
151 Bridgnorth Road, Wollaston, Stourbridge,
West Midlands DY8 3NU**

List of Subscribers

HOW is grateful to everyone who has supported this project by paying in advance for their copies of this book. We are especially grateful to the first 100 people to do so, for their long-term support:

1	Elsie M Chambers	35	Roger Hems	67	Jean Perks
2	Margaret Checketts	36	Patrticia Furze	68	Joyce Boaler
3	Nina Hodnett	37	Eric Stanton	69	Frances Davis
4	Bill & Muriel Williams	38	Susan Satchell	70	Les & Peggy Martin
5	Robert & Yvonne Newton	39	Paul Riley	71	Valerie Welsh
6	Anna Willetts	40	John Kirkham	72	Sue, Gary & Sons Edwards
7	Valerie & Barry Harper	41	Audrey Dainty	73	Mike & Vicki Horton
8	John Cartwright	42	Irene Johnson	74	Doreen Rutter
9	John Porter	43	Andrew Price	75	Hilary Phillips
10	Stan & Lillian Green	44	Gwendoline Hill	76	Alison Sheenhan-Hunt
11	Margie Postings	45	Megan Baxter	77	Deborah & Stephen Hudson
12	Richie J Lewis	46	Vi Morgan	78	Susan Rock
13	John & Janet Tribbel	47	Eric Davies	79	Margaret Jones
14	Derek Brookes	48	Lorraine Hayward	80	Gary Marsden
15	Helen Turner	49	Colin Clark	81	Sarah Hodnett
16	Lynn Andrews	50	Barbara Beavon	82	Rita & William Dudley
17	Ken Ison	51	Dennis Howard	83	Stuart Dudley
18	Andrew Briney	52	Robert J Clarke	84	Hazel & Kenneth Bull
19	Barbara Booker	53	Phyllis Turner	85	Vera & Raymond Taylor
20	Ethel Rowley	54	Marjorie Jones	86	Margaret Frances
21	Dorothy Dunn	55	Carol-Ann & Geoffrey Longmore	87	Rosemary & John Kirton
22	Gladys Williams			88	Joan White
23	Kathleen Fox	56	Nigel Chapman	89	Beryl Blackmore
24	Judith Dangerfield	57	Mick & Chris Parkin	90	David Gouldney
25	Robert Perks	58	Malcolm & Madelaine Dunn	91	Joy Cook
26	Joan Hackett			92	Andrew Waterhouse
27	Pat Southall	59	Gerald Darby	93	Ann Jankowska
28	Pamela Eccleston	60	Doreen & Louis Williams	94	Judith Godefroy-Chance
29	Harry Mobberley	61	Norman Allen	95	Stan Hill
30	Ian Wardle	62	Joan Price	96	Sylvia Rose Butcher
31	Jeremy Humphries	63	Vivienne Myers	97	Margaret Irene Parkes
32	Lorna Singleton	64	Stella Young	98	Beryl Wright
33	Shirley McArthur	65	Anne Daly	99	Margaret Cartwright
34	Margaret Shillingford	66	Pauline Devereux	100	Janet Peters